Covenants and Third-Party Creditors

Daniela Matri

Covenants and Third-Party Creditors

Empirical and Law & Economics Insights Into a Common Pool Problem

Springer

Daniela Matri
Law Department
University of Bremen
Bremen, Germany

ISBN 978-3-319-62035-0   ISBN 978-3-319-62036-7 (eBook)
DOI 10.1007/978-3-319-62036-7

Library of Congress Control Number: 2017948242

Printed on acid-free paper

This Springer imprint is published by Springer Nature
The registered company is Springer International Publishing AG
The registered company address is: Gewerbestrasse 11, 6330 Cham, Switzerland

Acknowledgements

It is my genuine pleasure to express my deep sense of thanks and gratitude to my doctorate supervisor Prof. Dr. Moritz Renner, Lichtenberg Professorship for Transnational Economic Law and Theory of Economic Law, University of Bremen.

I also owe a deep sense of gratitude to Prof. Dr. Thilo Kuntz and Prof. Dr. Gralf-Peter Calliess as well as to all my colleagues, who participated in the privatissimum, for their honest and challenging feedback and advice.

I thank profusely the College of Law of the University of Iowa for the opportunity to conduct my research at their facilities as well as for their support. In this regard, I would also like to thank the DAAD for the financial support concerning my research stay at the University of Iowa.

I also owe a deep sense of gratitude to all my interview partners, who made the empirical study possible in the first place.

It is my privilege to thank my family and my husband, who always supported me with love.

Contents

List of Abbreviations

AktG	*Aktiengesetz* (Stock Corporation Act)
alt.	Alternative
AnfG	*Anfechtungsgesetz* (Avoidance of Transactions Act)
BaFin	*Bundesanstalt für Finanzdienstleistungsaufsicht* (German Federal Financial Supervisory Authority)
BFuP	*Betriebswirtschaftliche Forschung und Praxis*
BGB	*Bürgerliches Gesetzbuch* (German Civil Code)
BGH	*Bundesgerichtshof* (German Federal Supreme Court)
CEO	Chief executive officer
cf.	Confer
CFR	Code of Federal Regulations
CPR	Common pool resource
EBITDA	Earnings before interest, taxation, depreciation and amortisation
ECJ	European Court of Justice (now: Court of Justice of the European Union)
ed.	Editor/s
edit.	Edition
e.g.	Exempli gratia (for example)
et al.	Et alii/aliae/alia (and other/s)
et seq.	Et sequens (and the following page)
et seqq.	Et sequential (and the following pages)
EU	European Union
fn.	Footnote/s
GAAP	Generally Accepted Accounting Principles
GmbH	*Gesellschaft mit beschränkter Haftung* (company with limited liability)
GmbHG	*Gesetz betreffend die Gesellschaften mit beschränkter Haftung* (Limited Liability Companies Act)
HGB	*Handelsgesetzbuch* (Commercial Code)
i.a.	Inter alia (among others)

ibid.	Ibidem (in the same work, but this time at)
i.e.	Id est (that is)
IFRS	International Financial Reporting Standards
InsO	*Insolvenzordnung* (German Insolvency Code)
LMA	Loan Market Association
LSTA	Loan Syndications and Trading Association
MAC	Material adverse change
MoMiG	*Gesetz zur Modernisierung des GmbH-Rechts und zur Bekämpfung von Missbräuchen* (Law for the Modernisation of the German Limited Liability Company Law and the Prevention of Misuse)
no.	Number
nos.	Numbers
NYSE MKT	Name of an American stock exchange situated in New York City
OJ	*Official Journal of the European Union*
p.	Page/s
para.	Paragraph
paras.	Paragraphs
RG	*Reichsgericht* (Supreme Court of the (German) Reich)
SEC	Securities and Exchange Commission
UCC	Uniform Commercial Code
UK	United Kingdom/British
USA/US	United States of America/American
US Code	United States Code
v.	Versus
WpHG	*Wertpapierhandelsgesetz* (Securities Trading Act)

List of Figures

List of Tables

Part I
Theoretical Framework and Development of Research Question

Chapter 1
Introduction: Covenants and Third-Party Creditors

1.1 Covenants and Creditor Protection

Credit[1] is an ancient concept that forms a central part of business life. Its roots lie in the Latin word *credere*, which means "to believe". Creditors have to trust that the debtor will return or reimburse the borrowed resource.[2] They run the risk of default, i.e. that the debtor cannot or will not return or repay the debt.

To protect creditors, states have implemented different statutory measures.[3] However, these measures may come into effect too late to provide proper protection, or may not be effective at all. Therefore, creditors try to reduce the credit risk—i.e. the probability of loan default and the severity of the consequential loss over the life of the loan[4]—with self-help devices, such as evaluating the creditworthiness of potential debtors and adapting the interest rate accordingly,[5] monitoring the debtor's behaviour, or requiring collateral. Particularly in cross-border or high-volume loans, so-called covenants are used to secure contractual payment obligations. These covenants—also known as undertakings—refer to obligations entered

[1]For the purposes of the work the term "credit" refers to the provision of money or resources by one party (the creditor) to another party (the debtor) where the debtor returns or reimburses the borrowed source not immediately but at a later date. Cf. Law and Martin (2009), p. 143 et seq., 155.

[2]See for example Renner, in: Canaris et al. (eds) (2015), para. 2; Ganter, in: Schimansky et al. (eds) (2011), para. 1.

[3]Creditor protection is understood here in a broad sense to include all mechanisms in company law, bankruptcy law, property law and contract law that directly or indirectly ensure or enhance the creditor's position.

[4]Golin and Delhaise (2013), p. 23 et seq.

[5]See Posner (1976), 501; Enriques and Macey (2001), 1171 et seq., 1188; Schön (2004b), 439; Schön (2004a), 166; critically Landers (1976), 529 et seqq.

D. Matri, *Covenants and Third-Party Creditors*, DOI 10.1007/978-3-319-62036-7_1

into by a borrower as part of the loan agreement[6,7] and ensure financial performance, asset protection, and information provision.[8]

Originally, covenants were mainly prevalent in Anglo-American loan agreements.[9] Nowadays, however, they are also common in continental bank loan agreements.[10] A classical scenario would be the following:

Scenario 1

The public company "Papermaker" has been successfully active in the papermaking business for 50 years. Now, Papermaker wants to expand in Italy and buy a new papermaking machine for €250 million. To finance this acquisition, Papermaker approaches its main bank "Best Bank". Best Bank agrees with this and wants to provide a loan of over €250 million to Papermaker. The loan principal, however, is too big for Best Bank on its own. For that reason, it approaches four other banks to syndicate[11] the loan. Since all banks believe it to be a good investment, they agree to provide a syndicated loan. They also agree on Best Bank as their leading bank. The papermaking machine will serve as security. However, the banks also want some reassurance in the form of covenants, because the papermaking machine will be located in Italy.[12] To protect itself, the bank consortium insists on some standard covenants. The debtor company must also inform Best Bank about any new debt-relevant circumstances. The enforcement of these clauses is ensured by an event of default clause.[13]

After three productive years with the new papermaking machine, Papermaker decides that, due to strong competition, it needs to invest in its infrastructure. Papermaker wants to issue bonds to finance this investment. However, the negative pledge clause restricts Papermaker's options. It states:

"Papermaker shall (and the Company shall ensure that no other member of the Group will) create or permit to subsist any Security[14] over any of its assets. [. . .] the above does not apply to:

(i) any security listed in schedule X (listing existing security) except to the extent the principal amount secured by that security exceeds the amount stated in that schedule;

(ii) any netting or set-off arrangement entered into by any member of the group in the ordinary course of its banking arrangements for the purpose of netting debit and credit balances;

(iii) any lien arising by operation of law and in the ordinary course of trading."[15]

---

[6]For reasons of comprehension, the term "loan agreement" will be used to refer to bond indentures and credit agreements and other debt agreements.

[7]For a similar definition see Tighe (1984), para. 4.01 (1). For other definitions see Leichtling et al. (2013), § 11.02 [2].

[8]Also Wright (2006), p. 137, Adams (2003), p. 86.

[9]For an overview of the historical development see Fifoot (1970), p. 255 et seqq.

[10]Cf. Haghani et al. (2009).

[11]For further details on syndicated loans, see Bleifeld (2015), p. 11 et seqq.

[12]For movable collateral the principle of *lex rei sitae* applies (Germany: Art. 43 I EGBGB, Italy: Art. 51 I PIL-Act); cf. Mansel, in: Heinrich (ed) (2015), paras. 90 et seqq. Italy is regarded as rather problematic with regard to movable collateral and the enforcement of collateral can be expensive and take years; see for example Lipsky (2011).

[13]An event of default clause stipulates the circumstances under which a default occurs, e.g. a covenant violation. It also determines the rights of the creditor in case a default is triggered. See for further details below 3.4.3.

[14]Security is defined as a mortgage, charge, pledge, lien or any other security interest securing any obligation of any person or any other agreement or arrangement having a similar effect.

[15]Box 22.3. LMA Loan Term: Wright (2006), p. 149 et seqq.

Papermaker had some good experiences with issuing bonds before and would like to issue bonds again. However, the issuance of secured bonds would violate the negative pledge clause as all kinds of security are prohibited.[16] Best Bank has signalled that it will not waive a default of the negative pledge clause because it views the future investments in the infrastructure as untimely and risky. Moreover, it fears the dilution of its collateral and Papermaker's pool of assets. Because Papermaker relies on the syndicated loan and the bank consortium has a right to accelerate in case of a covenant default according to the event of default clause, it accommodates Best Bank's concerns and decides to issue unsecured bonds.

This example illustrates that covenants and the event of default clause provide banks—in this case, the bank consortium and its leader Best Bank—with leverage to protect themselves from, among other things, the dilution of a debtor company's asset pool. Covenants allow the creditor and the debtor company to manage their own affairs in a fast and effective way using private mechanisms and, hence, they establish a bilateral[17] private governance system.[18]

1.2 Relevance of Third-Party Creditor Protection

The bank consortium, however, is not Papermaker's only creditor. Usually, there are more creditors involved. For the purposes of this work, those other creditors who are not part of the concerned covenant-secured bank loan agreement will be called third-party creditors.[19] They are a heterogeneous group of strong and weak creditors with diverse interests. Some will be adjusting creditors due to their bargaining power, contractual rights or short credit period. These creditors are capable of adapting their claims to the particular circumstances of the debtor as well as to the effects of a new credit granted to other creditors.[20] They can be

[16]Cf. Wright (2006), p. 150.

[17]In case of a syndicated loan, the private governance system can still be referred to as bilateral in a broader sense. Covenants provide creditor protection to the bank consortium as a whole, even though the bank consortium consists of different creditors. Their internal relationship is regulated by intercreditor agreements.

[18]See below 3.5.

[19]Banks have been chosen as the starting point because they are still the most important covenant-secured lenders. For further explanations see below 7.2.

[20]The differentiation between adjusting and non-adjusting creditors is the common standard. For example see Keay (2007), p. 15 et seqq. *Gullifer* and *Payne* distinguish between three categories of creditors: "those who consciously extend credit to the company (whether in the form of loans or trade credit or otherwise), those who deal with the company without intending to extent credit, but become creditors because the company becomes liable to them for breach of contract or otherwise (such as customers of goods and services), and those who have no prior contact with the company before becoming creditors (this category is mainly tort victims and tax authorities)." Gullifer and Payne (2011), p. 74.

i.a. other banks or institutional lenders, bondholders,[21] trade creditors, employees,[22] or consumers.[23]

Nonetheless, not every adjusting creditor is necessarily strong. Some might be weak if they lack the necessary bargaining power, information or alternatives—as may be the case for some employees, trade creditors and consumers. This puts this group of creditors *de facto* in the same position as non-adjusting creditors, who are unable to adjust their claim. For this reason, weak creditors are often categorised as non-adjusting creditors[24] alongside tort claimants and the state.[25] The state and public agencies constitute the most significant group of non-adjusting creditors.[26] For the purposes of this work, however, they can be neglected. In fact, specific liability regimes are usually in place that extend liability to directors—and, in limited cases, even to dominant shareholders—in order to ensure satisfaction of the state and public agencies.[27] Third-party creditors will therefore refer to banks or other institutional lenders (if not part of the concerned covenant-secured bank loan agreement), and bondholders as third-party creditors, trade creditors, employees, consumers and tort creditors (see Fig. 1.1).

These third-party creditors can be affected by covenants that are part of the bilateral loan agreement between the debtor company and the covenant-secured creditor, who will for the purpose of this work be a bank.[28] The bilaterally agreed-upon contractual rights of the bank, namely covenants, influence the credit risk for third-party creditors and the relationship between the debtor company and third-party creditors. For Scenario 1,[29] this means that the loan agreement between Papermaker and the bank consortium under Best Bank's leadership can have positive or negative impact on third-party creditors, for example bondholders or

[21]The bondholder is owed a debt by the bond issuer. Depending on the terms of the bond, the issuer promises to pay the bondholder interest (the coupon) and/or to repay the principal of the bond at a later date. See for example Zahn and Lemke (2002); Wood (2007), para. 12-002.

[22]The employee qualifies as a creditor since payment for done work is only due at the end of the week or month.

[23]If the product is paid for in advance.

[24]See for example Blumberg (1986), 576, 618 et seq.; Posner (1976), 505; dissenting Easterbrook and Fischel (1985), 104 et seqq.; Meiners et al. (1979), 359 et seqq.

[25]For an exhaustive categorisation of non-adjusting, involuntary creditors see Bebchuk and Fried (1997), 1295 et seqq.; Armour (2000), 362 et seq.; Mokal (2002), 709. There is also an empirical study showing the composition of different claimants in bankruptcy cases in the US; Warren and Westbrook (2005), 1223 et seqq.

[26]It is disputed whether the state is a non-adjusting creditor because it could change the law so as to adapt to the specific situation of the debtor. This theoretical ability, however, does not change the fact that the state does *de facto* not adapt; cf. Bebchuk and Fried (1997), 1298 et seq.

[27]Mülbert (2006), 366; cf. also Klose-Mokroß (1997), p. 90 et seqq.

[28]The term "bank" will be used as synonymous to covenant-secured creditor. This, however, does not imply that a bank cannot be a third-party creditor. A third-party creditor can also be covenant-secured but is not part of particular bilateral loan agreement under which a covenant default occurs. See above 1.1.

[29]See above 1.1.

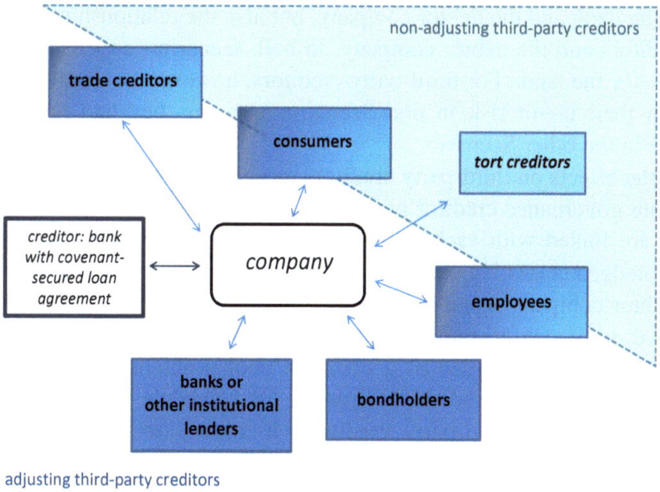

Fig. 1.1 Third party creditors (own illustration)

tort creditors. The prevention of secured bonds via the negative pledge clause is beneficial to all existing unsecured creditors, since the pool of assets available in bankruptcy[30] proceedings is less diluted through unsecured bonds than through secured bonds.

Scenario 2a

Years later after facing major financial difficulties Papermaker negligently feeds residues of the papermaking process into the ecosystem of a river and thousands of fish die as a consequence. Among other tort victims, the fish farmer "Angel" loses thousands of fish worth €18,000. Subsequently, Papermaker has to file for bankruptcy. Since Papermaker only issued unsecured bonds, more assets are available to all unsecured creditors, which leads to a higher recovery sum for Angel.

On the other hand, the bank could use covenants to minimise its own losses and, at the same time, maximise those of other creditors.

Scenario 2b

If Papermaker had to supply additional securities to the bank consortium after defaulting on a covenant that requires Papermaker to comply with environmental law, the pool of assets would be diluted and all unsecured creditors would suffer a higher loss.

These examples show that the self-protection device—the covenant enforced through an event of default clause—affects not only the bilateral relationship

[30]The term "bankruptcy" may sound misleading to UK lawyers with regard to companies because there, bankruptcy only refers to individuals. This work will, however, employ the term "bankruptcy" rather than insolvency to ensure comparability and comprehensibility. Moreover, the work will compare German and US law and in the US the correct term is bankruptcy. Bankruptcy will refer to both liquidation and reorganisation.

between the bank and the debtor company, but also the relationship between third-party creditors and the debtor company. In both scenarios, covenants reduced the credit risk for the bank. For third-party creditors, however, covenants had positive effects on their credit risk in one Scenario, whereas they had negative effects thereupon in the other Scenario.

Thus, the effects on third-party creditors provide a new dimension to covenants as a private governance creditor protection mechanism. This work will show that creditors are linked with each other directly via cross-default,[31] pari passu[32] or negative pledge clauses,[33] but also indirectly via the consequences of their actions on the debtor company's pool of assets. This link transforms the bilateral private governance into a multi-party private governance mechanism. If the conflict between creditors is regarded as a common pool problem, it becomes apparent that the link creates an incentive structure to solve the coordination problem between a bank and third-party creditors. It allows for the internalisation of potential externalities.

The value of covenants (enforced through an event of default clause) as a bilateral creditor protection device has been extensively analysed by the literature,[34] whereas the effects on third-party creditors have been merely treated as a side issue.[35] However, the focus of discussions in corporate governance, bankruptcy law and corporate law has recently moved onto third-party creditor effects.[36] The works by Peter Mankowski,[37] Wolfang Servatius[38] and Stefan Heinrich[39] in particular focus on third-party creditor effects. Their analyses are based on economic theories, but also on presumptions about the covenant-secured creditors' behaviour. Surprisingly, the factual conduct of covenant-secured creditors and therewith the incentive structure surrounding covenants barely appear in empirical research.[40] A profound understanding of both, however, is crucial for assessing the effects of covenants on third-party creditors. Similarly, the legal system impacts the

[31]Under the cross-default clause a default of the debtor company under another loan agreement (to which the creditor is not a party) puts the debtor company in default under the relevant loan agreement (to which the creditor is a party). See below 3.4.4.

[32]The pari passu clause stipulates that the debtor company's payment obligations under the loan agreement "rank at least pari passu (equally) with the claims of all its other unsecured and unsubordinated creditors, except for obligations mandatorily preferred by law applying to companies generally" Clause 19.12. LMA Term Loan: Wright (2006), p. 133; see also below 3.4.2.

[33]See above 1.1 and below 3.3.2.1.

[34]See only Bratton (2006); Garleanu and Zwiebel (2009); Gamba and Triantis (2013).

[35]Discussing third-party creditor effects on three pages for example Kästle (2003), p. 33, 230 et seq.

[36]See below 4.2.

[37]Mankowski, in: Lutter (ed) (2006b); Mankowski, in: Lutter (ed) (2006a).

[38]Servatius (2008).

[39]Heinrich (2009).

[40]There are only a handful of empirical studies. See Lou and Otto (2015); Lian (2014); Gao et al. (2013) 29.10.2015; Falato and Liang (2012).

incentive structure and thereby the third-party creditor effects of covenants if covenants are enforced in court or in the shadow of the law. This work will therefore investigate those aspects by combining an empirical and a law and economics approach, using the example of banks. Moreover, the form of covenant enforcement—in or out of court—will be researched to confirm that covenants and an event of default clause create a bilateral private governance system.

The first part will outline the theoretical foundation of self-help creditor protection to provide a general framework. Afterwards, the covenant's function as a bilateral private governance device of creditor protection between the bank and the debtor company will be presented. The most common covenants in relation to their function of credit risk reduction and other clauses that ensure the enforcement of covenants are discussed.

The second part will systematise and elaborate on the third-party creditor effects of covenants that have been discussed in the literature using a law and economics approach. First, to illustrate the importance of third-party creditor effects, three selected topics where third-party creditor protection and the external effects of covenants are relevant in the legal academic discussion will be presented. Then, the individual potential externalities (both positive and negative) will be specified. Finally, the likely self-interested conduct of banks and its theoretical consequences for the banks' behaviour after a covenant default will be concisely discussed. To illustrate the legal limitations for banks behaving in their own self-interest, a comparative study between the German and US legal systems using two significant examples will be conducted.

Subsequently, the third part will review the theoretical findings using an empirical qualitative study. As previously mentioned, the study will research the bank's conduct after a covenant default and the form of covenant enforcement—whether in or out of court. First, the study's design and methodology will be presented, followed by its findings. Those findings will then be discussed and the preliminary theory will be re-evaluated accordingly. The work will work out the incentive structure that allows internalising potential externalities of covenants by using the concept of common pool resources. Moreover, the implications of such an incentive structure as a CPR private governance system for both the above mentioned selected topics from the legal debates as well as the legal treatment of covenants and an event of default clause will be drawn up. Also, measures to foster the incentive structure will be developed. Finally, a conclusion will summarise all findings and a short outlook will be provided.

References

Adams D (2003) Corporate finance: banking and capital markets. Legal practice course 2002/03 series, 8th edn. Jordans, UK

Armour J (2000) Share capital and creditor protection: efficient rules for a modern company law. Mod Law Rev 63:355–378

Bebchuk LA, Fried JM (1997) The uneasy case for the priority of secured claims in bankruptcy: further thoughts ans a reply ro critics. Cornell Law Rev 82:1279–1348

Bleifeld M (2015) Akzessorische Kreditsicherheiten im Rahmen von syndizierten Krediten. Eine kreditsicherungsrechtliche und insolvenzrechtliche Überprüfung der Praxismodelle. Schriften zum Europäischen und Internationalen Privat-, Bank- und Wirtschaftsrecht, vol 56. De Gruyter, Berlin

Blumberg PI (1986) Limited liability and corporate groups. J Corp Law 11:573–631

Bratton W (2006) Bond covenants and creditor protection: economics and law, theory and practice, substance and process. Eur Bus Organ Law Rev 7:39–87

Easterbrook FH, Fischel DR (1985) Limited liability and the corporation. Univ Chic Law Rev 52:89–117

Enriques L, Macey JR (2001) Creditors versus capital formation: the case against the European legal capital rules. Cornell Law Rev 86:1165–1204

Falato A, Liang N (2012) Do creditor rights increase employment risk? Evidence from debt covenants. http://ssrn.com/abstract=2489115. Accessed 18 Feb 2016

Fifoot CHS (1970) History and sources of the common law. Tort and contract. reprinted edn. Greenwood Press Publishers, New York

Gamba A, Triantis AJ (2013) How effectively can debt covenants alleviate financial agency problems? http://ssrn.com/abstract=2101645. Accessed 25 Jan 2016

Ganter HG (2011) § 90. In: Schimansky H, Bunte H-J, Lwowski H-J (eds) Bankrechts-Handbuch. Beck, München

Gao Y, Khan M, Tan L (2013) Third-party costs of debt covenant violations: the case of audit fees. http://ssrn.com/abstract=2250750

Garleanu N, Zwiebel J (2009) Design and renegotiation of debt covenants. Rev Financ Stud 22:749–781

Golin J, Delhaise P (2013) The bank credit analysis handbook: a guide for analysts, bankers, and investors, 2nd edn. Wiley, Singapore

Gullifer L, Payne J (2011) Corporate finance law. Principles and policy. Hart, Oxford

Haghani S, Holzamer M, Voll S, Warnig C (2009) Financial Covenants in der Unternehmensfinanzierung. Roland Berger. http://www.rolandberger.com/media/pdf/Roland_Berger_Financial_Covenants_20090725.pdf. Accessed 07 Mar 2013

Heinrich S (2009) Covenants als Alternative zum institutionellen Gläubigerschutz. Eine rechtsvergleichende und ökonomische Analyse, vol 228. Schriften zum Wirtschaftsrecht. Duncker & Humblot, Berlin

Kästle M (2003) Rechtsfragen der Verwendung von Covenants in Kreditverträgen. Berlin

Keay A (2007) Company directors' responsibilities to creditors. Routledge-Cavendish, New York

Klose-Mokroß L (1997) Gläubigerschutz im Kapitalgesellschaftsrecht am Beispiel der Lehre von der verdeckten Sacheinlage. Lang, Frankfurt am Main [u.a.]

Landers JM (1976) Another word on parents, subsidiaries and affiliates in bankruptcy. Univ Chic Law Rev 43:527–540

Law J, Martin EA (2009) A dictionary of law. Oxford paperback reference, 7th edn. Oxford University Press, Oxford

Leichtling MA, Dubin BA, Wong JJ (2013) Commercial loan documentation guide. Mathew Bender, San Francisco

Lian Y (2014) Do bonholders receive benefits from bank interventions? http://www.nabet.us/proceedings-archive/NABET-ProceedingsFinal-2014.pdf-page=171. Accessed 06 Apr 2016

Lipsky MJ (2011) Statutenwechsel im italienischen Sachenrecht - Auswirkungen auf den Im- und Export von Mobiliarsicherheiten. Eine Untersuchung der rechtlichen Beständigkeit dinglicher Kreditsicherheiten im deutsch-italienischen Rechtsverkehr. Studien zum vergleichenden und internationalen Recht; 170. Lang, Frankfurt am Main [u.a.]

Lou Y, Otto CA (2015) Debt heterogeneity and covenants. http://ssrn.com/abstract=2297804. Accessed 08 Apr 2016

Mankowski P (2006a) Does contract suffice to protect the creditors of a company and their interests? In: Lutter M (ed) Legal capital in Europe, vol Spezial 1. European company and financial law review. De Gruyter, Berlin, pp 394–410
Mankowski P (2006b) Reicht das Vertragsrecht für einen angemessenen Schutz der Gesellschaftsgläubiger und ihrer Interessen aus? In: Lutter M (ed) Das Kapital der Aktiengesellschaft in Europa. de Gruyter Recht, Berlin, pp 488–507
Mansel H-P (2015) Art. 43 EGBGB. In: Heinrich D (ed) J. von Staudingers Kommentar zum Bürgerlichen Gesetzbuch. De Gruyter, Berlin
Meiners RE, Mofsky JS, Tollison RD (1979) Piercing the veil of limited liability. Del J Corp Law 4:351–367
Mokal RJ (2002) The search for someone save: a defensive case for the priority of secured credit. Oxf J Leg Stud 22:687–728
Mülbert PO (2006) A synthetic view of different concepts of creditor protection, or: a high-level framework for corporate creditor protection. Eur Bus Organ Law Rev 7:357–408
Posner RA (1976) The rights of creditors of affiliated corporations. Univ Chic Law Rev 43:499–526
Renner M (2015) Bankvertragsrecht, Vierter Teil. In: Canaris C-W, Habersack M, Schäfer C (eds) Staub, GroßkommHGB. de Gruyter, Berlin
Schön W (2004a) Die Zukunft der Kapitalaufbringung/-erhaltung. Der Konzern:162–170
Schön W (2004b) The future of legal capital. Eur Bus Organ Law Rev 5:429–448
Servatius W (2008) Gläubigereinfluss durch Covenants. Mohr Siebeck, Tübingen
Tighe R (1984) Structuring commercial loan agreements. Warren, Groham & Lamont, Boston
Warren E, Westbrook JL (2005) Contracting out of bankruptcy: an empirical intervention. Harv Law Rev 118:1197–1254
Wood P (2007) International loans, bonds, guarantees, legal opinions, vol 2. Sweet & Maxwell, London
Wright S (2006) International loan documentation. Palgrave Macmillan, New York
Zahn A, Lemke R (2002) Anleihen als Instrument der Finanzierung und Risikosteuerung. BKR:527–535

Chapter 2
Self-Help Devices of Creditor Protection

The following chapter will provide a general framework for creditor protection when the debtor is a limited (public or private) company. This will clarify the legitimacy of self-help devices and the varying vulnerability of third-party creditors in the face of potential externalities. It will begin by introducing the reason for self-help creditor protection, namely the reduction of credit risk. Afterwards, it will outline the extent to which particular creditor types can use self-help devices.

2.1 Credit Risk

Creditor self-help devices are part of a bank's risk management strategy. Risk management is becoming increasingly important for banks, because the international regulatory framework for banks—the Basel Accord III[1]—links the required bank capital to credit risk.

Credit risk is closely connected to the concept of asymmetric information.[2] The debtor company possesses more and better information about its own creditworthiness before and after being granted a loan than the creditor can collect without

[1]Basel III: A global regulatory framework for more resilient banks and banking systems - revised version June 2011, available at http://www.bis.org/publ/bcbs189.pdf, last accessed 31.01.2016; implemented within the European Union by Regulation (EU) No 575/2013 of the European Parliament and of the Council of 26 June 2013 on prudential requirements for credit institutions and investment firms; OJ 2013 L 176/1 and Directive 2013/36/EU of the European Parliament and of the Council of 26 June 2013 on access to the activity of credit institutions and the prudential supervision of credit institutions and investment firms; OJ 2013 L 176/338.

[2]Asymmetric information is rooted in the New Institutional Economics; see for example Fleischer (2001).

D. Matri, *Covenants and Third-Party Creditors*, DOI 10.1007/978-3-319-62036-7_2

disproportional costs. This can lead to opportunistic behaviour[3] and an agency conflict between shareholder[4] and creditors.[5]

Since creditors must provide advanced performance, they assume—with disbursement of the loan—the downside risk of the debtor company's financial situation. Credit is granted based on the creditworthiness of the debtor company at loan inception. The debtor company's internal credit rating[6] estimates the probability of default by the debtor company over a given time period[7]—typically 1 year.[8] These ratings are based either on statistical methods or purely expert judgements, but include similar risk factors. These are often in both qualitative (soft) and quantitative (financial data) factors, such as profitability, management experience, line of business and competitiveness,[9] industry prospective, cash flow,[10] and leverage.[11] If the credit risk is considered to be too high, the loan will not be granted or the high risk must be redeemed by the loan conditions, e.g. high interest rates.[12] Thus, both the loan approval and loan conditions[13] depend on a number of risk factors evaluated at a given time before granting a loan. If one of the factors subsequently deteriorates, the creditworthiness will decrease and, at worst, the debtor company will not fulfil its contractual obligations and bankruptcy proceedings may commence with respect to its assets.

---

[3]"Opportunistic behaviour occurs whenever one party attempts to obtain, at the expense of the other, a benefit not contemplated by the initial agreement, either explicitly or implicitly." Fischel (1989), 138.

[4]This presupposes that management acts on behalf of shareholders according to the shareholder value approach; see Armour et al., in: Kraakman et al. (eds) (2009), 117 et seq.; Bratton and Wachter (2010).

[5]Jensen and Meckling (1976); Myers (1977); Smith and Warner (1979); Malitz (1986); Bratton (2006); critically Graham and Harvey (2001); German literature: Schmidt (1980), p. 62; Eidenmüller (2001), 1048; Heinrich (2009), p. 222 et seq., 283 et seq.; Richter and Furubotn (2010), p. 173 et seqq.; Steffek (2011), p. 24 et seqq.; Servatius (2013), 15.

[6]Their importance also increased due to their consideration in Basel II as primary inputs to bank's minimum regulatory capital calculation. See Basel Committee on Banking Supervision (2005); Kästle (2003), p. 235 et seqq.

[7]Loan approvals depend in banking practice on ratings cf. Grunert et al. (2005), 510. One has to distinguish between the debtor company's rating and the loan rating. The former refers to the general default risk of the debtor company; the latter considers the actual loan agreement, i.e. collateral and covenants. Cf. Brunner et al. (2000), p. 5.

[8]Golin and Delhaise (2013), p. 24; Treacy and Carey (2000), 176.

[9]The competitiveness is evaluated by a comparative analysis in the market cf. Hale (1983), p. 7 et seq.

[10]Hale (1983), p. 3 et seqq.

[11]Cf. Golin and Delhaise (2013), p. 4 et seq., 21 et seqq., 59 et seqq.; Grunert et al. (2005), 511; Brunner et al. (2000), p. 8; Jacobson et al. (2006), 1906 et seqq.

[12]Cf. Admati and Hellwig (2013), p. 104.

[13]Cf. Merton (1974); but covenants, representations, warranties and collateral are also relevant.

These concerns can be broken down into three potential risks for creditors during the lifespan of a loan: The risk of false or lacking information; the risk of bankruptcy; and the risk of loss.[14]

2.1.1 Risk of False or Lacking Information

First, at the loan-granting stage, voluntary creditors face the risk that they might provide a loan that they otherwise would not have granted based on incomplete, false, belated or lacking information (risk of false or lacking information) that they otherwise would not have granted. *Ex ante* a debtor company might be inclined to provide false or misleading information about the value of corporate assets.[15] As a consequence, the creditor is not able to reliably compare potential debtor companies, which might lead to an adverse selection.[16] The creditor will therefore be undercompensated for risks. This might disrupt the functioning of the debt capital market.[17] In the case of non-adjusting creditors, the risk of information is often irrelevant as the majority has no choice in becoming a creditor anyway.[18]

2.1.2 Risk of Bankruptcy

After granting a loan, creditors then assume the downside risk of the debtor company's financial situation—i.e. that the debtor company cannot fulfil its contractual obligations and bankruptcy proceedings are commenced with respect to its assets (risk of bankruptcy). The need to reduce this risk is particularly pressing under the system of limited liability,[19] since the incentive for opportunistic behaviour is higher.[20] The debtor company—in the form of the acting manager of the borrowing company or directors and the shareholders[21]—might be inclined to perform worse or even to undertake a shift of wealth in its favour. Shareholders, for example, may have an incentive to keep all produced income in the case of

[14]Rausch (1985), p. 11 et seqq.; a different categorisation is followed by Mülbert (2006), 367 et seqq. and Thole (2010), p. 13 et seqq.

[15]Armour et al., in: Kraakman et al. (eds) (2009), p. 116.

[16]Akerlof (1970).

[17]Cf. Leland and Pyle (1977).

[18]Cf. Mülbert (2006), 369.

[19]For an evaluation of the economic usefulness of limited liability see Easterbrook and Fischel (1985); Hansmann and Kraakman (2000).

[20]For an elaboration of the relationship of limited liability and creditor protection see Teichmann (2006), p. 474 et seq.

[21]Cf. Bachner (2009), p. 21; Mülbert (2006), 368 et seq.

fixed-interest debts. Then, shareholders are willing to take higher risks since they have much to gain while their liability is restricted to their shareholder's equity. The chance to win and the risk of losing are asymmetrically distributed.[22] Thus, shareholders may act to the detriment of the debtholders, who will ultimately bear the consequences. The incentive for opportunistic behaviour is highest during a company's beginnings and when it is already facing a downwards trend that will eventually lead to bankruptcy. However, this does not mean that all bankruptcies are caused by opportunistic behaviour. The line between an inacceptable shift of wealth and an acceptable risk of loss is blurred.[23]

This opportunistic behaviour will incur costs, so-called agency costs.[24] The extensive literature[25] identifies three main types of agency costs for debts. First, asset substitution[26] occurs when a debtor company substitutes its low-risk assets for high-risk investments. As previously mentioned, the debtor company has an incentive to invest in high-risk projects as it benefits in case of success while being protected by limited liability in case of failure. Asset substitution also refers to asset dilution or withdrawal, where wealth is transferred from creditors to equity holders.[27] The second agency cost is called underinvestment.[28] There, a debtor company does not invest in low-risk projects because the return would only be used to pay off the debtholders, and the equity holder would be left with little or no excess return. As a consequence, the project, which would increase the overall value of the debtor company, will be rejected. The third agency cost of claim dilution[29] refers to the negative impact of the debtor company incurring subsequent debts.[30] The value of the claim (attached to a loan) can decline when subsequent borrowings are of the same or higher priority in bankruptcy. This also occurs when the creditor is not appropriately compensated for the increased credit risk by the interest rate.[31] At worst, the newly raised funds by the additional debts are distributed to the shareholders.[32]

---

[22]Known as overinvestment incentive by Jensen and Meckling (1976), 334 et seqq.

[23]Boese (2009), p. 22 et seq.

[24]This refers to the agency conflict between shareholder and creditors. See above 2.1.

[25]See only. Jensen and Meckling (1976); Myers (1977); Smith and Warner (1979); Malitz (1986); Bratton (2006); critically Graham and Harvey (2001).

[26]Cf. Jensen and Meckling (1976), 334 et seqq.; Green and Talmor (1986).

[27]This is sometimes dealt with as separate problem; see for example Bratton (2006), 45; Armour et al., in: Kraakman et al. (eds) (2009), p. 116.

[28]Cf. Myers (1977).

[29]Cf. Smith and Warner (1979).

[30]Other sources that dilute creditors' claims are also included in the concept of claim dilution, like pension claims, legal claims or tax penalties; cf. Tappeiner (2010), p. 36.

[31]Cf. Masulis (1980), 144 et seq.

[32]There are, of course, legal restrictions on such behaviour. However, these differ significantly in legal systems and do not always provide appropriate protection.

2.1.3 *Risk of Loss*

In the bankruptcy stage, creditors face the risk that during bankruptcy proceedings their claims will only be satisfied partially or not at all (risk of loss). This risk is closely related to the risk of bankruptcy, or can even be regarded as its materialisation. Creditors can suffer greater losses through opportunistic behaviour on the part of the debtor company. The value or number of assets available to satisfy creditors on bankruptcy can be diluted or the debtor company could pursue risky projects that lead to a shift of risk from the debtor company to the creditor. If there are only unsecured creditors, the pool of assets will generally be divided between them.[33] When there are secured creditors, however, they will enjoy priority and the collateral will not be available for the satisfaction of the other unsecured creditors. Thus, if a borrower obtains a secured credit *ex post*, the pool of assets for the satisfaction of the "first" creditor is diminished.[34] This can lead to a conflict between creditors.

2.1.4 *Corporate Groups as a Special Case*

The situation is more complicated when it involves a corporate group.[35] In these cases, the risk of bankruptcy and loss increases.[36] In addition, transfer prices and inter-company loans are problematic. Although the issue of corporate groups is important, a detailed analysis of this problem is not feasible within the scope of this work.[37] It suffices to be aware of the fact that when corporate groups are involved, the agency costs and the risks of bankruptcy and loss increase.

2.2 Mechanisms of Creditor Protection

Creditors can protect themselves against these risks by employing contractual and/or proprietary mechanisms.[38]

---

[33]The legal principal of *par conditio creditorum* is broadly accepted; cf. only UNCITRAL (2005), p. 11 et seq. and Thole (2010), p. 61.

[34]Thole (2010), p. 17 et seq.

[35]A general legal defintion of corporate groups is difficult to find; cf. only M. Hesselbarth, Conceptualising Transnational Corporate Groups. A Proposal for International Criminal Law, PhD thesis, forthcoming.

[36]The controlled company might provide the controlling company with constructive dividends and other concealed distributions. See, for example, Kühbacher (1993), p. 7.

[37]For more details see Armour et al., in: Kraakman et al. (eds) (2009), p. 127 et seq.

[38]The distinction between proprietary and contractual security devices is blurred. It helps, however, to comprehensively present the self-help devices.

2.2.1 Proprietary Devices

Proprietary devices help to minimise potential losses to creditors because they provide prior property rights over a particular asset—collateral. Thereby, the secured creditor can be reimbursed by realisation of the collateral before paying most of the debtor's other unsecured creditors. The collateral does not become part of the asset pool available for unsecured creditors in case of bankruptcy.[39]

The advantages of proprietary interest come with a number of disadvantages for other, less secured creditors—particularly, a higher risk of not being paid back in the event of bankruptcy. Moreover, it undermines the principle of equality in bankruptcy proceedings.[40] As a consequence, it is common for security interests to be statutorily limited in two ways. First, the priority can be statutorily altered on bankruptcy.[41] Second, proprietary interests must be disclosed.[42] Publicity rules in property law ensure that potential creditors know the debtor company's available assets before becoming creditors. Creditors consider the available assets in the credit risk analysis as well as when estimating the risk premium.[43] Information about possible claims attached to assets is therefore essential to reduce the risk of false or lacking information.

This function is fulfilled in German property law for movables by transfer of possession (*Besitzübergabe*).[44] However, the most common security interests—retention of title[45] and assignment as security[46]—are an exception to this concept: The retention of title allows for the transfer of possession, even though the buyer only becomes owner after full payment[47]; and the assignment as security does not require transfer of possession at all. This renders the notion somewhat irrelevant.[48]

---

[39]Wood (2008), para. 16-01. However, the sale price exceeding the loan principal is part of the bankruptcy estate; see below 9.3.2.

[40]See below 9.3.1.

[41]See Brinkmann, in: Eidenmüller, Kieninger (eds) (2008),; Eidenmüller, in: Eidenmüller, Kieniger (eds) (2008),; see further Gullifer and Payne (2011), p. 92 et seqq.; Sigman, in: Eidenmüller, Kieniger (eds) (2008), 159 et seq.; Stürmer, in: Eidenmüller, Kieniger (eds) (2008), 171 et seq.

[42]Gullifer and Payne (2011), p. 219; van Erp and Akkermans (2012), p. 75 et seqq.

[43]See above 2.1.

[44]Publicity refers to the possession transfer (*Besitzübergabe*) and registration in the Land Register (*Grundbucheintragung*); see only Stadler (2002), para. 40; Gaier, in: Säcker, Rixecker (eds) (2013), para. 22.

[45]*Eigentumsvorbehalt*: § 449 BGB. The retention of title is not always considered to involve the creation of security, see Ganter, in: Schimansky et al. (eds) (2011a), paras. 6 et seq. and McCormack (2004) p. 72. The author, however, follows a broader, functional approach. Similarly Westermann, in: Säcker, Rixecker (eds) (2012), paras. 1 et seqq.

[46]*Sicherungsübereignung*: see Ganter, in: Schimansky et al. (eds) (2011b), paras. 1 et seqq.

[47]Under the retention of title, the transfer of possession itself takes place according to the dominant view and under normal circumstances but the condition precedent (*aufschiebende Bedingung*) is not transparent. For a detailed analysis see Füller (2006), p. 361 et seqq.

[48]Similarly Wiegand (1990), 131.

The concept of *numerus clausus*, however, fulfils a similar function because it limits the number of available property rights.[49] There is an exhaustive list of property rights that the parties can enquire about during negotiations. This reduces search costs and respects banking discretion and confidentiality. Moreover, securities over real property must be registered in the Land Register.[50] The most common forms of security interests are the mortgage,[51] retention of title, and assignment as security.

In contrast, US property law recognises an unlimited number of security interests for personal property as it follows a functional approach in § 1-201(35) Uniform Commercial Code (UCC). According to § 1-201(35) UCC, a security interest is an interest in personal property or fixtures that secures payment or performance of an obligation. The creation of a security interest is a two-step process. First, the security interest is attached to the property, which makes it enforceable between the debtor and creditor.[52] Second, after filing notice with the appropriate public office, possessing or controlling the collateral, this security interest is perfected and made enforceable against third parties.[53] US property law therefore requires filing and, thus, publicity for the creation of a property right enforceable against third parties.[54] The law regarding collateral of real property is not coordinated in the US and is governed by state law.

2.2.2 Covenants and Other Contractual Devices

Despite all their benefits, security interests are not always the best option—or sometimes not an option at all—for securing a credit. This can be due to lack of bargaining power (e.g. against large corporate groups)[55] or appropriate collateral,[56] as well as to high transaction costs or contractual limitations in the case of international loans.[57]

---

[49]In the comparative law, context the *numerus clausus*' function is considered as informing other creditors about the existence of a security interest; see e.g. Armour, in: Eidenmüller, Kieninger (eds) (2008),, 25 et seqq. For the *numerus clausus* and its exceptions in Germany see e.g. Stadler (2002), paras. 41 et seq.; Gaier, in: Säcker, Rixecker (eds) (2013),paras. 11 et seqq.; critically Wieling (2007), p. 9.

[50]§ 1115 BGB.

[51]*Hypothek*: §§ 1113 et seqq. BGB; see for example Epp, in: Schimansky et al. (eds) (2011), paras. 3 et seqq.

[52]§ 9-203 UCC.

[53]See §§ 9-301 et seqq. UCC; the particular rules depend on the jurisdiction in which the collateral is located. Cf. McCormack (2004), p. 76 et seqq.

[54]For an overview of security interests in the US from a German perspective see Böckmann (2005), p. 163 et seqq.

[55]See Wood , para. 2-041.

[56]See Kästle (2003), p. 38 et seq.

[57]See Gullifer and Payne (2011), p. 160; Kästle (2003), p. 39 et seq.; Brinkmann (2011), p. 322 et seqq.

2.2.2.1 Other Contractual Devices

As a consequence, some creditors abstain from employing collateral and rely instead on other, contractual means of creditor protection. These include guarantees,[58] credit insurance,[59] subordination,[60] and set-off.[61]

2.2.2.2 Covenants

The most common contractual device in international loans is the covenant.[62] There is no exhaustive list of covenants and parties can, in principle, agree on any kind of covenant. Nevertheless, only a limited number of covenants will be sensible for a specific loan agreement—depending on the particular type of loan and the debtor company.[63] Covenants must be tailored to the specific needs of the given deal, i.e. take into consideration corporate structure, market context and purpose of the loan.[64] Thus, they will be negotiated anew for each loan and both parties will be eager for their interests to prevail. Debtor companies seek to ensure as much managerial freedom as possible as well as a low interest rate,[65] while creditors try to ensure that the risk attached to the loan does not unexpectedly deteriorate prior to maturity[66]—namely that the debtor company is willing and able to repay the loan plus interest according to the loan agreement. Furthermore, they seek a high profit margin.

Therefore, covenants try to ensure that the factors relevant to the credit analysis do not deteriorate, or at least allow the creditor to react to increased credit risk. This is achieved by providing a framework for actions and decision-making to prevent a fast and unchecked expansion of the debtor company that would endanger its sustainability and stability.[67] In this way, covenants can be regarded as providing

---

[58] Cf. Renner, in: Canaris et al. (eds) (2015), paras. 947 et seqq.; Davies (1998), 349 et seq. For US law from a German perspective see Böckmann (2005), p. 172 et seqq.

[59] Also including credit derivatives such as credit default swaps Chaplin (2005), p. 55 et seqq.; Wittinghofer (2010).

[60] Cf. Coogan et al. (1965); Berger, in: Säcker, Rixecker (eds) (2016), para. 105.

[61] Cf. Johnston and Werlen (2010).

[62] One reason for the widespread use of covenants is the uncertainty over security interests in international private law; see Khakzad (2009), p. 29 et seqq.

[63] For an overview of the specific covenants used in different loans see, for example, Wood (2007), paras. 5-049 et seq., 5-054 et seqq.; Kästle (2003), p. 42 et seqq.; Heinrich (2009), p. 135 et seqq. For an overview of specific debtor company's characteristics influencing the package of covenants see e.g. Demerjian (2010); Christensen and Nikolaev (2012).

[64] In more detail see Lloyd (1991), 449 et seqq.; Wood (2008), para. 8-01; cf. also Adams (2003), p. 100 et seq.

[65] It is believed that the type of covenant has no influence on the pricing of the loan cf. Moir and Sudarsanam (2007), 163.

[66] Fight (2004), p. 125.

[67] Similarly see Heinrich (2009), p. 143.

guidance.[68] Furthermore, covenants function as an early warning sign or "tripwire"[69] of financial distress, since they allow creditors to monitor the debtor company's financial situation and to take a number of corrective measures stipulated in the event of default clause in a timely manner. In that way, covenants allow for financial distress to be managed prior to entering the bankruptcy stage.[70]

To serve these purposes, covenants address three different areas: They ensure financial performance, protection of assets, and provision of information.[71] Classically, covenants are divided into the categories financial, affirmative and negative.[72] However, this categorisation is not binding.[73] For the purpose of this work, it is more convenient to categorise covenants according to their function. To provide creditor protection, it is crucial that covenants ensure financial performance, asset protection, and provision of information. The category of financial covenants deals mainly with financial performance. The protection of assets is ensured by both affirmative and negative covenants, whereas information is provided solely by affirmative covenants.

2.2.2.3 Mechanisms Suitable for Specific Creditor Types

As previously mentioned, not all creditors are able to use all types of creditor self-protection devices. The appropriate and available security device depends on the given leverage, economic power and the specific type of credit. The choice is also influenced by transaction costs incurred.[74] Frequently, there are contracting costs, enforcement costs and opportunity costs.[75] In the case of proprietary secured credit, the contracting costs include costs of negotiation and perfection of collateral. The enforcement costs are incurred through policing the security interest and the

[68]Cf. Tighe (1984), para. 4.01 (2)(a); Stern (2013), para. 5.01 (2)(a).

[69]In the US literature this function is often referred to as a "tripwire", cf. Lloyd (1991), 338.

[70]Cf. Thießen (1996), 22; Kästle (2003), p. 35; Servatius (2008), p. 71.

[71]Also Wright (2006), p. 137, Adams (2003), p. 86.

[72]Cf. Wight et al. (2009), p. 281.

[73]Wight et al. (2009), p. 281.

[74]See Davies (1998), 350; cf. also Kuntz (2008), 817 et seq.

[75]There are also reorganisation costs because secured creditors seem to prefer liquidation over reorganisation as they enjoy priority and liquidation is less risky. Listokin (2008), 1047; Zhang (2014), 797. Secured creditors may also hinder a reorganisation in cases where it would create greater value for all parties concerned; see Listokin (2008), 1047; Zhang (2014), 797; generally Baird and Jackson (1984), 106 et seq. This liquidation preference may, however, change due to the different interests of hedge-funds which are becoming more common, see Baird and Rasmussen (2010), 668 et seqq. In addition, secured creditors may create a hold-up problem in the negotiation process of reorganisation in order to obtain excess value since liquidation places a minor risk on their recovery chances. Misbehaviour by the debtor has little to no impact on the value of the pledged asset. Furthermore, secured creditors may push a speedy sale of assets to recover their investments in a timely manner. This may include selling the assets not for what they are worth, but just high enough to recover the loan. Renegotiation costs will, however, only rarely be considered by the parties when choosing a creditor self-help device.

opportunity cost reflects the fact that collateral might prevent efficient undertakings by the debtor company.[76] These three transaction costs identified for security interests also apply to covenants. Contracting costs refer to costs of negotiation and the tailoring of covenants to the specific characteristics of the debtor company and its industry. Enforcement costs include expenses for monitoring covenant compliance. Opportunity costs are incurred by preventing efficient undertakings by the debtor company.

Hence, not every self-help device is suitable for every creditor type. It will always depend on the specific situation. However, there are some *de facto* mechanisms that particular types of creditors commonly use.

2.2.2.3.1 Institutional Lenders

Due to their strong market position[77] institutional lenders can resort to nearly all types of self-help protection devices.[78] In the case of smaller debtor companies, institutional lenders prefer personal guarantees and collateral.[79] However, as the debtor company and the loan volume become bigger, a mixture of various self-help devices is employed. Covenants are standard. However, in recent years so-called "covenant-lite 2.0" loans have evolved in the US, which leave banks with nearly no protection and allow debtor companies to be hyper-leveraged.[80] This development was fostered by the low interest rate policy of the Federal Reserve System.[81]

2.2.2.3.2 Bondholders

Private bondholders are offered bonds on a "take it or leave it" basis, which might not allow for efficient self-protection. Bonds commonly include some covenants, but fewer than in bank loans.[82] Thus, they have a lower level of protection. The protection increases, however, when cross-default clauses are included. These allow bondholders to draw on the same level of protection that is provided by bank loans.[83] Nevertheless, bondholders often face a common action problem due

[76]Bebchuk and Fried (1996), 877.

[77]Cf. Davies (1998), 350; Aichberger (2013), p. 149.

[78]For a good but old overview see Drukarczyk et al. (1985), p. 62 et seq.

[79]Davies (1998), 349 et seq.

[80]See Richter (2014); Burne (June 12, 2014)for a more differentiated view see Choi and Triantis (2013).

[81]See Bean et al. (2015), p.71 et seqq.; Padgett (2013), p. 7 et seq.

[82]See Triantis and Daniels (1995), 1088 with further references. For a comparison of bank loans and bonds see Bratton, in: Eidenmüller, Schön (eds) (2008), p. 62 et seqq.

[83]US bonds included a cross-default clause in 2013 of 65 percent in case of non-investment grade and of 95 percent in case of investment grade, Çelik et al. (2015), p. 43. For further details on the cross-default clause see below 3.4.4.

to a large number of creditors.[84] They also depend on a trustee, who will rarely take steps to actively protect the rights of bondholders.[85] There are, however, a growing number of institutional bondholders who can better protect themselves due to higher volume investments.[86] Nevertheless, hedge funds have recently adopted a more aggressive approach with regard to enforcing covenants that might have forced the issuer to return to more covenant-lite[87] bonds.[88] This active behaviour, however, has sometimes also benefited all bondholders, i.e. when the "compensation" for a covenant default is granted to all creditors.[89]

2.2.2.3.3 Trade Creditors

The ability of trade creditors to protect themselves may be limited by market pressure.[90] However, some trade creditors—especially those who are essential for the debtor's business—will trade with the company on a daily basis and will therefore possess more information about the debtor's financial situation than, for example, banks.[91] They can therefore react promptly to most financial difficulties.[92] Moreover, due to the short time frame of transactions, trade creditors are interested in the solvency of the debtor company rather than in its creditworthiness.[93] The transaction costs of securing information about the debtor company are also relatively low, as trade creditors can rely on the information of other trade creditors who have dealt with the specific debtor company before.[94]

Generally, trade creditors have at their disposal the following devices to protect themselves: a general or individual reflection of credit risk in the price charged[95]; retention of title clauses in the case of goods; collateral from the company; personal guarantees from shareholders; advance payment requirements[96]; diversification of

84 See for example Schmidtbleicher (2010); Allen (2012), 65 et seqq.

85 Çelik et al. (2015), p. 52.

86 Çelik et al. (2015), p. 54.

87 Covenant-lite refers to the lack of maintenance covenants.

88 Çelik et al. (2015), p. 52 et seqq.

89 Cf. Kahan and Rock (2009).

90 See Finch (1999), 642, 644.

91 Cf. Finch (1999), 643.

92 This is regarded as trade creditors' main means of protection by Manning and Hanks (1990), p. 98.

93 See Enriques and Macey (2001), 1189.

94 Similarly see Kronman and Jackson (1979), 1160 et seq.; Böckmann (2005), p. 182 et seq.; Escher-Weingart (2001), p. 114 et seqq.; critically Mankowski, in: Lutter (ed) (2006), p. 498 et seqq.

95 It may often be impossible or inefficient for the trade creditor to estimate the particular credit risk of the debtor. They might be able free-ride to some extent on the information provided by banks, cf. Böckmann (2005), p. 183 et seqq.

96 Then they are, by definition, no longer creditors.

credit risk by contracting with a large number of different customers; and monitoring the financial situation of customers in order to stop supplying them in case of financial difficulties (contractual right to termination in case of financial difficulties or separate contracts for supplies required).[97]

If no information is available, the trade creditor can also employ rating agencies,[98] factoring[99] or trade credit insurers.[100]

2.2.2.3.4 Customers

Customers may protect themselves by refusing to pay in advance,[101] ensuring that goods or ownership[102] pass on payment and not on delivery,[103] or set-off in the case of running accounts, or diversification.[104] This, however, is not always possible since goods are sometimes offered on a "take it or leave it" basis. Then, the customer can only opt for the most trusted retail company, which will not always provide sufficient protection. For example, in the recent bankruptcy of the hardware stores Praktiker AG and Max Bahr GmbH & Co. KG, many customers ended up as unsecured creditors in the bankruptcy proceedings.[105]

2.2.2.3.5 Employees

Employees are unlikely to diversify by working for more than one employee,[106] but may—depending on the market situation and their educational background—change jobs. However, the majority of employees will be unable to change jobs quickly.[107] Employees are nonetheless partially secured through unemployment

---

[97] Gullifer and Payne (2011), p. 75; see also Drukarczyk et al. (1985), p. 65, Enriques and Macey (2001), 1189.

[98] However, this incurs high costs, cf, Böckmann (2005), p. 498 et seq.

[99] For the current use of factoring in Germany see Hartmann-Wendels (2012); see generally Renner, in: Canaris et al. (eds) (2015), paras. 436 et seqq.

[100] For an overview of trade credit insurances, see Baumann (1966), p. 18 et seqq.; Greulich (1975), p. 20 et seqq.; Grauschopf, in: Veith et al. (eds) (2016), paras. 10, 21 et seqq.; Jus (2013).

[101] Then, they are by definition no longer creditors.

[102] Depending on the jurisdiction, the tradition system or the consensual system and the principle of abstraction or causality is applied; cf. van Erp and Akkermans (2012), p. 783 et seqq.

[103] Retention of title.

[104] Gullifer and Payne (2011), p. 75.

[105] Cf. Sievers (06.08.2013).

[106] Cf. Warren and Westbrook (2005), 1232; Funke (2011), p. 80 et seq.

[107] Cf. Gullifer and Payne (2011), p. 76. However, a legal protection mechanism might be provided by labour representatives in boards as in Germany; cf. Fauver and Fuerst (2006); Arthurs et al., in: Wright et al. (eds) (2013), p. 696.

insurance provided by the state.[108] In some countries, even private insurances are available.[109]

2.2.2.3.6 Tort Creditors

Tort creditors have no benefit of contractual protection, since they are unaware of becoming a tort creditor *ex ante*. Arguably, the majority of tort claims arising from a company's actions are covered by compulsory insurance schemes—namely work and traffic accidents.[110]

References

Adams D (2003) Corporate finance: banking and capital markets. Legal practice course 2002/03 series, 8th edn. Jordans, UK

Admati A, Hellwig M (2013) The bankers' new clothes. what's wrong with banking and what to do about it. Princeton University Press, Oxfordeshire

Aichberger T (2013) Gläubigerschutz durch Ausschüttungssperren. Eine ökonomische Analyse anhand des deutschen, englischen und US-amerikanischen Regelungsmodells. Peter Lang, Frankfurt am Main

Akerlof GA (1970) The market for "lemons": quality uncertainty and the market mechanism. Q J Econ 84:488–500

Allen JG (2012) More than a matter of trust: the German Debt Securities Act 2009 in international perspective. Cap Mark Law J 7:55–85

Armour J, Hertig G, Kanda H (2009) Transaction with creditors. In: Kraakman RH, Armour J, Davies P et al (eds) The anatomy of corporate law. A comparative and functional approach, 2nd edn. Oxford University Press, Oxford, pp 115–151

Arthurs JD, Hoskisson RE, White RE, Wyatt C (2013) Multiple agency theory. An emerging perspective on corporate governance. In: Wright M, Siegel DS, Keasey K, Filatotchev I (eds) The Oxford handbook of corporate governance, 1st edn. Oxford University Press, Oxford, pp 673–702

Bachner T (2009) Creditor protection in private companies. Anglo-German perspectives for a European legal discourse. Oxford University Press, Oxford

Baird DG, Jackson TH (1984) Corporate reoganizations and the treatment of diverse ownership interests: a comment on adequate protection of secured creditors in bankruptcy. Univ Chic Law Rev 51:97–130

Baird DG, Rasmussen RK (2010) Antibankruptcy. Yale Law J 119:648–699

Basel Committee on Banking Supervision (2005) Studies on the validation of internal rating systems. Bank for international settlements. http://www.bis.org/publ/bcbs_wp14.htm. Accessed 22 Oct 2013

Baumann HA (1966) Factoring, Warenkreditversicherung, Zessionskredit. Eine vergleichende Darstellung. Schön, München

[108] Blaurock, in: Damm (ed) (2005), p. 10; Funke (2011), p. 82 et seqq.

[109] Klose-Mokroß (1997), p. 148; Aichberger (2013), p. 152.

[110] Cf. Klose-Mokroß (1997), p. 87; Blaurock, in: Damm (ed) (2005), p.10 et seq.; Gullifer and Payne (2011), p. 142.

Bean C, Broda C, Ito T, Kroszner RS (2015) Low for long? Causes and consequences of persistently low interest rates. http://www.icmb.ch/ICMB/Home_files/GenevaReportN%C2%B017.pdf. Accessed 20 Jan 2016
Bebchuk LA, Fried JM (1996) The uneasy case for the priority of secured claims in bankruptcy. Yale Law J 105:857–934
Berger KP (2016) Vorb. zu § 488. In: Säcker FJ, Rixecker R (eds) Münchener Kommentar zum BGB. Beck, München
Blaurock U (2005) Mindestkapital und Haftung bei der GmbH. In: Damm R (ed) Book Mindestkapital und Haftung bei der GmbH. Series Mindestkapital und Haftung bei der GmbH. De Gruyter, Berlin, pp 3–22
Böckmann T (2005) Gläubigerschutz bei GmbH und close corporation. Eine rechtsvergleichende Untersuchung nach deutschem und US-amerikanischem Recht unter besonderer Berücksichtigung des Rechts von Delaware, Kalifornien und New York, vol Band 151. Abhandlungen zum deutschen und europäischen Handels- und Wirtschaftsrecht. Carl Heymanns, Köln
Boese S (2009) Strukturprinzipien im Gläubigerschutz: eine rechtsvergleichende Untersuchung zur GmbH und zur englischen limited company. Studien zum vergleichenden internationalen Recht - comparative and international law studies, vol 159. Peter Lang, Frankfurt am Main
Bratton W (2006) Bond covenants and creditor protection: economics and law, theory and practice, substance and process. Eur Bus Organ Law Rev 7:39–87
Bratton WW (2008) Bond covenants and creditor protection: economics and law, theory and practice, substance and process. In: Eidenmüller H, Schön W (eds) The law and economics of creditor protection. A transatlantic perspective. T.M.C. Asser Press, The Hague, pp 37–85
Bratton WW, Wachter ML (2010) The case against shareholder empowerment. Univ Pa Law Rev 158:653–728
Brinkmann M (2008) The position of secured creditors in insolvency. In: Eidenmüller H, Kieninger E-M (eds) The future of secured credit in Europe, pp 248–283
Brinkmann M (2011) Kreditsicherheiten an beweglichen Sachen und Forderungen. Eine materiell-, insolvenz- und kollisionsrechtliche Studie des Rechts der Mobiliarsicherheiten vor dem Hintergrund internationaler und europäischer Entwicklungen. Jus Privatum, vol 156. Mohr Siebeck, Tübingen
Brunner A, Krahnen JP, Weber M (2000) Information production in credit relationships: on the role of internal ratings in commercial banking. http://publikationen.ub.uni-frankfurt.de/opus4/frontdoor/index/index/docId/4519. Accessed 22 Oct 2013
Çelik S, Demirtaş G, Isaksson M (2015) Corporate bonds, bondholders and corporate governance. doi:10.1787/5js69lj4hvnw-en. Accessed 19 Jan 2016
Chaplin G (2005) Credit derivatives. Risk management, trading and investing. Wiley, Chichester
Choi A, Triantis GG (2013) Market conditions and contract design: variations in debt contracting. N Y Univ Law Rev 88:51–82
Christensen HB, Nikolaev VV (2012) Capital versus performance: covenants in debt contracts. J Account Res 50:75–115
Coogan PF, Kripke H, Weiss F (1965) The outer fringes of article 9: subordination agreements, security interests in money and deposits, negative pledge clause and participation agreements. Harv Law Rev 79:229–277
Davies P (1998) Legal capital in private companies in Great Britain. AG:346–354
Demerjian PR (2010) Financial covenants, credit risk, and the resolution of uncertainty. http://ssrn.com/abstract=1559232. Accessed 10 Jan 2014
Drukarczyk J, Duttle J, Rieger R (1985) Mobiliarsicherheiten. Rechtstatsachenforschung. Bundesanzeiger, Köln
Easterbrook FH, Fischel DR (1985) Limited liability and the corporation. Univ Chic Law Rev 52:89–117
Eidenmüller H (2001) Kapitalgesellschaftsrecht im Spiegel ökonomischer Theorie. JZ 21:1041–1051

Eidenmüller H (2008) Secured creditors in insolvency proceedings. In: Eidenmüller H, Kieniger E-M (eds) The future of secured credit in Europe. European company and financial law review. De Gruyter Recht, Berlin, pp 273–283
Enriques L, Macey JR (2001) Creditors versus capital formation: the case against the European legal capital rules. Cornell Law Rev 86:1165–1204
Epp W (2011) § 94. In: Schimansky H, Bunte H-J, Lwowski H-J (eds) Bankrechts-Handbuch. Beck, München
van Erp S, Akkermans B (2012) Cases, materials and text on national, supranational and international property law. Ius Commune casebooks for the common law of Europe. Hart, Oxford
Escher-Weingart C (2001) Reform durch Deregulierung im Kapitalgesellschaftsrecht. Eine Analyse der Reformmöglichkeiten unter besonderer Berücksichtigung des Gläubiger- und Anlegerschutzes. Mohr Siebeck, Tübingen
Fauver L, Fuerst ME (2006) Does good corporate governance include employee representation? Evidence from German Corporate Boards. J Financ Econ 82:673–710
Fight A (2004) Syndicated lending: essential capital markets. Butterworth Heinemann, UK
Finch V (1999) Security, insolvency and risk: who pays the price? Mod Law Rev 62:633–670
Fischel DR (1989) The economics of lender liability. Yale Law J 99:131–154
Fleischer H (2001) Informationsasymmetrie im Vertragsrecht. Beck, München
Füller JT (2006) Eigenständiges Sachenrecht? Jus privatum 104. Mohr Siebeck, Tübingen
Funke MC (2011) Gläubigerschutz durch Information im Recht der Aktiengesellschaft, vol 60. Heidelbergerschriften zum Wirtschaftsrecht und Europarecht. Nomos, Baden-Baden
Gaier R (2013) Einleitung Sachenrecht. In: Säcker FJ, Rixecker R (eds) Münchener Kommentar zum BGB. Beck, München
Ganter HG (2011a) § 90. In: Schimansky H, Bunte H-J, Lwowski H-J (eds) Bankrechts-Handbuch. Beck, München
Ganter HG (2011b) § 95. In: Schimansky H, Bunte H-J, Lwowski H-J (eds) Bankrechts-Handbuch. Beck, München
Golin J, Delhaise P (2013) The bank credit analysis handbook: a guide for analysts, bankers, and investors, 2nd edn. Wiley, Singapore
Graham JR, Harvey CR (2001) The theory and practice of corporate finance: evidence from the field. J Financ Econ 60:187–243
Grauschopf J (2016) § 22 Kreditversicherung. In: Veith J, Gräfe J, Gebert Y (eds) Der Versicherungsprozess. Nomos, Baden-Baden
Green RC, Talmor E (1986) Asset substitution and the agency costs of debt financing. J Bank Financ 10:391–399
Greulich H (1975) Die Kreditversicherung, vol 43. Taschenbücher für Geld, Bank und Börse. Fritz Knapp, Frankfurt am Main
Grunert J, Norden L, Weber M (2005) The role of non-financial factors in internal credit ratings. J Bank Financ 29:509–531
Gullifer L, Payne J (2011) Corporate finance law. Principles and policy. Hart, Oxford
Hale RH (1983) Credit analysis. A complete guide. Wiley, New York
Hansmann H, Kraakman RH (2000) The essential role of organizational law. Yale Law J 110:387–440
Hartmann-Wendels T (2012) Factoring: ein Finanzierungsinstrument mit Wachstumspotenzial. Ergebnisse einer Befragung deutscher Unternehmen. Finanzierung, Leasing, Factoring 59 (1):14–19
Heinrich S (2009) Covenants als Alternative zum institutionellen Gläubigerschutz. Eine rechtsvergleichende und ökonomische Analyse, vol 228. Schriften zum Wirtschaftsrecht. Duncker & Humblot, Berlin
Jacobson T, Lindé J, Roszbach K (2006) Internal ratings systems, implied credit risk and the consistency of banks' risk classification policies. J Bank Financ 30:1899–1926
Jensen M, Meckling W (1976) Theory of the firm: managerial behavior, agency costs and ownership structure. J Financ Econ 3:305–360
Johnston W, Werlen T (2010) Set-off law and practice: an international handbook, 2nd edn. Oxford University Press, Oxford

Jus M (2013) Credit insurance. Elsevier Science, San Diego
Kahan M, Rock E (2009) Hedge fund activism in the enforcement of bondholder rights. Northwest Univ Law Rev 103:281–322
Kästle M (2003) Rechtsfragen der Verwendung von Covenants in Kreditverträgen. Duncker & Humblot, Berlin
Khakzad F (2009) Die Bedeutung von Financial Covenants in der internationalen Finanzkrise. Eul, Lohmar
Klose-Mokroß L (1997) Gläubigerschutz im Kapitalgesellschaftsrecht am Beispiel der Lehre von der verdeckten Sacheinlage. Lang, Frankfurt am Main [u.a.]
Kronman AT, Jackson TH (1979) Secured financing and priorities among creditors. Yale Law J 88:1143–1182
Kühbacher U (1993) Darlehen an Konzernunternehmen. Besicherung und Vertragsanpassung, vol 3. Konzern, Konzernrecht und Konzernfinanzierung. Duncker & Humblot, Berlin
Kuntz T (2008) Haftung von Banken gegenüber anderen Gläubigern nach § 826 BGB wegen Finanzierung von Leveraged Buyouts? ZIP:814–823
Leland HE, Pyle DH (1977) Informational asymmetries, financial structure, and financial intermediation. J Finance 32:371–387
Listokin Y (2008) Is secured debt used to redistribute value from tort claimants in bankruptcy? An Empirical Analysis. Duke Law J 57:1037–1079
Lloyd RM (1991) Financial covenants in commercial loan documentation: uses and limitations. Tenn Law Rev 58:335–366
Malitz I (1986) On financial contracting: the determinants of bond covenants. Financ Manag 15:18–25
Mankowski P (2006) Reicht das Vertragsrecht für einen angemessenen Schutz der Gesellschaftsgläubiger und ihrer Interessen aus? In: Lutter M (ed) Das Kapital der Aktiengesellschaft in Europa. de Gruyter Recht, Berlin, pp 488–507
Manning B, Hanks JJ (1990) Legal capital, 3rd edn. Foundation Press, Westbury
Masulis RW (1980) The effects of capital structure change on security prices: a study of exchange offers. J Financ Econ 8:139–178
McCormack G (2004) Secured credit under English and American law. Cambridge studies in corporate law. Cambridge University press, Cambridge
Merton RC (1974) On the pricing of corporate debt. The risk structure of interest rates. J Finance 29:449–470
Moir L, Sudarsanam S (2007) Determinants of financial covenants and pricing of debt in private debt contracts. The UK evidence. Account Bus Res 37(2):151–166
Mülbert PO (2006) A synthetic view of different concepts of creditor protection, or: a high-level framework for corporate creditor protection. Eur Bus Organ Law Rev 7:357–408
Myers SC (1977) Determinants of corporate borrowing. J Financ Econ 5:147–175
Padgett C (2013) Signs of a "covenant bubble" suggest future risks for investors. http://online.wsj.com/public/resources/documents/CovenantQualityMay2013.pdf. Accessed 20 Feb 2016
Rausch W (1985) Gläubigerschutz im Insolvenzverfahren - Eine ökonomische Analyse einschlägiger rechtlicher Regelungen. Josef Eul, Bergisch Gladbach
Renner M (2015) Bankvertragsrecht, Vierter Teil. In: Canaris C-W, Habersack M, Schäfer C (eds) Staub, GroßkommHGB. De Gruyter, Berlin
Richter W (2014) Biggest credit bubble in history flashes warning-'seek cover'. http://www.nakedcapitalism.com/2014/04/wolf-richter-biggestcredit-bubble-in-history.html. Accessed 20 Jan 2016
Richter R, Furubotn EG (2010) Neue Institutionenökonomik, 4th edn. Mohr Siebeck, Tübingen
Schmidt RH (1980) Ökonomische Analyse des Insolvenzrechts. Band 18 von Neue betriebswirtschaftliche Forschung
Schmidtbleicher R (2010) Die Anleihegläubigermehrheit. Untersuchungen zur Ordnungstheorie und Ordnungspolitik. Mohr Siebeck, Tübingen
Servatius W (2008) Gläubigereinfluss durch Covenants. Mohr Siebeck, Tübingen
Servatius W (2013) Covenants in der Restrukturierung. Corp Financ Law:14–22

Sigman HC (2008) Perfection and priority of security rights. In: Eidenmüller H, Kieniger E-M (eds) The future of secured credit in Europe. European company and financial law review. De Gruyter Recht, Berlin, pp 143–165
Smith CWJ, Warner JB (1979) On financial contracting: an analysis of bond covenants. J Financ Econ 7:117–161
Stadler A (2002) Einleitung Sachenrecht. Soergel Kommentar Bürgerliches Gesetzbuch, 13th edn. Stuttgart
Steffek F (2011) Gläubigerschutz in der Kapitalgesellschaft. Krise und Insolvenz im englischen und deutschen Gesellschafts- und Insolvenzrecht. Mohr Siebeck, Tübingen
Stern S (2013) Structuring and drafting commercial loan agreements, vol 1, Revised Edition edn. A.S. Pratt, USA
Tappeiner F (2010) Structure and determinants of financial covenants in leveraged buyouts, vol Dissertation. Technische Universität München, München
Teichmann C (2006) Binnenmarktkonformes Gesellschaftsrecht. De Gruyter, Berlin
Thießen F (1996) Covenants in Kreditverträgen: Alternative oder Ergänzung zum Insolvenzrecht? ZBB:19–37
Thole C (2010) Gläubigerschutz durch Insolvenzrecht - Anfechtung und verwandte Regelungsinstrumente in der Unternehmensinsolvenz. Beiträge zum ausländischen und internationalen Privatrecht. Mohr Siebeck, Tübingen
Tighe R (1984) Structuring commercial loan agreements. Warren, Groham & Lamont, Boston
Treacy WF, Carey M (2000) Credit risk rating systems at large US banks. J Bank Financ 24:167–201
Triantis GG, Daniels RJ (1995) The role of debt in interactive corporate governance. Calif Law Rev 83:1073–1114
UNCITRAL (2005) Legislative guide on insolvency. United Nations, New York. https://www.uncitral.org/pdf/english/texts/insolven/05-80722_Ebook.pdf. Accessed 14 Jan 2016
Warren E, Westbrook JL (2005) Contracting out of bankruptcy: an empirical intervention. Harv Law Rev 118:1197–1254
Westermann HP § 449. In: Säcker FJ, Rixecker R (eds) (2012) Münchener Kommentar zum BGB. Beck, München
Wiegand W (1990) Die Entwicklung des Sachenrechts. AcP 190:112–138
Wieling HJ (2007) Sachenrecht. Springer-Lehrbuch, 5th edn. Springer, Berlin
Wight R, Cooke W, Gray R (2009) The LSTA's complete credit agreement guide. McGraw-Hill, New York
Wittinghofer S (2010) Fachbegriffe aus M & A und Corporate Finance. Credit Default Swaps als Instrument zur Absicherung von Kreditrisiken. NJW (16):1125–1127
Wood P (2007) International loans, bonds, guarantees, legal opinions, vol 2. Sweet & Maxwell, London
Wood P (2008) Law and practice of international finance. Law and practice of international finance. Sweet & Maxwell, London
Wright S (2006) International loan documentation. Palgrave Macmillan, New York
Zhang W (2014) The paradoxes of secured lending: is there a less uneasy case for the priority of secured claims in bankruptcy? Univ Pa J Bus Law 16:789–841

Chapter 3
Covenants and Bilateral Creditor Protection

The following chapter will explain how covenants function as a bilateral creditor protection device between a bank and a capital debtor company. It will illustrate the debtor company's obligations and, with it, the bank's rights and potential for influencing the debtor company. First, the common covenants will be presented according to their ability to reduce the three credit risks. Afterwards, the clauses ensuring that covenants are enforceable will be discussed. They transform the self-help device—the covenant—into a bilateral private governance mechanism that addresses norm setting, application, and enforcement. This bilateral private governance system will be described in the subsequent section and will form the basis for assessing third-party creditor effects and the multi-party private governance system.

3.1 Protection Against the Risk of False or Lacking Information

Covenants play at most only a limited role in reducing the risk of false or lacking information.[1] Other clauses—namely representations and the event of default clause—ensure that the information provided is accurate. This is relevant for both the *ex ante* and *ex post* asymmetrical information problem. However, reducing *ex ante* informational asymmetry and, hence, the risk of false or lacking information depends on a number of factors. If the parties have contracted before and included covenants in these contracts, the bank will most likely possess more information because data was already collected over the lifespan of the earlier loan. This information will include financial data as well as data regarding past defaults, which will—if a cross-default clause was stipulated—also contain defaults with

[1] Similarly Heinrich (2009), p. 124.

D. Matri, *Covenants and Third-Party Creditors*, DOI 10.1007/978-3-319-62036-7_3

other creditors. If there has been no past contractual relationship, the bank has less information. In the US, however, the bank can ask for information from the Securities and Exchange Commission (SEC), as public companies have to file any default[2] with the SEC.[3]

3.2 Protection Against the Risk of Bankruptcy

The risk of bankruptcy is mainly addressed by financial covenants and some negative covenants.

3.2.1 *Financial Covenants*

The following subsections will only outline the most common financial covenants, which are interest coverage ratio, leverage ratio, tangible net worth, gearing, and current ratio covenants.[4]

[2]Both covenant (technical) and payment (non-technical) defaults are included.

[3]See below 5.2.1.1.2.2.

[4]The interest coverage ratio covenant is the most common financial covenant, with a frequency of 61.82 (Demerjian (2007), p. 34) to 83.80 (When including the interest coverage, cash interest coverage, debt service coverage and fixed charge coverage as in 2006; Demerjian and Owens (2013), p. 35 et seqq.) percent. The leverage ratio covenant has a frequency of 39.70 (Demerjian (Demerjian (2007), p. 34) to 48.90 (When including "debt to EBITDA" and "senior debt to EBITDA" as in 2006; Demerjian and Owens (2013), p. 38 et seq.) percent. The frequency of the tangible net worth covenant lies between 39.49 (Demerjian (2007), p. 34) and 49.60 (When including net worth and tangible net worth as in 2006; Demerjian and Owens (2013), p. 43 et seq.) percent. The gearing covenant has a frequency of 30.04 (Demerjian (2007), p. 34) to 48.20 (When including leverage, sr. leverage, "debt to tangible net worth" and "debt to equity" as in 2006; Demerjian and Owens (2013), p. 39 et seqq.) percent. The frequency of the current ratio covenant lies between 9.64 (Demerjian (2007), p. 34) and 13.5 (When including current ratio as in 2006; Demerjian and Owens, Measuring Financial Covenant Strictness in Private Debt Contracts, available at: http://ssrn.com/abstract=2232880, last accessed 10.01.2014, p. 41 et seq.) percent. Information on the prevalence of these covenants is taken from two empirical studies by Peter R. Demerjian, who analysed financial covenants in private loan contracts in the US from 1987 to 2007. There are also other empirical studies on how frequently different financial covenants are employed. However, these are not comparable as they use different parameters or refer to research in other countries; for Germany see Haghani et al. (2009), for Australia see Mather and Peirson (2006); for the UK see Moir and Sudarsanam (2007). For an interesting early study of the hierarchy and grouping of financial ratios, see Pinches et al. (1975). His findings broadly correspond with the list of the most common covenants; cf. Pinches et al. (1975), 303 et seqq.

3.2.1.1 Framework of Financial Covenants

Usually, two financial figures will be compared in the form of financial ratios and set as a limit. A bank may, for example, stipulate that the ratio of EBITDA (earnings before interest, taxation, depreciation and amortisation) to finance charges must not exceed 1:1.[5] Financial covenants help to reduce the credit risk by ensuring the debtor company's financial maintenance and solvency as long as it complies with the set ratios. They ensure that the debtor company's liquidity suffices to service the loan and meet other financial obligations. If the credit risk increases, a default will be triggered and the bank will be given the power to counteract at an early stage of financial distress. Since financial covenants reflect the business' performance, they also function as an indicator of managerial quality and thereby coerce the management to maintain financial planning and discipline to a degree.[6]

3.2.1.1.1 Setting of Financial Covenants

The starting point for most financial covenants is EBITDA.[7] However, this is only the basic definition: Parties can agree to deduct or add other items back in, such as acquisition costs or profits and losses of any member of the company group.[8] Depending on the particular definition, financial covenants can be more or less effective. As a general principle, the more items that are added back, the less effective the financial covenant.[9]

Banks use a number of different financial covenants, which have to be adapted to the specific business plan of the debtor company. Banks will set the ratios based on the agreed financing case. They will also allow for headroom overlaid on top. This headroom averages at 20%, but there are three different methods of headroom calculation.[10]

[5]Cf. Adams (2003), p. 87 et seq.

[6]Adams (2003), p. 87.

[7]Cf. Wood (2007), para. 5-040; Wight et al. (2009), p. 153.

[8]Cf. Loan Market Association (24.12.2012), p. 2, 6 et seq.; Wight et al. (2009), p. 153 et seq.; Wood (2008), para. 8-36.

[9]Wood (2008), para. 8-36.

[10]Cf. Ballo (2010), p. 318. Firstly, and most commonly, one can apply the 20 percent just to EBITDA; secondly, it can be applied to EBITDA and net debt; and thirdly, it can be applied to the forecast ratio. The second option provides the most headroom, whereas the last results in the least. Therefore, parties mainly agree on the first method, as this is the one that serves as the middle ground. Cf. Achleitner et al. (2009), p. 22 et seqq.

3.2.1.1.2 Inclusion of Subsidiaries

Covenants often apply to both the parent company and its subsidiaries, since the debtor's (parent company's) strength is equal to the strength of the entire corporate group.[11] The definition of a subsidiary is crucial for the effect of covenants, since covenants will only apply to the covered subsidiaries. In loan agreements, a subsidiary is usually defined as a company "more than 50 percent of whose outstanding voting shares is owned by its parent and/or the parent's other majority-owned subsidiaries".[12] However, a bank might try to broaden the definition by including directly or indirectly controlled shares.[13]

3.2.1.1.3 Compliance with Financial Covenants

Compliance with financial covenants can be measured on different bases. They can either be tested at a specific date (date-specific covenants) or for one or more agreed fiscal periods (performance covenants). Usually, the so-called rolling period—comprising the two or four most recent fiscal quarters of the debtor company[14]—serves as testing basis. Occasionally, covenants combine both date-specific and performance elements (hybrid covenants).[15]

3.2.1.2 Interest Coverage Ratio Covenant

The interest coverage ratio covenant stipulates that the ratio of EBITDA to finance charges[16] must not be less than X:1.[17] It measures the debtor company's ability to generate sufficient cash profit to cover its interest costs,[18] thereby restricting excessive debt and warning against shortfalls in the current year's operation profits.[19]

---

[11] Wight et al. (2009), p. 282.

[12] 17 CFR § 210.1-02 (n).

[13] Cf. Simpson (1973), 1165 et seqq.; Wight et al. (2009), p. 282.

[14] Wight et al. (2009), p. 294 et seq.

[15] Wight et al. (2009), p. 293 et seqq.

[16] Finance charges refer to the sum of the accrued interests, commissions, discounts, fees, prepayment fees, premiums or charges and other finance payments related to borrowings paid or payable. Cf. Loan Market Association (24.12.2012), p. 8; Wood (2008), para. 8-37; Wight et al. (2009), p. 302 et seq.

[17] Wood (2008), para. 8-35; see also Box 7.10. LSTA Guide: Wight et al. (2009), p. 302.

[18] Wight et al. (2009), p. 302.

[19] Fight (2004), p. 131.

3.2.1.3 Leverage Ratio Covenant

The leverage ratio covenant (also called debt ratio or cash flow ratio) stipulates that the consolidated net debt[20] on the last day of the relevant period will not be more than X times consolidated EBITDA (or cash flow[21]) in respect of the relevant period.[22] It indicates the payback period for the loan because it measures how the debt level compares to operating profits. Moreover, it functions as an early warning sign of corporate failure.[23]

3.2.1.4 Tangible Net Worth Covenant

The tangible net worth covenant stipulates that the consolidated tangible net worth[24] must not be less than X.[25] The test excludes intangibles since they are not realisable or worthless on liquidation.[26] The tangible net worth covenant tests the shareholders' equity on the debtor company's balance sheet at a specific date to safeguard a minimum level of reserves and, hence, to prevent excessive dividend payouts.[27] It may also function as an early warning sign, as declining net worth often indicates that a company is heading towards bankruptcy.[28]

3.2.1.5 Gearing Covenant

The gearing covenant[29] stipulates that total indebtedness (minus the subordinated debt) must not exceed X percent of tangible net worth.[30] It measures the sufficiency of

[20]The total net debt is the sum of all obligations of group members for or in respect of borrowings at that time, but excluding obligations to any other group members; cf. Loan Market Association (24.12.2012), p. 10. It commonly refers to borrowings as well as to debt akin to borrowings; Wood (2008), paras. 8-34, 8-38; cf. also Adams (2003), p. 89 et seq.

[21]Cash flow can either refer to the "traditional" cash flow, including the sum of net income plus depreciation, or the "operating" cash flow, defined as "working capital provided by operations plus or minus changes in the noncash working capital accounts, except for short-term debt"; Casey and Bartczak (1984), 62.

[22]Cf. Box 7.15. LSTA Guide: Wight et al. (2009), p. 309; Wright (2006), p. 142.

[23]Cf. Harrison et al. (2011), p. 714 et seq.

[24]The tangible net worth consists of the stated net worth minus the accounts and notes receivable from the debtor's owners, officers or directors, goodwill and any other intangible assets, but adding back subordinated debt; right Wright (2006), p. 142; Wood (2008), para. 8-33; Wight et al. (2009), p. 297 et seq. Occasionally, the stipulated minimum net worth increases over the life of a loan; cf. Runge (2010), p. 37.

[25]Cf. Box 7.7. LSTA Guide: Wight et al. (2009), p. 297 et seq.

[26]Wood (2008), para. 8-33.

[27]Fight (2004), p. 131; Wight et al. (2009), p. 298.

[28]Lloyd (1991), 341.

[29]Confusingly, sometimes also referred to as leverage ratio covenant.

[30]Box 7.8. LSTA Guide: Wight et al. (2009), p. 300; Wood (2008), para. 8-34.

the debtor company's equity capital to meet the liabilities carried on its balance sheet.[31] The gearing covenant is date-specific and has an incidence of 30.04%[32] to 48.20%.[33] The gearing covenant restricts excessive debt. It particularly protects against debt-financed acquisition of goodwill and other intangibles. It also prevents excessive dividend payouts, as it safeguards both reserves and liquid assets (out of which dividends have to be paid) and signals low cumulative profits as an early warning.[34] In contrast to the net worth covenant, the gearing covenant does not require compliance with a fixed limit but is relative, thus allowing for more flexibility.[35]

3.2.1.6 Current Ratio Covenant

The current ratio covenant stipulates that the ratio of current assets to current liabilities must not be less than X:1.[36] The current ratio covenant ensures sufficient liquid assets for the debtor company to meet its liabilities due over the subsequent 12 months.[37] It therefore restricts excessive debt as it guards against funding fixed asset expansion with short-term debt. Furthermore, it prevents excessive dividend payouts as it safeguards liquid asset levels.[38]

3.2.2 *Negative Covenants*

The problem of asset dilution—one aspect of the risk of bankruptcy—is addressed by negative covenants, which restrict, for example, the disposal of assets and change of business or manager and merger.

3.2.2.1 No Disposal Clause

The no disposal clause stipulates that no debtor company shall "enter into a single transaction or a series of transactions (whether related or not) and whether voluntary or involuntary to sell, lease, transfer or otherwise dispose of any asset."[39]

---

[31] Wight et al. (2009), p. 300.

[32] Demerjian (2007) p. 34.

[33] When including leverage, sr. leverage, "debt to tangible net worth" and "debt to equity" as in 2006; Demerjian and Owens (2013), p. 39 et seqq.

[34] Fight (2004), p. 131.

[35] Runge (2010), p. 38.

[36] Box 7.9. LSTA Guide: Wight et al. (2009), p. 300.

[37] Wight et al. (2009), p. 301.

[38] Fight (2004), p. 131.

[39] Clause 22.4 LMA Loan Term: Wright (2006), p. 156.

It commonly "does not apply to any sale, lease, transfer or other disposal made in the ordinary course of trading of the disposing entity"[40] or "of assets in exchange for other assets comparable or superior in type, value and quality"[41] as long as "the higher of the market value or consideration receivable"[42] does not exceed X in any financial year. The purpose of this clause is to ensure that the debtor company will still be able to service the loan since the debtor company's ability to conduct its business may be adversely affected by any material disposal of fixed assets.[43] It also relates to cash flow problems and changes in business strategies. The composition of major assets would change in the event of a change in the business strategy,[44] whereas a company might sell its assets to generate money when facing cash flow problems.[45]

3.2.2.2 No Merger Clause

Banks may wish to restrict or prohibit any merger, demerger, amalgamation or corporate reconstruction to ensure the debtor company's identity.[46] In the case of a merger with the surviving corporation being the debtor company, the loan agreement will usually permit it.[47]

3.2.2.3 No Change of Business/Management Clause

A merger might also lead to a change of business, which banks fear. The nature of business at the closing date constitutes a main factor in the credit analysis of the debtor company.[48] Thus, a change of the general nature of business might lead to a different creditworthiness and financial covenants may no longer reflect the business reality or fulfil their functions.[49] Covenants therefore prohibit a change of business[50] and/or management.[51] Regularly, management-change clauses do not

---

[40] Wright (2006), p. 156.

[41] Wright (2006), p. 156. Sometimes the disposal of assets may also be conditional on the approval of the creditor.

[42] Wright (2006), p. 157.

[43] Adams (2003), p. 98.

[44] Called "asset stripping"; Wright (2006), p. 156.

[45] Adams (2003), p. 98.

[46] See Clause 22.5. LMA Term Loan: Wright (2006), p. 157; LSTA Guide: Wight et al. (2009), p. 360.

[47] Wight et al. (2009), p. 360 with further examples of exceptions.

[48] Clause 22.6. LMA Term Loan: Wright (2006), p. 158; LSTA Guide: Wight et al. (2009), p. 368.

[49] Wight et al. (2009), p. 368.

[50] Wright (2006), p. 158.

[51] Wight et al. (2009), p. 432.

require that the management remains satisfactory to the bank, but are rather limited to disability, death or other termination events.[52]

3.2.2.4 Other Negative Covenants

The bank may also want to restrict other undertakings of the debtor company to ensure its ability to service the loan. For example, a restriction or prohibition of distributions,[53] prepayment of debts[54] or of sale-leasebacks[55] are common. Often, banks also want a restriction on additional (unsecured) debt unless made in the ordinary course of business to avoid the risk of non-payment.[56]

3.3 Protection Against the Risk of Loss

The main problem of the risk of loss, namely claim dilution,[57] can be addressed by combining covenants.[58]

3.3.1 Affirmative Covenants

First, affirmative covenants will normally oblige the debtor company to provide insurance for all its major assets,[59] maintenance of its properties (in good working condition),[60] preservation of its corporate existence as well as its rights and franchises and those of its subsidiaries.[61] Affirmative covenants further stipulate that the debtor company needs to comply with all laws in all respects, if a failure to comply would lead to a material impairment of the debtor company's ability to perform its obligations under the loan agreement.[62]

---

[52]Due to potential lender liability, cf. *State National Bank v. Farah Manufacturing Co., Inc.*, 678 S.W.2d 661 (Tex. Ct. App. 1984); Wight et al. (2009), p. 432 et seq.

[53]Wright (2006), p. 158 et seq.

[54]LMA Term Loan: Wright (2006), p. 159; LSTA Guide: Wight et al. (2009), p. 377 et seqq.

[55]LSTA Guide: Wight et al. (2009), p. 362 et seq.

[56]LMA Term Loan: Wright (2006), p. 159; LSTA Guide: Wight et al. (2009), p. 352 et seqq.

[57]Claim dilution and asset dilution must be differentiated; see above 1.1.2.

[58]The pari passu clause, the cross-default clause and the event of default clause reduce claim dilution as well. However, they will be dealt with in more detail later on, since they do not belong to the category of covenants. See below 3.4.2 et seqq.

[59]Cf. Adams (2003), p. 96; Wight et al. (2009), p. 320 et seqq.

[60]Cf. Wight et al. (2009), p. 326.

[61]Cf. Wight et al. (2009), p. 326 et seq.

[62]Clause 22.2. LMA Term Loan: Wright (2006), p. 147; see also LSTA Guide: Wight et al. (2009), p. 327. For further affirmative covenants see Wight et al. (2009), p. 310 et seqq.

3.3.2 *Negative Covenants*

Second, a number of negative covenants aim at reducing claim dilution.

3.3.2.1 Negative Pledge Clause

The most important negative covenant in the context of claim dilution is the negative pledge clause. As shown in Scenario 1,[63] this clause prohibits the creation of any security (security and quasi-security)[64] over the debtor company's assets unless the given security is covered by one of the exceptions to the clause. The debtor company may want to exclude, for instance, existing security; "netting or set-off in the course of ordinary banking arrangements"[65]; "any lien arising by operation of law and in the ordinary course of trading"[66]; "any Security over or affecting any asset acquired by a member of the Group after the date of this Agreement"[67]; and "any security entered into pursuant to any Finance Document".[68]

The purpose of this clause in an unsecured loan is self-evident: it aims to preserve equality between different creditors, to protect the bank's leverage in case of debtor company's bankruptcy, to provide advance warning if a change of financial conditions occurs, and to protect the original debtor company's pool of assets.[69] In a secured loan, the negative pledge also helps protect a floating charge security[70] and supports the creditor's control over the company.[71]

[63]See above 1.1.

[64]LMA Term Loan: Wright (2006), p. 149 et seqq.; LSTA Guide: Wight et al. (2009), p. 339 et seqq.

[65]Clause 22.3(c)(ii) LMA Term Loan: Wright (2006), p. 152.

[66]Clause 22.3(c)(iii) LMA Term Loan: Wright (2006), p. 152.

[67]Clause 22.3(c)(iv) LMA Term Loan: Wright (2006), p. 153. The negative pledge clause is mainly concerned with the protection of the existing pool of assets.

[68]Clause 22.3(c)(vi) LMA Term Loan: Wright (2006), p. 154. Generally see Clause 22.3. (c) LMA Term Loan, Wright (2006), p. 151 et seqq.; LSTA Guide: Wight et al. (2009), p. 339 et seqq. For further possible exceptions see Wright (2006), p. 154 et seq.; Adams (2003), p. 97 et seq.

[69]Wright (2006), p. 148; Wood (2007), para. 5-009. There are also negative pledge clauses that include a provision for "automatic security". Those clauses provide an even broader spectrum of protection, see Hill (2008).

[70]Wright (2006), p. 273; Adams (2003), p. 97.

[71]Wright (2006), p. 148, listing further advantages.

3.3.2.2 CAPEX Covenant

The CAPEX covenant[72] limits capital expenditure spent on permitted acquisitions and reinvested insurance to an annual amount subject to carryovers.[73] Its purpose is to avoid excessive expenditures beyond the debtor company's capacity.[74] The CAPEX covenant can be set as a ratio or an absolute limit.

3.3.2.3 Dividend Restrictions Clause

Dividend restrictions aim to secure capital adequacy and make it difficult for wealth to be shifted from creditors to shareholders. The dividend restrictions are generally measured using the net profit earned at the time of contracting, but dividends can also be prohibited all together.[75] For example, a complete restriction on dividends is quite common with smaller debtor companies. However, caution is necessary if a debtor company has issued preference shares, since the debtor company might be obliged under its articles of association to provide a fixed rate of dividends to the shareholders.[76]

3.3.3 Financial Covenants as Supplements

The dividend restrictions are supplemented by financial covenants. The gearing covenant, for example, prevents excessive dividend payouts as it safeguards both reserves and liquid assets (out of which dividends have to be paid).[77] Furthermore, the current ratio covenant protects liquid asset levels[78] and the tangible net worth covenant tests the shareholder's equity on the debtor company's balance sheet at a specific date to prevent excessive dividend payouts.[79]

[72]The CAPEX covenant is regarded as financial covenant in the LMA Term Loan but is better characterised as negative covenant; cf. Wight et al. (2009), p. 307.

[73]Wight et al. (2009), p. 307.

[74]Borrowers may, however, negotiate so called "excess" cash flow for a specific period; cf. Wight et al. (2009), p. 308 et seq.

[75]Cf. Box 7.45. LSTA Guide: Wight et al. (2009), p. 371 et seq.; see also Wüstemann et al. (2007), 15; Heinrich (2009), p. 149.

[76]Adams (2003), p. 100.

[77]Fight (2004), p. 131.

[78]Fight (2004), p. 131.

[79]Fight (2004), p. 131; Wight et al. (2009), p. 298.

3.4 Clauses That Ensure the Enforcement of Covenants

3.4.1 Information Undertakings

The aforementioned covenants can only function properly if compliance with them is monitored. Monitoring refers to the acquisition, procession, interpretation and verification of information about the debtor company.[80] It addresses the problem of *ex post* informational asymmetry and, thus, the risk of opportunistic behaviour. For that reason, and to comply with the principles of safe and sound banking, positive covenants ensure the provision of information.[81]

Usually, debtor companies have to provide annually audited statements and half-yearly[82] or quarterly[83] unaudited statements in both a consolidated and individual form[84] that are certified by a director[85] or a senior officer.[86] The LMA Term Loan stipulates that the accounting rules according to which the financial statements are made must either be GAAP[87] as it changes from time to time[88] or the original GAAP at closing time.[89] Consistency of accounting is important to ensure comparability.[90] Therefore, frozen accounting standards are common. Rolling accounting standards are problematic because changes might lead to an unintended covenant default. One solution would be a procedure for re-setting financial covenants.[91] Notwithstanding the above, any change in GAAP must be reported.[92] Furthermore, the bank may ask for a compliance certificate stipulating compliance with financial covenants issued by two directors,[93] a financial officer[94] or an auditor.[95] Moreover, a bank may require

---

[80]Gilson and Kraakman (1984), 594 et seq.

[81]Wight et al. (2009), p. 310.

[82]So clause 20.1. LMA Term Loan: Wright (2006), p. 137.

[83]So the LSTA Guide: Wight et al. (2009), p. 311.

[84]This is only standard in the LMA Term Loan, cf. clause 20.3. (b) LMA Term Loan: Wright (2006), p.137. In the LSTA Guide consolidating statements are often stipulated, see Wight et al. (2009), p. 312.

[85]Clause 20. 3. (a) LMA Term Loan: Wright (2006), p. 138.

[86]In the LSTA Guide only the unaudited statements have to be certified by a senior financial officer of the debtor, cf. Box 7.16. (b) LSTA Guide: Wight et al. (2009), p. 311.

[87]Generally Accepted Accounting Principle.

[88]Clause 20.3. (b). LMA Term Loan: Wright (2006), p. 138.

[89]Clause 20.3. (c) called frozen GAAP; LMA Term Loan: Wright (2006), p. 138 et seq.

[90]Cf. Wight et al. (2009), p. 289.

[91]Wood (2008), para. 8-32.

[92]Clause 20.3. (c) LMA Term Loan: Wright (2006), p. 139; Box 7.17. (c) LSTA Guide: Wight et al. (2009), p. 313.

[93]Clause 20.2. (b) LMA Term Loan: Wright (2006), p. 138.

[94]Box 7.17. (a) LSTA Guide: Wight et al. (2009), p. 313 et seq.

[95]This is unlikely, however, as prior approval by the auditor is needed and an increase of audit fees follows as consequence, cf. Wight et al. (2009), p. 314.

notification of any default.[96] This clause, however, is only useful if a default of that clause has more severe consequences for the debtor company than the triggering (original) default—e.g. if the clause provides no or only a limited grace period.[97] Thus, a debtor company can trigger a default by failing to notify despite the non-expiration of the grace period of the underlying default.[98] The bank can also reserve the right for itself to request any information "regarding the operations, business affairs and financial condition of the debtor company or any subsidiary, or compliance with the terms of this Agreement"[99] if reasonable.[100]

3.4.2 *Pari Passu Clause*

To ensure equality of creditors, the pari passu clause is of equal importance and therefore often accompanies the negative pledge clause. The pari passu clause can be spelled out as representation,[101] affirmative covenant,[102] or event of default.[103] Often, however, it will be stipulated as repeated representation.[104] Then, the pari passu clause requires that the debtor company's payment obligations under the loan agreement must "rank at least pari passu [equally] with the claims of all its other unsecured and unsubordinated creditors, except for obligations mandatorily preferred by law applying to companies generally."[105] Hence, the purpose is to ensure an equal ranking with other unsecured creditors, whereas the negative pledge clause ensures that there is no subordination of the bank's right to repayment to secured creditors.[106] At this time, the pari passu clause merely addressed ranking in bankruptcy proceedings.[107] Then, the pari passu clause stated for most countries only the obvious—namely that the creditor ranks equally with all other creditors except for secured creditors, subordinated creditors and creditors preferred by law applying to companies. Commonly, these three stipulated exceptions are the only

[96]Clause 20.5. LMA Term Loan: Wright (2006), p. 140.

[97]See below 3.4.3.

[98]Wright (2006), p. 140 et seq.

[99]Box 7.19. LSTA Guide: Wight et al. (2009), p. 317.

[100]For further information undertakings, see, for example, Wright (2006), p. 141; Wight et al. (2009), p. 315 et seqq.

[101]Cf. Adams (2003), p. 59; Wright (2006), p. 133.

[102]Cf. Wight et al. (2009), p. 334.

[103]Adams (2003), p. 98.

[104]Adams (2003), p. 98; also Wood (2008), para. 8-24.

[105]Clause 19.12. LMA Term Loan: Wright (2006), p. 133; see also LSTA Guide: Wight et al. (2009), p. 334.

[106]Adams (2003), p. 98.

[107]Pucher, in: Krauskopf, Babey (eds) (2015), p. 71. For an overview of the history of covenants (in sovereign bond lending) see Weidemaier et al. (2013).

cases of different priorities in bankruptcy proceedings.[108] Thus, the pari passu clause seemed to be of minor importance. Now, however, the ambit of the pari passu clause is understood in a broader sense as to require all creditors to be satisfied equally, even outside bankruptcy.[109] This understanding increases the importance of the pari passu clause.

3.4.3 Event of Default Clause

Covenants are enforced through the contractual remedies stipulated in the event of default clause. This clause includes a number of agreed events that cause a default by the debtor company—such as non-payment, breach of covenants, cross-default concerning other creditors, material adverse change and bankruptcy proceedings.[110] Since each covenant is independent, any undertaking by the debtor company must comply with all covenants.[111] However, there is a difference between incurrence and maintenance tests for defaulting. Whereas incurrence covenants are only tested when a specific event occurs or on a specific date, maintenance covenants are ongoing covenants and must be met at all times.[112] Covenants in private loan agreements are mainly maintenance covenants. But some covenants may grant a grace period[113] during which the debtor company can cure the potential technical default.[114] If it is still uncured after the period expires, the potential covenant default will become an actual covenant default and will provide the bank with contractual remedies.[115] The typical event of default clause reads as follows:

> If any of the following events ("Events of Default") shall occur and be continuing: [...]
> (d) the Borrower shall fail to observe or perform (i) any covenant, condition or agreement contained in Sections [______] or (ii) any other covenant, condition or agreement contained in this Agreement or any of the other Loan Documents (other than those specified

[108]There may be some exceptions – i.e. in Spain where, without giving security and without consent of the subordinated creditor, a claim can be preferred over another by "escritura publica"; Wright (2006), p. 133 et seq.

[109]Pucher, in: Krauskopf, Babey (eds) (2015), p. 71; critically Wood (2003), 372 et seqq.; dissenting Diem (2013), paras. 60 et seqq.

[110]Clause 23. LMA Term Loan: Wright (2006), p. 168 et seqq.; Box 9.1.-9.17. LSTA Guide: Wight et al. (2009), p. 411 et seqq.; see further Adams (2003), p. 104 et seqq.

[111]Wight et al. (2009), p. 218.

[112]Wight et al. (2009), p. 338 et seq.

[113]The grace period can begin either from occurrence of the potential default or its acknowledgment by the borrower, cf. Wright (2006), p. 169 et seq.

[114]In the UK it is good practice to stipulate a grace period in the covenant clause (Adams (2003), p. 105; for different practice, however, Wright (2006), p. 169) whereas in the USA it seems commonplace to include it in the event of default clause itself (Box 9.4. LSTA Guide: Wight et al. (2009), p. 418).

[115]Clause 23.13. LMA Term Loan: Wright (2006), p. 184; Box 9.14.-9.16. LSTA Guide: Wight et al. (2009), p. 437 et seqq.

in paragraphs (a) or (b) [Payment Defaults] or the preceding clause (i)), and such failure shall continue unremedied for a period of [30] days after notice thereof from the Administrative Agent to the Borrower (which notice will be given at the request of any Lender).[116]

In principle, parties can agree on any number of events triggering a technical default as well as on any contractual remedy. However, in practice, a number of common remedies evolved. The main remedy, albeit the last resort, represents the right to immediate acceleration of the loan:

On and at any time after the occurrence of an Event of Default [which is continuing] the Agent may, and shall if so directed by the Majority Lenders, by notice to the Company:

(a) cancel the Total Commitments whereupon they shall immediately be cancelled;

(b) declare that all or part of the Loans, together with accrued interest, and all other amounts accrued or outstanding under the Finance Documents be immediately due and payable, whereupon they shall become immediately due and payable; and/or

(c) declare that all or part of the Loans be payable on demand, whereupon they shall immediately become payable on demand by the Agent on the instructions of the Majority Lenders.[117]

Since this can have adverse effects on the bank, the debtor company and other creditors in the form of the debtor company filing for bankruptcy, banks seldom use it.[118] However, it provides good leverage for forcing terms onto the debtor company. The bank may reserve the right to recall the loan at any time and, hence, convert it into a right to a recall on demand. Another option is the cancelation of any undrawn commitments when only parts of the loan have been utilised. Alternatively, the bank can issue a waiver, conditional on renegotiation and often on a waiver fee. Renegotiation may lead to an adjustment in interest rates, bringing in external advisors, a debt-equity swap, or the provision of additional collateral. A bank may also waive the covenant default only for a short period of time without renegotiation if the debtor company's financial situation is expected to improve. Furthermore, in cases of negligible defaults, the bank can also opt for an unconditional waiver without renegotiation.[119]

The contractual remedies are usually set to be available "on or at any time after an event of covenant default has occurred".[120] This is a great advantage compared to remedies under general law, where it might take some time to establish and enforce them.[121] The contractual remedies can be enforced immediately and therefore ensure a timely reaction to changes in the debtor company's financial situation in order to secure the bank's position.

---

[116]Boxes 9.1 and 9.4 LSTA Guide: Wight et al. (2009), p. 411 et seqq.

[117]Clause 23.13. LMA Term Loan: Wright (2006), p. 184.

[118]Beneish and Press (1993); Chen and Wei (1993); Gopalakrishnan and Parkash (1995), 20 et seqq.; Roberts and Sufi (2009), 1666; Wight et al. (2009), p. 438.

[119]Cf. Thießen (1996), 21 et seq.

[120]Adams (2003), p. 110. However, as previously mentioned a grace period may be included.

[121]In the UK, for example, the remedies depend on the type of the term breached (i.e. condition, warranty or intermediate term). Especially in cases of intermediate terms the appropriate remedy is not easy to determine. Moreover, in cases of misrepresentation remedies are based on common law, cf. Adams (2003), p. 103.

3.4.4 *Cross-Default Clause*

A cross-default or cross-acceleration clause is part of the event of default clause and can take a variety of forms. A common example is the following:

> If any of the following events ("Events of Default") shall occur and be continuing[122]
>
> (e) the Borrower or any Subsidiary shall fail to make any payment (whether of principal or interest and regardless of amount) in respect of any Material Debt, when and as the same shall become due and payable [(after giving effect to any period of grace)];
>
> (f) any event or condition occurs that results in any Material Debt becoming due prior to its scheduled maturity or that enables or permits [Alternative 1: (with or without the giving of notice, the lapse of time or both)] [Alternative 2: (with or without the giving of notice, but without any further lapse of time)] the holder or holders of any Material Debt or any trustee or agent on its or their behalf to cause any Material Debt to become due, or to require the prepayment, repurchase, redemption or defeasance thereof, prior to its scheduled maturity.[123]

A cross-default clause links the loan agreement with third-party creditors' contracts.[124] The cross-default clause can be distinguished from the cross-acceleration clause with regard to their triggers. The cross-acceleration clause is only triggered in cases of actual acceleration of another debtor company's obligation, whereas the mere default under another debtor company's obligation suffices in the case of cross-default clauses (see Alternative 1 above). Since these clauses come in all shapes, an in-between version is also possible, i.e. where the cross-default is only triggered when immediate acceleration without lapse of time (grace period) or further notice is possible—often called "cross-event of default" or "cross-acceleration" (see Alternative 2 above).[125]

The cross-default, cross-acceleration or cross-event of default clause is used to monitor and ensure the debtor company's ability to repay the loan. It functions as a general signal for any credit-related problems of the debtor company and can therefore reduce the risk of bankruptcy and loss. The secured creditor has a right to accelerate on its own if other creditors accelerate, which can either impact the debtor company's ability to repay or lead to bankruptcy proceedings. The problem of claim dilution is further reduced since the secured creditor is not left out of the renegotiation process.[126] Otherwise, a renegotiation of the defaulting loan agreement may occur that results in improvements for the other creditor that could be to the disadvantage of the creditors with the not defaulted loan agreements that have not defaulted.[127]

---

[122]Box 9.1. LSTA Guide: Wight et al. (2009), p. 411.

[123]Box 9.5. LSTA Guide: Wight et al. (2009), p. 419; see also clause 23.5. LMA Term Loan: Wright (2006), p. 171 et seqq.

[124]If stipulated by other creditors, it also links the third-party creditor's contract with that of all other creditors including the bank loan agreement. See below 8.4.1.

[125]Wight et al. (2009), p. 421.

[126]Wright (2006), p. 171.

[127]Wight et al. (2009), p. 420.

The cross-acceleration clause does not achieve this purpose, as a creditor will not be part of the renegotiation process and will only have rights after the negotiation took place and the other loan has already been accelerated.[128]

3.4.5 MAC Clause

The material adverse change (MAC) clause stipulates the right to accelerate when "circumstances arise which may give rise to a Material Adverse Change."[129] The ambit of an MAC, however, is unclear and subjective.[130] That is why the MAC clause should clearly refer to specific situations that constitute an MAC, such as financial conditions, prospects, validity and enforceability of documents, and ability of the debtor company to perform its obligations under the loan agreement.[131] The MAC clause can be connected to specific financial ratios laid down in covenants to highlight their importance and to ensure their legal enforceability.[132]

In domestic US loan agreements, it is mainly used as a representation or condition and seldom as an event of default clause based on an MAC (MAC default).[133] However, in international loan agreements the MAC default is more common.[134]

3.4.6 Performance Pricing Clause

The performance pricing clause—or grid pricing clause—often excludes the interest rate from the renegotiation process following a covenant default.[135] It regulates *ex ante* how the interest rate spread will (automatically) adjust to changes in credit quality gauged by either credit ratings or accounting ratios. The accounting-based measures often relate to the "debt to EBITDA" ratio, gearing, or interest coverage. The LSTA Guide[136] includes both the grid pricing relating to credit ratings and to

[128]Wright (2006), p. 174.

[129]Box 1.14. LMA Term Loan: Wright (2006), p. 48; similarly in the LSTA "any event or other condition shall occur and be continuing that is reasonably likely to result in a Material Adverse Effect"; Box 9.13. LSTA Guide: Wight et al. (2009), p. 436.

[130]Wright (2006), p. 179 et seq.

[131]Wright (2006), p. 182 et seqq.

[132]For possible limits on the legal enforceability see below 6.2.

[133]Wight et al. (2009), p. 177 et seqq., 236.

[134]Wight et al. (2009), p. 436.

[135]Shadab (2014), 1109.

[136]See generally Box 3.5.; for grid pricing based on credit rating see Box 3.6.; and for grid pricing based on financial test see Box 3.7. LSTA Guide: Wight et al. (2009), p. 72 et seqq.

accounting ratios, whereas the LMA Term Loan lacks them altogether. However, an unpublished empirical study shows that, in particular, performance pricing covenants based on a financial test were used in the UK from 1992 to January 2002.[137] Recently, the German literature[138] and a European trend report[139] have also recognised the use of performance pricing covenants.[140]

The grid pricing has a disciplinary effect.[141] It encourages the debtor company to improve its performance, because the grid is often set to be expensive at the beginning of the loan's life and then to decrease over time according to the debtor company's performance.[142] It transparently sets a reward structure for improved performance by offering a cheaper debt without further negotiation.[143]

3.5 Creating a Bilateral Private Governance System

As shown above, covenants and their related clauses constitute an efficient self-help mechanism for creditor protection in the private sphere. Thereby, they allow the creditor and debtor to create a bilateral private governance system.

As mentioned previously, covenants in combination with the event of default clause function as private governance mechanisms because they regulate all three stages of creditor protection in the private sphere[144]: norm setting, monitoring and sanctioning. Principally, covenants can be regarded as a two-sided (bilateral) form of private governance within the theory of private governance according to Williamson; see Figs. 3.1 and 3.2.[145]

Banks set relational norms in the form of covenants to measure the debtor company's financial performance. Covenants also ensure the recovery of the loan plus interest, using norms to protect the businesses assets. Compliance with the covenants is then monitored with the help of information undertakings. In case of default, the norms are applied via renegotiation and enforced via severe consequences in the event of default clause—namely termination as a last resort.

[137] Chatterjee (2006).

[138] See, for example, Wortmann (2001), p. 221, fn. 237; Stupp and Mucke (2005), 21; Becker (2013), p. 184, 222.

[139] Pappalarado Bonelli Erede et al. (2014), p. 5.

[140] Di Pietra et al. (2014), p. 172.

[141] Cf. Shadab (2014), 1088.

[142] Dichev et al. (2002); see also with further references Tung (2009), 148 et seq.

[143] Cf. Asquith et al. (2005), 102 et seqq. There is, however, also interest-increasing performance pricing, cf. Tung (2009), 149 et seq.; Asquith et al. (2005), 102 et seqq., 127.

[144] This can be regarded as complete privatisation of a governance structure, see Calliess (2006), p. 199 et seq.

[145] Williamson (1985), p. 75; see also von Harder (2016), p. 72et seqq.

function / regulator	norm setting	norm application	norm enforcement
state	legislature	courts	legal enforcement
private three-sided	social norms	alternative dispute resolution	reputation/exclusion
private two-sided	relational norm	negotiation	termination/collateral
Private one-sided	company norms	board of directors	hierarchy

Fig. 3.1 Private governance according to Williamson (Calliess and Renner 2008, p. 206)

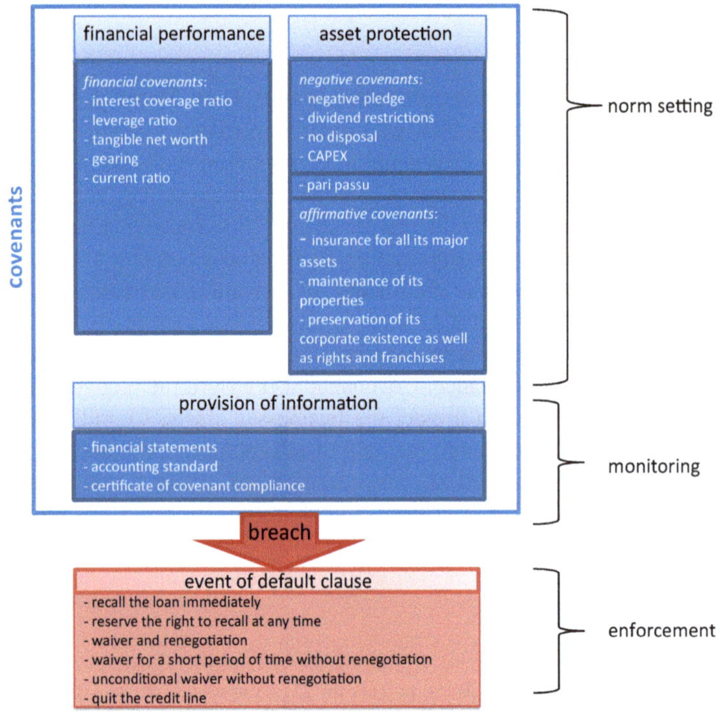

Fig. 3.2 Bilateral private governance through covenants (own illustration)

In Scenario 1,[146] the bank consortium and Papermaker first concluded a loan agreement and thereby set relational norms in the form of covenants and the event of default clause. When Papermaker wanted to issue secured bonds, a potential default of the negative pledge clause ensured that Papermaker and the bank

[146] See above 1.1.

consortium negotiated again. By applying the covenants and the event of default clause, the bank consortium prevented the issuance of secured bonds. Then, in Scenario 2b[147] when Papermaker had violated a covenant, the bank consortium demanded additional collateral and thereby enforced the covenants and the event of default clause.

This enforcement outside the court works because covenants are "deliberately drafted to be self-governing".[148] They create a contractual regime, which is "of a more thoroughly transaction-specific, ongoing-administrative kind".[149] Covenants are self-enforcing[150] as they create a situation in which the value of continuing the contractual relationship is accepted by both parties to be higher than the gain of non-compliance in the present. As long as this is given, the parties will comply with the contract and no further governance mechanisms are necessary.[151] The threat of breaking off the future relationship in case of non-compliance might suffice in the event of repeated interaction. A problem arises where the number of repetitions is fixed from the beginning, i.e. the problem of endgame. Another mechanism of private governance—reputation—can complement the self-enforcing contract.[152] Such mechanisms are needed for protection against the *ex post* opportunism of the debtor company.

In the case of a loan agreement, the relationship between a bank and debtor company is fundamentally transformed.[153] A conversion of dependency occurs: An at arm's lengths relationship (with a large number of bidding companies) changes into a bilateral (monopoly like) exchange relationship with transaction-specific investments. Thus, dependency is created through specificity. On the one hand, the debtor company depends on the continuous renewal and enlargement of the credit (line), and thus gains no advantage from opportunistic behaviour. Furthermore, defaulting can create enormous costs for the debtor company if the bank decides to accelerate. Acceleration could even lead to a cross-default, which would incur even more costs. One or both events can bankrupt the debtor company. Moreover, a default would damage the debtor company's reputation, as authorities and companies might collect such debt information and present it to any potential future lender. On the other hand, the bank carries the risk of loss in the event of default. This creates a special relationship of interdependency and an individualised transaction,[154] which in turn allows for an enforceable private governance system.

---

147 See above 1.2.

148 Wells and Amin (2013), 571. Cf. also Heinrich (2009), p. 349.

149 Williamson (1985), p. 71.

150 Cf. Telser (1980); Klein (1985). Self-enforcing contracts are also relational contracts. See for relational contracts MacNeil (1974); Macaulay (1963). For the role of self-enforcing contracts in the bilateral private ordering sphere see von Harder (2016), p. 74.

151 Dietz (2010), p. 17 et seq.

152 Okun (1981), 89; Furubotn and Richter (2005), p. 172 et seq., 258 et seqq.; Richter and Furubotn (2010), p. 182 et seqq., 279 et seqq.

153 Williamson (1985).

154 So-called "lock in" situation, cf. McMillan and Woodruff (2000), 2426.

The bilateral governance system is created by covenants and an event of default clause and it shifts the management of financial distress from bankruptcy proceedings to an earlier stage that falls outside the scope of bankruptcy law.[155]

References

Achleitner A-K, Braun R, Tappeiner F (2009) Determinants of financial covenants in leveraged buyouts-evidence from an economy with strong creditor rights. http://papers.ssrn.com/sol3/papers.cfm?abstract_id=1523264. Accessed 7 Mar 2013

Adams D (2003) Corporate finance: banking and capital markets. Legal practice course 2002/03 series, 8th edn. Jordans, UK

Asquith P, Beatty A, Weber J (2005) Performance pricing in bank debt contracts. J Account Econ 40:101–128

Ballo EHF (2010) Die AGB-Kontrolle von Kreditverträgen in der Akquisitionsfinanzierung. Lang, Frankfurt am Main

Becker HP (2013) Investition und Finanzierung: Grundlagen der betrieblichen Finanzwirtschaft, 6th edn. Springer, Wiesbaden

Beneish MD, Press E (1993) Costs of technical violation of accounting-based debt covenants. Account Rev 68(2):233–257

Calliess G-P (2006) Grenzüberschreitende Verbraucherverträge. Rechtssicherheit und Gerechtigkeit auf dem elektronischen Weltmarktplatz. Mohr Siebeck, Tübingen

Calliess G-P, Renner M (2008) Rechtssicherheit ohne Staat? Eine empiriegestützte Theorie. In: Gosewinkel D, Schuppert GF (eds) Politische Kultur im Wandel von Staatlichkeit. edition sigma, Berlin, pp 205–222

Casey CJ, Bartczak NJ (1984) Cash flow – it's not the bottom line. Harv Bus Rev:61–66

Chatterjee R (2006) Performing pricing and covenants in debt contracts. https://www.jbs.cam.ac.uk/fileadmin/user_upload/research/workingpapers/wp0607.pdf. Accessed 02 Feb 2016

Chen K, Wei KCJ (1993) Creditors' decisions to waive violations of accounting-based debt covenants. Account Rev 68:218–232

Demerjian PR (2007) Financial ratios and credit risk: the selection of financial ratio covenants in debt contracts. http://ssrn.com/abstract=929907. Accessed 19 Aug 2013

Demerjian PR, Owens EL (2013) Measuring financial covenant strictness in private debt contracts. http://ssrn.com/abstract=2232880. Accessed 10 Jan 2014

Di Pietra R, McLeay S, Ronen J (2014) Accounting and regulation. New insights on governance, markets and institutions. Springer, New York

Dichev ID, Beatty A, Weber J (2002) The role and characteristics of accounting-based performance pricing in private debt contracts. http://ssrn.com/abstract=318399. Accessed 02 Feb 2016

Diem A (2013) § 22. Akquisitionsfinanzierungen. Kredite für Unternehmenskäufe, 3rd edn. Beck, München

Dietz T (2010) Institutionen und Globalisierung. Eine empirische Untersuchung am Beispiel grenzüberschreitender Softwareentwicklungsverträge. Mohr Siebeck, Tübingen

Fight A (2004) Syndicated lending: essential capital markets. Butterworth-Heinemann, UK

Furubotn EG, Richter R (2005) Institutions and economic theory. The contribution of the new institutional economics, 2nd edn. The University of Michigan Press, Michigan

Gilson RJ, Kraakman RH (1984) The mechanisms of market efficiency. Va Law Rev 70:549–644. doi:10.2307/1073080

[155]A covenant default is triggered between a crisis of success and a liquidation crisis. See e.g. Krolak et al. (2009), 1420.

Gopalakrishnan V, Parkash M (1995) Borrower and lender perceptions of accounting information in corporate lending agreements. Account Horiz 9:13–26
Haghani S, Holzamer M, Voll S, Warnig C (2009) Financial Covenants in der Unternehmensfinanzierung. Roland Berger. http://www.rolandberger.com/media/pdf/Roland_Berger_Financial_Covenants_20090725.pdf. Accessed 07 Mar 2013
von Harder S (2016) Unternehmensinternes Vertragsrecht. Normsetzung, Streitschlichtung und Vollstreckung im firmeninternen Handel. Nomos, Baden-Baden
Harrison WTJ, Horngren CT, Thomas CW, Suwardy T (2011) Financial accounting: international financial reporting standards, 8th edn. Pearson, Singapore
Heinrich S (2009) Covenants als Alternative zum institutionellen Gläubigerschutz. Eine rechtsvergleichende und ökonomische Analyse, vol 228. Schriften zum Wirtschaftsrecht. Duncker & Humblot, Berlin
Hill G (2008) Negative pledge with provision for 'automatic security' on breach: a form of floating charge? Butterworths J Int Bank Financ Law:528–531
Klein B (1985) Self-enforcing contracts. ZgS 141:594–600
Krolak T, Morzfeld K, Remmen J-D (2009) Financial Covenants als Instrument der Krisenfrüherkennung und der normierten Krisenbewältigung. DB 62(27):1417–1422
Lloyd RM (1991) Financial covenants in commercial loan documentation: uses and limitations. Tenn Law Rev 58:335–366
Macaulay S (1963) Non-contractual relations in business: a preliminary study. Am Sociol Rev 28:55–67
MacNeil I (1974) Many futures of contract. South Calif Law Rev 47:691–816
Mather P, Peirson G (2006) Financial covenants in the markets for public and private debt. Account Financ 46(2):285–307
McMillan J, Woodruff C (2000) Private order under dysfunctional public order. Mich Law Rev 98:2421–2458. doi:10.2307/1290349
Moir L, Sudarsanam S (2007) Determinants of financial covenants and pricing of debt in private debt contracts. The UK evidence. Account Bus Res 37(2):151–166
Okun AM (1981) Prices and quantities: a macroeconomic analysis. Blackwell, Oxford
Pappalarado Bonelli Erede, Bredin Prat, De Brauw Blackstone Westbroek, Hengeler Müller, Slaughter and May, Uria Menéndez (2014) Loan documentation in Europe: recent trends and current issues. http://www.uria.com/documentos/publicaciones/4230/documento/BF001.pdf?id=539. Accessed 02 Feb 2016
Pinches GE, Eubank AA, Mingo KA, Caruthers JK (1975) The hierarchical classification of financial ratios. J Bus Res:295–310
Pucher M (2015) Die Pari-passu-Klausel. In: Krauskopf PL, Babey F (eds) Internationales Wirtschaftsrecht: Schiedsverfahren und Prozessführung | Internationales Handelsrecht | Wettbewerbsrecht und Regulierung. Nomos, Baden-Baden, pp 62–78
Richter R, Furubotn EG (2010) Neue Institutionenökonomik, 4th edn. Mohr Siebeck, Tübingen
Roberts MR, Sufi A (2009) Control rights and capital structure: an empirical investigation. J Finance 64:1657–1695
Runge JC (2010) Covenants in Kreditverträgen. Grenzen der Einflussnahme von Kreditgebern. RWS-Verlag, Köln
Shadab HB (2014) Performance-sensitive debt: from asset-based loans to startup financing. Univ Pa J Bus Law 16:1077–1110
Simpson DB (1973) The drafting of loan agreements: a borrower's viewpoint. Bus Law 28:1161–1196
Stupp A, Mucke J (2005) Die Auswirkungen kreativer "Zins"-Vereinbarungen auf die ordentlichen Kündigungsmöglichkeiten des Darlehensnehmers. BKR:20–27
Telser JG (1980) A theory of self-enforcing agreements. J Bus 53:27–44
Thießen F (1996) Covenants in Kreditverträgen: Alternative oder Ergänzung zum Insolvenzrecht? ZBB:19–37
Tung F (2009) Leverage in the board room: the unsung influence of private lenders in corporate governance. UCLA Law Rev 57:115–181

Weidemaier M, Scott R, Gulati M (2013) Origin myths, contracts, and the hunt for pari passu. Law Soc Inq 38:72–105
Wells C, Amin D (2013) Till default do us part: facility agreements and acceleration. J Int Bank Financ Law:571–575
Wight R, Cooke W, Gray R (2009) The LSTA's complete credit agreement guide. McGraw-Hill, New York
Williamson OE (1985) The economic institutions of capitalism. The Free Press, New York
Wood P (2003) Pari passu clauses. What do they mean? Butterworths J Int Bank Financ Law 18:371–374
Wood P (2007) International loans, bonds, guarantees, legal opinions, vol 2. Sweet & Maxwell, London
Wood P (2008) Law and practice of international finance. Law and practice of international finance. Sweet & Maxwell, London
Wortmann A (2001) Shareholder value in mittelständischen Wachstumsunternehmen. Dt. Univ.-Verl, Wiesbaden
Wright S (2006) International loan documentation. Palgrave Macmillan, New York
Wüstemann J, Bischof J, Kierzek S (2007) Internationale Gläubigerschutzkonzeptionen. BB Beilage 5:13–19

Part II
The Systematisation of Third-Party Creditor Effects of Covenants: Preliminary Framework

Chapter 4
Academic Discussion and the Relevance of Third-Party Creditor Protection

The bilateral private governance system allows the bank to react to a debtor company's worsened financial situation before the debtor company is bankrupt. The bank can use the information advantage provided by information undertakings to take corrective action before (adjusting) third-party creditors can react. This, for example, enables the bank to receive additional collateral from the debtor company. The additional collateral, however, may lessen the chances of third-party creditors' claims being satisfied, because it reduces the debtor company's pool of assets. This shows that the bilateral governance system created by covenants and the event of default clause can affect third-party creditors' claims. To understand these effects, the work will first describe their treatment as externalities under law and economics theory. Then, their relevance for the current legal discussion will be shown. Afterwards, the specific potential externalities of the bilateral governance system will be presented. This part will systematise the theoretical considerations in the literature to allow for an overall assessment. It will be completed by the subsequent chapter, which will establish the general presumption that banks behave in a self interested way as well as show the legal limits of such behaviour under German and US law.

4.1 Covenants Creating a Bilateral Private Governance System with Externalities

The following section will describe the third-party creditor effects according to law and economics as potential externalities. Subsequently, the relevance of these potential externalities for current legal debates will be presented. This will be done with three selected topics that are prevalent in the German and US literature. The first two debate from the German literature concern covenants as an alternative to institutional creditor protection in company or bankruptcy law. The third

D. Matri, *Covenants and Third-Party Creditors*, DOI 10.1007/978-3-319-62036-7_4

discussion, which mainly appears in the US literature, concerns banks and their means of influencing a debtor company as part of corporate governance.

4.1.1 The Law and Economics Term of Externalities

In law and economics theory, some third-party effects are called externalities. The definition of an externality, however, is not very clear-cut and its concept has been over-used.[1] Hence, the problem of externalities should be treated with caution.

Broadly speaking, there are two different approaches.[2] One is based on modern welfare theory,[3] while the other is based on the Coase theorem.[4] This work will follow the second approach understanding externalities to occur in situations where the actions of one economic agent directly affect another agent without the acting agent incurring the costs or benefits (indirect effects through the market price are excluded).[5] Externalities can be either negative—in the form of costs—or positive—in the form of benefits. Potential externalities may be internalised privately when it is economically feasible for the concerned parties to negotiate with each other about incurring the costs and/or benefits.[6] In that case, an externality—technically speaking—does not occur.

With that in mind, the following chapters will only refer to potential externalities.

4.1.2 Covenants and Externalities

The bank's action under the bilateral private governance system, created by covenants and an event of default clause, directly affects third-party creditors. Generally, the bank will neither incur the costs for third-party creditors nor will it benefit from the positive third-party creditor effects.

In Scenario 2a,[7] for example, the disciplinary function of the negative pledge clause benefits third-party creditors by preventing asset dilution. The bank

[1]For a detailed analysis of the historical development see Papandreou (1998). See also Dahlman (1979); he states i.a. that "It is thus doubtful whether the term "externality" has any meaningful interpretation, except as an indicator of the political beliefs and value judgments of the person who uses (or avoids using) the term." Dahlman (1979) 156. See further Cornes and Sandler (1996), p. 39.

[2]Cf. Dahlman (1979), 142 et seq.

[3]This approach aims at the evaluation of the actual economic performance according to the maximum welfare solution (*Walrasian* general equilibrium); Pigou (1932).

[4]Coase (1960); cf. Furubotn and Richter (2005), p. 101 et seqq.

[5]Cf. Furubotn and Richter (2005), p. 101; Richter and Furubotn (2010), p. 109.

[6]Furubotn and Richter (2005), p. 106; Richter and Furubotn (2010), p. 114.

[7]See above 1.2.

consortium, however, will not benefit from the maintained value of the third-party creditor's claim. By the same token, if the bank consortium demands new collateral, the bank would not incur the costs for the third-party creditors' claim dilution (Scenario 2b[8]). These externalities are not assumed to be internalised, because third-party creditors are presumed to have no impact on the renegotiation after a covenant default. This is particularly true for smaller third-party creditors.[9]

4.2 The Relevance of Externalities

The fact that the bilateral private governance system created by covenants and an event of default clause causes potential externalities has a significant influence on the legal academic discussion. A detailed examination of those debates will not form part of this work. The work will, however, provide considerable insight for such discussions by systematising and empirically analysing the potential externalities of that bilateral private governance system. To illustrate the implications of this task, three examples from the German and US academic literature will be given.

4.2.1 Covenants as an Alternative to Institutional Creditor Protection

First, covenants will be discussed as an alternative to institutional creditor protection by either company law or bankruptcy law. Generally, covenants can only be an alternative to institutional creditor protection if they achieve the aims of statutory creditor protection. In fact, externalities should be regulated if they contradict these aims.

Despite this general consideration, the academic discussion comes in various shapes in different legal systems. This work will concentrate on the German literature, because it is here that the debate has been particularly prominent in the last decade.[10]

---

[8]See above 1.2.

[9]Cf. Siegel (1998), 594; Hopt, in: Wank et al. (eds) (2002), 1019; Merkt (2004), 313 et seq.; Mankowski, in: Lutter (ed) (2006), 496.

[10]Seminal for covenants as alternative to bankruptcy law Thießen (1996); for an overview about the debate regarding Company Law see e.g. Nikoleyczik (2007), p. 1 et seqq.

4.2.1.1 Company Law

The introduction of the MoMiG[11] and the release of the European Commission's Action Plan on Company Law[12] sparked a debate about the effectiveness of creditor protection through legal capital rules and about whether—and if so to what extent—covenants could substitute them.[13] The crucial part of this discussion concerns the protection of non-adjusting creditors, because it is widely accepted that adjusting creditors can protect themselves via self-help devices—in particular via covenants.[14]

To protect non-adjusting creditors is also the main rationale for creditor protection in company law. The historical reason for legal creditor protection lies in its function as a corrective mechanism for the incentive structure and risk of moral hazard created by the limited liability of shareholders.[15] The principle of limited liability allows for the externalisation of the risk of failure.[16] It is therefore sometimes stated that creditor protection through law is an ethical necessity[17] or based on a notion of fairness[18] and common sense.[19] However, adjusting corporate creditors are able to protect themselves using contract law, credit agencies and self-help mechanisms, which render the corrective basis for them a rather theoretical one. The argument is, nevertheless, still widely accepted.[20] The ECJ, for example,

[11]*Gesetz zur Modernisierung des GmbH-Rechts und zur Bekämpfung von Missbräuchen* (Law for the Modernisation of the German Limited Liability Company Law and the Prevention of Misuse).

[12]Communication from the Commission to the Council and the European Parliament - Modernising Company Law and Enhancing Corporate Governance in the European Union - A Plan to Move Forward COM/2003/0284.

[13]See, for example, Zur entwicklung des europäischen gesellschaftsrecht: Stellungsnahme der arbeitsgruppe europäisches gesellschaftsrecht (group of german experts on corporate law) zum report of the high level group of company law experts on a modern regulatory framework for company law in Europe (2003); Merkt (2004); Nikoleyczik (2007); Grade and Wauters, in: Geens, Hopt (eds) (2010).

[14]See, for example, *Centros Ltd v. Erhvervs- og Selskabsstyrelsen* (1999) C-212/97, ECR [1999] I-1459, para. 36; *Kamer van Koophandel en Fabrieken voor Amsterdam v. Inspire Art Ltd* (2003) C-167/01 ECR [2003] I-10155, para. 135; nuanced Bezzenberger (2005), 108 et seqq.; Heinrich (2009), p. 43, 45. Both argue that the information asymmetry obscures an appropriate risk allocation by adjusting creditors. This argument is particularly questionable in the context of covenants. The adjusting creditors might not be able to evaluate the credit risk properly *ex ante* but covenants allow them to adjust *ex post* and to collect more information over the life of the loan.

[15]As previously mentioned this work considers the debtor company as a limited (public or private) company.

[16]See above 4.2.1.1. Generally see Heinrich (2009), p. 42 et seqq. with further references.

[17]Wiedemann (1980), p. 515.

[18]Nikoleyczik (2007), p. 11 et seq.

[19]Rickford (2004), 967, 971; cf. Mülbert (2006), 365.

[20]Cf. Schön (2004a), 293 et seqq.; Bachner (2009), p. 7; Thole (2010), p. 15; Mülbert (2006), 370; Teichmann (2006), p. 455; Heinrich (2009), p. 41 et seqq. (he, however, classifies the argument as an economic one but at the same time acknowledges that the concept of limited liability does not endanger the creditors' interests).

classifies creditor protection as an overriding requirement relating to the general interest that can potentially justify restrictions on the freedom of establishment.[21] This seems reasonable, as creditors are not always able to negotiate. In fact, as previously mentioned creditors can be too weak—if a transaction is too small or a creditor too naïve—or may belong to the group of involuntary creditors who cannot adjust to the higher risk attached to the limited liability concept.[22] The rationale of creditor protection in company law, therefore, is best understood in law and economics terms: creditor protection in corporate law aims at correcting negative externalities caused by the incentive structure of limited liability.[23]

To protect non-adjusting creditors from negative externalities, three different means of creditor protection are used in the legal capital approach: initial minimum equity capital, distribution restrictions, and the requirement that specific action is taken after a significant loss of capital.[24] The value of prescribing a minimum legal capital for creditors is questionable and widely accepted to be symbolic.[25] The minimum legal capital, even if protected by rules on provision and maintenance of capital, will rarely suffice to satisfy non-adjusting creditors in a winding-up.[26] However, the rules on provision and maintenance of capital can—depending on their implementation—provide significant creditor protection for non-adjusting creditors.

The question of whether covenants can substitute legal capital rules in that aspect is highly disputed. Proponents of covenants argue that covenants provide creditor protection "reflexively" to other creditors.[27] Translated into the language of this work, they put forward that the bilateral governance system produces positive externalities for third-party creditors and internalises some of the negative externalities of limited liability with its disciplinary function. If that is the case, covenants could indeed be considered an alternative to institutional creditor protection by company law.

However, opponents argue that while reflexive creditor protection by covenants may be possible, covenant-secured creditors will always act selfishly and will thus create significant negative externalities.[28] These negative effects will outweigh the positive effects. If that is the case, the bilateral private governance system created by covenants and an event of default clause actually contradicts the legal ratio of

[21] *Überseering BV v. Nordic Construction Company Baumanagement GmbH* [2002] C-208/00, ECR I-9919, para. 92.

[22] Cf. Armour et al., in: Kraakman et al. (eds) (2009), p. 120.

[23] In that direction, probably, Grundmann, in: Grundmann et al. (eds) (2010), p. 85 et seqq.

[24] Publicity duties can be regarded as a fourth instrument. For a detailed overview see Wiedemann (1980), p. 520 et seq., 552 et seqq.; Escher-Weingart (2001), p. 107 et seqq.

[25] Cf. Armour (2000), 371 et seq.; Kübler, in: Hopt, Wymeersch (eds) (2003), p. 100 et seq.; Schön (2004b), 437 et seq.

[26] See for Germany Schulte (2016), p. 105; see also, generally, Armour (2000), 372. For the European legal capital doctrine see Enriques and Macey (2001), 1185 et seqq.

[27] Cf. Siegel (1998), 594; Hopt, in: Wank et al. (eds) (2002), p. 1018 et seq.; Merkt (2004), 313.

[28] Cf. Servatius (2008), p. 367; Burger and Buchhart (2001), 101.

creditor protection in company law. Hence, the bilateral private governance system should be regulated. To achieve that, some authors support a subordination of covenant-secured debts.[29] Others suggest a super-priority or compulsory insurance for tort creditors.[30]

4.2.1.2 Bankruptcy Law

A similar discussion can be found in the literature on German bankruptcy law—namely on whether covenants create a "more efficient" creditor protection system than bankruptcy law. Proponents[31] argue that covenants can be better tailored to the specific needs and circumstances of the debtor. Moreover, non-covenant secured creditors can protect themselves with cross-default clauses. Opponents[32] argue that covenants can only be used by creditors with market power and that non-covenant secured creditors will be unprotected in case of financial difficulties. Their main argument is that the collective protection of bankruptcy law is more efficient than that of covenants.[33]

This argument reflects the rationale of bankruptcy law. Bankruptcy law provides pari passu—or *par conditio creditorum* — between unsecured creditors. Thereby, the conflict between creditors in case of bankruptcy is reduced. In bankruptcy, only a limited pool of assets is available, which is insufficient to satisfy all creditors' claims. Each creditor therefore tries to collect first. A "run to assets"[34] begins and, with it, a piecemeal dismantling of the debtor company. A piecemeal dismantling leads to a lack of operating assets and a decrease in the aggregated value of assets.[35] This problem is described in the literature as a multi-party prisoner's dilemma[36] or a common pool problem.[37] To reduce the problem, the individualistic approach of debt collection is replaced by a collective enforcement mechanism that ensures the equal satisfaction of all claims.[38] This functions as a deterrent prior to bankruptcy, structures the process of creditor satisfaction and limits creditors' losses after bankruptcy.[39]

---

[29]Servatius (2008), p. 426 et seqq.; Engert (2012); Majic (2013), p. 45 et seqq.

[30]Cf., for example, Mankowski, in: Lutter (ed) (2006), p. 491 et seqq.

[31]Thießen (1996), 31 ("markwirtschaftlich Alternative zum staatlichen Insolvenzrecht").

[32]Burger and Buchhart (2001); Thole (2010), p. 46.

[33]Burger and Buchhart (2001), 101 et seqq. with further references; similarly see Köndgen, in: Prütting (ed) (1997), 154.

[34]See e.g. BGH WM 2013, 1504, 1507 ("Windhundrennen").

[35]Cf. Schmidt (1980), p. 37; Rausch (1985), p. 33.

[36]Rapoport and Chammah (1965); Engel (2004), p. 55 et seqq.; Grünewald (2015), p. 97 et seqq.

[37]Jackson (1986), 10 et seq.; Eidenmüller (1999), p. 19 et seqq.; Zirener (2005), p. 186 et seqq.; Thole (2010), p. 56 et seqq.; Eidenmüller (2016), 145.

[38]This collective enforcement mechanism is based on the bargaining theory. It represents the mechanism to which all creditors would have agreed *ex ante* (before bankruptcy) without knowing what will happen; cf. Jackson (1982), 861 et seqq.; Rausch (1985), p. 21 et seq.

[39]Cf. Schmidt (1980), p. 35; Rausch (1985), p. 25 et seqq.

This highlights the fact that covenants can only be efficient if they provide collective creditor protection. The debate therefore centres around the question of externalities through covenants.[40] If potential negative externalities of covenants can be internalised or are rather small and, at the same time, potential positive externalities are significant, the bilateral private governance system created by covenants and an event of default clause would also protect third-party creditors. Hence, it would provide collective creditor protection.

So far, both debates present mainly theoretical remarks with regard to positive and negative externalities of covenants. There is a lack of empirical and in-depth research on the topic. Furthermore, as Horst Eidenmüller pointed out, the efficiency of covenants can only be assessed if the relationship between positive and negative externalities is gauged.[41] This work will therefore tackle this task in particular and attempt to fill the gap in the legal literature.

4.2.2 Rethinking Corporate Governance

Another debate where externalities are relevant centres around the theory of corporate governance in the US literature.[42] Originally, Oliver Williamson claimed that the external disciplinary force of debt is significantly limited due to its rule-based nature.[43] He argued that compared to the governance structure of equity, the contractual rules of a debt offer less discretion. So, Williamson considered debt governance only suitable for simple transactions and when highly redeployable assets are involved.[44] It could only be applied to simple transactions. In practice, however, the bank's sanction mechanisms have proven to be more flexible.[45]

In light of recent events, such as Enron[46] or the current financial crisis, the corporate governance debate refocused on the role of stakeholders other than shareholders.[47] Particular attention was drawn to the interdependency among

[40]Cf. Schmidt (1980), p. 28 et seqq.

[41]"Entscheidend ist vielmehr, daß [sic.] Effekte zu Lasten und zugunsten Dritter auftreten können, daß [sic.] unklar ist, in welchem Verhältnis diese Effekte stehen und daß [sic.] deshalb auch unklar ist, wie die Effizienz von *covenants* zu beurteilen ist."; Eidenmüller (1999), p. 148.

[42]Similar discussions can, of course, be found in other legal jurisprudences. For Germany see e.g. Schmidt, in: Jürgens (ed) (2007).

[43]Seminal for debt as part of corporate governance Williamson (1988); for an current perspective see e.g. Tirole (2006), p. 51 et seqq. and Gullifer and Payne (2011), p. 80 et seqq.

[44]Williamson (1988), 579 et seqq.

[45]Triantis and Daniels (1995), 1082; the immense creditor influence was proven in the empirical study by Nini et al. (2012).

[46]Cf. Deakin and Konzelmann, in: Armour, McCahery (eds) (2006).

[47]This conflict goes back to the *Berle-Dodd* debate: Berle (1931); Berle and Means (1947); Dodd (1932); Dodd (1935).

different creditors.[48] That all stakeholders interact and are part of the corporate governance is particularly embedded in the theories of team production[49] and interactive corporate governance.[50] The theory of interactive corporate governance implies that "all stakeholders share a common goal of constraining managerial slack that is only partly offset by the conflicts of interest among stakeholders. In other words, the governance activities of one stakeholder generally yield positive net externalities to others."[51] Yet, not all creditors are able to play an active part in corporate governance. The acting creditor has usually gained its disciplinary force through covenants. However, this powerful (covenant-secured) creditor will, from a common sense perspective, likely use its significant influence to enhance its own position and thereby weaken the third-party creditor's position.[52] This can lead to creditor opportunism, which occurs whenever a covenant-secured creditor tries to obtain a benefit not explicitly or implicitly stipulated in the initial agreement at the expense of third-party creditors.[53] The covenant-secured creditor takes corrective action that produces negative externalities.

Although the opportunistic behaviour of creditors is particularly a problem with hedge funds in the US,[54] similar tendencies can be seen in banks. The traditional motivation of banks, however, will be different from that of hedge funds. Thus, the question of whether creditors have a disciplinary effect on debtor companies and thereby play an important part in corporate governance is, once again, connected to the question of whether the bilateral private governance system created by covenants and an event of default clause causes mainly positive or negative externalities. However, the corporate governance discussion focuses on the shareholder-creditor conflict and not—like the work—on the creditor-creditor conflict.

4.3 Summary

To understand the negative and positive effects of the bilateral private governance system, created by covenants and an event of default clause, their treatment under law and economics theories as externalities was introduced. Generally, the bank will neither incur the costs for third-party creditors nor will it benefit from the positive third-party creditor effects. So, potential negative and positive externalities can occur. These externalities are relevant for current legal debates. The topics concerning covenants as an alternative to institutional creditor protection by either

[48] Levmore (1982); Triantis and Daniels (1995), 1077.

[49] Blair and Stout (1999).

[50] Triantis and Daniels (1995).

[51] Triantis and Daniels (1995), 1079.

[52] Hoffmann (2012).

[53] Fischel (1989), 138.

[54] Cf. Lipson (2010) with further references.

company law or bankruptcy law in Germany and the role of covenant-secured creditors in corporate governance in the US literature were selected to demonstrate the impact of externalities. All three legal debates relate to the question of whether the bilateral private governance system created by covenants and an event of default clause causes mainly positive or negative externalities.

References

Armour J (2000) Share capital and creditor protection: efficient rules for a modern company law. Modern Law Rev 63:355–378

Armour J, Hertig G, Kanda H (2009) Transaction with creditors. In: Kraakman RH, Armour J, Davies P et al (eds) The anatomy of corporate law. A comparative and functional approach, 2nd edn. Oxford University Press, Oxford, pp 115–151

Bachner T (2009) Creditor protection in private companies. Anglo-German perspectives for a European legal discourse. Oxford, Oxford

Berle AA (1931) Corporate powers as powers in trust. Harv Law Rev 44:1049–1076

Berle AA, Means GC (1947) The modern corporation and private property. [1932] edn. Macmillan, New York

Bezzenberger T (2005) Das Kapital der Aktiengesellschaft: Kapitalerhaltung – Vermögensbindung – Konzernrecht. Dr. Otto Schmidt, Köln

Blair MM, Stout LA (1999) A team production theory of corporate law. Va Law Rev 85:247–328

Burger A, Buchhart A (2001) Financial Covenants statt Insolvenzordnung. Finanz Betrieb:99–104

Coase RH (1960) The problem of social cost. J Law Econ 3:1–44

Cornes R, Sandler T (1996) The theory of externalities, public goods, and club goods, 2nd edn. Cambridge University Press, Cambridge

Dahlman CJ (1979) The problem of externality. J Law Econ 22:141–162

Deakin S, Konzelmann S (2006) Corporate governance after Enron. An age of enlightenment? In: Armour J, McCahery J (eds) After Enron. Improving corporate law and modernising securities regulation in Europe and the US. Hart Publishing, Oxford/Portland, pp 155–158

Dodd EM (1932) For whom are corporate managers trustees? Harv Law Rev 45:1145–1163

Dodd EM (1935) Is effective enforcement of the fiduciary duties of corporate managers practicable? U Chi L Rev 2:194–207

Eidenmüller H (1999) Unternehmenssanierung zwischen Markt und Gesetz. Mechanismen der Unternehmensreorganisation und Kooperationspflichten im Reorganisationsrecht. Otto Schmidt, Köln

Eidenmüller H (2016) Was ist ein Insolvenzverfahren? ZIP 37:145–151

Engel T (2004) Die Insolvenz und optionsbasierte Reorganisationsmodelle. Deutscher Universitäts-Verlag/GWV Fachverlage GmbH, Wiesbaden

Engert A (2012) Drohende Subordination als Schranke einer Unternehmenskontrolle durch Kreditgeber. ZGR 41(6):835–874

Enriques L, Macey JR (2001) Creditors versus capital formation: the case against the European legal capital rules. Cornell Law Rev 86:1165–1204

Escher-Weingart C (2001) Reform durch Deregulierung im Kapitalgesellschaftsrecht. Eine Analyse der Reformmöglichkeiten unter besonderer Berücksichtigung des Gläubiger- und Anlegerschutzes. Mohr Siebeck, Tübingen

Fischel DR (1989) The economics of lender liability. Yale Law J 99:131–154

Furubotn EG, Richter R (2005) Institutions and economic theory. The contribution of the new institutional economics, 2nd edn. The University of Michigan Press, Michigan

Grade J-MN, Wauters M (2010) Reforming legal capital: harmonisation or fragmentation of creditor protection. In: Geens K, Hopt KJ (eds) The European company law action plan revisited. Leuven University Press, Leuven, pp 25–59
Grundmann S (2010) Welche Einheit des Privatrechts? Von einer formalen zu einer inhaltlichen Konzeption des Privatrechts. In: Grundmann S, Haar B, Merkt H, Mülbert P, Wellenhofer M (eds) Welche Einheit des Privatrechts? Von einer formalen zu einer inhaltlichen Konzeption des Privatrechts. Series Welche Einheit des Privatrechts? Von einer formalen zu einer inhaltlichen Konzeption des Privatrechts, vol Series. De Gruyter, Berlin, pp 61–91
Grünewald P (2015) Mehrheitsherrschaft und insolvenzrechtliche Vorauswirkung in der Unternehmenssanierung. Mohr Siebeck, Tübingen
Gullifer L, Payne J (2011) Corporate finance law. Principles and policy. Hart, Oxford
Heinrich S (2009) Covenants als Alternative zum institutionellen Gläubigerschutz. Eine rechtsvergleichende und ökonomische Analyse, vol 228. Schriften zum Wirtschaftsrecht. Duncker & Humblot, Berlin
Hoffmann G (2012) Grenzen der Einflussnahme auf Unternehmensleitungsentscheidungen durch Kreditgläubiger. WM:10–19
Hopt KJ (2002) Gesellschaftsrecht im Wandel. In: Wank R, Hirte H, Frey K, Fleischer H, Thüsing G (eds) Book Gesellschaftsrecht im Wandel. Series Gesellschaftsrecht im Wandel, vol Series. Beck, München, pp 1013–1032
Jackson TH (1982) Bankruptcy, non-bankruptcy entitlements, and the creditors' bargain. Yale Law J 91:857–907. doi:10.2307/796070
Jackson TH (1986) The logic and limits of bankruptcy law. Beard Books, Washington
Köndgen J (1997) Financial Covenants. “Symbiotische” Finanzierungsverträge im Spannungsfeld von Vertrags-, Gesellschafts- und Insolvenzrecht. In: Prütting H (ed) Insolvenzrecht 1996, vol 1. RWS, Köln, pp 127–157
Kübler F (2003) The rules of capital under pressure of the securities markets. In: Hopt KJ, Wymeersch E (eds) Capital markets and company law. Oxford Press, Oxford, pp 95–114
Levmore S (1982) Monitors and freeriders in commercial and corporate settings. Yale Law J 92:49–83
Lipson JC (2010) Controlling creditor opportunism. http://works.bepress.com/jonathan_lipson/3. Accessed 21 Feb 1014
Majic M (2013) Covenants und Insolvenz: Risiken covenant-gesicherter Kreditgeber im Falle der Insolvenz des Kreditnehmers. De Gruyter, Berlin
Mankowski P (2006) Reicht das Vertragsrecht für einen angemessenen Schutz der Gesellschaftsgläubiger und ihrer Interessen aus? In: Lutter M (ed) Das Kapital der Aktiengesellschaft in Europa. De Gruyter Recht, Berlin, pp 488–507
Merkt H (2004) Der Kapitalschutz in Europa – ein rocher de bronze? ZGR:305–323
Mülbert PO (2006) A synthetic view of different concepts of creditor protection, or: a high-level framework for corporate creditor protection. EBOR 7:357–408
Nikoleyczik T (2007) Gläubigerschutz zwischen Gesetz und Vertrag. Alternativen zum System eines festen Nennkapitals. Steuer, Wirtschaft und Recht, vol Band 281. Eul, Köln
Nini G, Smith DC, Sufi A (2012) Creditor control rights, corporate governance, and firm value. Rev Financ Stud 25:1713–1761
Papandreou AA (1998) Externality and institutions. Oxford Press, Oxford
Pigou AC (1932) The economics of welfare, 4th edn. Macmillan, London
Rapoport A, Chammah AM (1965) Prisoner's dilemma: a study in conflict and cooperation. University of Michigan Press, Ann Arbor
Rausch W (1985) Gläubigerschutz im Insolvenzverfahren - Eine ökonomische Analyse einschlägiger rechtlicher Regelungen. Steuer, Wirtschaft und Recht, vol Band 17. Verlag Josef Eul, Bergisch Gladbach, Köln
Richter R, Furubotn EG (2010) Neue Institutionenökonomik, 4th edn. Mohr Siebeck, Tübingen
Rickford J (2004) Reforming capital report of the interdisciplinary group on capital maintenance. Eur Bus Law Rev:919–1027

Schmidt RH (1980) Ökonomische Analyse des Insolvenzrechts. Band 18 von Neue betriebswirtschaftliche Forschung

Schmidt RH (2007) Stakeholderorientierung, Systemhaftigkeit und Stabilität der Corporate Governance in Deutschland. In: Jürgens U (ed) Perspektiven der Corporate governance. Bestimmungsfaktoren unternehmerischer Entscheidungsprozesse und Mitwirkung der Arbeitnehmer. Nomos, Baden-Baden, pp 31–54

Schön W (2004a) The future of legal capital. EBOR 5:429–448

Schön W (2004b) Zur "Existenzvernichtung" der juristischen Person. ZHR 168:268–297

Schulte L-P (2016) Zum Beitrag von Insolvenzeröffnungsgründen und Financial Covenants zum Gläubigerschutz. In: Eine empirische Analyse ihrer Warnfunktion und ihres Einflussess auf den Wert der Ansprüche von Fremd- und Eigenkapitalgebern. Betriebswirtschaftlische Schriften. Band 169. Duncker & Humblot, Berlin

Servatius W (2008) Gläubigereinfluss durch Covenants. Mohr Siebeck, Tübingen

Siegel T (1998) Zweitwertbilanzierung für das deutsche Bilanzrecht? BFuP 50(5):593–603

Teichmann C (2006) Binnenmarktkonformes Gesellschaftsrecht. De Gruyter, Berlin

Thießen F (1996) Covenants in Kreditverträgen: Alternative oder Ergänzung zum Insolvenzrecht? ZBB:19–37

Thole C (2010) Gläubigerschutz durch Insolvenzrecht - Anfechtung und verwandte Regelungsinstrumente in der Unternehmensinsolvenz. Beiträge zum ausländischen und internationalen Privatrecht. Mohr Siebeck, Tübingen

Tirole J (2006) The theory of corporate finance. Princeton University Press, Princeton

Triantis GG, Daniels RJ (1995) The role of debt in interactive corporate governance. Calif Law Rev 83:1073–1114

Wiedemann H (1980) Gesellschaftsrecht I. Beck, München

Williamson OE (1988) Corporate finance and corporate governance. J Financ 43:567–591

Zirener J (2005) Sanierung in der Insolvenz. Handlungsalternativen für einen wertorientierten Einsatz des Insolvenzverfahrens. Deutscher Universitätsverlag, Wiesbaden

Zur Entwicklung des Europäischen Gesellschaftsrecht: Stellungsnahme der Arbeitsgruppe Europäisches Gesellschaftsrecht (Group of German Experts on Corporate Law) zum Report of the High Level Group of Company Law Experts on a modern Regulatory Framework for Company Law in Europe (2003). ZIP:863–880

Chapter 5
Potential Externalities of the Bilateral Governance System

To answer that question, the following chapter will discuss the potential positive and negative externalities of the bilateral private governance system of covenants. First, it will describe the concept of delegated monitoring, as this theory provides a suitable starting point for analysing potential externalities of a bank's conduct after a covenant default. Subsequently, the potential positive externalities of providing information as well as a disciplinary effect on the debtor company will be discussed. This will be followed by an examination of the potential negative externalities—namely influencing the debtor company's management in a way that is not in the interest of all creditors, reducing the pool of assets, and causing unnecessary bankruptcy or a domino effect. Then, the general limits of potential positive or negative externalities due to covenants being based on financial data will be discussed. Finally, the feasibility of positive and negative externalities will be deduced. Overall, the chapter will show that the scale of positive and negative effects mainly depends on the bank's conduct after a covenant default.

5.1 Banks as Monitoring Agents for Third-Party Creditors

That a bank's behaviour can have positive or negative effects on third-party creditors is no new idea: this concept is at the core of the theory of delegated monitoring.[1] According to this theory, financial intermediaries monitor and control debtor companies on behalf of other creditors. It would be too expensive for each creditor to monitor individually—particularly for smaller investors.[2] Moreover, multi-monitoring will

[1]Leland and Pyle (1977); Campbell and Kracaw (1980); Diamond (1984); Fama (1985). The delegated monitoring is considered to be an important reason for the existence of banks.

[2]It is often said that bondholders delegate monitoring to bank creditors via cross-acceleration clauses, cf. Beatty et al. (2012), 556.

D. Matri, *Covenants and Third-Party Creditors*, DOI 10.1007/978-3-319-62036-7_5

lead to duplications of effort and inefficiencies. That is why financial intermediaries—in particular banks—act as agents for other creditors (principals) when monitoring a debtor company.[3] For example, banks may monitor on behalf of bondholders. The relationship between a bank and a debtor company is closer than that between the various bondholders and the debtor company.[4] Furthermore, the trustee—who represents the collective interest of bondholders—has limited incentives to monitor, because the trustee is permitted—in the absence of any actual knowledge or notice to the contrary—to assume that the issuer is complying with its obligations.[5]

The delegation of monitoring, however, incurs agency costs (delegation costs) because it leads to an information asymmetry between banks and other non-monitoring creditors, thus creating the problem of moral hazard. These delegation costs represent the potential negative externalities, whereas the positive effects of monitoring represent the potential positive externalities.

Covenants play an important role in ensuring the positive effects of delegated monitoring because they function as an incentive to monitor.[6] Monitoring is costly for banks because it covers "the ongoing acquisition, provision, interpretation, and verification of information about the firm".[7] Banks must incur those monitoring costs, but other creditors can benefit or "free-ride" on the bank's efforts. This leads to an adverse incentive structure, namely that banks monitor too little. Covenants correct the incentive structure caused by free-riding amongst creditors.[8] Due to the early warning of financial distress provided by covenants, a recovery of the debtor company is possible and taking corrective actions is still promising for the bank.

5.2 Potential Positive Externalities

5.2.1 Information Production

In this way, covenants foster the potential positive externalities of banks being financial intermediaries—namely the production of information[9] that is not known to the public.[10] Apart from providing an incentive to monitor, covenants also

---

[3]The theory of delegated monitoring bases on the agency theory, see only Diamond (1984).

[4]Ferran and Ho (2014), p. 296; Triantis and Daniels (1995).

[5]Committee (2004), p. 18 and clause 1.1.8.; Wood (2007), para. 17-017 et seqq.; Hill and Beech (2010), 6; Schmolke (2009), 17.

[6]Rajan and Winton (1995); Park (2000).

[7]Triantis and Daniels (1995), 1079.

[8]Armour (2000), 361.

[9]"Information ist handlungs- und zweckorientiertes Wissen um Tatsachen." (Information is action-oriented and purposive knowledge of facts); Funke (2011), p. 99. Here the purposive knowledge is relevant as it fosters the decision process, Funke (2011), p. 99 et seqq.

[10]Leland and Pyle (1977); Campbell and Kracaw (1980); Diamond (1991).

produce information on their own. This production of information already starts during the negotiating process of covenants, because they are tailored to the specific conditions of the debtor company.[11] The information collecting process continues via information undertakings until the relationship between the bank and the debtor company comes to an end. Covenants that require the debtor company to request an exception foster the gathering of information.[12]

The information produced can either concern the covenant default itself or the bank's reaction to the default. Both types of information reflect the debtor company's financial situation. This information, however, is only valuable for third-party creditors if they have access to it. The subsequent sections will describe the different ways in which information is shared with third-party creditors. First, the publication of direct information about a covenant default in the case of a privately held and a publicly traded debtor company will be discussed. Then, indirect information regarding the bank's reaction to a covenant default and its disclosure will be described. Afterwards, the general value of the information will be outlined.

5.2.1.1 Direct Information About a Covenant Default

5.2.1.1.1 Privately Held Companies

Information regarding a covenant default by a privately held company is only made available to third-party creditors in rare cases.

Under German accounting law, private debtor companies may be bound by a duty to disclose covenant defaults. If a private debtor company is large pursuant to § 267 III HGB,[13] it can opt to disclose its financial statements according to International Financial Report Standards (IFRS),[14] § 325 IIa HGB.[15] In this case, IFRS 7.18 et seq. requires that information is disclosed about details of the covenant default, the loan principal involved and whether it was cured or waived and—if not remedied—whether the breaches permitted the lender to demand accelerated repayments.[16] Also, modifications of the loan agreement affecting the credit and/or liquidity risk must be disclosed according to IFRS 7.33 et seqq. All other private debtor companies, however, must prepare their financial statements according to HGB. Here, midsized (§ 267 II HGB) and large (§ 267 III HGB) private debtor

[11] Cf. Tighe (1984), para. 4.01 (2)(c).

[12] Cf. Tighe (1984), para. 4.01 (2)(c).

[13] *Handelsgesetzbuch* (Commercial Code).

[14] For the history and transnational character of IFRS see e.g. Renner (2013), 952 et seqq.

[15] The financial statements according to IFRS only regard the duty to disclose; the company still has to provide a financial statement according to HGB for tax purposes, for example. The consolidated financial statements can also be prepared according to IFRS, § 315a HGB.

[16] Cf. Zwirner (2011), 61 et seq.; Hannen (2013), 1435.

companies may only be obliged to disclose a covenant default if an acceleration of the defaulted loan is reasonably likely. They have to publish, among other things, a management report (*Lagebericht*) pursuant to § 325 I No.1 HGB.[17] This management report must include a risk report and forecast (*Risiko- und Lagebericht*) according to § 289 HGB. Covenant defaults are not explicitly mentioned in § 289 HGB. However, when an acceleration of the defaulted loan is reasonably likely due to a covenant default, the debtor company's liquidity risk is adversely affected. Thus, a discussion in the risk report and forecast seems advisable. This is supported in particular by the fact that covenant defaults are taken into consideration during the audit of annual accounts.[18] Nevertheless, a covenant default will only be disclosed in rare cases. The more extensive duty to disclose under IFRS concerns few private companies; only large private companies have the possibility to use IFRS. Of those eligible companies, only a limited number voluntarily opt for IFRS. A study from 2005 showed that only 8% of the interviewed companies had already opted for IFRS accounting and 11% were planning to do so.[19] All other large and midsized private debtor companies may only be obliged to publish a covenant default if an acceleration of the defaulted loan is reasonably likely, which will rarely be the case.[20]

In the US, private companies are under no duty to disclose covenant defaults.[21] For that reason—and particularly because informal exchange is restricted by banking secrecy—disclosure to third-party creditors seems unlikely in the US. However, information can be disclosed with the debtor company's consent. Additionally, loan agreements include confidentiality clauses that clarify under what conditions non-public information can be disclosed to third parties and who these parties can be.[22] Similarly, confidentiality agreements are used when loans are traded on the secondary market.

Once the loan matures, information collected via covenants may be shared with new potential creditors with the consent of the debtor company. This reduces the information asymmetry between the debtor company and future creditors. As a result, credit rationing is decreased and more efficient credit terms can be negotiated, as the debtor company can credibly signal its good creditworthiness.[23]

---

[17] § 326 I HGB excludes small private companies (§ 267 I HGB) from the duty to disclose a management report.

[18] Schmidt, in: (2016), para. 136; similar Zwirner (2011), 62; Krommes (2015), p. 1206.

[19] Deutsche Industrie- und Handelskammertag and AG (2005), p. 5.

[20] For an acceleration being improbable see below 5.3.3 and for the legal limits of an acceleration see below 6.2.1.

[21] There is no duty to disclose annual financial statements at all for private companies under US law; see, for example Haas (2004), p. 10 et seq.; Gros (2010), p. 64 et seq.

[22] Clause 24.7. LMA Loan Term: Wright (2006), p. 205 et seq.; Meloni (2008).

[23] Bennardo et al. (2014), p. 3 et seqq. with further references.

5.2.1.1.2 Publicly Traded Companies

The law with regard to the disclosure of covenant defaults in the case of publicly traded debtor companies is different.

5.2.1.1.2.1 German Law

Under German law the difference is marginal. Capital market-oriented parent companies must disclose covenant defaults in their annual financial statements under IFRS 7.18 et seq. according to § 315a HGB. Other public companies preparing their financial statements under HGB may have to discuss them in their (annual) managerial report only if an acceleration of the defaulted loan is reasonably likely.

Aside from that, a public debtor company can be under an ad hoc duty to disclose covenant defaults pursuant to Art. 17 I of the Market Abuse Regulation.[24] Art. 17 I states that an issuer has to inform the public of inside information directly concerning that issuer as soon as possible. The inside information has to be made public in a manner which enables fast access and complete, correct and timely assessment of the information by the public. In Art. 7 I (a) of the Market Abuse Regulation[25] inside information is defined as

> information of a precise nature, which has not been made public, relating, directly or indirectly, to one or more issuers or to one or more financial instruments, and which, if it were made public, would be likely to have a significant effect on the prices of those financial instruments or on the price of related derivative financial instruments.

It is unclear whether information about current or likely future covenant defaults falls under the category of insider information. The covenant default itself will probably not significantly affect the prices. However, the potential action to be taken by the bank in response to the default may. It is, yet, questionable if this information can be considered of a precise nature. Art. 7 II of the Market Abuse Regulation clarifies that

> information shall be deemed to be of a precise nature if it indicates a set of circumstances which exists or which may reasonably be expected to come into existence, (...) where it is specific enough to enable a conclusion to be drawn as to the possible effect of that set of circumstances (...) on the prices of the financial instruments (...) also the intermediate steps of that process which are connected with bringing about or resulting in those future circumstances or that future event, may be deemed to be precise information.

Recital 16 of the Regulation also provides some guidance by clarifying that it is suffices if based on an overall assessment of the factors existing at the relevant time

---

[24] EU Regulation No 596/2014 of the European Parliament and of the Council of 16 April 2014 on market abuse (market abuse regulation) and repealing Directive 2003/6/EC of the European Parliament and of the Council and Commission Directives 2003/124/EC, 2003/125/EC and 2004/72/EC (Text with EEA relevance), OJL 2014 173/1. For all cases before 03.07.2017 the old § 15I WpHG (*Wertpapierhandelsgesetz* (Securities Trading Act)) is still applicable.

[25] Before 03.07.2016 the old § 13 I WpHG defined insider information in a similar way.

there is a realistic prospect that the event affecting the prices will occur.[26] In line with the ECJ jurisprudence in *Markus Geltl v. Daimler AG*[27] the Recital also excludes a probability-magnitude test, i.e. the magnitude of the effect of that set of circumstances or that event on the prices should not be considered when determining the probability. However, the event following the covenant default must be able to significantly affect the prices. Thus, in accordance with the academia and the Issuer Guideline of the BaFin (both commenting on the old § 15 WpHG),[28] the knowledge about current or likely future covenant defaults only has a significant effect on the stock exchange or market price when the acceleration of a material credit is reasonably likely.[29] The covenant default may then be considered an intermediary step in a protracted process and is pursuant to Art. 7 III of the Market Abuse Regulation itself deemed to be an inside information.

An ad hoc duty to disclose according to Art. 17 I of the Market Abuse Regulation is therefore only assumed when, after a covenant default, the acceleration of the (material) credit is reasonably likely. An acceleration of a bank loan after a covenant default, however, is rare.[30] Thus, the circumstances under which a covenant default will trigger the ad hoc duty are limited. Furthermore, it is currently only the mere fact that a termination is reasonably likely or has occurred which must be disclosed and not the underlying covenant default.[31] This does not produce any substantial information for third-party creditors.

---

[26]There is no need that the particular direction in which the price of the financial instrument will be affected can be determined; *Jean-Bernard Lafonta v. Autorité des marchés financiers* (2015) C-628/13 ECLI:EU:C:2015:162; cf. also Klöhn (2015), 809 et seqq.

[27]*Markus Geltl v. Daimler AG* (2012) C -19/11, ECR [2012] I-397. That no high probability of the circumstances or events in question coming into existence or occurring is required is also in line with this case, see ibid. para. 46.

[28]The Issuer Guideline includes a non-exhaustive list of information that is relevant for the stock exchange or market price, see *Bundesanstalt für Finanzdienstleistungsaufsicht, Emittentenleitfaden* 2013, available at http://www.bafin.de/SharedDocs/Veroeffentlichungen/DE/Fachartikel/2013/fa_bj_2013_09_emittentenleitfaden.html, last accessed on 14.02.2016, p. 52 et seq.

[29]Heinrich (2009), p. 266; Kocher and Widder (2010), 927 et seq. This is determined by an *ex ante* prognosis; cf. Schwark and Kruse, in: Schwark, Zimmer (eds) (2010), para. 44. The information must also be specific enough: "A piece of information allows a conclusion to be drawn about its impact on prices, either when it would enable a reasonable investor to take an investment decision without (or at very low) risk, or when it is likely to be exploited immediately on the market" CESR's Advice on Level 2 Implementation Measures for the proposed Market Abuse Directive, 2002, Ref.: CESR/02–089, para. 20, indent 3. This is given in case of covenant defaults, as the information about them is specific, calculable and demonstrable. See also Kumpan, in: Baumbach, Hopt (eds) (2014), para. 1.

[30]For an acceleration being improbable see below 5.3.3 and for legal limits of an acceleration see below 6.2.1.

[31]See for example SKW Stahl-Metallurgie Holding AG's ad hoc statement from 14.08.2014, which only states that some unspecified financial covenants were violated and that they hold constructive talks; available at http://www.skw-steel.com/investor-relations/pflichtmitteilungen/ad-hoc-meldungen/, last accessed on 23.05.2016.

5.2.1.1.2.2 US Law

Under US law, the disclosure duties for public companies are further reaching. A publicly traded company is obliged to disclose a covenant default immediately when it has material consequences, using the form 8-K (Item 2.04(a) et seqq.; Items 3.03 and 8.01 can also be relevant).[32] The consequences of a covenant default are deemed to be material if an acceleration of a loan of material size to the debtor company is immanent or reasonably likely, because management must discuss any known material trends, favourable or unfavourable, in the registrant's capital resources.[33] When evaluating, whether acceleration is reasonably likely, all circumstances surrounding the covenant default must be considered. This also includes, for example, cross-default clauses in other agreements. If acceleration is found reasonably likely, the following information must be filed: the date of the covenant default, a brief description of the loan agreement defaulted, a brief description of the covenant default, the amount involved and terms of acceleration, and any other material obligations that might be affected by the covenant default.[34] In addition, any material modifications of a (material) loan agreement must be disclosed under Item 1.01 of form 8-K. This disclosure must include the date of amendment and a brief description of the amendment.

In case of a non-material covenant breach, the default must be disclosed in the subsequent financial statements using forms 10-K or 10-Q.[35] Pursuant to 17 CFR § 210.4-08(c), any covenant default of a related indenture or agreement that existed at the date of the most recent balance sheet and has not been subsequently cured is to be stated in the notes to the financial statements' notes. The SEC Interpretation 2003 reads:

> companies that are, or are reasonably likely to be, in breach of such covenants must disclose material information about that breach and analyse the impact on the company if material. That analysis should include, as applicable and to the extent material:
>
> - the steps that the company is taking to avoid the breach;
> - the steps that the company intends to take to cure, obtain a waiver of or otherwise address the breach;

[32]Pursuant to Sec. 13 or 15(d) of the Securities Exchange Act of 1934 (15 US Code § 78m), Rule 13a-11 (17 CFR § 240.13a-11) and Rule 15d-11 (17 CFR § 240.15d-11). The form 8-K with filing instructions is under the OMB Number: 3235-0060. Similar requirements can also be found in the stock exchange listing requirements; see, for example § 401(a) NYSE MKT Company Guide which requires "immediate public disclosure of all material information concerning its affairs, except in unusual circumstances", and its explanation in § 402(a) NYSE MKT Company Guide including a "an event of technical default or default on interest and/or principal payments".

[33]17 CFR § 229.303 (Item 303 Regulation S-K), which provides the standard instructions for filling out any forms under (i.a.) the Securities Exchange Act of 1934.

[34]Form 8-K, Item 2.04(a)(1)-(4).

[35]The form 10-K with filing instructions is under the OMB Number: 3235-0063. The form 10-Q with filing instructions is under the OMB Number: 3235-0070.

- the impact or reasonably likely impact of the breach (including the effects of any cross-default or cross-acceleration or similar provisions) on financial condition or operating performance; and
- alternate sources of funding to pay off resulting obligations or replace funding.

> Second, companies should consider the impact of debt covenants on their ability to undertake additional debt or equity financing.[36]

This shows that the information provided under US law is detailed and provides sufficient content for evaluating the financial consequences for the debtor company. Nevertheless, it is possible that there will be a substantial delay before public disclosure of the violation (report date) occurs—up to 45 days for a 10-Q filing and 90 days for a 10-K filing.[37] This can provide the bank with a considerable information advantage during the time of default or renegotiation and SEC filing.[38]

5.2.1.2 Indirect Information Through the Bank's Reaction

Besides direct information about a covenant default, a bank also generates information through its reaction to a particular default. These reactions can be divided into two groups: voice and exit.[39] "Exit" refers to accelerating the loan, refusing to renew an existing debt or to issue an additional loan, or putting an existing credit facility on hold. "Voice" refers to an attempt to correct the default situation.[40] Covenants construct the framework for the situations in which the bank can exercise either the exit or voice strategy.[41]

A bank's exit may provide an early warning sign to third-party creditors, allowing them to react to the altered financial situation in a more timely manner.[42] In the case of a public corporation, the debtor company must immediately disclose a (material) bank's exit in Germany and the US.[43] Third-party creditors of large private companies in Germany may be annually informed via the management report.[44] In addition, information undertakings in the loan agreement between a third-party creditor and the private debtor company contractually oblige the debtor

---

[36]Interpretation: Commission Guidance Regarding Management's Discussion and Analysis of Financial Condition and Results of Operations Securities and Exchange Commission 17 CFR Parts 211, 231 and 241 [Release Nos. 33-8350; 34-48960; FR-72], VI.C.

[37]See general instructions A.(1)(b) of form 10-Q and A.(2)(c) of form 10-K.

[38]Insider trading can be a consequence. Outside investors with confidential access usually have to sign a confidentially agreement and are obliged not to trade until the information is made public. Thus, there will be no gain from the information advantage; cf. Griffin et al. (2014).

[39]The terms are borrowed from the corporate governance literature, cf. Hirschman (1970); Triantis and Daniels (1995), 1080.

[40]Triantis and Daniels (1995), 1079.

[41]The options are, however, limited by law; see below 6.2.

[42]Ofek (1993) (with empirical support).

[43]See above 5.2.1.1.2.

[44]See above 5.2.1.1.1.

company to inform the third-party creditor about any material changes.[45] In the absence of such a contractual duty on the part of the debtor company, third-party creditors may only gain knowledge of the exit by closely monitoring the debtor company's conduct. If none of the above apply, there will be no visible information for a third-party creditor and hence no potential positive externalities. This may even lead to a "run to assets" by informed adjusting creditors without the knowledge of some uninformed third-party creditors.

However, the bank might not opt for the exit strategy and decide instead to exercise its voice. An exit may be less attractive due to the transaction and regulatory costs of exit,[46] the search and transaction costs for new lending arrangements, and the loss of potential gains through further financing of the revitalised debtor company. Exercising a voice will only generate information in certain instances—namely when it becomes visible for third-party creditors. Visibility can, for example, be provided through perfection of collateral—if like in the US filed publicly.[47] Third-party creditors can even draw conclusions about the seriousness of the debtor company's financial difficulties from the type of collateral taken. If the collateral is relatively long-lived and stable, the financial difficulties of the debtor company can be assumed to be rather minor. However, a fast-depreciating or, in the short-term, risky collateral (e.g. accounts receivables) signals acute financial difficulties.[48] Moreover, some visibility is ensured for public debtor companies in the US, as public companies have to publish any non-material covenant default—including the steps the debtor company takes to address the default—in their financial statements.[49] In addition, material modifications of a (material) loan agreement must be disclosed by public companies in the US or under IFRS.[50] Additionally, third-party creditors can ensure visibility through contractual information undertakings as previously mentioned.

5.2.1.3 Value of Information for Third-Party Creditors

A cross-default clause provides the third-party creditor with a right to be heard in the renegotiation process when the bank takes corrective measures—exit or voice. Indeed, if the bank exits the loan agreement, a cross-acceleration clause also provides a third-party creditor with own rights. However, not all third-party creditors can demand cross-default or cross-acceleration clauses. Nonetheless, they may be

---

[45] See above 3.4.1.

[46] Triantis and Daniels (1995), 1087 fn. 57.

[47] Cf. Rajan and Winton (1995), 1115. For publicity requirements of collateral in the US and Germany see above 2.2.1. Under IFRS 7.14 et seq. information about collateral must be provided as well.

[48] Rajan and Winton (1995), 1116.

[49] See above 5.2.1.1.2.2.

[50] See above 5.2.1.1.2.2.

able to react to the changed conditions in a different way. Empirical studies show, for example, that if a bank obtains additional control rights after a covenant default, trade credit reduces. Furthermore, an even larger decrease in trade credit is found in cases of likely acceleration of a bank loan.[51] This demonstrates that as long as third-party creditors know about and can adjust to the altered situation, they benefit from the monitoring efforts of creditors. However, if a third-party creditor depends on the debtor company or is generally unable to adjust (tort creditor), the information value is non-existent.

In any case, the information is only valuable if it is correct. The covenant-secured creditor might, however, exit for reasons unrelated to misbehaviour (to escape a bad deal, for example)[52] or the bank might monitor too carelessly or react too late.[53]

5.2.2 Disciplinary Effect: Reducing the Shareholder-Creditor Conflict

Information generated by covenant defaults and the bank's subsequent conduct allows adjusting third-party creditors to take corrective measures, but does not help non-adjusting third-party creditors. Covenants and covenant defaults can, however, potentially benefit all third-party creditors due to their disciplinary function.

If a bank exercises its voice, misbehaviour by the debtor company can be reduced through the corrective action that is prompted and future misbehaviour can be deterred. In addition, an exit may not only generate information but actually motivate corrective action to be taken by the management or the board of directors.[54] In order to have a positive impact, the consequences of an exit must be serious enough to either deter managerial misbehaviour *ex ante* or to induce correctional action *ex post*—without eliminating all opportunity for the debtor company to change.[55] The leverage of the threat to exit is more credible if a bank can afford to opt for it. A big commitment—combined with loose covenants that trigger a default too late for the sufficient recovery of the loan principal—reduce the credibility of the threat. On the other hand, both collateral and tighter covenants strengthen the threat.[56]

Covenants deter managerial misbehaviour *ex ante* due to their "tripwire" function.[57] Specifically, the interest coverage ratio and the gearing covenants warn against

---

[51]Zhang (2015).

[52]Triantis and Daniels (1995), 1091 et seqq.

[53]Triantis and Daniels (1995), 1094 et seqq.

[54]Jensen (1989); Wruck (1990), 430 et seqq.; Triantis and Daniels (1995), 1085; Servatius (2008), 73 et seqq.

[55]Hirschman (1970), p. 22 et seqq.; Triantis and Daniels (1995), 1085.

[56]Cf. Triantis and Daniels (1995), 1087 et seq.

[57]Covenants foster the debtor company's self-control, see e.g. Grünewald (2015), p. 86.

shortfalls in the current operation profits: the leverage ratio covenant signals if the debtor company is close to becoming overindebted; and the tangible net worth covenant functions as an early warning sign that the debtor company is heading towards bankruptcy. Moreover, the CAPEX covenant limits excessive expenditures to those that are within the debtor company's capacity. Excessive payouts to shareholders are restricted by a negative covenant restricting distributions as well as by financial covenants—namely the tangible net worth, gearing, and current ratio covenant.

All covenants taken together provide a particular framework within which the debtor company can conduct its business. As shown before in Chap. 3, this framework limits opportunistic behaviour by the debtor company with regard to claim and asset dilution as well as overinvestment. If the debtor company acts outside the framework, a default is triggered and serious action can be taken by the bank. At that moment, renegotiation provides the bank with control and the opportunity to take corrective action. The control shifts from the shareholders to the bank.[58] Until this shift of control, the disciplinary effect of covenants reduces the shareholder-creditor conflict for all creditors.

The disciplinary effect of covenants prior to a default can even be seen as a supplement or substitute for statutory creditor protection, if the creditor protection provided by covenants is higher than the statutory one. Third-party creditors can free-ride on the higher protection. Whether the creditor protection of covenants or statute is higher depends on the particular legal system and set of covenants. A superficial analysis would not provide any new insights, while an in-depth analysis would require a separate dissertation.[59] For the purposes of this work, it suffices to note that covenants can potentially supplement or even substitute statutory creditor protection. In any case, the disciplinary effect before a shift of control produces potential positive externalities. This is supported by an empirical study, which found that covenants influence the debtor company's policy in general even before a covenant default occurs.[60]

After the shift of control, however, the positive or negative third-party effects depend largely upon the bank's reaction. For example, claim dilution can be hampered for all creditors by a negative pledge clause or a pari passu clause as these ensure equality in bankruptcy proceedings by eliminating *ex post* creditors with a higher priority. However, when a negative pledge clause is violated, a bank might simply ask for the same priority level as the new creditor to permit the debtor company to proceed with the new secured debt. This reaction is not beneficial but rather detrimental to third-party creditors. The same applies to the limitation of asset dilution by a negative pledge clause. Third-party creditors only benefit from the clause if the bank enforces it in a way that prohibits other pledged loans. When the bank simply requires taking part in the collateral by way of a collateral pool, the assets available to third-party creditors are reduced.

[58]Chava and Roberts (2008), 2086.

[59]See only Heinrich (2009); Aichberger (2013).

[60]Gamba and Triantis (2013).

The positive effects were seen in Scenario 2a,[61] where the bank consortium enforced the negative pledge clause in a way that meant Papermaker could only issue unsecured bonds. This ensured more assets for all unsecured creditors, which led to a higher recovery sum for the tort victim Angel.

5.3 Potential Negative Externalities

Through monitoring—and with it, through the bank's information advantage—the bank can also "enhance its position at the expense of other stakeholders."[62] This can be done either actively by influencing the debtor company after a covenant default, or passively through a covenant's disciplinary effect.

A bank's active influence can be quite far-reaching. As shown in Sect. 3.4.3, banks can take a number of corrective measures ranging from the immediate acceleration and recall of the loan principal to an adjustment in interest rate, bringing in external advisors, debt equity swap, provision of additional collateral, or even a waiver conditional on the payment of a waiver fee. Furthermore, banks can influence the management.

5.3.1 Influencing the Management Not in the Interest of All Creditors

Returning to Scenario 1,[63] the influence on the debtor company can go as far as the CEO being replaced:

Scenario 3

Papermaker's CEO chairs the board of directors, which includes many of the CEO's friends. For the new investment in Papermaker's infrastructure, Papermaker wants to issue bonds. As mentioned previously, the issuance of secured bonds was prohibited by the negative pledge clause and not accepted by the bank consortium. For that reason, Papermaker has to issue unsecured bonds. However, this will still violate the leverage ratio covenant. During the negotiations for a waiver for that violation, the bank consortium kindly suggests implementing a new CEO. Although Papermaker's board of is CEO-friendly, it decides to replace the current CEO with a seasoned turnaround specialist. Papermaker follows the bank consortium's suggestion because it would likely face bankruptcy if the bank consortium accelerated.[64]

[61] See above 1.2.

[62] Triantis and Daniels (1995), 1091.

[63] See above 1.1.

[64] This is a realistic scenario; cf. the real case "Warnaco" described in Baird and Rasmussen (2006), 1209 et seqq.

This example also shows that the bank's influence on the (managerial) debtor company's conduct is not limited to a situation of financial distress, but can take place at any point in the loan's life when renegotiation is required. A bank will use its influence to improve its position and will rarely consider the interests of third-party creditors. Only when a third-party creditor has leverage on its own—for example another bank or bondholders—might its concerns be considered. However, a bank is usually interested in the maintenance of the debtor company, which is beneficial for most third-party creditors. Employees may be the exception, as a bank could use its influence to slim down the debtor company.

This potential negative externality for employees may be fostered by the *ex ante* disciplinary effect of covenants. Empirical studies show that there is a positive correlation between the deterioration of the financial conditions of debtor companies with tight covenants and a drop in employment.[65] Management seems to be more inclined to confront employees and unions in the shadow of a potential covenant default than without it. However, other third-party creditors—such as tort creditors—may benefit from this early intervention.

The disciplinary effect of covenants can also lead to an underinvestment, since lucrative investments may be restricted or prevented. The negative pledge clause in particular can reduce investments. Empirical studies have also shown that debtor companies reduce their leverage and cut back on investments after a covenant violation. On the one hand, this is beneficial to all creditors as the bankruptcy estate is not diluted. On the other hand, efficient investments might be missed.[66]

5.3.2 *Reducing the Pool of Assets*

A covenant-secured creditor can also demand an additional risk premium in the form of collateral in return for a default waiver or looser covenants. The (additional) collateral reduces the bankruptcy estate available to third-party creditors and thereby their chances of satisfaction in bankruptcy proceedings.[67] This was the case in Scenario 2b,[68] where Papermaker had to supply additional securities to the bank consortium after a covenant default. Thus when Papermaker filed for bankruptcy, fewer assets were available to satisfy third-party creditors' claims—for example the tort claim of the fish farmer Angel.

Similarly, other risk premiums—like a waiver fee or an increased interest rate—can cause asset dilution. Unlike collateral, the claims of other risk premiums take no priority in bankruptcy proceedings. The worst form of asset dilution, however, is

---

[65] Falato and Liang (2012); already in that direction Cronqvist et al. (2009).

[66] Chava and Roberts (2008); Roberts and Sufi (2009).

[67] Kronman and Jackson (1979), 1147; LoPucki (1994), 1892 et seqq.; Bebchuk and Fried (1996), 867 et seqq.; Mülbert and Birke (2002), 724; Engert (2006), 308; Aichberger (2013), p. 153.

[68] See above 1.2.

the immediate acceleration and recall of the loan principal. With it, the available assets are reduced by the total sum of the principal—whereas collateral and other risk premiums in particular only cover part of the loan principal.

Adjusting third-party creditors can protect themselves from negative consequences of additional risk premiums—as long as they are aware of them. In fact, the bank's reaction triggers similar corrective measures from adjusting third-party creditors. These self-protection measures, however, reduce the pool of assets even further. Taken together, those corrective actions can lead to a significant reduction in the debtor company's pool of assets. Particularly, non-adjusting creditors are exposed to this asset dilution, unless the risk premium was taken out in the reach-back period of bankruptcy.[69]

5.3.3 Unnecessary Bankruptcy and the Domino Effect

The acceleration and recall of the loan principal also increases the risk of a debtor company's subsequent bankruptcy.[70] Third-party creditors fear that the debtor company will not be able to repay their credit in full, because the debtor company's financial situation has deteriorated. Thus, all adjusting third-party creditors will either limit their risk exposure or will enforce their cross-default or cross-acceleration clauses and collect their credit as well. The result is thus a multi-party race to collect. A race to collect may occur anyway when a debtor company's financial situation deteriorates, but it is exacerbated by a bank loan's acceleration following a covenant default. This multi-party race to collect will likely lead to the debtor company's bankruptcy. Non-adjusting third-party creditors would be left with a small pool of assets to satisfy their remaining claims.

However, due to the frequent use of the cross-acceleration clause by adjusting third-party creditors, the debtor company will probably enter bankruptcy within the 3 months following the first acceleration. This would negate all collecting efforts of the bank and adjusting third-party creditors.[71] The cross-default or cross-acceleration clause establishes, therefore, "a constructive balance of terror among creditors"[72] because each creditor can destroy the collection efforts of the other creditor by driving the debtor company into bankruptcy. This is the reason why creditors will seldom opt for acceleration.

However, the credit volume available to the debtor company can be negatively affected by a covenant default, because it can damage the debtor company's financial reputation.[73] Depending on the market, this may be the "financial death

[69]See below 6.2.2.1.1 and 6.2.2.2.1.

[70]Wilhelmi (2006), 15 et seq.; Funke (2011), p. 377.

[71]See below 6.2.2.1.1 and 6.2.2.2.1.

[72]Hahn (2010), p. 3.

[73]Gullifer and Payne (2011), p. 160.

sentence"[74] for the debtor company. The consequences are not only determined by the market, but also by the seriousness and frequency of covenant defaults. An empirical study shows that a decrease in credit line is unlikely when the debtor company violates a financial covenant for the first time in the last four quarters. However, the likelihood significantly increases in case of a repeated financial covenant default in the last four quarters.[75] Other studies show that, in the early stages of financial distress, debtor companies often rely on trade credit to finance their business after a covenant default.[76] Trade creditors who continue a relationship with the distressed debtor company often charge an extra risk premium.[77] In that way, debtor companies can continue their business while the remaining trade creditors are being compensated for the increased credit risk.

5.4 General Limits

Both the potential positive and negative externalities of the bilateral private governance system are affected by some restrictions due to covenants being based on financial data. Covenants only produce valuable information and discipline the debtor company if they correctly depict the debtor company's financial situation. Similarly, a bank can only obtain an information advantage—and exploit it if covenants are adequately stipulated. It can be difficult, however, for covenants to properly reflect the debtor company's financial situation.

Firstly, covenants are based on financial data that is of a subjective and historical nature. Financial data is, in itself, imperfect because it tries to capture a complex financial reality in a shortened and thus, in a way, simplified report. For example, determination of the treatment of various accounting items is often left to the discretion of debtor companies.[78] Therefore, financial data must be interpreted and consequently takes on a subjective element. This, combined with the imperfections, leads to the conclusion that financial data can never entirely reflect the current debtor company's financial situation instead only providing an estimation of the debtor company's future development.[79] A degree of uncertainty will therefore always remain.

Secondly, financial covenants can only indicate a default in the period that the particular accounts cover. Accounting numbers reflect past performance and only

[74]Benjamin (2007), p. 169.

[75]Montoriol-Garriga and Zaytseva (2011).

[76]Montoriol-Garriga and Zaytseva (2011); Garcia-Appendini and Montoriol-Garriga (2015); Zhang (2015).

[77]Garcia-Appendini and Montoriol-Garriga (2015). Some trade creditors may, however, depend on the debtor company and have no other option than to continue their relationship.

[78]Golin and Delhaise (2013), p. 15.

[79]Golin and Delhaise (2013), p. 15.

provide limited insight into the current situation. A warning can come too late for the bank to react in a timely manner.[80]

Finally, covenants are only effective if they are monitored and enforced. However, if the credit risk is transferred, the economic risk is decoupled from the control rights.[81] After a loan is sold on the secondary market, there is no longer an incentive for the bank to monitor.[82]

The fact that the bilateral private governance system created by covenants and an event of default clause is limited by covenants being based on financial data, applies equally to both potential positive and negative externalities equally. Thus, the proper stipulation of covenants impacts both in the same way and can be disregarded in their further analysis.

5.5 Scale of Positive and Negative Effects Depends on the Covenant-Secured Creditor's Conduct

The above overview of potential negative and positive externalities demonstrates that the bilateral private governance system of creditor protection created by covenants and an event of default clause affects third-party creditors in various ways. Generally, third-party creditor effects occur in two different stages of time: *ex ante* and *ex post* a covenant default.

In the *ex ante* period, covenants benefit third-party creditors because they reduce the conflict of interest between shareholders and creditors. Covenants discipline the management into acting in the interest of all creditors by limiting the scope for opportunistic behaviour.

After a covenant default, however, the extent to which the bilateral private governance system of creditor protection negatively or positively affects third-party creditors mainly depends on the bank's reaction and the ability of the third-party creditor to adjust. The information produced by a covenant default only benefits adjusting third-party creditors and, particularly, those with cross-default or cross-acceleration clauses. The corrective action that is subsequently taken can benefit and harm both adjusting and non-adjusting third-party creditors. The bank

[80] Adams (2003), p. 93. However, if ratios are collected over a longer period, their value increases and they provide an important contribution towards the economic analysis of the debtor company's business; cf. Runge (2010), p. 32. A bank compares not only current ratios with previous ratios of the given debtor company, but also with those of competitors and with the management forecast. If those numbers give reason for concern, the bank may also request a spot test of covenants – provided it is stipulated in the loan agreement; see Adams (2003), p. 93 et seq. The analysis of ratios can, therefore, only function as guidance and should not be regarded as a cure-all; cf. Harrison et al. (2011), p. 796. It is, however, the most effective way of establishing a company's creditworthiness; see Golin and Delhaise (2013), p. 16.

[81] Whitehead (2008).

[82] Gorton and Haubrich (1987), p. 31 et seqq.

can use covenant defaults as leverage to get better conditions in renegotiations. These improved terms can be collateral, warrants, convertibility options or guarantees.[83]

Scenario 4

In Scenario 1,[84] Papermaker wanted to issue secured bonds. However, because Best Bank signalled that the bank consortium would not waive a default of the negative pledge clause, Papermaker was only able to issue unsecured bonds. This prevented an asset and claim dilution for all creditors.

However, Best Bank could have reacted in a different way. It could have allowed Papermaker to proceed with the issuance of secured bonds on the condition that it paid an additional risk premium. The risk premium may be an increased interest rate or the provision of additional collateral. This reaction would allow for the asset and claim dilution through the secured bonds and even amplify the process through the additional risk premium.

Hence, third-party creditors would be negatively affected. Adjusting third-party creditors could take corrective measures on their own and would likely be marginally affected. Those actions, however, would harm non-adjusting third-party creditors even more. So the scale of positive and negative externalities in the *ex post* period is mainly determined by the bank's conduct. To put it another way, the bilateral private governance system of creditor protection, created by covenants and an event of default clause is only collectivised if the bank takes specific corrective action that benefits all third-party creditors.

References

Adams D (2003) Corporate finance: banking and capital markets. Legal practice course 2002/03 series, 8th edn. Jordans, UK

Alchberger T (2013) Glaubigerschutz durch Ausschüttungssperren. Eine ökonomische Analyse anhand des deutschen, englischen und US-amerikanischen Regelungsmodells. Peter Lang, Frankfurt am Main

Armour J (2000) Share capital and creditor protection: efficient rules for a modern company law. Modern Law Rev 63:355–378

Baird DG, Rasmussen RK (2006) Private debt and the missing lever of corporate governance. Univ Pa Law Rev 154:1209–1251

Beatty A, Liao S, Weber J (2012) Evidence on the determinants and economic consequences of delegated monitoring. J Account Econ 53:555–576

Bebchuk LA, Fried JM (1996) The uneasy case for the priority of secured claims in bankruptcy. Yale Law J 105:857–934

Benjamin J (2007) Financial law. Oxford Press, Oxford

---

[83]The possibilities are only limited by law – particularly by bankruptcy law; see below 6.2.2.1.1 and 6.2.2.2.1. Generally, for the US see Triantis and Daniels (1995), 1096 et seqq. and for Germany see Kästle (2003), p. 113 et seqq.

[84]See above 1.1.

Bennardo A, Pagano M, Piccolo S (2014) Multiple bank lending, creditor rights, and information sharing. doi:10.1093/rof/rfu001. Accessed 09 Apr 2014
Campbell JL, Kracaw WA (1980) Information production, market signalling, and the theory of financial intermediation. J Financ 35:863–882
Chava S, Roberts MR (2008) How does financing impact investment? The role of debt covenants. J Financ 63:2085–2121
Cronqvist H, Heyman F, Nilsson M, Svaleryd H, Vlachos J (2009) Do entrenched managers pay their workers more? J Financ 64:309–339
Deutsche Industrie- und Handelskammertag, AG P (2005) International Financial Reporting Standards (IFRS) in mittelständischen Unternehmen. http://www.dihk.de/ressourcen/downloads/ifrs_studie.pdf. Accessed 16 Apr 2016
Diamond DW (1984) Financial intermediation and delegated monitoring. Rev Econ Stud 51:393–414
Diamond DW (1991) Monitoring and reputation. The choice between bank loans and directly placed debt. J Polit Econ 99(4):689–721
Engert A (2006) Solvenzanforderungen als gesetzliche Ausschüttungssperre bei Kapitalgesellschaften. ZHR 170:296–335
Falato A, Liang N (2012) Do creditor rights increase employment risk? Evidence from debt covenants. http://ssrn.com/abstract=2489115. Accessed 18 Feb 2016
Fama EF (1985) What's different about banks? J Monet Econ 15:29–39
Ferran E, Ho LC (2014) Principles of corporate finance law. Oxford University Press, Oxford
Financial Markets Law Committee (2004) Issue 62—trustee exemption clauses. http://www.fmlc.org/uploads/2/6/5/8/26584807/62.pdf. Accessed 14 Nov 2015
Funke MC (2011) Gläubigerschutz durch Information im Recht der Aktiengesellschaft, vol 60. Heidelbergerschriften zum Wirtschaftsrecht und Europarecht. Nomos, Baden-Baden
Gamba A, Triantis AJ (2013) How effectively can debt covenants alleviate financial agency problems? http://ssrn.com/abstract=2101645. Accessed 25 Jan 2016
Garcia-Appendini E, Montoriol-Garriga J (2015) Trade credit use as firms approach default. http://ssrn.com/abstract=2457750. Accessed 21 Feb 2016
Golin J, Delhaise P (2013) The bank credit analysis handbook: a guide for analysts, bankers, and investors, 2nd edn. Wiley, Singapore
Gorton GB, Haubrich JG (1987) Loan sales, recourse, and reputation: an analysis of secondary loan participations. http://finance.wharton.upenn.edu/~rlwctr/papers/8714.pdf. Accessed 18 Feb 2016
Griffin PA, Lont DH, McClune K (2014) Insightful insiders? Insider trading and stock return around debt covenant violation disclosures. Abacus 50:117–145
Gros M (2010) Rechnungslegung in Deutschland und den USA: Implikationen für eine zweckadäquate Fortentwicklung der deutschen Rechnungslegungskonzeption. Gabler Research. Gabler Verlag, Wiesbaden
Grünewald P (2015) Mehrheitsherrschaft und insolvenzrechtliche Vorauswirkung in der Unternehmenssanierung. Mohr Siebeck, Tübingen
Gullifer L, Payne J (2011) Corporate finance law. Principles and policy. Hart, Oxford
Haas JJ (2004) Corporate finance in a nutshell. West nutshell series. Thomson/West, St. Paul
Hahn D (2010) The roles of acceleration. http://ssrn.com/abstract=1547702. Accessed 03 Apr 2016
Hannen I (2013) Bilanzierung bei drohendem oder bereits eingetretenem Verstoß gegen Financial Covenants. DB 66:1432–1436
Harrison WTJ, Horngren CT, Thomas CW, Suwardy T (2011) Financial accounting: international financial reporting standards, 8th edn. Pearson, Singapore
Heinrich S (2009) Covenants als Alternative zum institutionellen Gläubigerschutz. Eine rechtsvergleichende und ökonomische Analyse, vol 228. Schriften zum Wirtschaftsrecht. Duncker & Humblot, Berlin

Hill S, Beech T (2010) The credit crisis: have trustees lived up to expectations? Capital Markets Law J 5:5–20. doi:10.1093/cmlj/kmp042
Hirschman AO (1970) Exit, voice, and loyalty: responses to decline in firms, organizations, and states. Harvard University Press, Cambridge
Jensen MC (1989) Eclipse of the public corporation. Harv Bus Rev 5:61–74
Kästle M (2003) Rechtsfragen der Verwendung von Covenants in Kreditverträgen. Duncker & Humblot, Berlin
Klöhn L (2015) Ad-hoc-Publizität und Insiderverbot nach “Lafonta”. NZG:809–817
Kocher D, Widder S (2010) Ad-hoc-Publizität in Unternehmenskrise und Insolvenz. NZI:925–932
Krommes W (2015) Handbuch Jahresabschlussprüfung, 4th edn. Springer, Wiesbaden
Kronman AT, Jackson TH (1979) Secured financing and priorities among creditors. Yale Law J 88:1143–1182
Kumpan C (2014) § 13 WpHG. In: Baumbach A, Hopt K (eds) Handelsgesetzbuch. Beck, München
Leland HE, Pyle DH (1977) Informational asymmetrics, financial structure, and financial intermediation. J Financ 32:371–387
LoPucki LM (1994) The unsecured creditor’s bargain. Va Law Rev 80:1887–1965
Meloni K (2008) Lender confidentiality undertakings: recent changes to LMA facility documentation—borrowers likely to call for tighter wording. Butterworths J Intern Banking and Financ Law 24:558
Montoriol-Garriga J, Zaytseva V (2011) Suppliers as lenders of last resort: an empirical analysis of trade credit in the event of financial covenants violation on bank loan contracts. http://demo.uib.es/IBEW/Papers2011/MasterThesis/VictoriaZaytseva.pdf. Accessed 14 Feb 2015
Mülbert PO, Birke M (2002) Legal capital—is there a case against the European legal capital rules? EBOR 3:695–732
Ofek E (1993) Capital structure and firm response to poor performance: an empirical analysis. J Financ Econ 34:3–30. doi:10.1016/0304-405X(93)90038-D
Park C (2000) Monitoring and structure of debt contracts. J Financ 55:2157–2195
Rajan RG, Winton A (1995) Covenants and collateral as incentives to monitor. J Financ 50:1113–1146
Renner M (2013) Occupy the system! Societal constitutionalism and transnational corporate accounting. Indiana Journal of Global Legal Studies 20:941–964
Roberts MR, Sufi A (2009) Control rights and capital structure: an empirical investigation. J Financ 64:1657–1695
Runge JC (2010) Covenants in Kreditverträgen. Grenzen der Einflussnahme von Kreditgebern. RWS Vlg, Köln
Schmidt S (2016) § 317 HGB. In: Beck’scher Bilanz-Kommentar. Beck, München
Schmolke KU (2009) Der gemeinsame Vertreter im Referentenentwurf eines Gesetzes zur Neuregelung des Schuldverschreibungsgesetzes - Bestellung, Befugnisse, Haftung. ZBB:8–19
Schwark E, Kruse D (2010) § 13 WpHG. In: Schwark E, Zimmer D (eds). Kapitalmarktrechts-Kommentar. Beck, München
Servatius W (2008) Gläubigereinfluss durch Covenants. Mohr Siebeck, Tübingen
Tighe R (1984) Structuring commercial loan agreements. Warren, Groham & Lamont, Boston
Triantis GG, Daniels RJ (1995) The role of debt in interactive corporate governance. Calif Law Rev 83:1073–1114
Whitehead CK (2008) The evolution of debt: covenants, the credit market, and corporate governance. http://ssrn.com/abstract=1205222. Accessed 17 Apr 2016
Wilhelmi R (2006) Das Mindestkapitai als Mindestschutz. Eine Apologie im Hinblick auf die Diskussion um eine Reform der GmbH angesichts der englischen Limited. GmBH-Rundschau 97(1):13–24
Wood P (2007) International loans, bonds, guarantees, legal opinions, vol 2. Sweet & Maxwell, London
Wright S (2006) International loan documentation. Palgrave Macmillan, New York

Wruck KH (1990) Financial distress, reorganization, and organizational efficiency. J Financ Econ 27:419–444. doi:10.1016/0304-405X(90)90063-6
Zhang Z (2015) Debt covenant violations and trade credit. http://ssrn.com/abstract=2482249. Accessed 16 Feb 2016
Zwirner C (2011) Financial Covenants im IFRS-Abschluss. IRZ:59–62

Chapter 6
The Self-Interested Behaviour of Banks and Its Legal Limits

The collective effect of covenants and the event of default clause depends, therefore, on the bank's conduct. This chapter will first describe the bank's probable self-interested behaviour and, subsequently, use examples to discuss the legal restrictions of such self-interested conduct under German and US law.

6.1 The Self-Interested Behaviour of Banks

A bank's conduct can be presumed to be determined only by self-interest.[1] Adam Smith pointed out that human behaviour is guided by self-interest when he said that it "is not from the benevolence of the butcher, the brewer, or the baker, that we expect our dinner, but from their regard to their own interest."[2] This is also the underlying assumption of the rational choice model of the *homo oeconomicus*: The *homo oeconomicus* is rational as well as opportunistic and aims at maximising its personal benefits.[3] This model often faces the critique that it does not reflect the behaviour of real people, because no one acts always in their own interests nor rationally.[4] This critique, however, overlooks the fact that the *homo oeconomicus* is merely an instrument to predict future decisions on an abstract level.[5] Hence, the decision model is helpful in determining the average behaviour of banks after a

---

[1]Servatius (2008), p. 367; Burger and Buchhart (2001), 101.

[2]Smith (1776), para. I.2.2.

[3]There are, of course, other versions of the *homo oeconomicus* model. The self-interest version is, however, the dominant model in the law and economics literature; cf. Korobkin and Ulen (2000), 1064 et seq. For a detailed analysis of the *homo oeconomicus* see, for example, Kirchgässner (2008), p. 11 et seqq.

[4]See, for example, Fezer (1986), 822. For an overview of the critique on the *homo oeconomicus* see Korobkin and Ulen (2000); Eidenmüller (2005), 218 et seqq.

[5]Eidenmüller (2001), 1042.

D. Matri, *Covenants and Third-Party Creditors*, DOI 10.1007/978-3-319-62036-7_6

covenant default. In light of the recent financial crisis, however, there may be doubtful over whether banks always act rationally,[6] but they still can be assumed to behave selfishly and to pursue the most advantageous corrective option. For Scenarios 2a and 2b,[7] this means that whether the bank consortium demands a risk premium or prohibits issuing secured bonds depends exclusively on the benefits at stake for the bank consortium. The decision may only be influenced by negative effects on the reputation of Best Bank and the bank consortium or by performance sensitive pricing. For example, a grid pricing clause would exclude the interest rate from the scope of renegotiation and limit the bank consortium's options for opportunistic behaviour.[8] It is doubtful that third-party creditors' interests would influence the bank consortium's decision. If the bank consortium's interests coincide with those of third-party creditors, the *ex post* influence via covenants will yield positive externalities. However, at least when Papermaker is in economic difficulties, the interests of the bank consortium and those of third-party creditors will clash.[9] In this case, only the threat of driving Papermaker into bankruptcy can influence the bank consortium's conduct. Thus, the bank consortium may not accelerate or demand additional collateral to avoid Papermaker's bankruptcy, because otherwise the chances of recovery decrease.[10]

6.2 Legal Limits of Bank's Self-Interested Conduct

Statutory law, of course, also has an impact on the bank consortium's conduct. The legal limits of a bank's conduct vary across jurisdictions. This work will not analyse them in detail, but will use two significant examples to compare legal limits under German and US law.[11] Obvious reasons for liability, such as fraud, will be excluded.[12] Generally, the validity of contractual rights will only be questioned and claims will only be brought by the debtor company if the "lock-in" situation between the bank and debtor company is resolved—namely, when the bank accelerates and recalls the loan principal or when the debtor company is bankrupt. In all other circumstances, enforcement out of court seems probable.[13]

[6]Cf. Akerlof and Shiller (2010).

[7]For both scenarios see above 1.2.

[8]Shadab (2014), 1109.

[9]Mankowski, in: Lutter (ed) (2006), p. 496 et seq.; Servatius (2008), p. 82 et seqq.; similar Merkt (2004), 314.

[10]Cf. Kuntz (2008), 817.

[11]For a detailed analysis of the US law see Cappello (2014), p. 239 et seqq. For the German law see Servatius (2008), p. 93 et seqq.

[12]Also excluded is how and if covenants can bind the board of directors; see Fettes (2014), p. 86 et seqq.; Kuntz (2016), 110 et seqq. For limits of influencing the debtor company's business under competition law; cf. Fettes (2014), p. 77 et seqq. For limits pursuant to § 117 AktG (analogous) see Servatius (2008), p. 132 et seqq.

[13]This is supported by the lack of relevant case law.

Hence, this work will analyse the legal limits in those two circumstances employing Scenario 1.[14] The legal consequences of the following two examples will be analysed under German and US law.

In the first example, the bank consortium accelerates the loan agreement.

<u>*Scenario 5*</u>

After issuing unsecured bonds in Scenario 1,[15] Papermaker is encountering financial difficulties. It has misjudged the costs and benefits of the improved infrastructure. Additionally, the last year has been poor for the paper industry. Consequently, Papermaker substantially violates two financial ratios under the syndicated loan for over 15 days – namely the interest coverage ratio and the leverage ratio covenants. Both covenants had a 20-percent headroom. After some communication between Papermaker and Best Bank, the bank consortium accelerates and recalls the loan principal. This acceleration is based on an event of default clause that allows immediate cancelation of the loan or for additional collateral to be demanded if

> any of the following events ("Events of Default") shall occur and be continuing: [...] (d) Papermaker shall fail to observe or perform (i) any covenant [...] which continues unremedied for a grace period of 15 days.[16]

Papermaker, however, refuses to repay because it believes that this is only a temporal problem and that the bank consortium has no right to accelerate. Hence, the bank consortium sues Papermaker to enforce the acceleration.

In the second example, the bank consortium receives additional collateral and, 89 days later, Papermaker files for bankruptcy.

<u>*Scenario 6*</u>

As in Scenario 5,[17] Papermaker violates both the interest coverage ratio and the leverage ratio covenants. But instead of accelerating, the bank consortium demands additional collateral from Papermaker because it is undersecured. This additional collateral only covers part of Papermaker's unpledged assets. 89 days later, Papermaker has to file for bankruptcy. Now, the unsecured bondholders (and the bankruptcy administrator) question whether the additional collateral is avoidable[18] or if the bank consortium may be liable towards them.

6.2.1 *Acceleration Based on Covenant Default*

Scenario 5,[19] where the bank consortium sues Papermaker to enforce the acceleration, will first be analysed under German and US law.

---

[14] See above 1.1.

[15] See above 1.1.

[16] Based on Boxes 9.1. and 9.4. LSTA Guide: Wight et al. (2009), p. 411 et seqq.

[17] See above 6.2.

[18] The term "avoidable" is used in the US when preferential treatment is voidable or contestable.

[19] See above 6.2.

6.2.1.1 German Law

Under German law, the acceleration may not be enforceable due to its violating the law of standard business terms (*Allgemeine Geschäftsbedingungen*), §§ 305 et seqq. BGB,[20] or unconscionability *(Sittenwidrigkeit)*, § 138 BGB.[21] Moreover, the duty of good faith (*Treu und Glauben*), § 242 BGB, restricts the legal right to terminate for cause and may give a right to damages.

6.2.1.1.1 Validity and Enforceability of Event of Default Clause

Generally, covenants and event of default clauses concretise §§ 490 I and 314 BGB.[22] Parties can allocate specific risks between them because § 490 BGB is merely dispositive[23] and § 314 BGB is only mandatory law at its core.[24] Unless the debtor is structurally inferior, parties can—within the limits of § 138 BGB—agree on situations that always give a right to accelerate.[25]

The right to accelerate based on a financial covenant default could be void as an unfair standard business term if it unreasonably disadvantages the debtor company pursuant to § 307 I 1 BGB. Usually an event of default clause and covenants will be regarded as standard business terms according to § 305 I BGB.[26] In fact, the event of default clause has not been seriously subjected to negotiations as required by constant jurisprudence of the BGH.[27] Particularly in syndicated loans, standardised terms are essential for market compatibility.[28] Thus, the right to accelerate based on

---

[20] *Bürgerliches Gesetzbuch* (German Civil Code).

[21] Generally, for § 138 BGB see Köndgen, in: Prütting (ed) (1997), p. 140 et seqq.; Kästle (2003), p. 84 et seqq.; for its application on the negative clause, see Köndgen, in: Prütting (ed) (1997), p. 144 et seq.; Heinrich (2009), p. 176 et seq.

[22] Renner, in: Canaris et al. (eds) (2015), para. 232; other authors have described it as objectivisation; cf. Merkel and Tetzlaff, in: Schimansky et al. (eds) (2011), para. 176; Berger, in: Säcker, Rixecker (eds) (2012), para. 57; Mülbert, in: von Staudinger (ed) (2015), para. 168.

[23] Heinrich (2009), p. 363; Gaier, in: Säcker, Rixecker (eds) (2016), para. 4; Weidenkaff, in: (2014), para. 1; Mülbert, in: von Staudinger (ed) (2015), para. 6.

[24] BGHZ 133, 316, 320; Gaier, in: Säcker, Rixecker (eds) (2016), para. 4; Grüneberg, in: Palandt (ed) (2014), para. 3; Teichmann, in: (2014), para. 9; see also government bill, BT-Drucks 14/6040, p. 176.

[25] Gaier, in: Säcker, Rixecker (eds) (2016), para. 4.

[26] Kästle (2003), p. 84; Eidenmüller (1995), p. 151; Ballo (2010), p. 89 et seqq.; Nouvertné (2012), 2143 et seq.; Renner and Leidinger (2015), 500; critically Heinrich (2009), p. 347 et seq.

[27] See only BGH WM 1977, 287; BGH WM 1978, 1384; BGHZ 143, 104, 111 et seq. And if the LMA standard contract was used, the applicability of § 307 I, II BGB will not be excluded by the policy of the law in § 310 I 3 BGB because in the proceedings of setting the LMA standard mainly the creditor interests are considered. Cf. Nouvertné (2012), 2144 et seq.; Renner and Leidinger (2015), 500; for the policy of the law see Maurer (2012), p. 168 et seq. In addition the exception of § 310 IV BGB is not applicable, see Weitnauer (2005), 1443 et seq.

[28] Weitnauer (2005), 1446; Nouvertné (2012), 2143; Renner, in: Canaris et al. (eds) (2015), para. 900.

a financial covenant default is generally not seriously negotiated and hence, subject to legal restrictions for standard business terms.[29]

The cause for the right to terminate stipulated in the event of default clause must be valid for the event of default clause to be effective.[30] Thus, the event of default clause combined with the relevant financial covenants must withstand the test of content (*Inhaltskontrolle*), § 307 BGB.[31]

The control standard is determined by § 307 I, II BGB.[32] The benchmark of reasonableness pursuant to §307II no. 1 BGB is compatibility with the essential principles of the statutory provision from which the clause deviates—here § 490 I BGB. § 490 I BGB allows for immediate termination if the repayment claim is jeopardised. It requires substantial deterioration in the debtor company's financial circumstances or in the value of a security given for the loan as a result of which the repayment of the loan is jeopardised, even if the security is realised. The event of default clause combined with covenants deviates from § 490 I BGB if they grant a right to terminate, but the conditions for a substantial deterioration in the debtor company's financial circumstances are not (yet) met.[33] Material reasons for this deviation from § 490 I BGB must be present in order for it to still be in compliance with justice and reasonableness (*Recht und Billigkeit*).[34] Horst Eidenmüller in particular suggests that, here, the function of covenants as "tripwires" has to be considered: An acceleration based on a covenant breach should be measured by whether the covenant default plausibly indicates an increased credit risk.[35] The creditor may have a legitimate interest in accelerating a loan if the credit risk significantly increases—particularly if the debt is unsecured. Furthermore, the acceleration seems reasonable for the debtor company because the debtor company cannot expect the bank to be bound to the original credit conditions under a substantially worsened financial situation.[36] However, it will always depend on the specific

---

[29]If it is regarded an individual agreement, § 138 BGB sets the legal limits. See for debtor gagging (*Schuldnerkebelung*) under § 138 BGB Kästle (2003), p. 126 et seqq.; Hoffmann (2012), 14 et seq.

[30]Cf. Weitnauer (2005), 1447.

[31]§ 310 I 1 BGB excludes §§ 305 II, III, 308 and 309 BGB for standard business terms that are used in contracts with an entrepreneur, a legal person under public law, or a special fund under public law.

[32]The concrete control standard of § 307 II BGB precedes the general one of § 307 I BGB. Covenants will regularly comply with the transparency requirement of § 307 I 2 BGB, because they stipulate the rights and obligations in detail. Kästle (2003), p. 98 et seq.; similar regarding § 305 c BGB Weitnauer (2005) 1446; critically Thießen (1996), 28 fn. 66.

[33]For a deviation of § 490 BGB see for example Eidenmüller (1999), p. 158 et seq.; Renner, in: Canaris et al. (eds) (2015), para. 900.

[34]See only BGH WM 1984, 931, 932; BGH WM 1998, 1289, 1291 et seq.

[35]Eidenmüller (1999), p. 159. See also Kästle (2003), p. 93 et seqq.; critically Nouvertné (2012), 2145 et seq.

[36]Eidenmüller (1999), p. 159; similarly X Fettes (2014), p. 65 et seq.

wording of the clause. This approach is also in line with the jurisprudence of the BGH on banks' standard business terms (*AGB-Banken*).[37] The BGH found that the reasonableness of the clause must be evaluated on a case-by-case basis and the interests of both parties must be weighed up.[38]

Nevertheless, the essential principles in § 490 I BGB could also be regarded as too rigid or unproductive for complex syndicated loans.[39] In this case, the other benchmark of reasonableness pursuant to § 307 II no. 2 BGB—that is, essential rights or duties inherent in the nature of the contract—must be considered. However, its narrow interpretation also seems to be unproductive: one ends up with a circular control standard if this standard term is measured by itself.[40] Moritz Renner, therefore, argues for a broader application—namely that the actual behavioural expectations of the parties are considered and, with them, all relevant standard terms.[41] Then, deviation from that general standard leads to a rebuttable presumption that the clause is unreasonable.[42]

A settlement of the dispute about the correct control standard is unnecessary, because both the indication of an increased credit risk (§ 307 II no. 1 BGB) and the market standard for acceleration clauses (§ 307 II no. 2 BGB) yield the same result for Scenario 5.[43] Although the event of default clause does not require a material default, the 20-percent headroom and the grace period of 15 days ensure that a covenant default is triggered in situations close to a substantial financial deterioration under § 490 I BGB. This is particularly true because the violated covenants—the interest coverage ratio and the leverage ratio covenants—form a probable indication of an increased credit risk.[44] Hence, the benchmark of § 307 II no. 1 BGB is met. The fact that both the 20-percent headroom and the grace period of 15 days concur with the market standard[45] ensure that the benchmark of § 307 II no. 2 BGB is also met but is furthermore an indication of reasonableness pursuant to § 307 II no. 1 BGB.[46] Therefore, the event of default clause combined with the interest

---

[37] BGH WM 1978, 234, 235 et seqq.; BGH WM 1991, 1452; BGH WM 2003, 1416; BGHZ 154, 146, 150 et seq.

[38] Cf. BGH WM 1985, 1437 concerning No.17 sentence 2 AGB-Banken (old version).

[39] Cf. Eidenmüller (1999), p. 159; Renner and Leidinger (2015), 501. Against the application of § 307 II BGB at all Heinrich (2009), p. 349 et seq.

[40] Cf. Renner and Leidinger (2015), 501. For the narrow interpretation see Lieb (1988), 951; Schulte-Nölke, in: Schulze et al. (eds) (2014), para. 17.

[41] Renner (2013), 681 et seqq.; Renner and Leidinger (2015), 501 et seq. Cf. also Wurmnest, in: Säcker, Rixecker (eds) (2016), para. 70.

[42] Renner and Leidinger (2015), 501 et seq.

[43] See above 6.2.

[44] The interest coverage ratio measures the debtor company's ability to generate sufficient cash profit to cover its interest costs and, thereby, warns against shortfalls in the current year's operation profits; cf. Fight (2004), p. 131; Wight et al. (2009), p. 302. The leverage ratio functions as an early warning for corporate failure; cf. Harrison et al. (2011), p. 714 et seq.

[45] See 3.2.1.1.1.

[46] Eidenmüller (1999), p. 158 et seqq.; Kästle (2003), p. 75 et seq.; Ballo (2010), p. 318 et seq.

coverage ratio and the leverage ratio covenants should be considered reasonable under § 307 BGB. Nevertheless, there is no case law as of yet and a different judgment is possible.

If the event of default clause, the interest coverage ratio covenant and the leverage ratio covenant are to be considered individual agreements, they could be null pursuant to § 138 BGB. However, the control standard of § 138 BGB is lower than that of § 307 BGB, under which the clauses are likely to be considered reasonable.[47] Consequently, it is improbable that the event of default clause combined with the interest coverage ratio and the leverage ratio covenants will be regarded as immoral.

6.2.1.1.2 Treu und Glauben in Case of Acceleration

As previously mentioned, the legal right to terminate for cause is concretised by the event of default clause. To exercise the right to terminate, however, it must comply with the duty of good faith (*Treu und Glauben*) according to § 242 BGB.[48] A termination for cause that violates *Treu und Glauben* is regarded as not considerable (*unbeachtlich*).[49] A termination can be in bad faith (*treuwidrig*) if the bank has contributed substantially to the cause of the acceleration and created the impression that it will not accelerate when the debtor company acts according to the bank's suggestions.[50] This is the case if the bank influences the debtor company's management and thereby causes the termination reason.[51] Similarly, a bank cannot terminate the loan if it is sufficiently secured. The only exception may be if substantial depreciation of the collateral is expected.[52] Furthermore, if a bank has given the impression that it will keep the credit (line) open despite the covenant breach, it must give advance notice.[53] In Scenario 5,[54] the bank consortium's acceleration would only violate § 242 BGB if it waived prior defaults of both the interest coverage ratio and the leverage ratio covenants, because they do not signal an increased credit risk.[55]

[47]Cf. Kästle (2003), p. 100. For the relationship of private autonomy and bank law see Schimansky (1995).

[48]Cf. OLG Schleswig WM 2006, 1338; in detail, see Kästle (2003), p. 118 et seqq.

[49]Cf. Renner, in: Canaris et al. (eds) (2015), para. 139 with further references.

[50]Mülbert, in: von Staudinger (ed) (2015), para. 42. In detail see Voglis (2001), p. 117 et seqq. Generally, see Kähler, in: Gsell et al. (eds) (07.04.2016), paras. 1099 et seqq.

[51]See, for example, BGH WM 1985, 1493; Mülbert, in: von Staudinger (ed) (2015), para. 227 et seqq.

[52]Obermüller (1980), 343.

[53]Based on the principle of *venire contra factum proprium* BGH WM 1978, 234; cf. Canaris (1979), 125 et seqq.; Obermüller (1980), 344; Runge (2010), p. 343 et seqq.

[54]See 6.2.

[55]Cf. Wittig (1996), 1388; Mülbert, in: von Staudinger (ed) (2015), para. 182.

Further restrictions on exercising the right to terminate are not applicable to Scenario 5[56]; only in cases of a restructuring loan can the bank not enforce its contractual right to accelerate if the recovery of the debtor company follows the recovery plan[57] and a recovery still appears promising.[58] Furthermore, a bank can also be liable for damages if the termination is untimely (*Kündigung zur Unzeit*).[59]

6.2.1.2 US Law

Under US law the acceleration may not be enforceable if the doctrine of unconscionability or the duty of good faith have been violated.

6.2.1.2.1 Validity and Enforceability of Event of Default Clause

The US doctrine of unconscionability under the leading case *Ora Lee Williams v. Walker-Thomas Furniture Company*[60] sets similar boundaries for the validity of covenants as the previously discussed German law.[61] US law generally recognises acceleration clauses not as penalties and hence as valid.[62] The clause will, however, not be enforced if it is unconscionable or if the bank acted in bad faith.[63] A clause is likely to be considered unconscionable if unfair bargaining as well as unfair substantive terms are shown. Unfair bargaining is indicated when a meaningful choice by the weaker party is absent.[64] This will, however, rarely be the case when a debtor

[56]Moreover, the bank can be liable for damages under §§ 280 I, 241 II BGB if it failed to properly consider the debtor company's interests. Fundamentally (but for the old law), see, for example, BGH WM 1960, 576; BGH WM 1968, 1214; BGH WM 1979, 1176; Renner, in: Canaris et al. (eds) (2015), para. 259. A bank is unlikely to be liable for damages to third-party creditors in case of an acceleration; cf. Mülbert, in: von Staudinger (ed) (2015), para. 322 et seqq.

[57]BGH WM 1956, 217, 220; BGH WM 2004, 2200, 2202 et seq.; Theewen (2003), 147.

[58]RG BankArchiv 1937/38, 311, 312; BGH WM 1956, 217, 220; BGH WM 2004, 2200, 2202 et seq.; Obermüller (1980), 343; Mülbert, in: von Staudinger (ed) (2015), para. 39.; Renner, in: Canaris et al. (eds) (2015), para. 254.

[59]In addition to § 242 BGB, the doctrine was developed in analogy to §§ 627 II, 671 II, 675 I 2 und 723 II BGB (old version). A *Kündigung zur Unzeit* only leads to damages and not to invalidity. See BGH, WM 1978, 234, 236; cf. Canaris (1979), 114; Kästle (2003), p. 117; Runge (2010), p. 339 et seqq.

[60]350 F.2d 445 (D.C. Cir. 1965). See also § 2-302 Uniform Commercial Code (UCC) and § 208 Restatement (Second) of Contracts.

[61]See e.g. Knapp, in: DiMatteo et al. (eds) (2013).

[62]*Harris v. Kessler*, 12 P.2d 467 (Cal.App. 1932).

[63]*Graf et al. v. Hope Bldg. Corporation*, 171 N.E. 884 (N.Y.App. 1930). See also Leaf (1970), 532.

[64]Seminally, *Ora Lee Williams v. Walker-Thomas Furniture Company*, 350 F.2d 445, 449 (D.C. Cir. 1965) (Unconscionability has generally been recognized to include an absence of meaningful choice on the part of one of the parties together with contract terms that are unreasonably favorable to the other party).

company and a bank agree on an acceleration clause. The termination might, however, be in bad faith. This is the case when the acceleration violates the bank's duty of good faith towards the debtor company.

6.2.1.2.2 Duty of Good Faith in Case of Acceleration

In the US, the doctrine of the duty of good faith[65] varies between jurisdictions. There are, however, some common features. The duty of good faith is closely connected to the fiduciary duty of controlling creditors. At arm's lengths, creditors have a less intensive duty of good faith in contrast to controlling creditors, because the debtor company can still act in its own self-interest as long as it complies with the terms of the contract.[66] The debtor company's ability to act in its own self-interest is still given after a covenant default. Hence, the mere leverage provided by a covenant default does not constitute a fiduciary duty and generally only compensatory damages can be sued for.[67] The enforcement of rights and remedies written in the loan agreement will generally not violate a duty of good faith. However, if a course of dealing has been established, the bank can only deviate from it with advanced notice.[68] Also, in most jurisdictions the bank can only accelerate a loan if a material default has occurred and if it believes in good faith that the prospect of performance or payment has deteriorated.[69] Whether the belief is in good faith or

---

[65] § 1-304 UCC and § 205 Restatement (Second) of Contracts; seminally, *Kirke La Shelle Co. v. Paul Armstrong Co. et al.*, 188 N.E. 163 (N.Y.App. 1933) and *Alan's of Atlanta. Inc v. Minolta Corp*, 903 F.2d 1414 (11th Cir. 1990) for an implied covenant of good faith and fair dealing. For example, if the creditor unreasonably or unilaterally refuses to advance funds under a line of credit without notice to the debtor company, the creditor can be held liable for breach of contract and the implied covenant of good faith and fair dealing (*KMC v. Irving Trust Co*, 757 F.2d 752 (6th Cir. 1985)).

[66] See for example *Jean Clark v. Harvey Rowe, Junior, & another*, 701 N.E.2d 624, 627 (Mass. 1998) (fiduciary relationships are never arm's length).

[67] *In re W.T. Grant Company v. Rodman,* 699 F.2d 599, 610 (2nd Cir. 1983) cert. denied, 464 U.S. 822 (1983). For compensatory damages, see *Rubin v. Pioneer Federal Savings & Loan Assn*, 214 Neb. 364 (Neb. 1983); *Indu Craft, Inc. v. Bank of Baroda*, 47 F.3d 490 (2nd Cir. 1995); however, see also *Robinson v. McAllen State Bank*, 48 Banking Rep (BNA) 1004 (Tex.Dist.Ct. 1987), where punitive damages were awarded because a bank breached its duty of good faith, resulting in the debtor company's bankruptcy.

[68] See e.g. *Sahadi v. Continental Ill. Nat'l Bank & Trust Co. of Chicago*, 706 F.2d 193 (7th Cir. 1983); *J.R. Hale Contracting Co Inc v. United N. M. Bank at Albuquerque*, 799 P.2d 581 (N.M. 1990).

[69] Although the duty of good faith is originally applied in cases of termination, which are at the creditor's discretion, the principle is also applied to a detailed event of default clause in most jurisdictions; cf. *Brown v. Avemco Inv. Corp.*, 603 F.2d 1367, 1375 et seqq. (9th Cir. 1979); *United States v. John Grayson,* 879 F.2d 620, 623 (9th Cir. 1989). Codified for termination including discretion: generally, § 1-309 UCC; for leases § 2A-109 UCC. For an overview and critic on the inconsistency between different jurisdictions see Mannino (2014), § 5.03(3) (ii).

not is usually measured by an objective standard—namely commercial reasonableness.[70] Generally, a default is more likely to be material if it relates to credit risk.

In Scenario 5,[71] Papermaker defaulted under the interest coverage ratio and leverage ratio covenants. As previously mentioned, both are closely related to the credit risk. The 20-percent headroom and the grace period also ensure that a covenant default is not triggered too easily. Taken together, they are likely to be considered sufficient in constituting a material default. However, the event of default clause does not require a material default itself. So, whether the court will consider the link between the interest coverage ratio/leverage ratio covenants and the credit risk sufficient to be material will depend on the particular wording of the covenants.[72] Similarly to under German law, therefore, it is probable that the acceleration will be effective but a different judgment is possible. The duty of good faith may also be heightened—namely a fiduciary duty may be owed—if the creditor exercised control over the debtor company. The concrete conditions for a fiduciary duty will be dealt with in Scenario 6[73].

6.2.1.3 Conclusion

The legal comparison shows that the right to accelerate in Scenario 5[74] is similarly limited under German and US law. Both legal systems require a material breach as cause for the termination to be effective, coupled with the termination not having been. In that way, the systems ensured that a bank cannot arbitrarily accelerate a loan and drive the debtor company into unnecessary bankruptcy.

6.2.2 *Additional Collateral Followed by Bankruptcy*

The following section will analyse the unsecured bondholders' rights[75] in Scenario 6[76] under German and US law, addressing whether the additional collateral is avoidable or if the bank consortium may be liable towards them.

---

[70] *Warren Mitchell v. Ford Motor Credit Company*, 688 P.2d 42 (Okl. 1984); *Richards Engineer, Inc. v. Charles Spanel* 745 P2.d 1031, 1033 (Colo.App. 1987); but see *Farmers Cooperative Elevator, Inc. v. State Bank*, 236 N.W.2d 674 (Iowa 1975) where a subjective standard was applied.

[71] See above 6.2.

[72] Under common law the burden of proof lies with the creditor *Leaf v. Reynolds*, 203 P. 458, 460 (Ida. 1921); *Spatuzzi v. Star Auto Truck Exchange, Inc.*, 119 N.J.L. 377 (Ct.Err.&App. 1938).

[73] See above 6.2.

[74] See above 6.2.

[75] Or the rights of the bankruptcy administrator.

[76] See above 6.2.

6.2.2.1 German Law

Within the legal systems, the legal doctrine of avoidable preference will be discussed first. Under German law, if potential wrongful and detrimental treatment of third-party creditors has occurred, the appropriate means for compensation are mainly found not in tort law but in bankruptcy law.[77] Subsequently, the possibility of nullity pursuant to § 138 BGB and liability issues will be analysed.

6.2.2.1.1 Avoidable Preference

A duty exists under German bankruptcy law to refund and restitute avoidable preferences (*Erstattungs- und Rückgewährpflicht*), which is reflected in § 143 InsO.[78] The coverage contesting (*Deckungsanfechtung*) according to §§ 130, 131 InsO regulates the preferential treatment of one creditor. A preferential transfer must be restituted to the bankruptcy estate if it grants a bankruptcy creditor either a security or a satisfaction (or facilitates it acquiring such).

Additional collateral will usually be regarded as incongruent coverage[79] because the event of default clause will not specify the particular security interest.[80] The bankruptcy administrator[81] can contest the additional collateral according to § 131 I InsO:

> A transaction granting or facilitating a bankruptcy creditor a security or satisfaction without his or her entitlement to such security or satisfaction, or to the kind or date of such security or satisfaction, may be contested if such a transaction was made 1) during the last month prior to the request to open bankruptcy proceedings or after such a request; 2) within the second or third month prior to the request to open bankruptcy proceedings, and the debtor was illiquid on the date of the transaction; or 3) within the second or third month prior to the

[77]For Germany, see Kuntz (2008), 818; Servatius (2008), p. 124; Thole (2010a), 688 et seq.; § 826 BGB is only applicable if challenging avoidable preferences under bankruptcy law does not offer sufficient compensation for the loss suffered by all creditors. See BGHZ 56, 339, 355; BGHZ 130, 314, 331; Oechsler (2013), para. 134, 336; dissenting, Wagner, in: Habersack (ed) (2013), para. 52. Under US law, both avoidable preference and fiduciary duty claims can be brought, parallel, before court; cf. *Harry G. Hager v. Ruth A. Gibson, Trustee for Preference , Ltd.*, 108 F.3d 35 (4th Cir. 1997).

[78]*Insolvenzordnung* (German Insolvency Code). It also reflected by § 11 AnfG (*Anfechtungsgesetz*, Avoidance of Transactions Act).

[79]An incongruent coverage refers to the situation where the particular transaction granting or facilitating a bankruptcy creditor a security or satisfaction is considerably not covered by the contractual relationship (including loan agreement and law). Agreements changing the original loan agreement so as to allow for the particular transaction are void within a one month period prior to the request to open bankruptcy proceedings but can be valid within a three month period if the debtor was not illiquid and there was no knowledge of the disadvantage to third-party creditors; BGHZ 59, 230, 235. In any case, the changing agreement can be contestable under § 133 InsO.

[80]Cf. Runge (2010), p. 376 et seq.; Wittig and Wulfers paras. 4/3108 et seq. Regarding *AGB-Banken* see BGHZ 174, 297, 301 et seq.

[81]§ 129 I InsO.

request to open bankruptcy proceedings, and the creditor was aware of the disadvantage to the bankruptcy creditors arising from such a transaction on its date.

In Scenario 6,[82] the additional collateral was provided 89 days[83] before filing for bankruptcy and, therefore, within the reach-back period of § 131 I nos. 2 and 3 InsO.[84] § 131 I no. 2 InsO, however, is not applicable because Papermaker was not illiquid on the date of the transaction. For § 131 I no. 3 InsO to apply, the creditor must have been aware of the disadvantage to the bankruptcy creditors arising from such a transaction on its date. A disadvantage to the bankruptcy creditors is given when the contestable transaction decreases the bankruptcy estate and reduces the satisfaction of other creditors' claims.[85] The element of awareness requires that the bank consortium positively knew about the disadvantage to the bankruptcy creditors.[86] In accordance with §131 II 1 InsO, this is commonly assumed by jurisprudence and literature, where the addressee of an avoidance knew about both the debtor company's distressed financial situation and its inability to satisfy all creditors in the foreseeable future.[87] Papermaker violated the interest coverage ratio and the leverage ratio covenants, which are both related to the credit risk. Thus, the bankruptcy administrator will probably be able to prove the bank consortium's positive knowledge.

Moreover, the bank consortium's awareness may be presumed pursuant to §§ 131 II 2, 138 II no. 2 alt. 2 InsO,[88] according to which the presumption is established for a debtor company having the opportunity, under a service contract, to become aware of the debtor company's financial circumstances. German jurisprudence only considers those service contract that aim at a function within the debtor company itself as relevant.[89] Christoph Paulus and Christoph Thole, however, argue that influence on the debtor company's management should be taken into account as a decisive factor.[90] Best Bank has not even influenced Papermaker's management.[91] Hence, the bank consortium's awareness will not be presumed.

---

[82]See above 6.2.

[83]The date of the transaction performance is determined by § 140 InsO.

[84]It is outside the one-month reach-back period of § 131 I 1 InsO.

[85]See only BGHZ 174, 314, 316. See also Majic (2013), p. 234 with further references.

[86]BGHZ 157, 242, 250; BGH WM 2004, 1837, 1839; Kayser, in: Kirchhof et al. (eds) (2013), para. 53.

[87]BGHZ 157, 242, 250 et seqq.; BGH WM 2004, 1837, 1839 et seq.; Hölzle (2006), 106 et seq.; Ede and Hirte, in: (2015), para. 22; Kayser, in: Kirchhof et al. (eds) (2013), para. 63.

[88]Positive knowledge may also be simulated by the analogous application of § 162 BGB; cf. Majic (2013), p. 237.

[89]See BGH WM 1997, 545, 548 for auditors; OLG Naumburg, WM 2006, 1677, 1678. This approach is based on the rationale of the government bill, BT-Drucks. 12/2443, p. 163.

[90]Paulus (2000), 2227; Thole (2010b), p. 342 et seqq. Maximilian Majic even considers the mere stipulation of information and influence rights as sufficient; Majic (2013), p. 223 et seqq. This, however, is too far reaching.

[91]Scenario 6 builds on Scenario 1 (above 1.1). Scenario 3 (above 5.3.1), where Best Bank influences the management, is excluded.

However, if the bankruptcy administrator could prove the bank consortium's positive knowledge, the additional collateral would be avoidable pursuant to § 131 I no. 3 InsO.

6.2.2.1.2 Nullity Under § 138 BGB

The material provision of additional collateral (*Verfügungsgeschäft*) may also be null pursuant to § 138 BGB. Therefore, additional elements to those of § 129 et seqq. InsO must be fulfilled.[92] The surety agreement must exploit one party or violate legitimate interests of third parties or the public in an immoral way.[93] This can be given in cases of debtor gagging (*Schuldnerkebelung*), which include sucking (*Aussaugung*) and silent business ownership (*stille Geschäftsinhaberschaft*).[94] "Sucking" refers to a situation where the debtor company is—due to selfish reasons of the secured party—left with so few assets and so little entrepreneurial freedom that the debtor company inevitably becomes bankrupt to the detriment of other creditors.[95] The doctrine of silent business ownership applies when the debtor company is merely a figurehead for the controlling bank. In addition, the controlling bank must receive all the gains without bearing any risks. This will, however, only be assumed if the debtor company has no—or only marginal—entrepreneurial freedom left.[96] For example, the secondment of a bank employee to play a part in the debtor company's financial recovery is considered problematic.[97]

Legitimate interests of third parties or the public can be violated in an immoral way when third-party creditors are harmed and/or misled. First, a surety agreement can be null resulting from failure to file for bankruptcy in due time (*Insolvenzverschleppung*), if it aims at using the bank's information advantage to secure its claims with collateral while the bank influences the debtor company to delay the filing for bankruptcy.[98] Second, according to the principle of

---

[92] BGHZ 53, 174, 180; BGHZ 130, 314, 331; Hefermehl, in: Soergel (ed) (1999), para. 67; Sack and Fischinger, in: von Staudinger (ed) (2011), para. 439.

[93] Armbrüster, in: Säcker, Rixecker (eds) (2015), para. 165; Ellenberger, in: Palandt (ed) (2016), para. 20; Hefermehl, in: Soergel (ed) (1999), para. 53; Sack and Fischinger, in: von Staudinger (ed) (2011), para. 169.

[94] RGZ 136, 247, 253 et seqq. (concerning § 826 BGB); Obermüller (1981), 352 et seqq.; Hefermehl, in: Soergel (ed) (1999), para. 119; Sack and Fischinger, in: von Staudinger (ed) (2011), paras. 304 et seq.

[95] RGZ 136, 247, 253 (concerning § 826 BGB); BGHZ 19, 12, 18; Obermüller (1981), 352 et seq.; Hefermehl, in: Soergel (ed) (1999), para. 119; Sack and Fischinger, in: von Staudinger (ed) (2011), para. 305.

[96] RGZ 136, 247, 253 et seq. (concerning § 826 BGB); LG Hamburg WM 1985, 163; Sack and Fischinger, in: von Staudinger (ed) (2011), para. 304.

[97] Cf. Ahnert (2002), 259; Sack and Fischinger, in: von Staudinger (ed) (2011), para. 304.

[98] BGH, WM 1964, 674; Hefermehl, in: Soergel (ed) (1999), para. 169.

endangerment of creditors (*Gläubigergefährdung*),[99] a surety agreement can be null if the collateral provided constitutes a reasonable risk due to its size and lack of transparency to third-party creditors and yet the bank knowingly proceeds.[100] If additional collateral is provided, it has to be ensured that new creditors will not be misled and existing creditors are not substantially damaged.[101] The scope of assessment, however, will always depend on the specific circumstances surrounding the surety agreement.[102] The dispute on whether the subjective element of knowing—or avoiding gaining knowledge of—the facts establishing immorality is required for § 138 BGB does not need to be settled because the subjective element will be given[103]: A bank will generally possess sufficient insight into the debtor company's financial situation due to information undertakings.[104] Thus, a bank's intention to disadvantage third-party creditors will be assumed.

In Scenario 6,[105] the surety agreement may be null for *Aussaugung* and *Gläubigergefährdung* according to § 138 BGB. The bank consortium used its leverage after a covenant default to receive additional collateral.[106] This on its own is not a transaction *contra bonos mores*.[107] For the *Aussaugung* to apply, Papermaker must have nearly no assets or entrepreneurial freedom left. The provided collateral only covers part of Papermaker's assets. If Papermaker's right to dispose of the provided collateral is restricted in such a way that it also significantly removes its entrepreneurial freedom, the surety agreement should be considered null.[108] Otherwise, the surety agreement should be valid.

Under the doctrine of *Gläubigergefährdung*, the bank consortium may face an intensified duty to investigate Papermaker's financial situation before demanding additional collateral, if there are indications that Papermaker may be experiencing financial difficulties.[109] The violation of both financial covenants indicates an

---

99The endangerment of creditors (*Gläubigergefährdung*) is difficult to distinguish from the legal instrument of credit deceit (*Kredittäuschung*); cf. e.g. Hönn, in: Soergel (ed) (2005), para. 147. Credit deceit also overlaps with failure to file for bankruptcy in due time (*Insolvenzverschleppung);* cf. e.g. Thole WM 2010, 686. For that reason, the work abstains from discussing the instrument of credit deceit and concentrates instead on *Gläubigergefährdung* and *Insolvenzverschleppung*.

100RGZ 136, 247, 248 (concerning § 826 BGB).

101BGHZ 10, 228, 233 et seq.; Koller (1985), 1014; Engert (2005), p.74.

102Cf. BGH WM 1961, 1103, 1106 (concerning § 826 BGB); BGHZ 90, 381, 399 (concerning § 826 BGB); BGH WM 1995, 995; Hefermehl, in: Soergel (ed) (1999), para. 171.

103For an overview of the debate, see e.g. Sack and Fischinger, in: von Staudinger (ed) (2011), paras. 74 et seqq.

104Similarly, for § 826 BGB see Engert (2005), p. 69.

105See above 6.2.

106This establishes the collaboration of Papermaker and the bank consortium; cf. Engert (2005), p. 69 et seq.

107BGH WM 1964, 671, 672 et seq.; Hefermehl, in: Soergel (ed) (1999), para. 120.

108BGH WM 1959, 964; Armbrüster, in: Säcker, Rixecker (eds) (2015), para. 73; Hefermehl, in: Soergel (ed) (1999), para. 120; Sack and Fischinger, in: von Staudinger (ed) (2011), para. 305.

109BGH WM 1995, 995; BGHZ 138, 291; Engert (2005), p. 72 et seqq.

increased credit risk and thereby warns of financial difficulties. Thus, the bank consortium must conduct a proper inquiry. After that inquiry, the bank consortium must be satisfied without gross fault that other creditors are not being misled or otherwise harmed by the provision of additional collateral.[110] The due diligence intensity may be even stricter than by collateral in connection with a new loan, because additional collateral has no counterpart in terms of new liquidity.[111] Nevertheless, the consistent case law requires an additional element of immorality, even in cases where all or nearly all assets of the debtor company are covered.[112] Here, the surety agreement leaves part of Papermaker's unpledged assets untouched. The surety agreement is thus unlikely to be null under the principle of *Gläubigergefährdung*.[113]

6.2.2.1.3 Treuepflicht of the Controlling Bank to Third-Party Creditors

The bank consortium could also be liable to third-party creditors.[114] In the German literature, it has been discussed whether a controlling bank owes third-party creditors a fiduciary duty (*Treuepflicht*) or not.[115] According to parts of the literature, the controlling creditor is obliged to pay damages pursuant to § 280 I BGB if it, or other third parties attributable to it, influence the debtor company to the detriment of other creditors.[116] However, establishing a special connection (*Sonderverbindung*) between creditors is problematic. The prevailing opinion assumes no special connection between creditors outside bankruptcy.[117] Some authors, nevertheless, argue for a *Sonderverbindung* and justify it with a responsibility under company law (*gesellschaftsrechtliche Mitverantwortung*) of control creditors.[118] However, a fiduciary duty would only lead to credit rationing.

[110]BGH WM 1955, 402, 403 et seq.; Sack and Fischinger, in: von Staudinger (ed) (2011), para. 421.

[111]BGH WM 1955, 402, 403; BGH WM 1971, 441, 442; Engert (2005), p. 74 et seq.; but see BGH WM 1995, 995, 996 et seq. For an ever stricter duty of care by additional collateral see Koller (1985), 1022 et seq.

[112]BGHZ 20, 43, 49 et seq.; BGH WM 1995, 995; BGHZ 138, 291, 300; Armbrüster, in: Säcker, Rixecker (eds) (2015), para. 73.

[113]Cf. BGH WM 1956, 527, 529; BGH WM 1995, 995; Engert (2005), p. 68 et seq.

[114]Avoidable preference does not regulate detrimental transaction to bankruptcy creditors exhaustively; see e.g. BGH WM 1974, 99, 100; Sack and Fischinger, in: von Staudinger (ed) (2011), para. 191.

[115]Seminally, Canaris (1979), 116 et seq.

[116]Köndgen, in: Prütting (ed) (1997), p. 127, 148; Kästle (2003), p. 144 et seqq.; Möllers (1991), p. 155 et seq.

[117]BGHZ 116, 319; Eidenmüller, in: Kirchhof et al. (eds) (2014a), para. 36. For a fiduciary duty within bankruptcy see Schulz (2003); Grünewald (2015), p. 155 et seqq., 197 et seqq.

[118]Möllers (1991), p. 156; similarly, Kästle (2003), p. 144; Eidenmüller, in: Kirchhof et al. (eds) (2014b), para. 65.

Moreover, the rationale for the fiduciary duty of a shareholder is based on a different situation because creditors do not decide collectively via resolution, but individually, and each adjusting creditor can protect itself.[119] Hence, the prevailing opinion seems preferable. The bank's managerial influence is unlikely to be limited by a fiduciary duty outside bankruptcy.

6.2.2.1.4 Liability Under § 826 BGB

A functionally similar liability is achieved by § 826 BGB, which covers intentional damage contrary to public policy. Although § 138 BGB and § 826 BGB can apply concurrently,[120] the elements of § 826 BGB are similar to those of § 138 BGB.[121] In contrast to §138 BGB, § 826 BGB sanctions immoral actions of a bank and requires intent to cause damage (*Schädigungsvorsatz*).[122] Moreover, their legal consequences have different effects on third-party creditors: Damages under § 826 BGB only benefit some third-party creditors whereas the nullity of the surety contract under § 138 BGB benefits all third-party creditors by increasing the bankruptcy estate.[123]

The four cases that have been explained under § 138 BGB also exist under § 826 BGB[124] and have already been summarised by the *Reichsgericht*[125] in 1932.[126] Those four cases—*Insolvenzverschleppung*,[127] *Aussaugung*, *stille Geschäftsinhaberschaft*[128] and *Gläubigergefährdung*—only serve as guidelines; the court still has to evaluate the conformity of the bank's conduct with what a decent person would consider just and reasonable on a case-by-case basis.[129]

---

[119] Kuntz (2008), 816 et seq.

[120] A surety agreement may be not null under § 138 BGB, but a bank may be liable for damages under § 826 BGB; Hönn, in: Soergel (ed) (2005), para. 98; Sack and Fischinger, in: von Staudinger (ed) (2011), para. 186.

[121] See e.g. BGH WM 1961, 776, 778; Engert (2005), p. 51.

[122] Cf. Hönn, in: Soergel (ed) (2005), para. 51 et seqq.; Wagner, in: Habersack (ed) (2013), para. 24 et seqq.

[123] Coing (1980), 1027; Hefermehl, in: Soergel (ed) (1999), para. 168.

[124] BGH WM 1963, 1093, 1093; BGH NJW 1970, 657, 659.

[125] Supreme Court of the (German) Reich.

[126] RGZ 136, 247, 258 et seq.

[127] BGH, WM 1964, 674. The damages cover the sum that third-party creditor would have recovered (*Quotenschaden*), or the suffered loss of third-party creditors who would have not contracted with the debtor company if bankruptcy were filed for properly (*Vertrauensschaden*). Seminally, BGH NJW 1994, 2220, 2222. Engert (2005), p. 29. For arguing for a liabilty under § 830 BGB, see Schmidt (1988), 1502.

[128] Cf. BGHZ 19, 12, 17; Engert (2005), p. 77 et seqq.

[129] BGH WM 1956, 283, 284; BGH WM 1961, 1103, 1106; BGHZ 90, 381, 399.

In Scenario 6,[130] the bank consortium may be liable to third-party creditors for *Gläubigergefährdung*.[131] The same remarks made with regards to § 138 BGB apply here. However, the suing third-party creditors must also prove that they suffered damages from the provision of additional collateral to the bank consortium and that the bank consortium knew—or purposefully avoided knowing—the facts establishing the possible endangerment of third-party creditors yet proceeded anyway.[132] This seems difficult, as the collateral provided only covers part of Papermaker's assets. Hence, a liability of the bank consortium under § 826 BGB is unlikely.

6.2.2.1.5 Liability as a Faktisches Organ

Another legal doctrine that could impact the bank's conduct after a covenant default is the *faktisches Organ*, the concrete conditions of which are highly disputed in the literature. An analysis of the different standpoints is, however, not indicated,[133] because a bank's conduct will not be impacted by *de lege ferenda* liability considerations: The BGH[134] jurisprudence applied to the case clearly denies liability as a *faktisches Organ* for banks that influence the management to the detriment of other creditors.[135] Banks are legal entities and so far only natural persons have been held liable.[136] Moreover, banks will not fulfil the criteria of visibly acting like an executive entity body[137] because a bank only influences the debtor company's behaviour and the debtor company still acts on its own.

6.2.2.2 US Law

Similarly to under German law, the additional collateral provided to the bank consortium in Scenario 6[138] may be avoidable under US law. Moreover, the bank consortium may be liable.

---

[130] See above 6.2.

[131] Third-party liability cannot be based on *Aussaugung* alone. An element of *Gläubigergefährdung* must be given as well. *Aussaugung* can, however, lead to liability towards the debtor company. Cf. Obermüller (1981), 355.

[132] BGHZ 160, 134, 144 et seqq.; BGH WM 2012, 260; Obermüller (1981) 356; Engert (2005), p. 75; Hönn, in: Soergel (ed) (2005), para. 52 et seq.; Wagner, in: Habersack (ed) (2013), para. 43.

[133] For an overview see Servatius (2008), p. 356 et seqq.; Majic (2013), p. 108 et seqq.

[134] *Bundesgerichtshof* (German Federal Supreme Court).

[135] Similarly, Fleischer (2004), 527; Engert (2005), p. 30 et seqq.; Majic (2013), p. 120. However, liability under § 117 AktG (analogously) is possible; cf. for example Hoffmann (2012), 13.

[136] BGHZ 150, 61, 68; critically Fleischer (2004), 526; Majic (2013), p. 116 et seq.

[137] "nach außen hervortretendes, üblicherweise der Geschäftsführung zuzurechnendes Handeln" BGHZ 104, 44, 48; BGHZ 150, 61, 69; critically Majic (2013), p. 115 et seq.

[138] See above 6.2.

6.2.2.2.1 Avoidable Preference

Pursuant to 11 US Code § 547(b), a trustee can avoid or recover preferential transfers. A transfer is only preferential if it is made in the sense of 11 US Code § 101(54),[139] it is in the interest of the debtor in property,[140] it is to or for the benefit of creditors,[141] it is for or on account of a pre-existing debt,[142] it results in greater distribution than under Chap. 7,[143] and it is made during the 90 days[144] immediately preceding the date of the filing of the petition.

However, if the benefiting creditor is regarded as an "insider", the reach-back period is extended to 1 year under 11 US Code § 547(b)(4)(B).[145] An insider, according to 11 US Code § 101(31)(B)(iii) is a person in control of the debtor company. Banks can be considered insiders in three ways. First, a bank can possess actual control from basic covenants by a pattern of general prohibition and frequent consents or waivers. Occasional interference by the bank after a covenant default, however, should not constitute control.[146] Second, covenants that prohibit a change of management or interfere in any other way with the debtor company's discretion regarding the management personality are likely to be considered a means of

[139]Pursuant to 11 US Code § 101(54), a "transfer" covers every mode – direct or indirect, absolute or conditional, voluntary or involuntary – of disposing of or parting with property or with an interest in property, including retention of title as a security interest and foreclosure of the debtor's equity of redemption.

[140]The element of "interest of the debtor in property" has been held in *Begier v. Internal Revenue Service*, 496 U.S. 53 (1990) to be property that would belong to the bankruptcy estate were it not for the transfer; equivalent to "property of the estate" as defined in 11 US Code § 541(A)(1).

[141]11 US Code § 101(10) defines "creditor" as an entity that has a claim against the debtor that arose at the time of or before the order for relief concerning the debtor. A claim is according to 11 US Code § 101(5) right to payment, whether or not such right is reduced to judgment, liquidated, unliquidated, fixed, contingent, matured, unmatured, disputed, undisputed, legal, equitable, secured, or unsecured; or right to an equitable remedy for breach of performance if such breach gives rise to a right to payment, whether or not such right to an equitable remedy is reduced to judgment, fixed, contingent, matured, unmatured, disputed, undisputed, secured, or unsecured.

[142]*Laws v. United Missouri Bank of Kansas City*, 98 F.3d 1047 (8th Cir. 1996). Exluded are down payments and gifts or donations; cf. *Robert Sullivan v. William Willock*, 854 F.2d 196 (7th Cir. 1988) and *Coleman Tidwell v. Glenda Galbreath,* 207 B.R. 309 (Bkrtcy.M.D.Ga. 1997).

[143]This requires a comparison between what the creditor would have received under Chapter 7 and what it *de facto* received. For example, fully secured creditors' claims are satisfied before the claims of unsecured creditors and because of that payments to a fully secured creditor are not considered avoidable preferences. Cf. *In re Tenna Corporation v. United States,* 801 F.2d 819 (6th Cir. 1986).

[144]This includes the two elements of "made while the debtor was insolvent" (11 US Code § 547(f)) and "within the applicable reach-back period" for non-insider creditors (11 US Code § 547(b)(4)(A)).

[145]11 US Code § 547(b)(4)(B). See, for example, *In re Crawford and Braunstein v. Crawford and Kamphaus*, 454 B.R. 262 (Bkrtcy.D.Mass. 2011). Also, the creditor's right to vote in Chapter 7 proceedings is forfeited, Bankruptcy Code, 11 US Code § 702(a)(3).

[146]Leichtling et al. (2013), § 11.05 (2.)(c.)(i.).

control.[147] Third, if the bank uses its inside information to gain an advantage at the expense of third-party creditors, control is likely to be assumed.[148]

In Scenario 6,[149] the additional collateral was provided 89 days before filing for bankruptcy and thus falls within the reach-back period of 90 days. The additional collateral, however, may not be avoidable because it may not result in greater distribution than under Chap. 7. This requires a comparison between what the creditor would have received under Chap. 7 and what it *de facto* received. For example, fully secured creditors' claims are satisfied before the claims of unsecured creditors. Because of this, payments to a fully secured creditor are not considered avoidable preferences.[150] The bank consortium was not fully secured, but undersecured. In these cases, the transfer will first be applied to the unsecured part of the loan,[151] which is probably not going to protect the bank consortium.[152] Furthermore, the defences of 11 US Code § 547(c) are not applicable. Hence, the additional collateral will probably be avoidable.

6.2.2.2.2 Fiduciary Duty of the Controlling Bank to Third-Party Creditors

Moreover, the bank consortium may be liable under the principle of fiduciary duty. As previously mentioned, a creditor in control owes the debtor company and its other creditors a fiduciary duty under US law when the debtor is under the lender's control.[153] The criteria, however, are indefinite and can only be outlined.[154] The

[147] *State National Bank of El Paso v. Farah Manufacturing Co.*, 678 S.W.2d 661 (Tex.Ct. App.1984) but judgment set aside; Leichtling et al. (2013), § 11.05 (2.)(c.)(ii.).

[148] Leichtling et al. (2013), § 11.05 (2.)(c.)(iii.).

[149] See above 6.2.

[150] *In re Schwinn Bicycle Co. v. Transamerica Insurance Finance Corporation* 200 B.R. 980 (Bkrtcy.N.D.Ill. 1996); For declining to follow and arguing that the hypothetical test must be performed also for fully secured creditors, see *In re Falcon Products, Inc., et al. v. First Insurance Funding*, 381 B.R. 543 (8th Cir.BAP 2008).

[151] *Murray Drabkin v. A.I. Credit Corporation,* 800 F.2d 1153 (D.C. Cir. 1986); *In re Lease-A-Fleet, Inc. v. Donald L. Wolk, Setven C. Wolk, Robins Le-Cocq Corp.*, 151 B.R. 341 (Bkrtcy.E.D. Pa. 1993).

[152] See, for example, *In re Powerine Oil Company v. Koch Oil Company,* 59 F.3d 969 (9th Cir. 1995).

[153] See *Taylor et al. v. Standard Gas & Elec. Co. et al.*, 59 S.Ct. 543 (1939).

[154] For a detailed analysis see, for example, Cappello (2014), p. 281 et seqq.

fairly dominant opinion regards creditors as being in control when the creditor takes active control and forces the debtor company to undertake things that were not part of the lending relationship from the beginning.[155] If the bank is not in control, it may also be required that the bank gained an unconscionable advantage by controlling the debtor company—in addition to a confidential relationship between the debtor company and the bank—in order to be held liable.[156] A bank can also be held liable for aiding and abetting a breach of a fiduciary duty owed by the directors or officers of the debtor company.[157] The bank, however, has a number of defences—the main one being *in pari delicto*.[158] This means that a party cannot sue the bank if both parties participated in the wrongdoing for which the bank is sued.[159]

The third-party creditor can sue for damages for losses suffered during the period of control[160] or for equitable subordination of the bank's claim.[161] Equitable subordination can be ordered by bankruptcy court under 11 US Code § 510 (c) and is generally based on the Deep Rock doctrine established by *Taylor v. Standard Gas & Electric Co.*[162] Equitable subordination has been commonly ordered in cases where the inequitable conduct of the creditor who had a special

---

[155]See *State National Bank of El Paso v. Farah Manufacturing Company, Inc.*, 678 S.W.2d 661 (Tex.Ct.App.1984) but judgment set aside; *Citibank, N.A. v. Data Lease Financial Corporation*, 828 F.2d 686 (11th Cir. 1987), cert. denied, 484 U.S. 1062 (1988). See also *A. Gay Jenson Farms Co. v. Cargill, Inc.*, 309 N.W.2d 285 (Minn. 1981). See also Restatement (Second) of Agency § 140 comment a: A security holder who merely exercises a veto power over the business acts of his debtor by preventing purchases or sales above specified amounts does not thereby become a principal. However, if he takes over the management of the debtor's business either in person or through an agent, and directs what contracts may or may not be made, he becomes a principal, liable as a principal for the obligations incurred thereafter in the normal course of business by the debtor who has now become the general agent. The point at which the creditor becomes a principal is that at which he assumes de facto control over the conduct of his debtor, whatever the terms of the formal contract with his debtor may be.

[156]See *Hoffman v. Lincoln National Bank and Trust Company,* 636 N.E.2d 185, 188 (Ind.App. 5 Dist. 1994); *Capital Bank v. MVB, Inc.*, 644 So.2d 515, 521 (Fla. Dist. Ct. App. 1994).

[157]*In re Fedders North America, Inc. v. Goldman Sachs Credit Partners L.P.*, 405 B.R. 527, 542 et seqq. (Bkrtcy.D.Del. 2009).

[158]Seminally, *Cenco Incorporated v. Seidman & Seidman*, 686 F.2d 449 (7th Cir. 1982).

[159]See, for example, *Official Committee of Unsecured Creditors v. R F Lafferty & Co*, Inc., 267 F.3d 340 (3rd Cir. 2001); *Bondi v. Citigroup, Inc*, 32 A.3d 1158 (N.J.Super.A.D. 2011).

[160]*State National Bank of El Paso v. Farah Manufacturing Co.*, 678 S.W.2d 661 (Tex.Ct. App.1984) but judgment set aside.

[161]See, for example, *Bergquist v. First National Bank of St. Paul (In re American Lumber Co.)*, 5 Bankr. 470 (Bankr.D.Minn.1980).

[162]*Taylor et al. v. Standard Gas & Electric Co. et al.*, 59 S. Ct. 543 (Sup.Ct. 1939).

relationship with the debtor company harmed the debtor company or other creditors.[163] Only in rare cases has a claim been subordinated without a special relationship.[164]

In Scenario 6,[165] the bank consortium was provided with additional collateral. This alone does not amount to control: "[...] there is generally no objection to a creditor's using his bargaining position, including his ability to refuse to make further loans needed by the debtor to improve the status of his existing claims."[166] The fact that the right to additional collateral was stipulated in the loan agreement renders a fiduciary duty particularly improbable.

6.2.2.3 Conclusion

The legal comparison shows that the right to additional collateral in Scenario 6[167] is restricted in similar ways under German and US law. Under both legal systems, the additional collateral is probably avoidable. The only difference may be that there is no distinction under US law between congruent and incongruent coverage. Nevertheless, the result is the same. The reach-back periods are similar—3 months compared to 90 days.

Moreover, for both a liability under § 826 BGB and the concept of fiduciary duty, more is required than under avoidable preference law. In Scenario 6,[168] the bank consortium is unlikely to be held liable for receiving additional collateral that only covers part of the debtor company's assets.

6.3 High Probability of Self-Interested Behaviour of Banks

This chapter has shown that the feasibility of positive or negative externalities depends largely on the bank's conduct after a covenant default. Prior to a covenant default, potential positive externalities are likely due to covenants reducing the agency conflict between shareholders and creditors. After a covenant default, however, the bank's reaction to the default determines the scale of potential positive and negative effects. Positive effects could be the production of information

---

[163]See, for example, *In re T. E. Mercer Trucking Company*, 16 B.R. 176 (Bankr.N.D.Tex. 1981); *In re Yellowstone Mountain Club, LLC v. Brian Glasser*, 2014 WL 1369363 (Dist.Ct.D.Mont. 2014) appeal filed.

[164]See *In re American Lumber Company v. First National Bank of St. Paul,* 5 B.R. 470 (Bankr. Minn. 1980) (construing § 67 of the old Bankruptcy Act).

[165]See above 6.2.

[166]*In re W.T. Grant Company v. Charles Rodman*, 699 F.2d 599, 610 (2nd Cir. 1983).

[167]See above 6.2.

[168]See above 6.2.

through both a covenant default and the subsequent reaction of the bank, as well as the disciplinary function of any corrective action taken. However, the information produced by a covenant default only benefits adjusting third-party creditors and, particularly, those with cross-default or cross-acceleration clauses. The corrective action subsequently taken may also harm as well as benefit both adjusting and non-adjusting third-party creditors. The corrective action can lead to an influence on the debtor company that is not in the interest of all creditors, to asset dilution, to unnecessary bankruptcy or to a domino effect.

This chapter found it likely that a bank will act purely in its own self-interest and will therefore base its decision for corrective action purely on the benefits it sees for itself. It will not consider the costs for third-party creditors. The occurrence of negative externalities, therefore, is probable. The bank's decision is only influenced by legal limits. A legal enforcement by the debtor company, however, is rather unlikely as long as the lock-in situation between the debtor company and the bank lasts. When this relationship is dissolved by bankruptcy or acceleration, the legal limits are relevant. In those cases, a bank may also become liable to third-party creditors under tort law for controlling the debtor company. In addition, avoidable preference under bankruptcy law sets a limitation for the bank's conduct. Otherwise, the bank can mainly act freely within its bilateral private governance system created by covenants and an event of default clause. This marginal impact of legal restrictions on the bank's behaviour suggests that banks will behave selfishly and produce negative externalities. This means that the potential negative externalities probably outweigh the potential positive externalities of that private governance system. Hence, it is doubtful that the bilateral private governance system provides collective creditor protection.

References

Ahnert S (2002) Zivilrechtliche Haftungsrisiken für Kreditinstitute bei krisenbehafteten Unternehmen. BKR:254–260

Akerlof GA, Shiller RJ (2010) Animal spirits: how human psychology drives the economy, and why it matters for global capitalism, 9th edn. Princeton University Press, Princeton

Armbrüster C (2015) § 138. In: Säcker FJ, Rixecker R (eds) Münchener Kommentar zum BGB. Beck, München

Ballo EHF (2010) Die AGB-Kontrolle von Kreditverträgen in der Akquisitionsfinanzierung. Lang, Frankfurt am Main

Berger KP (2012) § 490. In: Säcker FJ, Rixecker R (eds) Münchener Kommentar zum BGB. Beck, München

Burger A, Buchhart A (2001) Financial Covenants statt Insolvenzordnung. Finanz Betrieb:99–104

Canaris C-W (1979) Kreditkündigung und Kreditverweigerung. ZHR 143:113–138

Cappello AB (2014) Lender liability, 5th edn. Juris, New York

Coing H (1980) Eine neue Entscheidung zur Haftung der Banken wegen Gläubigergefährdung. WM:1026–1030

Ede C, Hirte H (2015) § 131. In: Insolvenzordnung Kommentar. Franz Vahlen, München

Eidenmüller H (1995) Effizienz als Rechtsprinzip. Möglichkeiten und Grenzen der ökonomischen Analyse des Rechts. Mohr Siebeck, Tübingen

Eidenmüller H (1999) Unternehmenssanierung zwischen Markt und Gesetz. Mechanismen der Unternehmensreorganisation und Kooperationspflichten im Reorganisationsrecht. Otto Schmidt, Köln

Eidenmüller H (2001) Kapitalgesellschaftsrecht im Spiegel ökonomischer Theorie. JZ 21: 1041–1051

Eidenmüller H (2005) Der homo oeconomicus und das Schuldrecht: Herausforderungen durch Behavioral Law and Economics. JZ:216–224

Eidenmüller H (2014a) § 225a. In: Kirchhof H-P, Eidenmüller H, Stürner R (eds) Münchner Kommentar zur Insolvenzordnung. Beck, München

Eidenmüller H (2014b) Vor §§ 217 bis 269. In: Kirchhof H-P, Eidenmüller H, Stürner R (eds) Münchner Kommentar zur Insolvenzordnung. Beck, München

Ellenberger J (2016) § 138. In: Palandt O (ed) Palandt. Beck, München

Engert A (2005) Die Haftung für drittschädigende Kreditgewährung. Münchener Universitäts schriften Reihe der Juristischen Fakultät, vol 189. Beck, München

Fettes MW (2014) Zur Verwendung von Covenants gegenüber Kapitalgesellschaften. Duncker & Humblot, Berlin

Fezer K-H (1986) Aspekte einer Rechtskritik an der economic analysis of law und am property rights approach. JZ:817–824

Fight A (2004) Syndicated lending: essential capital markets. Butterworth-Heinemann, UK

Fleischer H (2004) Zur aktienrechtlichen Verantwortlichkeit faktischer Organe. AG 49(10): 517–528

Gaier R (2016) § 314. In: Säcker FJ, Rixecker R (eds) Münchener Kommentar zum BGB. Beck, München

Grüneberg C (2014) § 314. In: Palandt O (ed) Palandt Bürgerliches Gesetzbuch. C.H. Beck, München

Grünewald P (2015) Mehrheitsherrschaft und insolvenzrechtliche Vorauswirkung in der Unternehmenssanierung. Mohr Siebeck, Tübingen

Harrison WTJ, Horngren CT, Thomas CW, Suwardy T (2011) Financial accounting: international financial reporting standards, 8th edn. Pearson, Singapore

Hefermehl W (1999) § 138. In: Soergel H-T (ed) Soergel Kommentar Bürgerliches Gesetzbuch. Kohlhammer, Stuttgart

Heinrich S (2009) Covenants als Alternative zum institutionellen Gläubigerschutz. Eine rechtsvergleichende und ökonomische Analyse, vol 228. Schriften zum Wirtschaftsrecht. Duncker & Humblot, Berlin

Hoffmann G (2012) Grenzen der Einflussnahme auf Unternehmensleitungsentscheidungen durch Kreditgläubiger. WM:10–19

Hölzle G (2006) Zahlungsunfähigkeit - Nachweis und Kenntnis im Anfechtungsprozess. ZIP:101–107

Hönn G (2005) § 826. In: Soergel H-T (ed) Soergel Kommentar Bürgerliches Gesetzbuch. Kohlhammer, Stuttgart

Kähler L (2016) § 242. In: Gsell B, Krüger W, Lorenz S, Mayer J (eds) Beck-Online Großkommentar. Beck, München

Kästle M (2003) Rechtsfragen der Verwendung von Covenants in Kreditverträgen. Duncker & Humblot, Berlin

Kayser G (2013) § 131. In: Kirchhof H-P, Eidenmüller H, Stürner R (eds) Münchner Kommentar zur Insolvenzordnung. Beck, München

Kirchgässner G (2008) Homo oeconomicus: the economic model of individual behavior and its applications in economics and other social sciences. European heritage in economics and the social sciences 6. Springer, New York

Knapp CL (2013) Unconscionability in American contract law: a twenty-first century survey. In: LA DM, Zhou Q, Saintier SV, Rowley K (eds) Commercial contract law. Transatlantic perspectives. Cambridge University Press, Cambridge, pp 309–338

Koller I (1985) Sittenwidrigkeit der Gläubigergefährdung und Gläubigerbenachteiligung. JZ 22: 1013–1024
Köndgen J (1997) Financial Covenants. "Symbiotische" Finanzierungsverträge im Spannungsfeld von Vertrags-, Gesellschafts- und Insolvenzrecht. In: Prütting H (ed) Insolvenzrecht 1996, vol 1. RWS, Köln, pp 127–157
Korobkin RB, Ulen TS (2000) Law and behavioral science: removing the rationality assumption from law and economics. Calif Law Rev 88:1051–1144
Kuntz T (2008) Haftung von Banken gegenüber anderen Gläubigern nach § 826 BGB wegen Finanzierung von Leveraged Buyouts? ZIP:814–823
Kuntz T (2016) Grundlagen und Grenzen der aktienrechtlichen Leitungsautonomie. AG:101–116
Leaf FP (1970) Acceleration clauses in sales and secured transactions: the debtor's burden under Section 1-208 of the U.C.C. Boston Coll Law Rev 11:531–544
Leichtling MA, Dubin BA, Wong JJ (2013) Commercial loan documentation guide. Mathew Bender, San Francisco
Lieb M (1988) Das Leitbild des Finanzierungs-Leasing im Spannungsfeld von Vertragsfreiheit und Inhaltskontrolle. DB 41(18):946–954
Majic M (2013) Covenants und Insolvenz: Risiken covenant-gesicherter Kreditgeber im Falle der Insolvenz des Kreditnehmers. De Gruyter, Berlin
Mankowski P (2006) Reicht das Vertragsrecht für einen angemessenen Schutz der Gesellschafts gläubiger und ihrer Interessen aus? In: Lutter M (ed) Das Kapital der Aktiengesellschaft in Europa. De Gruyter Recht, Berlin, pp 488–507
Mannino EF (2014) Lender liability and banking litigation. ALM, New York
Maurer A (2012) Lex maritima. Grundzüge eines transnationalen Seehandelsrechts. Studien zum ausländischen und internationalen Privatrecht, vol 272. Mohr Siebeck, Tübingen
Merkel H, Tetzlaff C (2011) § 98. In: Schimansky H, Bunte H-J, Lwowski H-J (eds) Bankrechts-Handbuch. Beck, München
Merkt H (2004) Der Kapitalschutz in Europa – ein rocher de bronze? ZGR:305–323
Möllers TMJ (1991) Die Haftung der Bank bei der Kreditkündigung. Ein Beitrag zu den Verhaltenspflichten der Banken bei der Kündigung von Krediten im deutschen und amerikanischen Recht. Duncker & Humblot, Berlin
Mülbert PO (2015) § 490. In: von Staudinger J (ed) J. von Staudingers Kommentar zum Bürgerlichen Gesetzbuch. De Gruyter, Berlin
Nouvertné R (2012) Der Interessenausgleich zwischen Bank und Kreditnehmer bei Financial Covenants. ZIP:2139–2147
Obermüller M (1980) Kredite vor Konkurseröffnung. ZIP 1(5):337–344
Obermüller M (1981) Nachträgliche Besicherung von Krediten. ZIP:352–357
Oechsler J (2013) § 826. In: von Staudinger J (ed) J. von Staudingers Kommentar zum Bürgerlichen Gesetzbuch. De Gruyter, Berlin
Paulus CG (2000) Der subjektive Tatbestand in der Insolvenzanfechtung. WM 54(45):2225–2230
Renner M (2013) Die "Natur des Vertrags" nach § 307 Abs. 2 Nr. 2 BGB. AcP 213:677–717
Renner M (2015) Bankvertragsrecht, Vierter Teil. In: Canaris C-W, Habersack M, Schäfer C (eds) Staub, GroßkommHGB. De Gruyter, Berlin
Renner M, Leidinger A (2015) Zur AGB-Kontrolle standardisierter Unternehmenskreditverträge. BKR:499–505
Runge JC (2010) Covenants in Kreditverträgen. Grenzen der Einflussnahme von Kreditgebern. RWS Vlg, Köln
Sack R, Fischinger PS (2011) § 138. In: von Staudinger J (ed) J. von Staudingers Kommentar zum Bürgerlichen Gesetzbuch. De Gruyter, Berlin
Schimansky H (1995) Bankvertragsrecht und Privatautonomie. WM:461–467
Schmidt K (1988) Konkursverschleppungshaftung und Konkursverursachungshaftung. ZIP 9(23): 1497–1508
Schulte-Nölke H (2014) § 307. In: Schulze R, Dörner H, Ebert I et al (eds) BGB Handkommentar. Beck, München

Schulz D (2003) Treuepflichten unter Insolvenzgläubigern. Rws Kommunikationsforum, Köln

Servatius W (2008) Gläubigereinfluss durch Covenants. Mohr Siebeck, Tübingen

Shadab HB (2014) Performance-sensitive debt: from asset-based loans to startup financing. Univ Pa J Bus Law 16:1077–1142

Smith A (1776) The wealth of nations. University of Chicago Press, Chicago

Teichmann A (2014) § 314. In: Soergel Kommentar Bürgerliches Gesetzbuch. Kohlhammer, Stuttgart.

Theewen E (2003) Haftungsrisiken der Kreditinstitute in der Krise ihrer Schuldner. BKR 3(4): 141–148

Thießen F (1996) Covenants in Kreditverträgen: Alternative oder Ergänzung zum Insolvenzrecht? ZBB:19–37

Thole C (2010a) Gläubigerbenachteiligung und Gläubigerbegünstigung unter § 826 BGB. Zur Dritthaftung von Kreditgebern wegen sittenwidrigen Verhaltens. WM 64:685–692

Thole C (2010b) Gläubigerschutz durch Insolvenzrecht - Anfechtung und verwandte Regelungsinstrumente in der Unternehmensinsolvenz. Beiträge zum ausländischen und internationalen Privatrecht. Mohr Siebeck, Tübingen

Voglis EG (2001) Kreditkündigung und Kreditverweigerung der Banken im Lichte von Treu und Glauben. Münchner Universitätsschriften. Reihe der Juristischen Fakultät, Band 156. Beck, München

Wagner G (2013) § 826. In: Habersack M (ed) Münchener Kommentar zum BGB. Beck, München

Weidenkaff W (2014) § 490. In: Palandt Bürgerliches Gesetzbuch. Beck, München

Weitnauer W (2005) Covenants und AGB-Kontrolle. ZIP 33:1443–1448

Wight R, Cooke W, Gray R (2009) The LSTA's complete credit agreement guide. McGraw-Hill, New York

Wittig A (1996) Financial Covenants im inländischen Kreditgeschäft. WM:1381–1391

Wurmnest W (2016) § 307. In: Säcker FJ, Rixecker R (eds) Münchener Kommentar zum BGB. Beck, München

Part III
Empirical Research: Results and Re-evaluation of Preliminary Theory

Chapter 7
Design and Methodology

The resulting conclusion that the bilateral private governance system created by covenants and an event of default clause does not provide collective creditor protection is based on the theoretical presumption that a bank will act selfishly. Therefore, the next step in this work will be to empirically investigate the factual behaviour of banks.

This chapter will provide the general framework of the empirical study. First it will define the research object as the factual behaviour of banks and the enforcement of covenants, as well as their effects on third-party creditors. Then, the research object—namely banks and their conduct after a covenant default—will be presented. The research design will subsequently be introduced as semi-structured expert interviews. Finally, the data collection process and the data assessment will be discussed, thereby taking into consideration potential limitations and bias. The results will then be presented and discussed in Chap. 8.

7.1 Research Objective: The Factual Behaviour of Covenant-Secured Creditors and Its Effects on Third-Party Creditors

The research object of the empirical study follows on from the theoretical observations made thus far. Therefore, the essential findings from the previous chapters will be summarised before presenting this research object.

Firstly, covenants function as a bilateral private governance system to provide creditor protection. This private governance system, however, also affects third-party creditors. The effects on third-party creditors are not irrelevant, as certain externalities can lead to market failure.

The bilateral private governance system produces both potential positive and potential negative externalities. The potential positive externalities are the provision of information and a disciplinary effect on the debtor company. The potential

D. Matri, *Covenants and Third-Party Creditors*, DOI 10.1007/978-3-319-62036-7_7

negative externalities, on the other hand, are influencing the debtor company's management in a way that is not in the interest of all creditors, reducing the pool of assets, and causing unnecessary bankruptcy or a domino effect.

Whether positive or negative third-party creditor effects prevail depends on the bank's conduct after a covenant default. Self-interested and non-cooperative behaviour is the most likely course of action. Thus, negative effects will probably prevail.

However, the factual behaviour of covenant-secured creditors and therewith its effects on third-party creditors has been the subject of very little empirical research. The study will therefore investigate this aspect using the example of banks. The empirical study will also research the closely connected question of how covenants are enforced by banks because the way in which banks enforce covenants influences their behaviour after a covenant default. In addition, this research question will help to confirm that covenants are mainly enforced out of court and thus, create a bilateral private governance system.

7.2 Research Object: Banks and Their Behaviour After a Covenant Default Under Bank Loans

When conceptualising the empirical study, the criteria for the selection of the research object must be established so as to achieve far-reaching significance of the results. Three criteria appear to be important.

First, the covenant-secured creditor must be economically strong and adjusting so as to have a choice between different courses of actions after a covenant default. Second, there should be a sufficiently large number of third-party creditors that can be affected. This can be achieved by looking for high-volume credits for larger corporations. Third, it might be best to investigate the most common covenant-secured creditor to reflect the average creditor conflicts.

Debt financing consists mainly of private debt. Between 1993 and 2001, public debts were issued half as frequently as private debts.[1] Within private debt, the bank loan still plays a predominant role in Europe, whereas market debt financing is more common in the US.[2] Nonetheless, bank loans still represent a significant part of covenant-secured debt. In addition, banks are economically stronger in comparison to bondholders, as a bank speaks with one voice[3] and usually has the greatest commitment.[4] Hence, banks and their behaviour—or the way that they enforce covenants after a covenant default—is the appropriate research objects.

[1]Tirole (2006), p. 96. For factors influencing the selection of public and private debts, see also Houston and James (1996).

[2]For Germany, see Deutsche Bundesbank (2012), p. 13; for the UK, see Lund and Wright (1999); for a comparison between the EU and the US, see Societe General (2014), p. 2.

[3]As opposed to bondholders, who are a diverse heterogeneous group.

[4]Taking into account that each bondholder has a lower commitment. However, the overall commitment of all bondholders can be larger.

A binational approach was chosen for the study in order to properly reflect the globalisation of credit markets. The author herself is a German researcher and hence German banks are naturally the objects of research. The second object was selected based on the importance of the US financial market and the Anglo-American origin of covenants. Consequently, US and German banks and their behaviour after a covenant default form the appropriate research objects.[5]

7.3 Expert Interviews

A qualitative study was chosen due to a lack of empirical research.[6] Through its exploratory character, a qualitative study enables new information to be gathered on specific areas of research.[7] The aim of this work will not be to produce statements with universal validity, but to gain a detailed understanding of a few particular cases. It is about the genesis of innovative theoretical knowledge.[8] Thus, a theory-generating method[9] in the form of semi-structured, in-depth expert interviews[10] was chosen. This method requires a semi-structured question guide[11] that provides the broader framework for the interviews but facilitates the theory-generating process.[12]

The expert interviewees were selected according to purposive sampling.[13] Experts are persons who—based on specific practical or experiential knowledge related to a clearly defined problem—have created the opportunity to meaningfully structure and guide the concrete actions of others with their interpretations.[14]

---

[5]The author also held two telephone interviews, which have more of an anecdotal character, with UK bankers who confirmed that the US and UK markets have many things in common, with the exception that the US market does not use the LSTA documents as blueprints while the UK does use the LMA documents as such.

[6]To the author's knowledge, only four empirical studies concerning the problem of third-party creditor protection have been conducted to date: Lou and Otto (2015); Lian (2014); Gao et al. (2013)29.10.2015; Falato and Liang (2012).

[7]For a comparison and overview of quantitative and qualitative research, see Creswell (2014), p. 3 et seqq., 155 et seqq.

[8]Cf. Mayring (2010), p. 16 et seqq.; Glaser and Strauss (1971), p. 1 et seqq.

[9]For an overview of the theory-generating expert interview, see Bogner et al. (2014), p. 25 et seq.

[10]Expert interviews are a prominent qualitative research method in Germany, and are becoming more popular internationally; see Bogner et al. (2014) p. 2.

[11]For further explanations and the interview guide, see Appendix 1.

[12]Bogner et al. (2014), p. 27 et seqq.

[13]Ritchie et al. (2014), p. 113 et seq.

[14]Bogner et al. (2014), p. 13: "die sich – ausgehend von einem spezifischen Praxis- oder Erfahrungswissen, das sich auf einen klar begrenzbaren Problemkreis bezieht – die Möglichkeit geschaffen haben, mit ihren Deutungen das konkrete Handlungsfeld sinnhaft und handlungsleitend für Andere zu strukturieren"; similarly, Sprondel, in: Sprondel, Grathoff (eds) (1979), p. 140 et seqq.

Since the research concentrates on the behaviour and perception of banks after a covenant default, the required expert knowledge must be about banks and their behaviour. Furthermore, the experts must have access to that knowledge through their position and must shape the concrete actions of banks. Thus, experts must be either in a managerial position in a bank or consultants and should have at least 8 years of experience in the field. They must either work for a bank or be legal advisors or consultants for banks or debtor companies.

7.4 Data Collection and Assessment

7.4.1 Conducting the Interviews

As the interviewees were contacted beforehand,[15] they already knew the general topic of the research being carried out—i.e. loan covenants and creditor protection. Furthermore, every interviewee was informed that the interviews would be digitally recorded and that their statements were to be handled anonymously and confidentially, unless specific consent by the interviewee was provided.

To ensure comparability between the interview results, a semi-structured interview type was chosen. An interview guide[16] was developed that included three question blocks. First, the understanding of how covenants function and are enforced was researched. Second, questions were asked that focused on the effects on third-party creditors. Third, the experts were asked about their understanding of the legal treatment of covenants.

The interviews were conducted exclusively by the author as personal or telephone interviews. Interview duration ranged from 16 to 77 min, with an average duration of 36 min. A total of 14 interviews were conducted between September 2014 and July 2015; see Table 7.1.[17]

The sample size was determined on the basis of theoretical saturation—i.e. when only a few new ideas are stated in the interviews.[18] The sampling process was mostly straightforward with few restrictions on access to experts. However, time restrictions might have led to shorter answers. Interview partners were chosen according to the criteria established above regarding what constitutes an expert, and were sought out via internet research.

[15]Via email or telephone.

[16]See Appendix 1.

[17]Some interviews were conducted with two interviewees at the same time. They were coded separately, but the context of the whole interview was taken into consideration.

[18]Glaser and Strauss (1998), p. 69.

Table 7.1 Interviews (own illustration)

Interview no.	Company	Country	Capacity	Interview type
1	Bank	US	Management	In person
2	Bank	US	Management	In person
3	Law firm	US	Legal counsel/consulting	In person
4	Law firm	US	Legal counsel/consulting	In person
5	Bank	Germany	Management	In person
6	Bank	Germany	Management	In person
7	Bank	Germany	Management	In person
8	Bank	Germany	Management	In person
9	Bank	Germany	Management	In person
10	Corporate consulting	Germany	Management	Via telephone
11	Bank	Germany	Management	In person
12	Bank	Germany	Management	In person
13	Law firm	Germany	Legal counsel	In person
14	Law firm	Germany	Legal counsel	In person

7.4.2 Transcription and Coding

The digital recordings were nearly fully transcribed (around 95%) and tagged with time stamps.[19] This process created about 132 pages of material to be used in the ensuing qualitative content analysis.[20] This analysis consists of eight steps. At this stage, the author had already taken the first and second step—deciding on the research question and selecting material. The third step was to build a coding frame. The structure of the coding frame is complex and consists of main categories and subcategories. The main categories were generated deductively by a concept-driven approach that drew upon the interview guide: Private governance, negative effects of covenants on third-party creditors, positive effects of covenants on third-party creditors, and behaviour including third-party creditors. The subcategories were later generated inductively by a data-driven approach.[21] Before and during this process, the fourth (division of material into units of coding), fifth (trying out of coding frame) and six (evaluation and modification of coding frame) steps were conducted. Afterwards, the author undertook the main analysis, which resulted in 319 coding units.

The coding aims to categorise the material and generate a theory.[22] The computer software MAXQDA was used for coding.[23]

[19]The software F4 was used.

[20]The qualitative content analysis was conducted according to Schreier (2013). For an overview of the different types of QCA, see Schreier (2014).

[21]The final coding system corresponds with the headings in Appendix 2.

[22]Flick (2006), p. 296.

[23]For the use and usefulness of computer programs in qualitative content analysis, see, for example, Flick (2006), p. 351 et seqq.; Bogner et al. (2014), p. 83 et seqq.

7.4.3 Limitations and Bias

Several limitations may apply to the research topic. First, the sample is restricted with regard to its diversity as the author was unable to find a female expert who was willing to participate in the study. Hence, the study lacks well-balanced gender distribution. However, this mirrors to a large extent the social structure of finance experts, particularly in Germany, who are predominantly male. The significance or validity of the sampling is therefore not affected.

This gender setting also relates to the issue of interaction. The manner in which the interviewer both interacts with the interviewee and asks questions affects the data that is collected.[24] The interaction method of the interviewer as an expert from a different knowledge culture[25] was chosen, which is best for theory-generating expert interviews.[26] The author sometimes shared some knowledge and thoughts to keep the interviewee interested and maintain a balanced position between the interviewer and interviewee. This procedure is methodologically unproblematic,[27] as experts are not easily influenced and are used to defending their position. However, the interaction method of the interviewer as a layperson[28] was used sporadically when the interviewee had a classical picture of gender roles. The female author exploited this to gain more information since the interviewee feels more confident and under pressure to explain.[29]

Another problem relates to the binational approach of the study. The interviews were conducted in the respective mother tongue of the interviewees to ensure flawless communication of ideas and opinions.[30] The author, who was the interviewer and coder, is fluent in German and English. To ensure that the meaning was not altered, the material was only translated after the author had finished the analysis. The translation is, therefore, not literal[31] and only aims at making the statements accessible to all English-speaking readers. The translations are used for presenting the results of the study but the original statements with their respective translations are reproduced in the Appendix 2.

[24]See, for example, Bogner and Menz (2001), 487 et seqq.

[25]Knowledge level of equal standing; knowledge of terminology but less of field, cf. Bogner and Menz, in: Bogner et al. (eds) (2009), p. 60 et seqq.

[26]Bogner and Menz, in: Bogner et al. (eds) (2009), p. 62.

[27]Bogner and Menz, in: Bogner et al. (eds) (2009), p. 56 describing the interaction even as productive.

[28]A layperson possesses a low level of knowledge of the field.

[29]For the general benefits of the interview interaction "layperson" see Bogner and Menz, in: Bogner et al. (eds) (2009), p. 62 et seqq.; Bogner et al. (2014), p. 52 et seq.; for specific considerations regarding gender aspects see Bogner et al. (2014), p. 55 et seqq.

[30]This is regarded the gold standard, cf. Enzenhofer and Resch (2011; Bogner et al. (2014), p. 44 et seq.

[31]This is a common procedure for international empirical research. See Behling and Law (2000), p. 54 et seq.

Some interviews were conducted with two interviewees at the same time. The author ensured that each question was answered by both experts. The answers of both experts were first transcribed in one document and subsequently separated. This ensured that the author could always compare the context of the passage from the separated interview with that of the combined interviews when ambiguities occurred during the coding process.

Furthermore, the study is limited to bank employees and legal advisors or consultants for banks or debtor companies. Third-party creditors—other than banks—were not interviewed personally, but were represented by legal advisors or consultants who have considerably more experience. Third-party creditors themselves may know of one or two instances where a bank acted in response to a covenant default, whereas advisors and consultants deal with such situations on a daily basis. A subsequent quantitative study is required to analyse the perception of third-party creditors in further detail.

References

Behling O, Law KS (2000) Translating questionaires and other research instruments. Quantitative applications in the social sciences. Sage, London

Bogner A, Menz W (2001) "Deutungswissen" und Interaktion: Zu Methodologie und Methodik des theoriegenerierenden Experteninterviews. Soziale Welt, vol 52. Nomos, Baden-Baden

Bogner A, Menz W (2009) The theory-generating expert interview: epistemological interest, forms of knowledge, interaction. In: Bogner A, Littig B, Menz W (eds) Interviewing experts. Palgrave Macmillan, UK, pp 43–80

Bogner A, Littig B, Menz W (2014) Interviews mit Experten. Eine praxisorientierte Einführung. Springer, Wiesbaden

Creswell JW (2014) Research design: qualitative, quantitative, and mixed methods, 4the edn. Sage, Los Angeles

Deutsche Bundesbank (2012) Die langfristige Entwicklung der Unternehmensfinanzierung in Deutschland-Ergebnisse der gesamtwirtschaftlichen Finanzierungsrechnung. Monatsbericht Januar 2012. https://www.bundesbank.de/Redaktion/DE/Downloads/Veroeffentlichungen/Monatsberichtsaufsaetze/2012/2012_01_unternehmensfinanzierung.pdf?__blob=publicationFile. Accessed 12 Nov 2015

Enzenhofer E, Resch K (2011) Übersetzungsprozesse und deren Qualitätssicherung in der quali tativen Sozialforschung. Forum Qual Soz Forsch/Qual Soc Res 12:Art. 10

Falato A, Liang N (2012) Do creditor rights increase employment risk? Evidence from debt covenants. http://ssrn.com/abstract=2489115. Accessed 18 Feb 2016

Flick U (2006) An introduction to qualitative research, 3rd edn. Sage Publications, London/Thousand Oaks/New Delhi

Gao Y, Khan M, Tan L (2013) Third-party costs of debt covenant violations: the case of audit fees. http://ssrn.com/abstract=2250750

Glaser BG, Strauss AL (1971) The discovery of grounded theory: strategies for qualitative research. Observations, 4th printing edn. Aldine, New York

Glaser BG, Strauss AL (1998) Grounded theory. Strategien qualitativer Forschung. Huber, Bern

Houston J, James CM (1996) Bank information monopolies and mix of private and public debt claims. J Finance 51:1863–1889

Lian Y (2014) Do bondholders receive benefits from bank interventions? http://www.nabet.us/proceedings-archive/NABET-ProceedingsFinal-2014.pdf-page=171. Accessed 6 Apr 2016

Lou Y, Otto CA (2015) Debt heterogeneity and covenants. http://ssrn.com/abstract=2297804. Accessed 8 Apr 2016

Lund M, Wright J (1999) The financing of small firms in the United Kingdom. Bank Engl Q Bull 39(2):195–201

Mayring P (2010) Qualitative Inhaltsanalyse. Grundlagen und Techniken, 11th edn. Beltz, Weinheim

Ritchie J, Lewis J, McNaughton Nicholls C, Ormston R (2014) Qualitative research practice: a guide for social science students and researchers, 2nd edn. Sage, Los Angeles

Schreier M (2013) Qualitative content analysis in practice, reprinted edn. Sage, London

Schreier M (2014) Varianten qualitativer Inhaltsanalyse: Ein Wegweiser im Dickicht der Begriff lichkeiten. Forum Qual Soc Res 15:Art. 18

Societe General Doeass (2014) Eurozone: corporate financing via market: an uneven development within the Eurozone. EcoNote 24:1–8

Sprondel WM (1979) "Experte" und "Laie": Zur Entwicklung von Typenbegriffen in der Wissenssoziology. In: Sprondel WM, Grathoff R (eds) Alfred Schütz und die Idee des Alltags in den Sozialwissenschaften. Enke, Stuttgart, pp 140–154

Tirole J (2006) The theory of corporate finance. Princeton University Press, Princeton

Chapter 8
Results: Covenants as a Reciprocal Private Governance Creditor Protection System

The following chapter will present a summary of the empirical study's results and expert statements will be used to illustrate the findings.[1] First, the results for the covenant's enforcement out of court will be described and discussed. Subsequently, the findings for potential negative externalities will be presented and analysed. This will be followed by the presentation and subsequent discussion of potential positive externalities. Finally, the results showing the influence of third-party creditors on the bank's conduct will be described and discussed.

8.1 Private Governance: Enforcement Out of Court

All interviewed experts implicitly agreed that covenants are commonly enforced out of court. Only four experts, however, stated this explicitly (3, 24; 9, 16; 13, 42; 14, 14). Such private enforcement[2] can also include banks possessing the power to interpret the loan agreement.

> And here we naturally see ourselves in a position to give advice to our customers – even though, from a purely legal perspective, we don't possess the power to interpret the loan agreement. Ultimately it would be only possible to solve this before the court, but this is a purely theoretical measure. Generally, you end up consulting your lawyer – the agent consults the lawyer of the consortium – and an opinion will end up being formed from this. (9, 16)

[1]Those statements as well as all findings are marked by first stating the interview number and then the passage. For example, a statement from Interview 4 in Passage 10 reads "(4, 10)". A complete overview of the coded phrases can be found in Appendix 2.

[2]Private enforcement refers here to the enforcement of contractual rights out of court.

D. Matri, *Covenants and Third-Party Creditors*, DOI 10.1007/978-3-319-62036-7_8

8.1.1 Motivation for Private Enforcement

The experts stated two main reasons as to why covenants are mainly enforced out of court.

First, private enforcement was considered by two experts to be better for both parties as legal enforcement was regarded as too costly and time-consuming. The incurred costs could lead to the bankruptcy of at least one party, but both parties would be left financially weakened (13, 42; 14, 19). The bank is generally more interested in the going-concern surplus and not in the unnecessary bankruptcy of the debtor company (3, 21).

> In contrast, a court trial regularly results in years of uncertainty until the matter is decided in the last instance. This takes years to happen, in which time a party might already become bankrupt. As a consequence you end up with a bankruptcy administrator or you have to build up reserves. No party is interested in doing that. (13, 42)

For that reason, one interviewee stated that the rather rigid framework for the debtor company's behaviour provided by covenants is actually more flexible due to regular communication between the debtor company and bank (9, 34). This regular communication is an important part of private enforcement.

Second, without acceleration of the bank loan, both parties are still in a lock-in situation. It is too costly for either party to default. An acceleration, however, is unlikely, because the legal enforcement of acceleration is considered rather difficult. Both in Germany and the US, there is legal uncertainty with regard to acceleration based only on a covenant default. One US expert stated that termination is difficult if loan payments are made on time, unless the situation is covered under the general insecurity clause (1, 44; 1, 54).

> It is because – for whatever reason – it is just sort of the mind-set that, if you are getting paid, unless you can convince the judge that you are invoking a default under the general insecurity clause it is really hard — probably almost impossible — to enforce a financial covenant. (1, 54)

Furthermore, one interviewee pointed out that, in the US, the risk of equitable subordination and liability leads to fewer intervention options (1, 40).

In Germany, another expert stated that banks are unlikely to accelerate before payment default.

> [...] it is great to have reasons for acceleration stipulated on multiple pages and to have very sophisticated contracts. However, at the end of the day no bank dares to accelerate before payment default. (14, 25)

In Germany, there are also other barriers such as language and knowledge.

> It already starts with the language – namely an English contract. At the moment, the language of the court is German. Except for maybe Cologne, you have to provide a translation. But how does someone translate 4,000 pages? Because we will fight with the other party over the appropriate translation for two years. (14,19)

> There are several areas self-regulated by the market. The market found a standard for itself that works. This standard has not yet been dealt with by current legal literature and the universities – that is why I am really happy that you are here. So it is nearly impossible for a third party to access the topic and understand what happens. (14, 19)

This uncertainty regarding the legal enforcement of covenants seems not always unwanted, because practical experts would like to maintain the status quo of the market.

> Many do that not entirely unintentionally. Many finance lawyers – colleagues you are talking with – know very well that there are topics we do not want to write about because the fear is there that it will have an adverse effect. In this situation you simply say: 'It is better – even though the situation is unsatisfactory – not to thematise this problem. To put it in the hands of judges or someone else would cause more problems than the current status quo'. (14, 13)

This status quo provides some degree of certainty with regard to market standards and supports the presumption that covenants are mainly enforced out of court. This is also corroborated by the fact that one interviewee stated that legal implications are not always considered when drafting a loan agreement (13, 61).

8.1.2 Method of Private Enforcement: Self-enforcing Agreements

The aforementioned lock-in situation ensures that loan contracts are self-enforcing contracts. The interviewed experts confirmed covenants being privately enforced based on leverage (1, 16; 1, 18; 4, 14; 5, 13; 6, 15; 9, 18; 13, 16; 13, 42; 14, 27) and/or the relationship between a bank and debtor company (1, 14; 5, 47; 8, 89; 8, 91; 9, 18; 13, 28; 13, 40).

A covenant breach seems to enable communication; it provides the creditor and the debtor company with the opportunity to adjust to changed circumstances. One expert pointed out that performance-sensitive pricing is a good instrument for ensuring that the debtor company initiates communication.

> Well, a good one is when you are kind of creating pain for the customer. A good way to do that is to have a default interest rate – meaning that the customer can disregard the covenant and can not pay any attention to it, but if the bank increases the interest rate by four hundred bases points, it gets their attention. (1, 16)

A bank generally seems to use the threat to accelerate as leverage (6, 15; 9, 18) and to re-enforce the threat by freezing undrawn credit lines (14, 27). However, the leverage can be weakened if the debtor company has already drawn all credit lines (14, 27).

In addition to the threat to accelerate, the disclosure duties for publicly trading companies in the US appear to strengthen the leverage, because disclosing a covenant default has a negative impact on stock prices.[3]

> If we fully enforced our rights, we would cost you to file with SEC certain documents. On the other hand, maybe there is something else that we can get that would make this more comfortable, where they would not have to file. (1, 18)

Moreover, both a bank and a debtor company want to avoid more creditors at the negotiating table. A debtor company may also try to prevent a cross default so that it is not forced to meet the interests of other creditors (4, 14). In addition, both parties seem to want to avoid high legal costs (see Sect. 8.1.1).

The private enforcement of covenants can also be based on or fostered by a close relationship between a bank and debtor company. Trust and open communication as part of such a close relationship appear to facilitate the bank and debtor company working together to find a solution (9, 18; 13, 28; 13, 40). One expert stated that this could even go so far as a debtor company paying a prepayment penalty that would probably not hold in court in order to save its good relationship with a bank:

> I believe that a long-term relationship of trust where one is also willing to give sometimes or to find a solution that both parties can live with is in the long-term interest of the debtor. And that is my experience with my customers. Some of them have been willing to comply with the demands of the bank even though they did not need to. And those demands concerned high sums. [...] one debtor even said: "No, we have had a relationship of trust for years – we don't want to ruin that because of €500,000. So we are going to pay the prepayment penalty even though we know that we would most likely win before a court." (13, 40)

This shows that a good relationship seems essential for monitoring and enforcing financial covenants (8, 89; 8, 91). However, if a loan is fully secured, the motivation to monitor may be lacking (1, 28).

8.1.3 Discussion

The private enforcement of covenants and an event of default clause is based on their self-enforcing nature: enforcement is ensured due to the bank's leverage in the form of the right to immediate acceleration and/or the relationship between the bank and debtor company. Generally, communication, relationship and covenants seem to go hand in hand. This finding is supported by Greg Nini (et al.), who shows

[3]See only *M. D. Beneish and E. Press*, The Resolution of Technical Default, 70 The Accounting Review (1995), 337; *B. Emser*, Essays in Empirical Corporate Finance: Covenants Violations, Merket Timing and Product Market Competition, PhD thesis, University of Iowa, 2011, available at: http://ir.uiowa.edu/etd/1219, last accessed 14.02.2016, p. 60 et seqq.; *Nini, Smith and Sufi*, 25 Review of Financial Studies (2012), 1713; *A. Ertan and S. A. Karolyi*, Debt Covenants, Expected Default Costs, and the Implicit Cost of Financial Reporting Manipulation, working paper, 2014, available at: https://server1.tepper.cmu.edu/seminars/docs/Karolyipaper.pdf, last accessed 14.02.2016.

that creditors use covenant violation as leverage to exert informal influence on a debtor company.[4] For Germany, the studies by Roland Berger in 2009 and 2014 show that covenant defaults are followed by privately enforced actions such as renegotiations, adaption of credit conditions, pressure to take corrective actions and freezing the credit line.[5]

Moreover, legal restrictions seem to have only a marginal impact on bank's actions; the relationship between the bank and debtor company seems more important.[6] The fact that legal restrictions play a minor role is supported by the empirical study of Adam Badawi.[7] It shows that changes in background legal rules (in Delaware) caused nearly no reaction in loan agreements, whereas bond contracts reacted strongly. Loan agreements are not affected by legal changes because they are privately enforced. This also makes it clear, however, that covenants in bonds are differently enforced due to the collective action problem between bondholders and that the results of this study are restricted to situations where bank creditors are involved.[8]

8.2 Negative Effects on Third-Party Creditors

The marginal impact of legal restrictions on the bank's behaviour suggests that banks will behave selfishly and produce negative externalities. All interviewees identified some form of negative effect for third-party creditors when banks enforce covenants. Two main negative effects were identified: the bank influencing the management not in the interest of all creditors—including the debtor company paying the bank first as well as additional risk premiums—and causing unnecessary bankruptcy or a domino effect.

8.2.1 *Influencing the Management Not in the Interest of All Creditors*

Two ways in which banks could influence the management not in the interest of all creditors were found. First, the debtor company can pay the bank first. This includes paying interest rates, amortisation payments or fees. Because of those payments to the bank, third-party creditors may only be paid partially or not at all. Second, additional premiums can dilute third-party creditors' claims and the debtor company's pool of assets.

[4]Nini et al. (2009); Nini et al. (2012); see also Chava and Roberts (2008).

[5]Haghani et al. (2009), p. 16 et seq.; Haghani et al. (2014), p. 17.

[6]For relational contracts seminal MacNeil (1974); Macaulay (1963).

[7]Badawi (2016).

[8]Cf. also Becker and Ivashina (2016).

8.2.1.1 Debtor Company Pays Bank First or Only Pays Bank

Contractually, a debtor company may only be able to pay third-party creditors under certain circumstances—namely if no covenants are violated (4, 10; 2, 49; 3, 19). In addition, maintenance covenants can generally restrict the payment options.

> If you imagine the same borrower with and without a maintenance covenant: In one scenario, the credit is deteriorating and the maintenance covenant kicks in and either the company is putting into proceeding or has to renegotiate some date. In the other scenario, there is no maintenance covenant and, as a result, maybe the company can continue using a bunch of cash and they can go on and find other places where they can get some cash or sell assets and they can make some additional number of interest payment on junior debt that they otherwise would not be able to make. In a situation like that, it is conceivable to me that there are junior creditors at some level of the capital structure that might end up recovering more money overall in the absence of a maintenance covenant than they would if the maintenance covenant were there. (4, 10)

Similarly, junior debt prepayment covenants can restrict the debtor company's ability to pay junior creditors.

> One of the things that you should always find in a first lien document is a junior debt prepayment covenant. That is what junior creditors do not like because that, in essence, says that the senior lenders are going to treat payments on debt that is junior to their own debt almost like it is an equity payment. In other words, there are going to be restrictions on your ability to, for example, prepay. There may also be limitations under subordination provisions where, if there is a default — payment or bankruptcy default — under senior debt, the subordination provision may even stop interest payments. The subordinated debt typically does not have principal payments until maturity. But it will have semi-annual interest payment, which can usually freely be made. But if there is a bankruptcy or payment default, they are blocked. And for a covenant default on a senior debt, they could have to stand by for a hundred and eighty days, typically — or at least for one interest payment; usually not more than one. (3, 19)

However, a debtor company may feel responsibility towards other third-party creditors and may disregard any contractual payment restrictions (2, 42).

> If it comes to paying back the loan, it is about whom the customer is feeling more obligated to. (2, 42)

This can also include the debtor company having a better relationship with a third-party creditor than with the bank (2, 7; 2, 49).

> So, whomever he has the closest relationship to is probably the one who is getting paid. Even though his loan documents may say that the other creditor is paid first. (2, 49)

8.2.1.2 Additional Risk Premiums

Third-party creditors can, however, be exploited in a different way when additional risk premiums are demanded. Of these additional risk premiums, other than collateral (7, 10; 8, 6; 9, 20; 10, 54; 11, 22; 13, 16; 14, 41; 3, 24; 14, 51), a waiver fee appears to be the most common (9, 20; 10, 54; 13, 16). In addition, margin increase (14, 41) or other accommodations by the debtor company in favour of the bank are likely (13, 16). If a bank is already fully secured then monetary premiums are enforced (4, 12).

Experts stated that if a bank is not fully secured, it is likely that additional security will be demanded (5, 13; 6, 15; 7, 10; 10, 56; 11, 28; 13, 16; 14, 51). One interviewee pointed out that additional security is not always demanded (7, 10). However, four interviewees stated that as long as there is potential collateral left over, it is likely that a bank will request additional collateral (6, 15; 10, 56; 11, 28; 14, 51).

> If there is something left and there is a covenant breach, the request for additional security is never far away. (10, 56)

> And, depending on the situation, there may be an increased need for credit protection. And then, the topic of additional security is on the table. (11, 28)

Nonetheless, the additional collateral may not lead to a fully secured loan.

> However, I have seen few credits that were paid solely by securities. (9, 84)

Regardless of the additional premium demanded, there are certain limits. For example, one interviewee pointed out that management only complies with the bank's requests to a certain extent. In fact, it is assumed they will not act in a way that will make them liable (10, 76).

Moreover, third-party creditors seem to be able to protect themselves (1, 30; 7, 70; 7, 104; 8, 22; 11, 30; 12, 2; 13, 20). This can generally be achieved by a cross-default clause (11, 34; 13, 20). The threat of a domino effect often seems sufficient to ensure that third-party creditor interests are considered.

> Cases where the domino effect occurred do exist – or at least it was used as a threat. That is already enough. So you have to find a way to reconcile all interests. (11, 34)

In that way, the bank and third-party creditors with a cross-default clause are perceived to all be in the same boat.

> If we are faced the situation that the debtor is in financial distress, one has to negotiate with all creditors because – due to the cross-default clause or most preferred clause or however one drafts those clauses – all creditors are finally in the same boat. (13, 20)

Bonds are considered to include cross-default clauses, but they often cannot use their individual rights to accelerate as a threat due to a collective action problem.

> [...] because they know the first-lien bonds, while they rank equal in the capital structure, they cannot get their act together. (3, 29)

Banks as third-party creditors in a syndicated loan (1, 30; 12, 2; 13, 20) are commonly protected through an intercreditor agreement, which ensures equal treatment.

> The tendency towards syndicated loans increases. [...] This provides protection to banks because all banks are in the same boat [...]. (12, 2)

Other creditors without a cross-default clause—like suppliers—can protect themselves or have leverage on their own. For example, a trade creditor may supply something that is critical to the debtor company's operational flow.

> So by the time a borrower gets a troubled credit and is in the situation where it finds out that it is 90 days past making payments to this supplier, everything delivered has to be paid for in cash. (1, 30)

In addition to payment in advance, trade creditors can protect themselves via retention of title (7, 70).

Another relevant class of third-party creditors that are considered to have leverage are factor or leasing creditors, who are often covered by first-class or first-ranking collateral (11, 30).

The majority of experts agreed that the interests of short-term and long-term third-party creditors are taken into consideration. However, it may be difficult for third-party creditors lending for a medium duration (7, 104).

Some third-party creditors are perceived as not only being heard during the renegotiations but also as using their leverage to benefit from the lock-in situation between a bank and debtor company.

> The moment I find myself in financial distress, I inevitably face the problem of small creditors trying to obtain the known 'nagging' premiums or 'nagging' influences. (8, 22)

Nevertheless, the bank's actions seem to have a great impact on third-party creditors' chances of recovery in bankruptcy proceedings.

> Even if the loan is unsecured, the bank will have *de facto* the most power in bankruptcy proceedings – just because the bank will be the biggest creditor. The bank has the power with regard to negotiations, reorganisation negotiations outside bankruptcy. And the bank has the biggest say or biggest influence because it has its finger on the trigger. (14, 51)

At that point, however, the junior debt is considered to be commonly worthless anyway (4, 12).

8.2.2 Unnecessary Bankruptcy and the Domino Effect

Bankruptcy of a debtor company is not always avoidable or uneconomic. Sometimes a debtor company may, however, be driven into avoidable bankruptcy by the domino effect.

> And those cross-default clauses can cause a domino effect that may not reflect the actual situation – it is triggered by the situation on paper. (6, 19)

This seems to be a particular problem if covenants are drafted wrongly (5, 28), if there is no cooperation between creditors (14, 27), and if one creditor regards a covenant default as an exit strategy (5, 17; 5, 30; 10, 34; 13, 12; 13, 38). This was described as the main problem for banks who wanted to continue the relationship with the debtor company, but other banks used the opportunity to exit (5, 30).

> In the offset of the financial crisis, when the companies performed worse than expected and the banks were also affected and everyone was looking for a way out, customers encountered problems – but so did the banks who wanted to continue the relationship. That is, we were not concerned about the debtor, even though his development was a little negative in that particular phase – and understandably so. But other banks activated the emergency brakes, so to speak, leaving little room to resolve the situation. (5, 30)

With acceleration and as a response to the preferential treatment of another creditor (5, 17), the debtor company may be driven into unnecessary bankruptcy (10, 34; 13, 38).

Bonded loans were perceived as a special problem, because under such loans various investors have the individual right to accelerate. Therefore, many creditors have to work together.

> There is a relatively narrow contractual basis for a bonded loan. That's why there are normally many different investors. Basically, each one of them has a right to accelerate when a covenant is violated. This means that if covenants are drafted incorrectly – it does not even have to be incorrect, but generally it is particularly true if covenants are drafted incorrectly – you enter a scenario of accelerations that immediately causes a liquidity shortage for the debtor company. (5, 28)

In addition to a lack of cooperation, unnecessary bankruptcy can also be caused by the primary cost structure of the bank loan, as it hinders the restructuring and recapitalisation of the debtor company (7, 104).

Two experts, however, pointed out that if a bank loan was accelerated the domino effect would be irrelevant, because the regular debtor company would be insolvent straight away (12, 31; 13, 36).

> [...] regardless of how solvent a debtor is, if the bank accelerates and immediately recalls its loan, every company is bankrupt. (13, 36)

Furthermore, it seems that the domino effect is rarely witnessed in reality (13, 36) but is more frequently used as threat to ensure equal treatment (11, 34). This is due to a number of reasons. First, for a domino effect to occur, a cross-default or cross-acceleration is required. These are generally regarded as standard in loan contracts, because they provide protection against a worsened position.

> So, the cross-default clause is standard because that is the only means to protect oneself when something happens from a third party. (11, 14)

Five interviewees confirmed the fact that, nowadays, both cross-default and cross-acceleration clauses seem to be standard in all loan agreements—not only bank loan agreements (3, 24; 3, 26; 11, 14; 12, 8; 14, 45; 13, 10). This does not mean that they must be triggered in all cases (3, 24; 4, 10; 10, 42; 12, 27); the bank has to actually accelerate the bank loan in order to trigger a domino effect.[9]

[9]In case of a default clause, a third-party creditor that is protected by a cross-default clause may, of course, be the first to accelerate and thereby start the domino effect. However, the domino effect will generally be triggered by a bank as it has the biggest commitment and thus the biggest signalling effect.

However, a termination was considered highly unlikely by eight interviewed experts (2, 17; 3, 24; 5, 10; 5, 17; 8, 6; 9, 18; 9, 52; 12, 31; 14, 25). This is due to a number of reasons.

First, a bank seems to be in no better position than other senior unsecured creditors in bankruptcy proceedings if it is unsecured (9, 82). Moreover, a bank appears to generally have the biggest commitment (9, 22; 9, 84) and, thereby, the most to lose.

> Then, there is a cross-default and the consortium banks are in the unattractive situation of having to provide the fresh money injection – because they commonly hold the greatest commitments – to keep the whole thing alive. (9, 22)

> [. . .] banks have a massive interest in putting the debtor company back into a reasonable situation to generate cash flows out of which the loan can be paid. (9, 84)

A bank may also be interested in the going-concern surplus of the debtor company. If a debtor company continues and is recapitalised, the bank's earnings are perceived to be higher (3, 21; 4, 12; 13, 38). A bank may also want to keep larger debtor companies that are commonly restructured as customers.

> It is particularly true for an investment bank in a sponsor deal or, for that matter, large companies that tend to go through bankruptcy but never go away. (3, 21)

Also, when a debt is undersecured, the interest in keeping the debtor company alive to produce cash flow seems higher (4, 12).

Finally, a bank may not accelerate due to a mere breach of covenant (2, 17; 3, 24) because it does not want to talk to all third-party creditors with a cross-acceleration clause.

> So once the lenders actually accelerate, the lenders are no longer the only ones with a seat at the table. (3, 24)

8.2.3 Discussion

These findings show that the provision of additional risk premiums and, thereby, a dilution of the debtor company's asset pool appears likely, whereas other potential negative externalities seem rather unlikely. Covenants can only restrict the payment behaviour of the debtor company to a certain extent. If a debtor company has a closer relationship to a third-party creditor, it may pay this third-party creditor first. Similarly, an unnecessary bankruptcy is improbable because banks seem averse to termination for four main reasons. First, the unsecured part of the bank loan ranks equal to all other unsecured creditors in bankruptcy. Second, the bank seems to have the most to lose because it commonly has the biggest commitment. Third, the bank appears to be interested in the debtor company's going concern surplus due to a higher overall profit. Finally, banks seem to dislike acceleration because, then, most creditors have a seat at the table.

This is supported by Yihui Wang's and Han Xia's empirical study from the US, which found that an acceleration following a covenant default only occurred in 6% of the cases.[10] Similar results were presented by Michael Roberts and Amir Sufi, who found a loan to be terminated after a covenant default 4% of the time.[11] The findings may be contradicted for Germany by the Roland Berger study from 2009, which found a termination occurred in 20% of cases.[12] Their study from 2014, however, found acceleration in zero cases.[13] The authors of the study attribute the discrepancy between 2009 and 2014 to the bad macro-economy in 2009.[14] The derivation of the numbers, however, is unclear. In the study from 2009, the authors themselves stated that a termination after a covenant default is rare and quantified it at 8% (compared to the aforementioned 20% stated in the study from 2014 for 2009).[15] Due to these inaccuracies, the Roland Berger study is inconclusive. The finding that an acceleration is improbable can thus be regarded as unrefuted.

The potential negative externality of an additional risk premium—namely asset dilution—depends on the demanded risk premium. The findings suggest that waivers are most common. This is supported i.a. by Wang's and Xia's empirical study, which found that banks waive the default in 50.4% of the cases.[16] The current study, however, also indicates that additional collateral is a common reaction after a covenant default. This is somewhat contrary to the results of Wang and Xia; they found that in 49.6% of cases, banks changed the terms of the loan after a covenant violation.[17] Hereby, banks decrease the size of existing loan facilities agreements in 47% of cases, increase interest rates in 41% of cases, and issue additional or new collateral in only 8% of cases.[18] Similar results were presented by Roberts and Sufi, where additional collateral was provided 7% of the time.[19]

The different results could be due to either a disparity in the US and German markets or the qualitative nature of the current study. It is questionable whether German banks are more likely to react to a covenant default by demanding additional collateral than US banks. In fact, the Roland Berger studies indicate that this is not the case. In 2009 it found that, in 14% of cases, a countermeasure was

[10] Wang and Xia (2014), 2383.

[11] Roberts and Sufi (2009), 1688.

[12] At least according to their study in 2014 Haghani et al. (2014), p. 17 but compare Haghani et al. (2009), p. 17.

[13] Haghani et al. (2014), p. 17.

[14] Haghani et al. (2014), p. 17.

[15] Haghani et al. (2009), p. 17.

[16] Wang and Xia (2014), 2383. See also Chen and Wei (1993) (where they found that 48 percent of covenant defaults were waived) and Roberts and Sufi (2009), 1688 (where they found that 63 percent of covenant defaults were waived).

[17] Similar Roberts and Sufi (2009), 1688 (where they found that 32 percent of covenant defaults were followed by a lender reaction other than waiver or acceleration).

[18] Wang and Xia (2014), 2383.

[19] Roberts and Sufi (2009), 1688.

taken.[20] This includes, among other things, additional collateral. In 2014, the frequency dropped to as low as 9%.[21] These results can only be regarded as indication due to the aforementioned inaccuracies.[22] Nevertheless, it seems reasonable to suggest that the different results are a consequence of distinct empirical methods (qualitative vs. quantitative). The current qualitative study reflects the bank's high desire to demand additional collateral. *De facto*, however, this may not always be possible. This is reflected in the results of the aforementioned quantitative empirical studies. The results of the current study should thus be considered in a different way: Banks would like to demand additional collateral after a covenant default. In the majority of cases, however, additional collateral may not be available due to a lack of sufficient or visible collateral, legal uncertainties, and/or high transaction costs.

8.3 Positive Effects on Third-Party Creditors

The experts also identified two positive effects for third-party creditors when banks enforce covenants. First, covenants and their enforcement discipline the debtor company. Second, covenants facilitate the reduction of information asymmetry between third-party creditors and the debtor company.

8.3.1 Disciplinary Effects

Covenants and their enforcement may discipline the debtor company in three ways. Third-party creditors seem to obtain similar rights to banks. Covenants may also ensure a larger pool of assets and keep the debtor company solvent.

8.3.1.1 Similar Rights for Third-Party Creditors

Three experts explicitly stated that debtor companies must comply with the strictest covenant (3, 24; 4, 10; 6, 12) before a covenant default.

[20] Haghani et al. (2009), p. 16.

[21] Haghani et al. (2014), p. 17.

[22] Also for countermeasures, discrepancy exists between the reported numbers in the 2014 study for 2009 and the numbers in the 2009 study itself. Haghani et al. (2014), p. 17 (reporting 40 % for counter measures in 2009); Haghani et al. (2009), p. 16 (reporting 14 % for counter measures in 2009).

> The company always needs to adhere to its stricter covenants. [...] The more strengthened covenants and the more senior the debt, the more they serve some practical protection for the junior lenders. (3, 24)

> Oftentimes, an issuer has both bank loans and bonds in its capital structure. So, effectively, the tighter of the two sets of covenants are the ones that control. There might be transactions that a borrower might want to undertake that it could under one set of covenants but it could not under the other, and the undertaking could be risky. Obviously the creditors behind the looser document are benefitting from the tighter of the two, as a practical matter. (4, 10)

In addition, to ensure uniformity of conditions (9, 28; 13, 26; 14, 49), financial ratios may be assimilated as far as is sensible to facilitate documentation and monitoring for the debtor company (9, 28).

> That is why it is often sensible from the debtor's perspective to accept maybe slightly stricter or tighter covenants – but that are still homogenous in all financing agreements – so that basically all you have to do is create one checklist and work through it. (13, 26)

After a covenant default, the third-party effects depend on the bank's behaviour. Two interviewed experts stated that the negative pledge clause has been enforced to ensure that no collateral is provided (6, 12; 12, 10). However, one of them also said that the negative pledge clause is regularly enforced to achieve equal treatment in the form of a collateral pool.

> 'You are prohibited from collateralising anyone, but if you do then you have to treat us equally.' If you find out that someone got collateral, then you have to say: "I want to participate, or at least I want an equivalent collateral." And then you get into a situation where you create a collateral pool. (6, 7)

On the other hand, the principle of equal treatment is regarded as an essential basis for the relationship between a creditor and debtor company and, thereby, also between creditors (9, 42; 12, 10).

> Equal treatment is a really, really important topic. It should go without saying that you do not suddenly provide another bank with collateral. (9, 42)

In addition, cross-default clauses (1, 22; 9, 48; 11, 14; 11, 32; 12, 8; 13, 12; 14, 45) are stipulated for precisely this purpose of equal treatment.

> I believe that banks in particular fear that the devil will take the hindmost. They naturally want to be able to pull the plug and make a fast to exit in case of financial distress – and a default under a different contract also constitutes financial distress. (13, 12)

One interviewee pointed out that the cross-default clause may not provide you with the same rights, but does provide you with a means of being involved in the negotiation process.

> The cross-default clause is an important thing to have. Even though it might not help you necessarily, it brings everybody to the table so you are able to discuss what the issues are with the credit. (1, 22)

Three experts supported the statement that cross-default clauses nowadays seem to be standard in all loan agreements, not just in bank loan agreements (11, 14; 12, 8; 14, 45). Two interviewees, however, claimed that often only a cross-acceleration clause is stipulated (3, 24; 3, 26; 13, 10). Both types of clauses face, to a certain extent, the problem that terms of the loan agreement between the bank and debtor company can be changed without the consent of third-party creditors (3, 18; 3, 24; 4, 10; 9, 34; 12, 27).

> [...] because they can be changed through renegotiations with the consortium banks without triggering a cross-default, or via a different method of refinancing. (12, 27)

A cross-default clause may also not be triggered due to the default being waived or cured within a specified grace period. This allows the debtor company and the bank to avoid dealing with third-party creditors, as including other creditors can cause coordination and cooperation problems. This seems particularly true for bondholders.

> That is, when a cross-default between a syndicated loan and bond occurs, you face the situation that you can control and steer the syndicated loan with a majority of consortium banks, but you must get all bondholders on board. And the more heterogeneous the bondholder structure, the more difficult it becomes. (11, 32)

On the other hand, this also weakens the ability of bondholders to enforce their rights. Bondholders are perceived as too diverse to coordinate (3, 29).

8.3.1.2 Ensuring a Larger Pool of Assets

Covenants can also ensure a larger pool of assets if the negative pledge clause is enforced to ensure that no collateral is provided (6, 12; 12, 10). However, as shown before, the negative pledge clause may also be enforced to achieve equal treatment. In that case, the bank participates in a collateral pool (6, 7; 9, 52), which reduces rather than ensures the debtor company's asset pool. Furthermore, a bank may demand additional security after a covenant default in some cases if the debt is not fully secured (see Sect. 8.2.3), which will further decrease the debtor company's pool of assets.

8.3.1.3 Keeping the Debtor Company Solvent

The enforcement of covenants, however, appears to often aim at keeping the debtor company solvent, the motivation for which seems manifold. First, interviewees pointed out that banks have a sense of responsibility to society and the debtor company's employees (9, 86; 11, 46; 13, 38).

> A company depends on the continuation of the credit and, thereby, on the relationship it has with the bank. And because the company may be in a special situation, perhaps there is no other bank the company could approach and therefore I basically cannot exit this relationship. It is an ethical responsibility of the bank not to abuse this position of power. However, it is not condemnable *per se* but actually normal that the bank should try to occupy the best negotiation position. (11, 46)

Second, the bank may have the biggest commitment, and thereby, the most to lose (9, 18; 9, 84; 11, 36).

> However, every bank has to consider whether it is rewarding to recall the loan principal in such a situation when you have the biggest commitment outstanding and it is usually not paid back. (9, 18)

Thus, interviewees give greater consideration to the going-concern value of the debtor company than its cut-off value (4, 12; 13, 38). Generally, the motivation of creditors depends on the duration of the credit—namely short-term, mid-term or long-term. A bank's investment intentions are mainly long-term, and therefore banks usually seem to make relationship investments (2, 44; 9, 26; 9, 32; 11, 20; 11, 48; 13, 28; 13, 40; 14, 35). Due to the relationship, a bank is considered more likely to support the debtor company if in financial distress.

> We know that life is not all sunshine and roses and we are ready to face those situations with companies. However, the customer has to take you on the journey with him and inform you on time when there is an issue [. . .]. (9, 32)

However, some banks that should find it easier to establish a relationship due to geographical closeness, may not be able to use this advantage or do not even try to.

> The worst thing is that regional and local banks – which should have a better on-site relationship – don't adopt that position, choosing instead to participate fully in the margin business. It's also possible that they have to participate, but apparently they are not heard when they say – or maybe they don't even try to say – "So, you can obviously go with this cheap loan, but in the long run it is not worth it because those who give the money today so easily are the first who take it away." (11, 48)

Those banks may be faster to accelerate a loan than banks that are interested in the relationship.

> [. . .] these stable relationships and trust one has built also lead to better communication with the bank in times of crisis, and the bank is also more willing to go along with you than they would be without those years spent building a relationship. (13, 28)

Relationship lenders seem not only interested in the repayment of the loan principal and interest rate, but also in relationship rents (3, 21; 14, 39).

> A lot of the investment banks are relationship lenders. They do a lot of things with these sponsors, more than just this one loan deal – M&A advisory and other things. You want to maintain the relationship as much as possible. (3, 21)

One interviewee pointed out that a relationship is valuable because the acquiring costs are high and the competition between banks is intensive (14, 39). Moreover, some bigger companies are perceived

> [. . .] to go through bankruptcy but never go away. (3, 21)

The general motivation of banks seems to be to preserve equity value. This will reduce the shareholder creditor conflict for all creditors to some extent (3, 15; 9, 84; 10, 48; 12, 35; 13, 38).

> On the one hand it – that is, financial covenants – can have a disciplinary effect that the company is anxious to comply with the financial ratios and that it is not too optimistic regarding investments – that it does not go down the wrong track. (13, 38)

Nevertheless, one interviewee stated that the efforts to support and discipline a debtor company are limited due to overregulation (8, 81).

8.3.2 *Information Sharing*

As worked out in the theoretical section of this work, covenants produce information for third-party creditors. This information, however, must be shared with third-party creditors to be of value to them.

8.3.2.1 Information Shared by the Debtor Company

If a contractual duty to inform exists, interviewees generally assessed that debtor companies take such a duty seriously (1, 26; 6, 2; 9, 32; 13, 55; 13, 57). In case of default under another loan, the debtor company may be obliged to inform third-party creditors with a cross-default clause (1, 22; 1, 26; 13, 55).

> It is standard practice – and will be stipulated in the loan agreement of bank X – to include a clause requiring the debtor to inform about any reasons for acceleration. And a cross-default constitutes, of course, a reason for acceleration – namely that there is a default under the loan contract of bank Y. (13, 55)

Early communication is particularly likely to be initiated by the debtor company for syndicated loans and if the debtor company is larger (6, 2).

One interviewee pointed out that, generally, it is a smart move for the debtor company to be transparent with all creditors.

> So if the company is smart, it will deal with other creditors in an appropriately transparent way. The other creditors will hear about it anyway. (10, 66)

Another interviewee stated that a good consultant could also play an important role in initiating the communication between a debtor company and creditors (14, 29). A bank may also instigate a dialogue when it requires a guarantee from other creditors that their credits are continued (11, 30).

8.3.2.2 Informal Exchange Between Creditors

A multi-party negotiation seems likely when a substantial problem occurs (1, 24; 7, 35; 9, 26; 11, 40; 12, 6; 13, 36; 14, 27; 14, 45).

> If you get into that situation where you might find yourself trying to exchange information in case of a troubled credit, there might be a meeting of creditors called — informally,

outside of court – where you have an exchange of ideas and all lenders are there. You are certainly not handing everybody what your loan agreements are, but you could certainly say: "I have got a default and I am willing to do this or that if I get X". Then, it is kind of a multiple-party negotiation with the original borrower and the other creditors. (1, 24)

Those multi-party negotiations are described as following an informal structure, similar to that of bankruptcy court proceedings (1, 56; 14, 29).

In bankruptcy court proceedings there is a lot of opportunity cost and reputation cost involved. You essentially set up a structure that mirrors what you get in bankruptcy court, but without that additional time, expense and money. If everyone is in agreement with it, it works out great. But it only takes one rogue lender or one party that maybe has a material interest so that it does not want to agree to that for the whole thing to fall apart. (1, 56; for the US)

By now, in Germany, such a committee of creditors has been established. [...] Now we have terms in these transactions – like a steering committee – and then that means five or six banks out of the big circle with one leading bank. However, they must form themselves; there are no legal means to force a formation. (14, 29; for Germany)

The information exchange is fostered by the fact that the market is interlinked. Creditors are perceived as networked (5, 49; 6, 34; 6, 36) and may talk with each other on a regular basis (1, 26; 6, 36; 14, 47). This seems to be particularly true for banks (6, 36; 14, 47).

One has to be in the market, close to the customer and to know who is also close to the customer. Basically, one must be networked. Otherwise it won't work. (5, 49)

The statement from an expert regarding the use of involuntary bankruptcy for information sharing in the US provides further proof that information sharing is considered beneficial (1, 26; 1, 54):

Banks typically do not like to get into bankruptcy court. But sometimes you do, due to the fact that you have this general information sharing, and then you have a structure around what is occurring. (1, 54)

This also shows that there are problems with the informal information exchange. For example, the first discussion may only include the creditor or those creditors that have the strictest terms. The other creditors appear to be left out (4, 14; 13, 57).

Then, you normally speak with the bank under whose contractual terms the matter was prohibited and not with other banks. You settle the problem with, for example, bank X, and bank Y is left out. Only if bank X is not willing to waive the default would you maybe start talking to bank Y. (13, 57)

Also, debtor companies are seen to dislike disclosure. One interviewee pointed out that public companies

[...] go private if they are in a work-out situation or if there is some strategy that they are trying to implement that might be viewed unfavourably by the investment community. And so they have private investors, obviously, that they have to answer to, but there is less pressure to perform immediately. So you have got more flexibility to take a longer view or a longer tag if you need to. (1, 20)

Moreover, information exchange faces legal restrictions (1, 24; 12, 43).

> [...] if we talk about lasting deterioration, then everybody must be at the table. However, only the company can initiate that. We have banking secrecy. You cannot initiate that as a creditor, even if you know about the other from the accounting records. (12, 43)

And as a practical matter, a debtor company can conceal problems (5, 49). The bank has to trust that the debtor company will inform it of these problems in a timely manner (6, 22; 11, 16). This highlights once again the importance of relationship lending.

8.3.2.3 Information Provided by Third Parties

Information can also be provided by third parties. General information regarding market standards, for example, is provided by the LMA and the LSTA, but in the US also by specialised law firms (3, 31). Two interviewed experts also suggested that covenants or covenant defaults may influence the rating of the debtor company (7, 47; 8, 53). Another interviewee pointed out that as long as covenant default exists, auditors will only give a qualified opinion (9, 74).

Communication through legal practitioner publications is, to a certain extent, deliberately avoided (14, 13).

8.3.2.4 Discussion

First, covenants seem to provide similar rights before a covenant default to ensure uniformity of covenants or due to the disciplinary effect of the strictest covenants. This disciplinary effect is confirmed by Yili Lian, who found that bank intervention positively affects the value of bondholders.[23] Similarly, Scott Dyreng found that the debtor company's management may adjust investment decisions to meet covenants.[24] After a covenant default, third-party creditors have similar rights due to cross-default or cross-acceleration clauses. A Cross-default clause seems to be regarded as more common than the cross-acceleration clause.

Second, the potential positive externality of preventing asset dilution and keeping the debtor company solvent depends on the bank's conduct after a covenant default. The findings are inconclusive regarding whether a negative pledge clause is enforced to prevent an asset dilution for all creditors or only to ensure equal treatment for the bank (additional collateral for the bank or a collateral pool). Further empirical research is required to clarify the banks' conduct after a breach of a negative pledge clause.

Nevertheless, banks generally appear to be interested in keeping the debtor company solvent. First, banks seem to have a sense of responsibility to society and

[23] Lian (2014).

[24] Dyreng (2009). See also Bulan and Hull (2013) (where they found that after a covenant default, the likelihood of a dividend reduction significantly increases in the subsequent quarter).

employees. Initially, this appears contrary to the two empirical studies that found a positive correlation between the deterioration of financial conditions of debtor companies with tight covenants and a decrease in employment.[25] However, Nuri Ersahin (et al.) shows that the employment reduction is concentrated within the peripheral business activities of the debtor company, resulting in a refocus on the core and productive business of the debtor company.[26] This increases the overall value of the debtor company. Although fewer employees may be employed after a covenant default, their long-term employment can be ensured. Moreover, banks appear to have the most to lose due to their holding the biggest commitment and the most to gain from long-term relationship with a debtor company (relationship rents).

Finally, the value of the produced information by a covenant default depends on information sharing with third-party creditors. This study found that the debtor company seems likely to inform at least the largest third-party creditors about a covenant default. If a substantial problem occurs, a multi-party negotiation seems to be common. This process may also be fostered by third-parties such as advisors, auditors and rating agencies.

8.4 Influence of Third-Party Creditors on the Bilateral Private Governance System

Why and how third-party creditors are included in renegotiations after (or in anticipation of) a covenant default will be discussed next.

8.4.1 Linked Contracts

Third-party creditors can influence the bank's conduct if their contracts are linked via a cross-default, pari passu or negative pledge clause. Because of this linkage, they are perceived to have the ability to drive the debtor company into bankruptcy and can use that as leverage to influence the bank (1, 22; 6, 22; 7, 33; 7, 35; 9, 22; 9, 26; 11, 32; 11, 34; 11, 36; 12, 6; 12, 10; 13, 20; 14; 27; 14, 45). This is particularly true for bondholders and other banks.

Their leverage, however, is limited if only a cross-acceleration clause is stipulated. Three interviewees supported the statement that, nowadays, the cross-default clause is a standard component of all loan agreements, not only bank loan agreements (11, 14; 12, 8; 14, 45). However, two experts claimed that often only a cross-acceleration clause is present (3, 24; 3, 26; 13, 10). In any case, banks can avoid the

[25] Falato and Liang (2012), ; already in that direction Cronqvist et al. (2009).

[26] Ersahin et al. (2016).

cross-default or cross-acceleration clause being triggered (3, 24; 4, 10; 10, 42; 12, 27). Provided there is early communication, a bank can waive a default or the debtor company can cure it within the grace period. For the cross-acceleration clause, it is also sufficient to simply abstain from accelerating the loan.

Third-party creditors may face the problem that they lack relevant information (5, 41; 11, 16; 11, 46) due to information asymmetry (11, 46). Even if they have the relevant information, third-party creditors may have a collective action problem—bondholders in particular are often too diverse to bundle their interests (3, 29).

8.4.2 Banks as Third-Party Creditors in a Small Community

When other banks are third-party creditors, the informal exchange appears to be facilitated by the fact that the banking community is small (8, 34; 9, 36; 11, 38; 14, 19).

> In the end – at least this is my impression – it is like a round of poker. Everyone knows the documents in detail, is prepared well in advance and everyone knows their rights. And even those who hold all the aces will make concessions, because they know that "if I do not come up to meet the other banks – in which way whatsoever – then there will be a second case with a different company where we are interlinked again and then they are going to punch me in the face". (8, 34)

One interviewee, however, pointed out that this incentive structure has its limits.

> Let's say, for example, that there is a Mr. Y at the bank in Osnabrück. If he wants to play tough, he won't care if we are also holding negotiations with his colleague Z in Hannover. So it always depends on the situation. (11, 38)

8.4.3 Third-Party Creditors That Are Essential for Operational Business

Third-party creditors such as trade creditors are perceived to have leverage on the bank when they are essential for the debtor company's operational business (1, 30; 9, 26).

> And then you might have other creditors that might not have a formal loan agreement, but they supply something that is critical to the operational flow of the company. They probably do not have covenants. But, on the other hand, they are usually delivering something on a relatively frequent basis to the customer that the customer needs to keep its doors open. (1, 30)

One interviewee stated that leasing creditors (11, 30; 11, 40) can also be essential for the operational business and therefore must be included in negotiations.

> [...] making use of leased items would be a risk in the sense of: Is the company still able to produce or trade? (11, 30)

Not all trade creditors can be involved in negotiations with banks. For that reason, trade creditors may often be represented by their trade credit insurers (9, 26; 12, 43; 14, 51).

> Generally, you have the trade credit insurer on board because they ensure active life on the supplier side. For that reason, efforts are made to find a solution that is acceptable to all involved parties. There, the smallest is sometimes the one who can make the difference and the banks in bank consortiums are first bound together. (9, 26)

> A really important group, which is not directly on balance sheet, is, for example, trade credit insurers. In that moment in which a trade credit insurer says: "For heavens' sake, I'm out", it's possible that delivery will stop is and the company may not be able to operate anymore. (12, 43)

A trade credit insurer reimburses the insured party (trade creditor) for any loss incurred by their debtor's non-payment of valid debt.[27] The insured trade creditor must assign its claim against the debtor company to the trade credit insurer if it uses the insurance. In case of bankruptcy, therefore, the debtor company has usually to deal with the trade credit insurer anyway.

8.4.4 Sense of Responsibility

Generally, banks may consider third-party creditors' interests due to a sense of responsibility. Three experts stated that they believe that banks try to act responsibly (9, 86; 11, 46; 13; 38).

> And I believe that banks, on the other hand, are very responsible in most cases and try to manage the whole thing in a way that is fair for everyone – even in difficult times. (9, 86)

> My experience is that banks are really reluctant to drive a company into bankruptcy because banks are aware of the fact that they have a certain responsibility both to society and the employees of the company. (13, 38)

This shows that banks are at least aware of the fact that their actions can deeply affect third-party creditors such as employees.

8.4.5 Discussion

Third-party creditors influence the bank's reaction to a covenant default in different ways. In fact, an interdependency between a bank and the third-party creditors can be observed. First, the bank's loan agreement may be linked with that of third-party

[27] For an overview of trade credit insurances, see Baumann (1966), p. 18 et seqq.; Greulich (1975), p. 20 et seqq.; Grauschopf, in: Veith et al. (eds) (2016), paras. 10, 21 et seqq.; Jus (2013).

creditors by a cross-default, negative pledge or pari passu clause. Second, the interests of a bank and third-party creditors may be connected. This alignment of interests is created by third-party creditors, who are essential for the operational business threatening to drive the debtor company into bankruptcy. It is also fostered by the fact that the banking community is small and that trade credit insurers represent trade creditors. The empirical study by Yun Lou and Clemens Otto, which finds that covenants can also address conflicts between creditors and that heterogeneity of debts influences covenant settings, supports the interdependency theory of creditors.[28]

8.5 Conclusion

The empirical study proved the presumption that banks disregard third-party creditor's interests wrong. Covenants and the event of default clause are indeed enforced out of court. Therefore, they create a bilateral private governance system and legal restrictions only have a marginal impact on the bank's conduct. This private governance system yields potentially positive and negative externailities for third-party creditors. The main potential negative externality is asset dilution due to additional risk premiums, whereas the main potential positive externalities are keeping the borrower solvent and producing information after a covenant default that is likely to be shared with third-party creditors. The fact that the positive externalities seem to outweigh the negative externalities is due to the interdependency between the bilateral private governance system and the third-party creditors; see Fig. 8.1.

This interdependency transforms the bilateral private governance into a multiparty private governance system, which allows for the internalisation of potential negative externalities. The interdependency is based on two aspects: First, the bank's loan agreement can be linked with that of third-party creditors via a cross-default, negative pledge or pari passu clause. Second, the interests of a bank and third-party creditors may be connected. This is achieved by third-party creditors who are essential for the operational business threatening to drive the debtor company into bankruptcy. This is particularly true for trade creditors. Banks are willing to consider the trade creditors' interests to ensure the continuancy of the debtor company because banks regularly have the biggest commitments and stand to lose the most in case of bankruptcy. In addition, banks are interested in the relationship rents.

Furthermore, the fact that the banking community is small and that trade credit insurers represent trade creditors fosters an alignment of interests. The bank industry—and particularly the international lending community—is small enough so that banks will have various common debtors with different rights and priorities. Similarly, trade credit insurers will be involved with different debtor companies of

[28]Lou and Otto (2015).

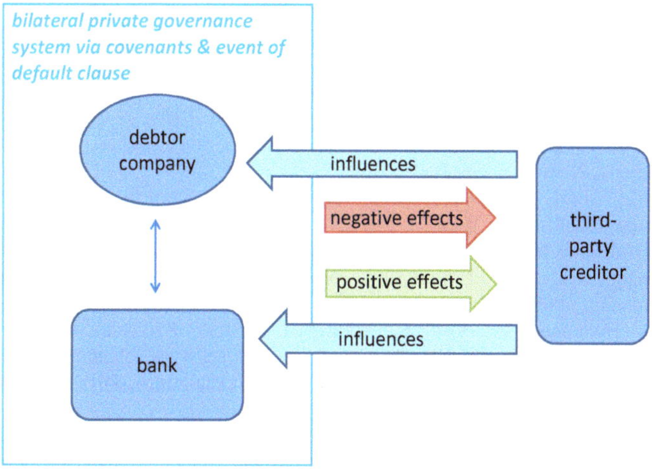

Fig. 8.1 Reciprocal system (own illustration)

the bank. Thus, even if a bank could theoretically have all the advantages, it might not use them in order to ensure the cooperation of a third-party creditor in a different case.

Nevertheless, further studies should be conducted concentrating on other covenant-secured creditors and the perception of third-party creditors to concretise, broaden or limit the theory developed.

References

Badawi AB (2016) Debt contract terms and creditor control. http://scholarship.law.berkeley.edu/law_econ/Spring2016/Schedule/11/. Accessed 6 Apr 2016

Baumann HA (1966) Factoring, Warenkreditversicherung, Zessionskredit. Eine vergleichende Darstellung. Schön, München

Becker B, Ivashina V (2016) Covenant-light contracts and creditor coordination. http://ssrn.com/abstract=2756926. Accessed 6 Apr 2016

Beneish MD, Press E (1995) The resolution of technical default. Account Rev 70:337–353

Bulan L, Hull T (2013) The impact of technical defaults on dividend policy. J Bank Financ 37(3): $32#814–823

Chava S, Roberts MR (2008) How does financing impact investment? The role of debt covenants. J Finance 63:2085–2121

Chen KCW, Wei KCJ (1993) Creditors' decisions to waive violations of accounting-based debt covenants. Account Rev 68:218–232

Cronqvist H, Heyman F, Nilsson M, Svaleryd H, Vlachos J (2009) Do entrenched managers pay their workers more? J Finance 64:309–339

Dyreng SD (2009) The cost of private debt covenant violation. http://www.kellogg.northwestern.edu/accounting/papers/Dyreng.pdf. Accessed 6 Apr 2016

Ersahin N, Irani RM, Le H (2016) Creditor control rights and resource allocation within firms. http://business.illinois.edu/rirani/ErsahinIraniLe_CovenantsResourceAllocation.pdf. Accessed 6 Apr 2016

Falato A, Liang N (2012) Do creditor rights increase employment risk? Evidence from debt cove nants. http://ssrn.com/abstract=2489115. Accessed 18 Feb 2016

Grauschopf J (2016) § 22 Kreditversicherung. In: Veith J, Gräfe J, Gebert Y (eds) Der Versicherungsprozess. Nomos, Baden-Baden

Greulich H (1975) Die Kreditversicherung, vol 43. Taschenbücher für Geld, Bank und Börse. Fritz Knapp, Frankfurt am Main

Haghani S, Holzamer M, Voll S, Warnig C (2009) Financial Covenants in der Unternehmens finanzierung. Roland Berger. http://www.rolandberger.com/media/pdf/Roland_Berger_Finan cial_Covenants_20090725.pdf. Accessed 7 Mar 2013

Haghani S, Holzamer M, Voll S, Warnig C (2014) Financial Covenants in der Unternehmensfinanzierung 2014. Roland Berger. http://www.rolandberger.de/media/pdf/Roland_Berger_Financial_Covenants_Unternehmensfinanzierung_20141210.pdf. Accessed 7 Apr 2016

Jus M (2013) Credit insurance. Elsevier Science, San Diego

Lian Y (2014) Do bondholders receive benefits from bank interventions? http://www.nabet.us/proceedings-archive/NABET-ProceedingsFinal-2014.pdf-page=171. Accessed 6 Apr 2016

Lou Y, Otto CA (2015) Debt heterogeneity and covenants. http://ssrn.com/abstract=2297804. Accessed 8 Apr 2016

Macaulay S (1963) Non-contractual relations in business: a preliminary study. Am Sociol Rev 28:55–67

MacNeil I (1974) Many futures of contract. South Calif Law Rev 47:691–816

Nini G, Smith DC, Sufi A (2009) Creditor control rights and firm investment policy. J Financ Econ 92:400–420. doi:10.1016/j.jfineco.2008.04.008

Nini G, Smith DC, Sufi A (2012) Creditor control rights, corporate governance, and firm value. Rev Financ Stud 25:1713–1761

Roberts MR, Sufi A (2009) Control rights and capital structure: an empirical investigation. J Finance 64:1657–1695

Wang Y, Xia H (2014) Do lenders still monitor when they can securitize loans? Rev Financ Stud 27:2354–2391

Chapter 9
Re-evaluation: Collectivisation of Creditor Protection Through Private Governance

The empirical study showed that the bilateral private governance system created by covenants and an event of default clause provides collective creditor protection to a certain extent. A bank does not act in a purely self-interested way after a covenant default, but will include third-party creditors for two main reasons: both the contracts and their interests are interlinked. This leads to a multi-party private governance system and an incentive structure that allows to internalise potential negative externailities of covenants. Thus, the preliminary theory about the bilateral private governance system must be re-evaluated. The following chapter will tackle this task by applying the common pool resource theory. Potential externalities of covenants and the bank's conduct after a covenant default can only be properly understood when applying the common pool resource scheme.

For this purpose, the nature of a common pool resource (CPR) will be explained and applied to the coordination problem between banks and third-party creditors. Afterwards, three instruments used to address the coordination problem will be presented—namely bankruptcy law, collateral and the incentive structure surrounding the bilateral private governance system created by covenants and an event of default clause. This will clarify their interrelationship and thereby also their function in addressing the coordination problem. Those findings will then be considered in the next chapter.

9.1 Common Pool Resources

A CPR refers to a natural or man-made resource, the appropriation[1] of which is subject to rivalry and for which the exclusion of potential beneficiaries is too costly. The rivalry relates to the fact that if one appropriator[2] consumes from a CPR, the

[1]Appropriation refers to "the process of withdrawing resource units from a resource system [...]." Ostrom (1990), p. 30.

[2]"Those who withdraw such units are called "appropriators" Ostrom (1990), p. 30.

D. Matri, *Covenants and Third-Party Creditors*, DOI 10.1007/978-3-319-62036-7_9

ability of other users to do the same is adversely affected. This is the reason for possible overuse or destruction of a CPR (potential negative externality). The problem that potential beneficiaries cannot be excluded by providers or producers[3] leads to free riding (potential positive externality).[4]

A CPR can be explained by using a simple example[5]: You own a lake with fish and there are no restrictions on how many fish you are allowed to catch. Furthermore, you are the only person permitted to fish there. You have two options: either you harvest all the fish right away, sell them for €80,000 and have no income in the following years as no fish are left, or you harvest only half of the fish and leave them to multiply again so that you have a steady income of €40,000 each year, which has a present value of, say, €400,000. All other things being equal, the latter option, is obviously better.

The situation changes, however, if you bring in other people who also have rights to harvest the fish. The optimal solution remains to limit your fishing, but you cannot be sure that there will be fish left to multiply because you are not the only one fishing in the lake. Thus, the incentive structure has changed. If you cannot control the others, it might be better to harvest as many fish as you can because you do not know if there will be any fish next year. This reasoning applies to all fishermen, so that at the end of the year the stock will be depleted.

The fishermen are in an *n*-person prisoner's dilemma[6] and cooperation of all fishermen would internalise potential externalities (stock depletion/overuse) and ensure an optimal equilibrium; see Fig. 9.1.

9.2 Aggregated Value of the Debtor Company's Pool of Assets as a CPR

The same considerations can be applied to the situation between creditors of a (distressed) debtor company. This is no new idea: It is employed to justify the imposition of a collective resolution in bankruptcy law[7] and of collateral in property law.[8]

The concrete CPR, however, varies due to different starting points.[9] Covenants aim at the prevention of the debtor company's bankruptcy and the preservation of

[3]Providers are "those who arrange for the provision of a CPR" and producer is "anyone who actually [...] ensure[s] the long-term sustenance of the resource system itself" Ostrom (1990), p. 31.

[4]Cf. Dolšak and Ostrom, in: Dolšak, Ostrom (eds) (2003), p. 7 et seq.

[5]The example is based on Jackson (1986), p. 11 et seq.

[6]See Hamburger (1973); Goetze (1994).

[7]See e.g. McCormack (2016), 139.

[8]See e.g. Picker (1992), 646 et seqq.

[9]The aggregated value of the pool of assets is often regarded as CPR in bankruptcy law or property law literature, cf. Jackson (1986), 14; Picker (1992), 669 et seq. Outside this literature, also the debtor company's solvency or the avoidance of bankruptcy (costs) have been regarded as CPR, see Schmidtbleicher (2010), p. 45 (solvency as CPR for bondholders); Roe (1987), 238 (avoidance of bankruptcy costs as CPR for bondholders but noting that this also true for all creditors).

		fisherman 1	
		harvest as much as you can	hold off
fisherman 2	harvest as much as you can	€80,000; €80,000	€80,000; €40,000
	hold off	€40,000; €80,000	€400,000; €400,000

Fig. 9.1 Prisoner's dilemma of fishermen (own illustration)

the debtor company's going-concern value.[10] The same aim is pursued by all creditors if the debtor company is in financial distress. Thus, the aggregated value of the debtor company's pool of assets (as going-concern value) can be regarded as CPR.[11] The aggregated value of the debtor company's pool of assets is non-exclusive. A collective action that is directed at protecting or enhancing the debtor company's going-concern value benefits all creditors—at least to some extent. The CPR also creates rivalry because if one creditor exploits the debtor company's asset pool, the going-concern value will decrease and all creditors will harvest less from the debtor company's asset pool. Generally, it would be socially desirable for all adjusting creditors to cooperate. However, the bank is in a prisoner's dilemma with adjusting third-party creditors: no creditor knows when and under what conditions the other creditor might demand additional risk premiums or accelerate and demand repayment.

For example, similar to in Scenario 5,[12] Papermaker has financial difficulties after issuing unsecured bonds in Scenario 1.[13] Papermaker had misjudged the costs and benefits of the improved infrastructure and the last year has been poor for the paper industry. Consequently, Papermaker substantially violates the interest coverage ratio and the leverage ratio covenant under the syndicated loan for over 15 days. The bank consortium could waive the default on the condition that Papermaker provides additional collateral as in Scenario 6.[14] Due to legal restrictions and limited suitable assets, the bank consortium could secure €80,000 for repayment of the loan principal. Papermaker will consequently, as in Scenario 6,[15] become bankrupt. Alternatively, Papermaker could discipline the debtor company

[10]For a detailed analysis of the going concern surplus, see, for example, Butler and Gilpatric (1994), 280 et seqq.

[11]Negatively formulated, the avoidance of bankruptcy (costs) is the CPR. See Roe (1987), 238 (avoidance of bankruptcy costs as CPR for bondholders but noting that this also true for all creditors); Klein and Coffee (1991), 1240 et seq. (avoidance of bankruptcy as CPR for bondholders); Brudney (1992), 1858 (for bondholders: "The collective good - payment of all at more than market price, albeit at less than principal [...]"); Liebenow (2015), p. 22 et seq. (avoidance of bankruptcy (costs) for bondholders).

[12]See above 6.2.

[13]See above 1.1.

[14]See above 6.2.

[15]See above 6.2.

		third-party creditor: harvest as much as you can (risk premium)	third-party creditor: discipline
bank consortium	harvest as much as you can (risk premium)	€80,000; €80,000	€80,000; €40,000
	discipline	€40,000; €80,000	€400,000; €400,000

Fig. 9.2 Prisoner's dilemma of bank consortium and third-party creditor (own illustration)

by demanding a management change (like in Scenario 3), other investment decisions, or a slimmer employment structure and then adjust the covenants accordingly. This could lead to a recovery of Papermaker and the bank consortium could recover say €400,000 over the next 10 years. However, the outcome also depends on the actions of third-party creditors, who can also decide between disciplining and harvesting. Provided that the bank consortium and the third-party creditor have equal means, this leads to the following prisoner's dilemma; see Fig. 9.2.

This illustrates that it would be beneficial to cooperate. The decrease or increase of the third-party creditor's recovery chances due to the bank consortium's conduct, and vice versa, is the manifestation of externalities.

9.3 Mechanisms to Reduce the Coordination Problem

The question of whether—and if so how—the cooperation of users (fishermen or creditors) can be ensured to internalise negative externalities has been debated in the literature for over five decades.[16] First, Garret Hardin argued that externalities of a CPR can be internalised and thereby the "tragedy of the commons" avoided when a CPR is privatised or appropriated by national governments and managed by governmental agencies.[17] Later, Elinor Ostrom challenged this by arguing that incentive structures are more complex than assumed and that communities can evolve rules without external regulation to avoid the tragedy of the commons.[18]

[16]The debate really started with Garret Hardin (Hardin (1968)) but can be tracked back to Aristoteles (1872), p. 58 et seqq.

[17]Hardin (1968), 1247 but Hardin's work is actually about open access resources. Arguing for state regulation as the superior method for CPR e.g. Ophuls (1973), p. 229, 367 et seqq.; Hardin, in: Brokaw (ed) (1978), p. 314; Ehrenfeld (1972), p. 322. Arguing for privatization as the superior method e.g. Demsetz (1967); Johnson (1972); Smith (1981), 467 et seq.

[18]Ostrom (1990). Already Mancur Olson recognised that cooperation may be possible in case of small groups with homogeneous claims and repeated interaction, Olson (1965).

9.3.1 State Regulation: Bankruptcy Law

As shown above, there is a multi-party prisoner's dilemma between a bank and third-party creditors that underlies the common pool problem in the event of distressed debtor companies[19] as outside bankruptcy law, the principle of "first-come, first-serve"[20] applies. If there are insufficient assets to satisfy all creditors, a premium on racing to the debtor company's assets occurs and the individual creditor remedies may lead to a result that is bad for all creditors as a group. Even in the case of an insolvent debtor company, creditors might be better off if the assets stay together rather than a piecemeal disposal.[21] In fact, a lack of operating assets or an inefficient sale can leads to a decrease in the aggregated value of the debtor company's assets. Secured creditors may push for a fast sale of assets to recover their investments in good time. This may include selling the assets not for what they are worth, but just high enough to recover the loan principal.

To avoid this tragedy of the commons, bankruptcy law imposes "a *collective* and *compulsory* proceeding on [creditors]."[22] It replaces the individualistic approach of debt collection with a collective enforcement mechanism that ensures the equal satisfaction of all claims. This mechanism, however, is different from classical CPR solutions since it is only applicable within a limited time frame.[23] Bankruptcy law regulates the common pool problem after bankruptcy proceedings have been commenced and shortly before this, in the reach-back period of avoidable preferences.

In Germany, reasons to open bankruptcy proceedings are insolvency (*Zahlungsunfähigkeit*, § 17 InsO),[24] immediate insolvency (*drohende Zahlungsunfähigkeit*, § 18 InsO)[25] and overindebtness (*Überschuldung*,

---

[19]Seminally, Baird and Jackson (1984), 105 et seqq.; Jackson (1986), 10 et seq. For an overview of the literature discussing whether this is the only purpose of bankruptcy law, see Armour (2001), 8 et seqq.; for Germany see Thole (2010), p. 56 et seqq.

[20]Cf. Jackson (1986), 8 et seq.; Mokal (2005), p. 35; see for a comparative overview Dirix, in: Eidenmüller, Kieniger (eds) (2008), p. 223 et seqq.

[21]Cf., for example, Rausch (1985), p. 23 et seq., 33; Mokal (2005), p. 35; Thole (2010), p. 53.

[22]Jackson (1986), p. 13. See also for the USA Baird (1991), 223 and for Germany see government bill BT-Drucks. 12/2443, p. 77; Balz (1988), 1439; Engel (2004), p. 44 et seqq.; Mock, in: Uhlenbruck et al. (eds) (2015a), paras. 2 et seq.

[23]Cf. Jackson (1986), p. 13.

[24]§ 17 II InsO: The debtor shall be deemed illiquid if he is unable to meet his mature obligations to pay. Insolvency shall be presumed as a rule if the debtor has stopped payments. See Pape (2008); Plagens and Wilkes (2010).

[25]§ 18 II InsO: The debtor shall be deemed to be faced with imminent insolvency if he is likely to be unable to meet his existing obligations to pay on the date of their maturity. See Drukarczyk, in: Kirchhof et al. (eds) (2013), paras. 20 et seqq.; Mock, in: Uhlenbruck et al. (eds) (2015b), paras. 18 et seqq.

§ 19 InsO).[26,27] When either *Zahlungsunfähigkeit* or *Überschuldung* is given, the debtor company must[28]—or in case of *drohende Zahlungsunfähigkeit* can[29]—file a petition for bankruptcy proceedings (§§ 13 I, 16 InsO). A creditor can also file a petition pursuant to § 14 I InsO if the creditor has a legal interest in opening bankruptcy proceedings and can provide its claim and the reason why bankruptcy proceedings should be opened to the satisfaction of the court. The reach-back period of bankruptcy law regularly covers three months, but can be extended to 4 years in cases of gratuitous benefit and up to 10 years for wilful disadvantage.[30]

Similarly to that, in the US the debtor company can file a voluntary petition with the bankruptcy court pursuant to § 301 Bankruptcy Code[31] or an involuntary petition can be filed by creditors according to § 303 Bankruptcy Code.[32] Contrary to Germany, an element of insolvency or overindebtness is not required for a voluntary petition.[33] Moreover, involuntary petitions can only be brought by three creditors. Their non-contingent, undisputed claims must aggregate at least

---

[26]§ 19 II InsO: Overindebtedness shall exist if the debtor's assets no longer cover his existing obligations to pay, unless it is highly likely, considering the circumstances, that the enterprise will continue to exist. As regards claims in respect of the restitution of shareholder loans or claims deriving from legal transactions corresponding in economic terms to such a loan, for which the creditors and the debtor have agreed, in accordance with § 39 II, that they shall rank lower behind the claims set out in § 39 I, Nos. 1 to 5 in the insolvency proceedings – consideration shall not be given to the obligations under the first sentence. See Drukarczyk and Schüler, in: Kirchhof et al. (eds) (2013), paras. 21 et seqq.; Mock, in: Uhlenbruck et al. (eds) (2015c), paras. 38 et seqq.

[27]See, generally, Gehrlein (2012); Frystatzki (2014).

[28]§ 15a InsO. See instead of many Klöhn, in: Kirchhof et al. (eds) (2013), paras. 47 et seqq. with further references.

[29]This is only a reason to open bankruptcy proceedings if requested by debtor (§ 18 I InsO), but this is rarely used. Cf. Drukarczyk, in: Kirchhof et al. (eds) (2013), paras. 2 et seq.; Uhlenbruck, in: Richter et al. (eds) (2003), p. 441 et seqq. Furthermore, a reason to open bankruptcy proceedings must be presented in a material and understandable way by the debtor. See BGHZ 153, 205; BGH WM 2005, 472, 473 et seq.

[30]See above 6.2.2.1.1. for incongruent coverage (§ 131 InsO). §§ 130, 131, 132 InsO have a three-month reach-back period. § 133 InsO stipulates a reach-back period of ten years for a transaction with the intention to disadvantage creditors if the other party was aware of the debtor's intention on the date of such transaction, and of two years for an onerous contract entered into by the debtor with a person with a close relationship to him (§ 138 InsO). § 134 InsO states a four year reach-back period for a gratuitous benefit.

[31]11 US Code § 301. For the history of voluntary bankruptcy see MCCoid (1988). A debtor company can regularly choose between filing under either Chapter 7 (liquidation) or Chapter 11 (reorganisation). Chapter 10 is only available to small companies, whose accumulated debt may not be more than $2,500,000.

[32]11 US Code § 303. An involuntary petition may also be commenced under Chapter 7 or 11; 11 US Code § 303(a).

[33]*In re Johns-Manville Corporation, et al.*, 36 B.R. 727 (Bkrtcy.S.D.N.Y.1984), appeal denied 39 B.R. 234, reargument denied 39 B.R. 998, mandamus denied 749 F.2d 3. However, the voluntary petition must be in in good faith see *In re Dolton Lodge Trust No. 35188*, 22 B.R. 918 (Bkrtcy.N.D.Ill.1982); *In re SGL Carbon Corporation*, 200 F.3d 154 (3rd Cir. 1999).

$15,775[34] or more than the value of any collateral securing such claims (§ 303(b)(1) Bankruptcy Code).[35] Alternatively, when there are less then twelve creditors, one or two creditors whose claims aggregate at least $15,775 can file for involuntary bankruptcy (§ 303(b)(2) Bankruptcy Code).[36] However, the bankruptcy court will only order a relief according to § 303(h)(1) and (2) Bankruptcy Code[37] if the debtor company is generally not paying its debts as they become due[38] or if, within the 120 days prior to the date the petition is filed, a custodian[39] was appointed or took possession of substantially all of the debtor company's property. The reach-back period of bankruptcy law regularly covers 90 days, but in cases of fraudulent transfer can be extended to 2 years.[40]

Outside of this time frame, bankruptcy law does not avoid the "tragedy of the commons". There is still a period between a debtor company triggering a covenant default and entering into financial distress and the application of bankruptcy law. This gap is intentional so that bankruptcy law does not intervene too early and hinder the chances of recovery outside the court.[41] Nevertheless, the gap limits the ability of bankruptcy law to address the common pool problem.

9.3.2 *Privatisation of Rights: Collateral*

The common pool problem is also addressed by the allocation of rights to individual users rather than to the group of users (privatisation).[42] For the aggregated value of

---

[34]Dollar amount as adjusted by the Judicial Conference of the US; cf. 11 US Code § 104.

[35]11 US Code § 303(b)(1). The US courts, however, have made exceptions from the express requirements in specific cases: For example, for a sole creditor that may otherwise be without adequate remedy; cf. *In the Matter of 7H Land & Cattle Co.*, 6 B.R. 29 (Bankr.D.Nev. 1980). Also a single petitioning creditor may be successful in instances that involve fraud, artifice or scam is involved; *Concrete Pumping Services Inc. v. King Construction Co. Inc.*, 943 F.2d 627 (6th Cir. 1991). In another case, where only two creditors petitioned even though the debtor had more than twelve creditors, the special circumstances exception was applied due to preferential and fraudulent treatment; *In re Jan McLendon Moss*, 249 B.R. 411 (Bankr.N.D.Tex. 2000).

[36]11 US Code § 303(b)(2).

[37]11 US Code § 303(h)(1), (2).

[38]Unless such debts are the subject of a bona fide dispute as to liability or amount.

[39]Other than a trustee, receiver, or agent appointed or authorised to take charge of less than substantially all of the debtor company's property, for the purpose of enforcing a lien against such property.

[40]See above 6.2.2.2.1 but note the extention for insiders of one year. For fraudulent transfer see 11 US Code § 548.

[41]Cf. Schmidt (1982), 166; Baird (1991), 223 et seqq.; Uhlenbruck, in: Richter et al. (eds) (2003), p. 445; Mock, in: Uhlenbruck et al. (eds) (2015a), para. 4.

[42]Dolšak and Ostrom, in: Dolšak, Ostrom (eds) (2003), p. 8.

the debtor company's asset pool, this is achieved by collateral.[43] The pledged assets are no longer part of the CPR.

This approach, however, has some problems. First, the pledged assets may be worth more than the secured claim and the remaining value still belongs to the aggregated value of the debtor company's pool of assets.[44] This is particularly problematic when questioning the willingness of secured creditors to sell pledged assets at a lower price. An adequately secured creditor will merely need to sell the assets at a price high enough to recover the loan principal; everything above that price holds no advantage for the secured creditor.[45] Thus, the secured creditor may still reduce the CPR by not selling at the highest sale price.

The aggregated value of the debtor company's pool of assets may also be adversely affected by a secured creditor's lack of motivation to monitor the debtor company because it does not suffer the consequences of the debtor company's misbehaviour. The incentive to monitor decreases according to the extent to which the loan is secured.[46] This decreased level of monitoring may also lead to a lower level of precaution on the part of the debtor company. An unsecured creditor might be more keen to monitor the behaviour of the debtor company and thus might, for example, intensify the incentive of the debtor company to prevent tort liabilities.[47] Tort liabilities further diminish the aggregated value of the debtor company's pool of assets.

The instrument of collateral to avoid the tragedy of the commons is also limited by the availability and *de facto* enforceability of collateral. A debtor company may, for example, not possess assets that are suitable to pledge. This is often the case for project financing or start-ups. Furthermore, the enforceability of the collateral can be hampered—for example in cases of acquisition in good faith. In Germany, acquisition in good faith (*gutgläubiger Erwerb*) is generally possible according to §§ 932 et seqq. BGB and the buyer takes the pledged asset free of security interests (§ 936 BGB).[48] In the US, pursuant to § 9-317 b) UCC the collateral is not

---

[43] Cf. only Dorndorf (1986), p. 30 et seq.; Picker (1992); Engel (2004), p. 62.

[44] Similarly, Engel (2004), p. 38, 64 et seqq.

[45] The secured creditor may however under a duty to realise collateral in a considerate and best possible way. In Germany see for the *Grundsatz der schonenden und bestmöglichen Verwertung*; BGH WM 1961, 243, 244; BGH WM 1967, 397, 397.

[46] Zhang (2014), 810. Secured debt can lead to cost-efficient monitoring and thereby, reduce the agency costs, when unsecured creditors adjust their monitoring efforts as a consequence of the issuance of a secured loan. This is, however, seldom the case. Thus, the overall monitoring efforts decrease since the incentives for secured creditors to monitor are reduced. They are shielded from negative effects of the debtor's misbehaviour by the stable value of the collateral; Adler (1993), 89; Bebchuk and Fried (1997), 1317 et seq.; Buckley (1986), 1440, 1443; Triantis (1992), 244 (stating that creditors only have incentives to monitor the collateral); Zhang (2014), 800.

[47] Bebchuk and Fried (1996), 898 et seqq.; Bebchuk and Fried (1997), 1319; Zhang (2014), 801 et seq.

[48] Restrictions on disposal rights can hamper the acquisition; Wiegand, in: von Staudinger (ed) (2011), para. 7. Also, a duty to investigate for security interests may apply: for retention of title positive RGZ 147, 321, 331; BGHZ 10, 14, 17. For this not applying in case of a general security interest, see BGH WM 1966, 792; BGH WM 1970, 120; BGHZ 86, 300, 311. Critically, see Wiegand, in: von Staudinger (ed) (2011), paras. 55 et seqq.

enforceable against a third party who is in good faith if the security interest is not perfected.[49] Following perfection of the security interest, a third party can, pursuant to § 9-320 UCC, only take the pledged asset free of said interest if it is a buyer in the ordinary course of business.[50]

Collateral is even more problematic in international transactions.[51] The transaction costs are higher because foreign lawyers must be consulted. This may ensure legal certainty and enforceability for immovables to some extent. Pledged movables, however, can cross borders after perfection and the security interest may become unenforceable. In fact, the enforceability of the security interest in the pledged movable will generally be determined—according to the conflict of laws principle *lex rei sitae*—by the law where the property is located.[52]

All in all, the above considerations show that collateral can—in a similar way to bankruptcy law—only provide a partial solution to the common pool problem.

9.3.3 Self-governing CPR Institutions

This patchwork of state regulation and privatisation, however, does not necessarily lead to a coordination problem. Creditors may also regulate the CPR privately. The aggregated value of the debtor company's pool of assets must be protected from overuse. To devise rules that regulate use is costly and requires a large portion of resource users, here creditors, to work together. This, however, is rarely achieved because the collective action dilemma—that is, all creditors benefiting from the

[49] § 9-317(b) UCC: Except as otherwise provided in subsection (e), a buyer, other than a secured party, of tangible chattel paper, documents, goods, instruments, or a certificated security takes free of a security interest or agricultural lien if the buyer gives value and receives delivery of the collateral without knowledge of the security interest or agricultural lien and before it is perfected.

[50] A buyer in ordinary course of business is defined in § 1-201(b)(9) UCC as a person that buys goods in good faith, without knowledge that the sale violates the rights of another person in the goods, and in the ordinary course from a person, other than a pawnbroker, in the business of selling goods of that kind. A person buys goods in the ordinary course if the sale to the person comports with the usual or customary practices in the kind of business in which the seller is engaged or with the seller's own usual or customary practices. A person that sells oil, gas, or other minerals at the wellhead or minehead is a person in the business of selling goods of that kind. A buyer in ordinary course of business may buy for cash, by exchange of other property, or on secured or unsecured credit, and may acquire goods or documents of title under a preexisting contract for sale. Only a buyer that takes possession of the goods or has a right to recover the goods from the seller under Article 2 may be a buyer in ordinary course of business. "Buyer in ordinary course of business" does not include a person that acquires goods in a transfer in bulk or as security for or in total or partial satisfaction of a money debt.

[51] See, generally, Schmidtchen and Schmidt-Trenz (1991), 331 et seq.; Basedow, in: Witzleb et al. (eds) (2014), p. 254 et seqq.

[52] In Europe, for example, this is codified in Germany in Art. 43 I EGBGB, in Italy in Art. 51 I PIL-Act, in Spain in Art. 10 I Civil Code; For the US, see, for example, *Curry v. McClanless*, 59 S. Ct. 900, 904 (1939). However, the law of another country may apply in special circumstances; see for example Art. 46 EGBGB (in case of a substantially closer connection).

rules (free-riding) while only some incur the costs—must be overcome.[53] A common property institution must therefore address threats of overuse and free-riding.[54] Empirical research by Ostrom showed that this is possible. Although Ostrom was not the first to analyse the self-regulation of CPRs,[55] she was the first to systematise self-governing CPR institutions.[56] She found that there is no single institutional design, but rather a set of general principles that foster the self-governing CPR institution's performance.[57]

The self-governing CPR institution must have clearly defined boundaries, rules adjusted to the specific circumstances, and participation of appropriators in collective choice to devise a proper set of rules.[58] Moreover, efficient monitoring and graduated sanctioning activities are essential for producing stable long-term cooperation, because even in repeated games reputation alone is insufficient.[59] Finally, the long-term maintenance of the self-governing CPR institution is fostered by conflict resolution mechanisms and minimal recognition of the appropriators' right to organise.[60]

The incentive structure surrounding the bilateral private governance system created by covenants and an event of default clause reflects those design principles. The findings of the empirical study will subsequently be systematised and presented accordingly.

9.3.3.1 Clearly Defined Boundaries

First, the set of individuals with rights to the CPR must be well defined. Clearly defined boundaries positively influence the incentives for cooperation and limit externalities. Here, the rights to the CPR are well defined as including all creditors of the debtor company. The CPR itself is also clearly determined as the aggregated value of the debtor company's pool of asset.

---

[53]Dolšak and Ostrom, in: Dolšak, Ostrom (eds) (2003), p. 6.

[54]Dolšak and Ostrom, in: Dolšak, Ostrom (eds) (2003), p. 8.

[55]For example, Robert Ellickson wrote about order without law Ellickson (1991). He cited Ostrom soon after her book was published in Ellickson (1993), p. 1319, 1366, 1391.

[56]Ostrom (1990).

[57]Ostrom (1990), p. 90 et seqq.; supported by e.g. Tucker (1999), 2, 4 et seqq.; cf. also Dolšak and Ostrom, in: Dolšak, Ostrom (eds) (2003), p. 22.

[58]Ostrom (1990), p. 93.

[59]Ostrom (1990), p. 93 et seq.

[60]Ostrom (1990), p. 101. The additional design principle of nested enterprises is only applicable to more complex institutions.

9.3.3.2 Congruence Between Appropriation, Provision Rules and Local Conditions

Second, the appropriation and provision rules must concur with local conditions. Covenant-secured creditors can appropriate or produce the aggregated value of the debtor company's pool of assets after a covenant default. Also, adjusting third-party creditors with cross-default clauses may harvest the aggregated value of the debtor company's pool of asset. The triggering covenants and the event of default clause, however, are adapted to the specific conditions of the debtor company's market. Financial covenants in particular are adjusted to the debtor company's business plan.

9.3.3.3 Collective-Choice Arrangements

Third, there must be collective-choice arrangements allowing for the participation of most creditors in the decision making process. During renegotiation, most creditors are included due linked contracts and interests.

9.3.3.3.1 Linkage of Contracts

Third-party creditors' contracts are linked with the bank loan agreement via a cross-default, pari passu and negative pledge clause. The use of such clauses is fostered by the standardisation process of the LSTA in the US and the LMA in the UK. This linkage, however, is not direct but occurs via the debtor company. All three clauses only oblige the debtor company to act in a specific way. There is no contractual relationship between a bank and a third-party creditor. Generally, the clauses cannot be enforced against another creditor.[61] Nonetheless, these clauses create an incentive structure for banks to consider third-party creditors' interests.

First, a negative pledge clause prohibits the debtor company from pledging assets to third-party creditors. Generally, creditors, who stipulate a negative pledge clause, ensure that they are involved when the debtor company takes out a secured loan. Moreover, the negative pledge clause regulates, if enforced properly, the use of the debtor company's pool of assets for new creditors and, thereby, its effects on the aggregated value of the debtor company's pool of assets. The empirical study was indecisive in determining whether a negative pledge clause is enforced to prevent asset dilution for all creditors or to ensure only equal treatment for the bank (additional collateral for the bank or a collateral pool). Thus, further empirical research should be conducted.

Second, the debtor company is bound by the pari passu clause to treat the bank and third-party creditors equally. This links the debtor company's behaviour

[61] See Bjerre (1999), 315 et seqq.; Jaschke (2006), p. 86 et seqq.

towards the bank with its conduct towards third-party creditors. If this contractual duty is violated, the third-party creditor may have a right to immediate termination. This can be used as a threat to consider their interests in renegotiations. In fact, the empirical study showed that banks have a strong interest in keeping the debtor company solvent and termination by a third-party creditor can negatively impact this.

Finally, a cross-default clause *de facto* binds the debtor company towards the stipulating third-party creditor to the same covenants as under the bank loan agreement. A covenant default under the bank loan agreement leads to a default under the third-party creditor's contract. A cross-acceleration clause, however, links the contracts only when the bank accelerates the loan. The empirical study showed that a cross-default clause is increasingly common. The exact distribution is a field for further quantitative research. However, both clauses establish "a constructive balance of terror among creditors",[62] because each creditor can destroy the collection efforts of the other creditor by driving the debtor company into bankruptcy. If done so within the reach-back period of bankruptcy law, this would negate all collecting efforts of the bank and adjusting third-party creditors. Moreover, the empirical study identified three further reasons why this creates an incentive structure to consider the interests of third-party creditors. First, the unsecured part of the bank loan ranks equal to all other unsecured creditors in bankruptcy. Second, the bank seems to have the most to lose because it commonly has the biggest commitment. Third, the bank appears to be interested in the debtor company's going-concern surplus due to a higher overall profit. The empirical study showed that, for those reasons, third-party creditors with a cross-default clause and, in serious cases, with a cross-acceleration clause are involved in the renegotiation process.

9.3.3.3.2 Linkage of Interests

This is closely connected to the second incentive for considering the interests of third-party creditors in renegotiations, namely leverage. This is achieved by the threat of third-party creditors who are essential for the operational business to drive the debtor company into bankruptcy. The empirical study identified two types of third-party creditors who are commonly essential for the debtor company's operational business: trade creditors (or trade credit insurers) and leasing creditors. Their interests are aligned because their approval of decided actions in renegotiations is essential for the operational business. The trade creditor or leasing creditor can—if disgruntled—paralyse the debtor company's operational business.

This linkage of interests is fostered by the reduction of players. Trade credit insurers will represent the interests of trade creditors more efficiently. In fact, including all suppliers might prove to be too difficult or expensive and trade credit insurers possess more bargaining power. The fact that smaller groups are more

[62] Hahn (2010), p. 3.

likely to achieve collective actions at all has already been stated by Mancur Olson.[63]

9.3.3.4 Effective Monitoring

Fourth, banks as third-party creditors or trade credit insurers who are part of or accountable to the group of the debtor company's creditors ensure effective monitoring when it comes to appropriating the aggregated value of the debtor company's asset pool. This is possible on the one hand through financial covenants stipulated in a third-party creditor's loan agreement, because excessive appropriation will cause a covenant default. On the other hand, it is possible because the *n*-person prisoner's game concerning the use of the CPR is not a one-off for banks and trade credit insurers; it is a repeated game. The empirical study found that banks and trade credit insurers will see each other on multiple occasions regarding different debtor companies. In fact, neither party can perceive an end to this repeated game.[64] This ensures that banks and trade credit insurers can monitor each other effectively. The presumption is also supported by other game theorists, who consider cooperation likely when both parties perceive the game as open-ended.[65] It is noteworthy that the open-ended prisoner's game does not involve the same CPR, but the aggregated value of the asset pools of different debtor companies. This, however, does not change the incentive structure for banks and trade-credit insurers.

9.3.3.5 Graduated Sanctions

Fifth, a graduated sanctioning system for creditors who overuse the debtor company's pool of assets is in place. Due to its being a repeated game for the main participants in the renegotiation process—namely banks and trade credit insurers—those creditors will punish each other for misbehaviour. The empirical study showed that the sanctioning will not occur immediately, but in a different renegotiation process with another debtor company. In the new constellation, the former stronger and misbehaving bank will likely have a weaker, or at least a different, position. The other bank(s) and trade credit insurer(s) will punish former misbehaviour by non-cooperation in the current instance. Trade credit insurers may decline further cooperation with a specific bank or vice versa. Alternatively, banks will sanction each other by not considering the interests of the former non-cooperating bank as they normally would. Moreover, non-cooperation may

---

[63] Olson (1992), p.8 et seqq.

[64] Seminal for repeated games and the "tit for tat" strategy Axelrod (1984).

[65] Gibbons, in: Cook (ed) (2001), p. 336 et seqq.; Gómez, in: Cafaggi (ed) (2011), p. 31 et seqq.; Watson (2013), p. 297 et seqq.

also significantly harm the bank's reputation.[66] In fact, the bank community was found to be particularly small so that misbehaviour would easily be noticed and affect the bank's reputation. Hence, the reputation network combined with the possibility of future sanctioning can be an effective enforcement mechanism.[67] This is also in line with Robert Ellickson's research, which found that coordination is more likely within close-knit communities and groups that possess a long tradition of mutual trust.[68]

9.3.3.6 Conflict-Resolution Mechanisms

Sixth, conflict-resolution mechanisms that are cheap and easy to access are required for the long-term stability of the system. This is generally ensured by cross-default clauses. Creditors with a cross-default clause or other leverage will be involved in the renegotiation process. During renegotiations, conflicts can be discussed and decisions can be made by the debtor company, who will also consider the interests of other third-party creditors—particularly those of employees. If this leads to an unsatisfying result, creditors can sue the misbehaving creditor for damages under aforementioned specific circumstances.[69] In addition, bankruptcy law will regulate the conflict if it escalates. Thus, the self-governing CPR institution surrounding the bilateral private governance system created by covenants and an event of default clause (CPR private governance system) only needs to regulate the "tragedy of the commons" to a certain extent.

The resolution of conflicts regarding the open-ended prisoner's game between the major creditors may be ensured by the LMA and LSTA. They create guidelines not only with regard to the contractual content, but also to the proper behaviour and market expectation.[70] Moreover, they provide a professional space for exchange.

9.3.3.7 Minimal Recognition of Rights to Organise

The same considerations apply to the seventh design principle: the creditor's right to devise its own institutions is accepted by external governmental authorities until bankruptcy law applies and within the general legal limits.

---

[66]For reputation as mechanism to ensure cooperation see McMillan and Woodruff (2000); McMillan and Woodruff (1999); Dietz (2014), p. 15 et seqq.; Ellickson (1991), p. 167 et seqq.

[67]Cf. Ostrom (1990), p. 94 et seqq.

[68]Ellickson (1993), p. 1366. Also arguing for the relevance of small groups that interact in a repeated game to solve the common pool problem Eidenmüller (1999), p. 421 et seqq.

[69]See above 6.2.2.1.4 and 6.2.2.2.2.

[70]See only the guides to specific markets and educational offers http://www.lma.eu.com/landing_documents.aspx and http://www.lma.eu.com/landing_education_events.aspx.

9.4 Collectivisation of Creditor Protection Through the CPR Private Governance System

The above considerations show that the *n*-person prisoner's dilemma between banks and third-party creditors concerning the aggregated value of the debtor company's asset pool (as a CPR) is privately regulated by the CPR private governance system. The CPR private governance system reflects the seven design principles identified by Ostrom. It has clearly defined boundaries, rules adjusted to the specific circumstances, and the participation of most creditors in collective choice so that a proper set of rules can be devised. Moreover, efficient monitoring and graduated sanctioning activities, which are essential in producing stable long-term cooperation, are ensured by banks and trade credit insurers as third-party creditors. Finally, the long-term maintenance of the CPR private governance system is fostered by conflict-resolution mechanisms in renegotiation processes and through the LSTA and LMA. Also, a minimal recognition of the bank's right to organise is given.

Due to the CPR private governance system, banks will not only act in a self-interested way but will cooperate with third-party creditors. Thus, banks will not merely appropriate from the aggregated value of the debtor company's pool of assets after a covenant default. Returning to our scenarios, it is unlikely that the bank consortium will use its influence on the management (Scenario 3[71]) to the detriment of third-party creditors. It is also improbable that the bank consortium can enforce the negative pledge clause so as to take part in a collateral pool without involving some third-party creditors. Similar considerations apply to demanding additional risk premiums after a covenant default (Scenario 2b[72] and 4[73]). Third-party creditors with a cross-default clause or who are essential for the operational business of Papermaker ensure that the bank consortium does not act merely in its own self-interest; see Fig. 9.3.

This CPR private governance system regulates the common pool problem before bankruptcy law applies. Moreover, unlike collateral, it is mainly enforced out of court and therefore avoids enforceability problems. This also highlights one of its main benefits, namely its transnational character. Covenants and the CPR private governance system are not limited to national jurisdictions. They can be enforced without problems connected with state jurisdictions and court enforcement mechanisms.[74] Questions about the applicable law or forum do neither hamper the enforcement of covenants in the bilateral private governance system nor the CPR private governance system regulating the common pool problem. The transnational

---

[71] See above 5.3.1.

[72] See above 1.2.

[73] See above 5.5.

[74] For the benefits of private governance's high transaction security and far-reach see e.g. *M. Renner*, Zwingendes transnationales Recht. Zur Struktur der Wirtschaftsverfassung jenseits des Staates, 2011, p. 69 et seqq.; Calliess et al., in: Hurrelmann et al. (eds) (2008), 165.

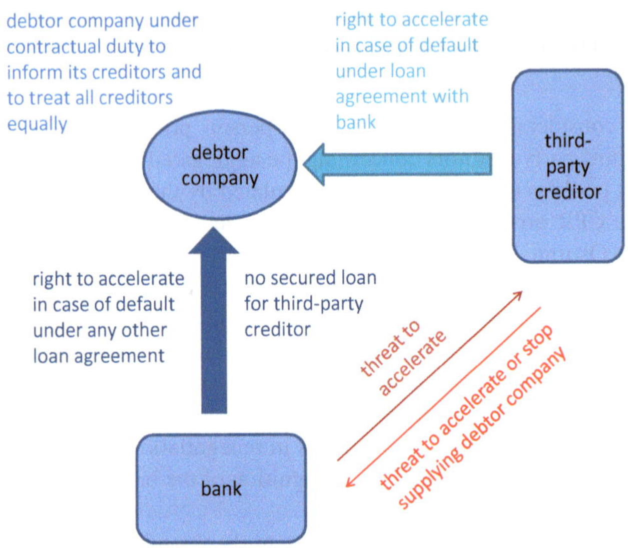

Fig. 9.3 Linkage between bank and third-party creditors (own illustration)

character of covenants and the CPR private governance system is further fostered by the standardisation process in the market due to the LMA and LSTA. This ensures that covenants and the event of default clause are internationally stipulated in a similar way. Moreover, the incentive structure surrounding covenants was found to be broadly alike in Germany and the US. Further qualitative research, however, should be conducted to support this theory. Generally, the transnational character allows for more certainty even though the CPR private governance system functions in the shadow of the law.[75]

References

Adler BE (1993) An equity-agency solution to the bankruptcy-priority puzzle. J Leg Stud 22(1): 73–98. doi:10.2307/3085634

Aristoteles JB (1872) Aristoteles' Politik: erstes, zweites und drittes Buch; mit erklärenden Zusätzen ins Deutsche übertragen von Jacob Bernays. Hertz, Berlin

Armour J (2001) The law and economics of corporate insolvency: a review. ERSC Centre for Business Research; Working Paper No. 197, Cambridge

Axelrod RM (1984) The evolution of cooperation. Basic Books, New York

Baird DG (1991) The initiation problem in bankruptcy. Int Rev Law Econ 11:223–232. doi:10.1016/0144-8188(91)90020-E

[75] Seminal Cooter et al. (1982).

Baird DG, Jackson TH (1984) Corporate reorganizations and the treatment of diverse ownership interests: a comment on adequate protection of secured creditors in bankruptcy. Univ Chic Law Rev 51:97–130

Balz M (1988) Logik und Grenzen des Insolvenzrechts. Zugleich eine Besprechung von Jackson, The Logic and Limits of Bankruptcy Law. ZIP (22):1438–1445

Basedow J (2014) Das Prinzip der gegenseitigen Anerkennung im internationalen Wirtschafts-verkehr. In: Witzleb N, Ellger R, Mankowski P, Merkt H, Remien O (eds) Festschrift für Dieter Martiny zum 70. Geburtstag. Mohr Siebeck, Tübingen, pp 243–258

Bebchuk LA, Fried JM (1996) The uneasy case for the priority of secured claims in bankruptcy. Yale Law J 105:857–934

Bebchuk LA, Fried JM (1997) The uneasy case for the priority of secured claims in bankruptcy: further thoughts and a reply to critics. Cornell Law Rev 82:1279–1348

Bjerre CS (1999) Secured transactions inside out: negative pledge covenants, property and per fection. Cornell Law Rev 84:305–393

Brudney V (1992) Corporate bondholders and debtor opportunism: in bad times and good. Harv Law Rev 105:1821–1878

Buckley FH (1986) The bankruptcy priority puzzle. Va Law Rev 72:1393–1470. doi:10.2307/1073043

Butler RV, Gilpatric SM (1994) A re-examination of the purposes of bankruptcy. Am Bankr Inst 2:269–292

Calliess G-P, Dietz T, Konradi W, Nieswandt H, Renner M, Sosa F (2008) Transformation des Handelsrechts? Neue Formen von Rechtssicherheit in globalen Austauschprozessen. In: Hurrelmann A, Leibfried S, Martens K, Mayer P (eds) Zerfasert der Nationalstaat? Campus, Frankfurt a.M., pp 143–175

Cooter R, Marks S, Mnookin R (1982) Bargaining in the shadow of the law: a testable model of strategic behavior. J Legal Stud 11:225–251

Demsetz H (1967) Toward a theory of property rights. Am Econ Rev 57:347–359

Dietz T (2014) Global order beyond law. How information and communication technologies facilitate relational contracting in international trade. International studies in the theory of private law (11). Hart, Oxford

Dirix E (2008) Remedies of secured creditors outside insolvency. In: Eidenmüller H, Kieninger E-M (eds) The future of secured credit in Europe. European company and financial law review. De Gruyter Recht, Berlin, pp 223–241

Dolšak N, Ostrom E (2003) The challenges of the commons. In: Dolšak N, Ostrom E (eds) The commons in the new millennium: challenges and adaptation. The MIT Press, Cambridge, pp 3–34

Dorndorf E (1986) Kreditsicherungsrecht und Wirtschaftsordnung. C.F. Müller, Heidelberg

Drukarczyk J (2013) § 18. In: Kirchhof H-P, Eidenmüller H, Stürner R (eds) Münchener Kommentar zur Insolvenzordnung. C.H. Beck, München.

Drukarczyk J, Schüler A (2013) § 19. In: Kirchhof H-P, Eidenmüller H, Stürner R (eds) Münchener Kommentar zur Insolvenzordnung. C.H. Beck, München

Ehrenfeld DW (1972) Conserving life on earth. Oxford University Press, New York

Eidenmüller H (1999) Unternehmenssanierung zwischen Markt und Gesetz. Mechanismen der Unternehmensreorganisation und Kooperationspflichten im Reorganisationsrecht. Otto Schmidt, Köln

Ellickson RC (1991) Order without law: how neighbors settle disputes. Harvard University Press, Cambridge

Ellickson RC (1993) Property in land. http://digitalcommons.law.yale.edu/fss_papers/411. Accessed 22 Apr 2016

Engel T (2004) Die Insolvenz und optionsbasierte Reorganisationsmodelle. Deutscher Universitäts-Verlag/GWV Fachverlage GmbH, Wiesbaden

Frystatzki C (2014) Die Beurteilung des Vorliegens von Insolvenzeröffnungsgründen – Entwurf eines neuen Standards des Instituts der Wirtschaftsprüfer (IDW ES 11). NZI:840–846

Gehrlein M (2012) Aktuelle Rechtsprechung zum Insolvenzeröffnungsverfahren. ZInsO 46: 2117–2127
Gibbons R (2001) Trust in social structures: Hobbes and Coase meet repeated games. In: Cook KS (ed) Trust in society. Russell Sage, New York, pp 332–353
Goetze D (1994) Comparing prisoner's dilemma, commons dilemma, and public goods provision designs in laboratory experiments. J Confl Resolut 38:56–86
Gómez F (2011) Cooperation, long-term relationships and open-endedness in contractual networks. In: Cafaggi F (ed) Contractual networks, inter-firm cooperation and economic growth. Edward Elgar, Cheltenham, pp 21–38
Hahn D (2010) The roles of acceleration. http://ssrn.com/abstract=1547702. Accessed 3 Apr 2016
Hamburger H (1973) N-person prisoner's dilemma. J Math Sociol 3:1–12
Hardin G (1968) The tragedy of the commons. Science 162:1243–1248
Hardin G (1978) Political requirements for preserving our common heritage. In: Brokaw HP (ed) Wildlife and America. Council on Environmental Quality, Washington, pp 310–317
Jackson TH (1986) The logic and limits of bankruptcy law. Beard Books, Washington
Jaschke ME (2006) Negativerklärungen nach deutschem und angloamerikanischen Recht: eine rechtsvergleichende Untersuchung. Peter Lang, Frankfurt am Main
Johnson OEG (1972) Economic analysis, the legal framework and land tenure systems. J Law Econ 15:259–276
Klein WA, Coffee JC (1991) Bondholder coercion: the problem of constrained choice in debt tender offers and recapitalizations. Univ Chic Law Rev 58:1207–1274
Klöhn L (2013) § 15a. In: Kirchhof H-P, Eidenmüller H, Stürner R (eds) Münchener Kommentar zur Insolvenzordnung. Beck, München
Liebenow P (2015) Das Schuldverschreibungsgesetz als Anleiheorganisationsrecht und Gesell schaftsrecht. Schriften zum Unternehmens- und Kapitalmarktrecht. Mohr Siebeck, Tübingen
McCoid JC (1988) Origins of voluntary bankruptcy. Bankr Dev J 5:361–390
McCormack G (2016) US exceptionalism and UK localism? Cross-border insolvency law in com parative perspective. Leg Stud 36:136–162
McMillan J, Woodruff C (1999) Dispute prevention without courts in Vietnam. J Law Econ Org 15:637–658. doi:10.1093/jleo/15.3.637
McMillan J, Woodruff C (2000) Private order under dysfunctional public order. Mich Law Rev 98:2421–2458. doi:10.2307/1290349
Mock S (2015a) § 16. In: Uhlenbruck W, Hirte H, Vallender H (eds) Insolvenzordnung Kommentar. Franz Vahlen, München
Mock S (2015b) § 18. In: Uhlenbruck W, Hirte H, Vallender H (eds) Insolvenzordnung Kommentar. Franz Vahlen, München
Mock S (2015c) § 19. In: Uhlenbruck W, Hirte H, Vallender H (eds) Insolvenzordnung Kommentar. Franz Vahlen, München
Mokal RJ (2005) Corporate insolvency law. Theory and Application. Oxford University Press, Oxford
Olson M (1965) The logic of collective action. Public goods and the theory of groups. Harvard economic studies 124. Harvard University Press, Cambridge
Olson M (1992) Die Logik des kollektiven Handelns: Kollektivgüter und die Theorie der Gruppen, 3rd edn. Paul Siebeck, Tübingen
Ophuls W (1973) Political theory of the steady state. Printed from microfilm edn. University Microfilms, Michigan
Ostrom E (1990) Governing the commons: the evolution of institutions for collective action. The political economy of institutions and decisions. Cambridge University Press, Cambridge
Pape G (2008) Zahlungsunfähigkeit in der Gerichtspraxis. WM 4:1949–1958
Picker RC (1992) Security interests, misbehavior, and common pools. University of Chicago Press 59:645–679

Plagens PW, Wilkes B (2010) Betriebswirtschaftliche Aspekte und offene Fragen im Zusammenhang mit der Definition des Begriffs Zahlungsunfähigkeit aufgrund der jüngeren BGH-Entscheidung. ZInsO (41):2107–2122

Rausch W (1985) Gläubigerschutz im Insolvenzverfahren - Eine ökonomische Analyse einschlägiger rechtlicher Regelungen. Josef Eul, Bergisch Gladbach

Roe MJ (1987) The voting prohibition in bond workouts. Yale Law J 97:232–280

Schmidt K (1982) Sinnwandel und Funktion des Überschuldungstatbestandes: rechtspolitische Perspektiven der Verfahrenseröffnung im Insolvenzrecht. JZ:165–174

Schmidtbleicher R (2010) Die Anleihegläubigermehrheit. Untersuchungen zur Ordnungstheorie und Ordnungspolitik. Mohr Siebeck, Tübingen

Schmidtchen D, Schmidt-Trenz H-J (1991) Private international trade in the shadow of the terri toriality of law: why does it work? South Econ J 58:329–338

Smith RJ (1981) Resolving the tragedy of the commons by creating private property rights in wildlife. Cato J 1:439–468

Thole C (2010) Gläubigerschutz durch Insolvenzrecht - Anfechtung und verwandte Regelungsinstrumente in der Unternehmensinsolvenz. Beiträge zum ausländischen und internationalen Privatrecht. Mohr Siebeck, Tübingen

Triantis GG (1992) Secured debt under conditions of imperfect information. J Legal Stud 21:225–258. doi:10.2307/724407

Tucker C (1999) Common property design principles and development in a honduran community. Fletcher J Dev Stud 14:1–23

Uhlenbruck W (2003) Zur fehlenden Akzeptanz des Insolvenzauslösers "drohende Zahlungsun fähigkeit". In: Richter F, Schüler A, Schwetzler B (eds) Zur fehlenden Akzeptanz des Insolvenzauslösers "drohende Zahlungsunfähigkeit". Vahlen, München, pp 441–453

Watson J (2013) Strategy: an Introduction to game theory. W.W. Nortan & Company, New York

Wiegand W (2011) § 932. In: von Staudinger J (ed) J. von Staudingers Kommentar zum Bürger lichen Gesetzbuch. De Gruyter, Berlin

Zhang W (2014) The paradoxes of secured lending: is there a less uneasy case for the priority of secured claims in bankruptcy? J Bus Law 16:789–841

Chapter 10
Consequences for Legal Discussion

The fact that the CPR private governance system works in the shadow of the law also points to the important issue of interaction between the different regulation spheres. Bankruptcy law, property law and the CPR private governance system address the same common pool problem regarding the aggregated value of the debtor company's pool of assets. However, they follow a different approach and apply in different yet overlapping instances. Collateral can, to a certain extent, avoid the cooperation problem by removing the pledged asset from the debtor company's pool of assets available to all creditors. Covenants and the event of default clause create a bilateral governance system that allows the bank to appropriate from, or produce the aggregated value of, the debtor company's asset pool. The CPR private governance system sets the incentive structure for banks to consider the interests of and effects on third-party creditors. Hence, banks will cooperate with other creditors and not merely appropriate from the CPR.

This incentive structure is influenced by bankruptcy law. Bankruptcy law undoes preferential treatment of some creditors in the aforementioned reach-back period to prevent overuse of the CPR. Moreover, after bankruptcy proceedings are commenced, bankruptcy law imposes a collective enforcement mechanism to ensure equal use of the CPR. This interaction must be considered by legal scholars. Thus, the following chapter will describe the change of perspective that should be made in the legal discussion. Covenants cannot be evaluated as an alternative to institutional regulation on its own, but the complete CPR private governance system and its interaction with institutional regulation must be considered. This will be presented first, followed by applying the same reflections to the corporate governance discussion. Moreover, institutional regulation should accept and respect the function of the CPR private governance system—namely, that of filling a gap in regulating the tragedy of the commons. The last section will therefore discuss the appropriate legal treatment of covenants and event of default clauses to foster the CPR private governance system.

D. Matri, *Covenants and Third-Party Creditors*, DOI 10.1007/978-3-319-62036-7_10

10.1 Covenants as a Supplement to Bankruptcy Law

First, the change of perspective—that is, covenants cannot be evaluated on their own but rather the complete CPR private governance system and its interaction with institutional regulation must be considered—will be a applied to the debate in German bankruptcy law literature on whether covenants create a "more efficient" creditor protection system than bankruptcy law.

Proponents argue that covenants can be better tailored to the specific needs and circumstances of the debtor company and that non-covenant secured creditors can protect themselves with cross-default clauses.[1] Opponents mainly argue that the collective protection of bankruptcy law is more efficient than that of covenants.[2] This shows that legal scholars recognise that covenants and bankruptcy law address the same problem, namely the common pool problem. However, the discussion fails to consider the concrete relationship between bankruptcy law, covenants and the CPR private governance system. Covenants and the surrounding CPR private governance system provide efficient collective creditor protection, but in the shadow of bankruptcy law. They supplement bankruptcy law by addressing the cooperation problem of creditors from the beginning of financial distress to the commencing of bankruptcy proceedings. The CPR private governance system was developed around bankruptcy law and partially depends on it for corrections of overuse. Thus, the question should not be whether covenants and the surrounding CPR private governance system can substitute bankruptcy law, but how an efficient interaction between them can be ensured.

10.2 Covenants as a Supplement to Capital Requirements

Second, the debate surrounding whether covenants and the CPR private governance system can substitute capital requirements must consider their different functions. The empirical study showed that covenants and the CPR private governance system provide collective creditor protection. In particular, covenants internalise externalities of limited liability before a covenant default. They reduce the shareholder-creditor conflict,[3] thereby achieving the aim of capital requirements before a covenant default occurs. After a covenant default, the CPR private governance system ensures that the debtor company's pool of assets is not overused. Nonetheless, rules on provision and maintenance of capital address a different conflict: whereas the CPR private governance system tackles the creditor-creditor conflict, rules on provision and maintenance of capital address the shareholder-creditor

[1]See above 3.4.4 and 8.4.1.

[2]See above 4.2.1.2.

[3]See above 5.2.2.

conflict. For this reason, covenants and the CPR private governance system cannot substitute but rather only supplement those capital requirements.

It is only the minimum initial capital requirement that appears to be dispensable. Currently, Germany provides in § 5a GmbHG[4] a private company form—the so-called *Unternehmergesellschaft*—that only requires €1 per business share.[5] For publicly trading companies, § 7 AktG[6] stipulates an initial minimum capital of €50,000.[7] By contrast, public companies within the US are generally under no duty to provide minimum capital.[8] Despite the differences for public companies, the factual impact seems to be minor, since the amount of €50,000 is marginal compared to the actual required capital of public companies. Furthermore, before companies enter bankruptcy proceedings, the initial capital is likely to be diminished.[9] Thus, minimum capital protects creditors negligibly at best.[10] As a consequence, it does not reduce the risk of bankruptcy or the loss appreciable.

Covenants, however, can ensure a minimum amount of assets and liquidity. Loan agreements including covenants are rarely negotiated before a company is incorporated and therefore cannot require an initial minimum capital. Nonetheless, if a company wants to take out a bank loan it has to be creditworthy. Creditworthiness includes, as previously mentioned the provision of sufficient funds. After the loan is granted, the debtor company must comply with financial covenants. This ensures a minimum amount of assets and liquidity.

All in all, the minimum initial capital requirement appears to be dispensable, whereas covenants and the CPR private governance system cannot substitute but rather only supplement rules on provision and maintenance of capital.

---

[4]*Gesetz betreffend die Gesellschaften mit beschränkter Haftung* (Limited Liability Companies Act).

[5]In late 2008, Germany introduced the corporate form Unternehmergesellschaft as the subform of the GmbH, requiring €1 as minimum capital, see, for example, Schall (2009); p. 101 et seqq.; von Rummel (2008), p. 249 et seqq.

[6]Aktiengesetz (Stock Corporation Act).

[7]Public companies within the EU are required to provide initial equity capital of €25,000 (Germany opted for a higher minimum capital requirement); Art. 6 Directive 2012/30/EU of the European Parliament and of the Council of 25 October 2012 on the coordination of safeguards that, for the protection of the interests of members and others, are required by Member States of companies within the meaning of the second paragraph of Art. 54 of the Treaty on the Functioning of the European Union, in respect of the formation of public limited liability companies and the maintenance and alteration of their capital, with a view to making such safeguards equivalent text with EEA relevance (recast), OJ 2012 L 315/74; applicable to i.a. SE, AG, plc and SpA.

[8]See, generally, Manning and Hanks (1990); Booth, in: Lutter (ed) (2006), and specifically Engert, in: Lutter (ed) (2006), p. 662.

[9]This is possible since minimum capital can be used at operating funds for the company. Only a return to shareholders is forbidden; see for Germany § 30 I GmbHG.

[10]Concurring Mülbert (2006), 387; Enriques and Macey (2001), 1185 et seqq. Partially dissenting Armour (2000), 365.

10.3 Creditors as Part of Corporate Governance

Third, taking both covenants and the CPR private governance system into account also carries implications for the corporate governance debate. Covenant-secured creditors can only play an important role for corporate governance when their interventions yield positive externalities. The common view assumes that a bank will act in a self-interested way and use its significant influence to enhance its own position, thereby impairing the third-party creditor's position.[11] The empirical study, however, found that banks will cooperate with third-party creditors and consider their interests due to the CPR private governance system. This supports the idea that covenant-secured creditors can play an important role in corporate governance—they can represent the interests of both creditors and long-term shareholders.

Under the current shareholder value approach, shareholders are deemed to only care about stock value.[12] However, there is no homogenous group of shareholders that only strive for short-term gain. Long-term investors exist.[13] However, they often abstain from interfering with management decisions as they mainly hold only limited shares due to diversification purposes. This short-term thinking may endanger the long-term performance of a company. In fact, short-term profit is often achieved by selling assets or discharging employees.[14] Thus, it reduces the aggregated value of the debtor company's pool of assets and harms creditors.[15] A lock-in of shareholder assets, on the other hand, can ensure that a manager is able to pursue long-term projects—such as research and development—without the immanent fear of having to pay back the shareholder's investment. This does not conceal the fact that short-term shareholders' interests can also benefit a company, and that banks and long-term shareholders may also have conflicting interest.[16] Nonetheless, covenants and the CPR private governance system ensure that managers mediate between the interests of both long-term and short-term investors.

All in all, covenant-secured creditors can represent the interests of both creditors and long-term shareholders. In addition, further research must consider the CPR private governance system in order to ensure proper reflections of the bank's incentive structure.

---

[11] See e.g. Hoffmann (2012).

[12] Stout (2012), p. 4.; cf., also Bebchuk (2013), 1646 et seqq.

[13] The conflict between short-term and long-term shareholders has been a major part of corporate governance discussions, cf. Lipton and Rosenblum (2003), 78; Kahan and Rock (2007), 1083; Anderson (2015), 19 et seq.

[14] See only, Moody's (2007), p. 3.

[15] See Maxwell and Rao (2003); Klein and Zur (2011). This, however, is at least in the short-term beneficial for shareholders as returns are higher Klein and Zur (2009).

[16] See Fried (2015); but Henry Hansmann and Reinier Kraakman declared the debate whether short-term or long-term shareholders' interests should be pursued by management as decided in favour of long-term shareholders' interests; Hansmann and Kraakman, in: Gordon, Roe (eds) (2004), 33.

10.4 Fostering the CPR Private Governance System in Germany

These three examples illustrate the important function of the bilateral private governance system created by covenants and an event of default clause combined with the CPR private governance system. Too much state regulation can threaten this private regulation.[17] This should be considered when discussing the legal treatment of covenant-secured loans. Moreover, more expensive mandatory duties to disclose covenant-defaults should and can apply, even *de lege lata*, to foster the CPR private governance system.

10.4.1 Legal Treatment of Covenants: § 138 v. § 826 BGB

First, the implications for the legal treatment of covenants and the event of default clause in Germany are elaborated.

The same consideration applies to the legal treatment of covenants and event of default clauses under § 138 BGB and § 826 BGB. The CPR private governance system ensures cooperative behaviour and that the debtor company's pool of assets is not overused. This should be considered when discussing the legal treatment of covenants and event of default clauses. Under § 138 BGB, they can be declared void if they exploit one party or violate legitimate interests of third parties or the public in an immoral way.[18] If in doubt, restrictive covenants and event of default clauses should not be declared void. In that way, covenants and the CPR private governance system can fulfil their function and reduce the common pool problem. In contrast, if declared null under § 138 BGB, no cooperative conduct would be created. The correction of CPR overuse should then occur based on factual misbehaviour. Thus, the *ex post* regulation under § 826 BGB is preferential in order to allow the CPR private governance system to function properly.

10.4.2 More Mandatory Disclosure

Furthermore, the CPR private governance system depends on information exchange. Third-party creditors must know about both the covenant default and the renegotiation to take part in the renegotiation process. The empirical study found that this is generally ensured by the debtor company and sometimes even via an informal information exchange between the bank and third-party creditors.

[17] Poteete et al. (2010), p. 112.

[18] See above 6.2.1.1.1.

Nonetheless, more mandatory disclosure duties of covenant defaults would foster the CPR private governance system.

This could be achieved by Art. 17 I of the Market Abuse Regulation even *de lege lata*. As previously mentioned, an ad-hoc duty to disclose according to Art. 17 I of the Market Abuse Regulation is assumed in the event of insider information pursuant to Art. 7 of the Market Abuse Regulation. Information about current or likely future covenant defaults falls under the category of insider information when the knowledge about current or likely future covenant defaults has the ability to significantly affect the stock exchange or market price.[19] In accordance with the academia and the Issuer Guideline of the BaFin (both commenting on the old § 15 WpHG),[20] an ad hoc duty to disclose a covenant default is only assumed when the acceleration of a material credit is reasonably likely.[21] The presumption that covenant defaults only affect the stock price when the acceleration of the credit is reasonably likely is questionable in light of empirical studies from the US. These show that covenant violations do, in fact, have an impact on the stock market price.[22] For example, Nini (et al.) found that the stock price performance improves significantly after disclosure of a covenant default.[23] Taking this data into consideration, a more far-reaching ad-hoc disclosure duty is possible *de lege lata*.[24] However, there are two main problems with this. First, the recommended interpretation of Art. 7 of the Market Abuse Regulation will cause compliance costs for the debtor companies.[25] Second, the problem of self-fulfilling prophecy can impede the rescue of a debtor company in financial distress. The rescue mainly depends on both belief and trust in the debtor company within the market. If nobody believes in the debtor company, its bankruptcy will be fast-tracked and the chances of rescue are

---

[19]For further elaborations see 5.2.1.1.2.1.

[20]The Issuer Guideline includes a non-exhaustive list of information that is relevant for the stock exchange or market price, see *Bundesanstalt für Finanzdienstleistungsaufsicht, Emittentenleitfaden* 2013, available at http://www.bafin.de/SharedDocs/Veroeffentlichungen/DE/Fachartikel/2013/fa_bj_2013_09_emittentenleitfaden.html, last accessed on 14.02.2016, p. 52 et seq.

[21]Heinrich (2009), p. 266; Kocher and Widder (2010), 927 et seq. This is determined by an *ex ante* prognosis; cf. Schwark and Kruse, in: Schwark, Zimmer (eds) (2010), para. 44. The information must also be specific enough: "A piece of information allows a conclusion to be drawn about its impact on prices, either when it would enable a reasonable investor to take an investment decision without (or at very low) risk, or when it is likely to be exploited immediately on the market" CESR's Advice on Level 2 Implementation Measures for the proposed Market Abuse Directive, 2002, Ref.: CESR/02–089, para. 20, indent 3. This is given in case of covenant defaults, as the information about them is specific, calculable and demonstrable. See also Kumpan, in: Baumbach, Hopt (eds) (2014), para. 1.

[22]See only Beneish and Press (1995); Emser (2011), p. 60 et seqq.; Nini et al. (2012); Ertan and Karolyi (2014).

[23]Nini et al. (2012).

[24]For the line between interpretation *de lege lata* and the development of the law, see Kuntz (2015).

[25]Cf. Aichberger (2013), p. 132.

diminished.[26] Nevertheless, belief and trust will be stronger if the coordination problem is resolved by a strengthened CPR private governance system. As previously shown, the ad-hoc disclosure duties under German and US law are triggered in a similar way: both require acceleration after a covenant default to be reasonably likely. Under US law, however, an ad-hoc disclosure duty can also be triggered by any material modifications of a (material) loan agreement. This lower trigger might prove particularly difficult with regard to the self-fulfilling prophecy problem. On the other hand, it substantially fosters the CPR private governance system.

In any case, the content that must be provided once an ad-hoc disclosure duty is triggered should be amended under German or rather EU law. The ad-hoc duty to disclose under Art. 17 I of the Market Abuse Regulation only requires the disclosure of the fact that a termination is reasonably likely. However, a more substantial catalogue of information is needed for the information to be of any value for third-party creditors. US law and the IFRS can be regarded as guidelines for a more meaningful disclosure. This could include *de lege ferenda* the date of the covenant default, a brief description of the loan agreement defaulted, a brief description of the covenant default, the amount involved and terms of acceleration, any other material obligations that might be affected by the covenant default, the time period waived for (if waived), and steps the company intends to take to cure or otherwise address the covenant default. Similarly, the risk report and forecast according to § 289 HGB should be read as requiring information about a covenant default. A detailed list of information that must be provided similar to that proposed for the ad hoc disclosure duty is desirable. This would ensure more transparency for private debtor companies. Thanks to the new electronic commercial register, this information will also be easy to access and reasonably up-to-date.[27] Those more extensive mandatory duties to disclose also facilitate the debtor company's self control.[28]

10.5 Summary

Interaction between the different regulation spheres—bankruptcy law, property law and the CPR private governance system—has important implications for current legal debates and the legal treatment of covenants and event of default clauses. Covenants cannot be evaluated as an alternative to institutional regulation on its own; the complete CPR private governance system and its interaction with institutional regulation must be considered. This change of perspective leads to the conclusion that covenants and the CPR private governance system are not a substitution but rather a supplement to bankruptcy law and capital requirements.

[26]See e.g. Buschmeyer (1993), p. 122 et seq.

[27]Easy access, reasonable up-to-dateness and standardised information reduce the costs; cf. Mülbert, in: Eidenmüller, Schön (eds) (2008), p. 384; Aichberger (2013), p. 135.

[28]Haas (1997), p. 110 with further references.

Only the initial minimum capital requirement seems to be dispensable. Moreover, covenant-secured creditors can also play an important role in corporate governance by mediating between short-term and long-term interests.

This work further discussed the legal treatment of covenants and event of default clauses because institutional regulation must accept and respect, to a certain extent, the function of the CPR private governance system. They fill a gap in the tragedy of the commons regulation by bankruptcy law and collateral. Accordingly, covenants and event of default clauses must not be declared null under § 138 BGB, if in doubt. Rather, factual misbehaviour must be sanctioned under § 826 BGB to ensure that covenants can still fulfil their function. Also, more extensive mandatory duties can foster the CPR private governance system. Any covenant breach that is reasonably likely to cause an acceleration should lead to an ad-hoc duty to disclose substantial information about the covenant default under Art. 17 I of the Market Abuse Regulation and a risk report and forecast pursuant to § 289 HGB should similarly include substantial information about covenant defaults.

References

Aichberger T (2013) Gläubigerschutz durch Ausschüttungssperren. Eine ökonomische Analyse anhand des deutschen, englischen und US-amerikanischen Regelungsmodells. Peter Lang, Frankfurt am Main

Anderson RI (2015) The long and short of corporate governance. Geo Mason Law Rev 23:19–68

Armour J (2000) Share capital and creditor protection: efficient rules for a modern company law. Mod Law Rev 63:355–378

Bebchuk LA (2013) The myth that insulating boards serves long-term value. Columbia Law Rev 113:1637–1694

Beneish MD, Press E (1995) The resolution of technical default. Account Rev 70:337–353

Booth RA (2006) Capital requirements in United States cooperations. In: Lutter M (ed) Legal capital in Europe, ECFR special volume 1. De Gruyter Recht, Berlin, pp 620–645

Buschmeyer K-D (1993) Publizität als Korrelat der Haftungsbeschränkung. Reihe: Finanzierung, Steuern, Wirtschaftsprüfung; 21. Müller Botermann, Köln

Emser B (2011) Essays in empirical corporate finance: covenants violations, market timing and product market competition. http://ir.uiowa.edu/etd/1219. Accessed 14 Feb 2016

Engert A (2006) Life without legal capital: lessons from American law. In: Lutter M (ed) Legal capital in Europe, ECFR special volume 1. De Gruyter Recht, Berlin, pp 646–694

Enriques L, Macey JR (2001) Creditors versus capital formation: the case against the European legal capital rules. Cornell Law Rev 86:1165–1204

Ertan A, Karolyi SA (2014) Debt covenants, expected default costs, and the implicit cost of financial reporting manipulation. https://server1.tepper.cmu.edu/seminars/docs/Karolyipaper.pdf. Accessed 14 Feb 2016

Fried JM (2015) The uneasy case for favoring long-term shareholders. Yale Law J 124:1554–1627

Haas U (1997) Geschäftsführerhaftung und Gläubigerschutz. Unternehmerische Verhaltenspflichten des GmbH-Geschäftsführers zum Schutz Dritter. Schriftenreihe Wirtschaftsrecht in Europa (4). Beck, München

Hansmann H, Kraakman R (2004) The end of history for corporate law. In: Gordon JN, Roe MJ (eds) Convergence and persistence in corporate governance, 1st edn. Cambridge University Press, Cambridge, pp 33–68

Heinrich S (2009) Covenants als Alternative zum institutionellen Gläubigerschutz. Eine rechtsvergleichende und ökonomische Analyse, vol 228. Schriften zum Wirtschaftsrecht. Duncker & Humblot, Berlin

Hoffmann G (2012) Grenzen der Einflussnahme auf Unternehmensleitungsentscheidungen durch Kreditgläubiger. WM:10–19

Kahan M, Rock EB (2007) Hedge funds in corporate governance and corporate control. Univ PA Law Rev 155:1021–1093

Klein A, Zur E (2009) Entrepreneurial shareholder activism: hedge funds and other private investors. J Finance 64:187–229

Klein A, Zur E (2011) The impact of hedge fund activism on the target firm's existing bondholders. Rev Financ Stud 24:1735–1771. doi:10.1093/rfs/hhr016

Kocher D, Widder S (2010) Ad-hoc-Publizität in Unternehmenskrise und Insolvenz. NZI:925–932

Kumpan C (2014) § 13 WpHG. In: Baumbach A, Hopt K (eds) Handelsgesetzbuch. Beck, München

Kuntz T (2015) Die Grenze zwischen Auslegung und Rechtsfortbildung aus sprachphilosophischer Perspektive. AcP 215:387–449

Lipton M, Rosenblum SA (2003) Election contests in the company's proxy: an idea whose time has not come. Bus Lawyer 59:67–94

Manning B, Hanks JJ (1990) Legal capital, 3rd edn. Foundation Press, Westbury

Maxwell WF, Rao RP (2003) Do spin-offs expropriate wealth from bondholders? J Finance 58:2087–2108

Moody's (2007) Short-term shareholder activists degrade creditworthiness of rated companies. https://www.moodys.com/sites/products/AboutMoodysRatingsAttachments/2006600000441326.pdf. Accessed 10 May 2016

Mülbert PO (2006) A synthetic view of different concepts of creditor protection, or: a high-level framework for corporate creditor protection. Eur Bus Organ Law Rev 7:357–408

Mülbert P A synthetic view of different concepts of creditor protection, or: a high-level framework for corporate creditor protection. In: Eidenmüller H, Schön W (eds) (2008) The law and economics of creditor protection. A transatlantic perspective. T.M.C. Asser Press, The Hague, pp 361–412

Nini G, Smith DC, Sufi A (2012) Creditor control rights, corporate governance, and firm value. Rev Financ Stud 25:1713–1761

Poteete AR, Janssen MA, Ostrom E (2010) Working together. Collective action, the commons, and multiple methods in practice. Princeton University Press, Princeton

von Rummel A (2008) Institutioneller Gläubigerschutz im Recht der kleinen Kapitalgesellschaft. Die englische private company limited by shares vor dem Hintergrund der deutschen GmbH. Mohr Siebeck, Tübingen

Schall A (2009) Kapitalgesellschaftsrechtlicher Gläubigerschutz. Grund und Grenzen der Haftungsbeschränkung nach Kapitaldebatte, MoMiG und Trihotel. Beck, München

Schwark E, Kruse D (2010) § 13 WpHG. In: Schwark E, Zimmer D (eds) Kapitalmarktrechts-Kommentar. Beck, München

Stout LA (2012) The shareholder value myth: how putting shareholders first harms investors, corporations, and the public. Berrett-Koehler, San Francisco

Part IV
Summary and Outlook

Chapter 11
Summary

The value of covenants as a bilateral creditor protection device has been extensively analysed by the literature. In Chap. 1, the Scenario 1 presented the standard situation for applying covenants, where a bank consortium provides a loan to a debtor company—Papermaker—and the loan agreement includes covenants. Here, the negative pledge clause allows the bank consortium to protect itself from both asset and claim dilution. However, covenants and their related clauses also affect third party creditors. The effects, as shown in Scenarios 2a and 2b, can be either positive or negative. Some third-party creditors can adjust to these effects, whereas non-adjusting creditors—like tort creditors—are exposed. This illustrates the importance of considering the effects of covenants on third-party creditors when discussing the value of covenants as a bilateral creditor protection device. The research into the effects on third-party creditors, however, has so far been insufficient. The work therefore tackled this task by first systematising potential externalities of covenants and then empirically testing the presumptions about the bank's conduct after a covenant default. In that way, the work reached an empirically backed theory about the effects of covenants on third-party creditors.

To achieve this, Chaps. 2 and 3 provided the general framework for discussing the function of covenants. Creditors need to protect themselves from the credit risk—which includes the risk of false or lacking information, the risk of bankruptcy and the risk of loss. The appropriate and available security device for a specific creditor depends on the given leverage, economic power and the type of credit. The choice is also influenced by the transaction costs incurred. Covenants are, as presented in Scenario 1, usually stipulated when a bank or a bank consortium provides a loan to a debtor company. Those other creditors who are not part of the specific covenant-secured bank loan agreement are known as third-party creditors. They can be other institutional lenders, bondholders, trade creditors, customers, employees or tort creditors. Some may also use covenants or other self-help devices. For example, institutional lenders can—due to their strong market position—resort to nearly all types of self-help protection devices; bondholders commonly use covenants and collateral; trade creditors can employ a number of

D. Matri, *Covenants and Third-Party Creditors*, DOI 10.1007/978-3-319-62036-7_11

self-help devices, but mainly rely on retention of title clauses, collateral from the debtor company, personal guarantees from shareholders, or payment in advance; and customers may protect themselves by refusing to pay in advance, ensuring that goods or ownership pass on payment and not on delivery, or set-off in the event of running accounts or diversification. In contrast, employees and tort creditors are usually unable to protect themselves.

Chapter 3 showed that covenants and their related clauses provide efficient means for self-help creditor protection. Covenants play only a limited role—if at all—in reducing the risk of false or lacking information. Other clauses, namely representations and the event of default clause, ensure that the provided information is accurate. However, protection against the risk of bankruptcy is ensured via financial covenants—namely via an interest coverage ratio covenant, a leverage ratio covenant, a tangible net worth covenant, a gearing covenant or a current ratio covenant. In addition, negative covenants—particularly a no disposal clause, a no merger clause and a clause restricting change of business or management—protect against this risk. Protection against the risk of loss is provided primarily by a negative pledge clause, a CAPEX covenant and a dividend restriction clause. The enforcement of said covenants is guaranteed by information undertakings, a pari passu clause, an event of default clause, a cross-default clause (often included in the event of default clause), an MAC clause and performance pricing.

These covenants, in combination with the clauses ensuring their enforcement, function as bilateral private governance mechanisms because they regulate all three stages of creditor protection in the private sphere—norm setting, monitoring and sanctioning. First, banks set relational norms in the form of covenants to measure the debtor's financial performance. Covenants also ensure the recovery of the loan principal plus interest, using norms to protect the businesses assets. Second, compliance with covenants is monitored with the help of information undertakings. Third, covenants are applied after a covenant default via renegotiation and enforced via severe consequences in the event of default clause, namely termination as a last resort.

This bilateral private governance system shifts the management of financial distress from bankruptcy proceedings to an earlier stage outside the scope of bankruptcy law. Thereby, it allows the bank to react to a worsened debtor company's financial situation before the debtor company is bankrupt. The bank can use its information advantage gained through information undertakings to take corrective action before (adjusting) third-party creditors can react. This enables the bank, for example, to receive additional collateral from the debtor company. The additional collateral, however, may hamper the chances of third-party creditors' claims being satisfied, because it reduces the debtor company's pool of assets. This shows that the bilateral governance system created by covenants and the event of default clause can affect third-party creditors' claims.

Chapter 4 then explained the relevance of these third-party creditor's effects. In law and economic theory, those effects are described as externalities. Generally, the bank will neither incur the costs for third-party creditors nor will it benefit from the positive third-party creditor effects. Thus, potential negative and positive externalities can occur. These externalities are relevant for the current legal debates. The selected topics concerning covenants as an alternative to institutional creditor protection by either company law or bankruptcy law in Germany and the role of covenant-secured creditors in corporate governance in the US literature were discussed using examples. All three legal debates concern the question of whether the bilateral private governance system created by covenants and an event of default clause causes mainly positive or negative externalities. If the positive outweigh the negative externalities, covenants can provide collective creditor protection and play a role in corporate governance.

Chapter 5 then systematised the debated potential positive and negative externalities of covenants. This chapter showed that the probability of positive or negative externalities depends largely on the bank's conduct after a covenant default. Prior to a covenant default, potential positive externalities are likely due to covenants reducing the agency conflict between shareholders and (all) creditors. After a covenant default, however, the bank's reaction to the default determines the scale of potential positive and negative effects. Potential positive externalities are the production of information through a covenant default and the subsequent reaction of the bank, as well as the disciplinary function of the corrective action taken. However, the information produced by a covenant default only benefits adjusting third-party creditors, particularly those with cross-default or cross-acceleration clauses. The corrective action subsequently taken may not only benefit but also harm both adjusting and non-adjusting third-party creditors. The corrective action can lead to potential negative externalities, namely to an influence on the debtor company that is not in the interest of all creditors, asset dilution, unnecessary bankruptcy or a domino effect.

Chapter 6 establishes the working hypothesis that a bank probably acts purely in its own self-interest and will therefore base its decision for a specific corrective action merely on the benefits it sees for itself, not considering the costs for third-party creditors. The occurrence of negative externalities is thus probable. The bank's decision is only influenced by legal limits. A legal enforcement by the debtor company, however, is rather unlikely as long as the lock-in situation between the debtor company and the bank lasts. When this relationship is dissolved by bankruptcy or acceleration, the legal limits become relevant. In those cases, a bank may also become liable to third-party creditors under tort law for controlling the debtor company. In addition, avoidable preference under bankruptcy law sets a limitation for the bank's conduct.

These limitations were subsequently presented in a legal comparison between US and German law. It showed that the bank's right to accelerate after a covenant default (Scenario 5) is similarly limited under German and US law. Roughly, both legal systems require a material breach as a cause for the termination to be effective and that the termination is not done in bad faith. In that way, it is ensured that a bank cannot arbitrarily accelerate a loan and drive the debtor company into unnecessary bankruptcy. Also, the undersecured bank's right to demand additional collateral after a covenant default (Scenario 6) is restricted in similar ways. Additional collateral is probably avoidable under both legal systems, when the bank's loan agreement was undersecured and the provision of collateral falls in the reach-back period—namely 3 months in Germany or 90 days in the US. For liability under § 826 BGB or the concept of fiduciary duty, more is required than under avoidable preference law. As long as additional collateral only covers parts of the debtor company's assets, a bank is unlikely to be held liable for demanding and receiving additional collateral.

Chapters 7 and 8 empirically tested the presumptions about the bank's conduct after a covenant default. Because the conclusion that negative externalities of covenants predominate is merely based on presumptions about a bank's behaviour the chapters investigated the *de facto* conduct of banks with a qualitative empirical study. First, the Chap. 7 presented the design and methodology of the empirical study. The research objective was identified as factual behaviour of covenant-secured creditors and its effects on third-party creditors. Moreover, the form of covenant enforcement—in or out of court—was researched to confirm that covenants and an event of default clause create a bilateral private governance system. The appropriate research object was found to be banks and their behaviour after a covenant default. Due to the lack of empirical studies on the factual conduct of banks and its effects on third-party creditors, a qualitative design was chosen in the form of expert interviews. The interviews were exclusively conducted by the author as personal or telephone interviews. A total of 14 interviews were conducted between September 2014 and July 2015.

Two main limitations apply to the empirical study. First, the binational approach of the study could pose a language barrier. However, the interviews were conducted in the respective mother tongue of the interviewees to ensure the flawless communication of ideas and opinions. The author, who was the interviewer and coder, is fluent in German and English. To ensure that the meaning was not altered, the material was only translated after the author had finished the analysis. The translation is, therefore, not literal and only aims at making the statements accessible to all English-speaking readers. Second, third-party creditors other than banks were not interviewed personally, but were represented by legal advisors or consultants who have considerably more experience. Third-party creditors themselves may know of one or two instances where a bank acted in response to a covenant default, whereas advisors and consultants deal with such situations on a daily basis. A subsequent quantitative study is required to analyse the perception of third-party creditors in further detail. The scope of the empirical study is limited due to the fact that it mainly focuses on the perception of banks. Further studies should thus concentrate on other covenant-secured creditors and the perception of third-party creditors to concretise, broaden or limit the theory developed.

Chapter 8 presented the results of the empirical study. It was found that covenants and the event of default clause are indeed enforced out of court and, thus, create a bilateral private governance system. It also shows that legal restrictions impact the bank's conduct only marginally. Moreover, the empirical study found that the presumption that banks disregard third-party creditors' interests is wrong. The findings suggest that the only substantial, potential negative externality is asset dilution due to additional risk premiums, whereas the main potential positive externalities are keeping the borrower solvent and producing information after a covenant default, which is likely to be shared with third-party creditors. However, further research regarding the enforcement of the negative pledge clause is required.

The fact that the positive externalities found seem to outweigh the negative externalities is due to the interdependency, or reciprocity, between the bilateral private governance system and third-party creditors. First, the bank's debt contract can be linked with that of third-party creditors via a cross-default, negative pledge and pari passu clause. Second, the interests of a bank and of third-party creditors can be linked because third-party creditors who are essential for the operational business can threat to drive the debtor company into bankruptcy. This leads to a multi-party private governance system and an incentive structure that allows to internalise potential negative externalities of covenants.

Chapter 9 re-evaluated the preliminary theory about externalities of the covenants' bilateral private governance system based on the findings of the empirical study by applying the concept of CPRs. The aggregated value of the debtor company's asset pool is the CPR. Around this CPR, an *n*-person prisoner's dilemma exists between banks and third-party creditors: No creditor knows when and under what conditions the other creditor will appropriate from or produce the debtor company's asset pool. This coordination problem is addressed by three means: bankruptcy law, collateral and the incentive structure surrounding covenants created by the interdependency found (CPR private governance system). The CPR private governance system changes the incentives for banks, so that banks will not only act in a self-interested way. It can also be correlated to the seven design principles identified by Ostrom: The CPR private governance system has clearly defined boundaries, rules adjusted to the specific circumstances and participation of most creditors in collective choice, so that a proper set of rules can be devised. Moreover, efficient monitoring and graduated sanctioning activities, which are essential to produce stable long-term cooperation, are ensured by banks and trade credit insurers as third-party creditors. Finally, the long-term maintenance of the CPR private governance system is fostered by conflict resolution mechanisms in renegotiation processes and through the LSTA and LMA. Also, a minimal recognition of the bank's right to organise is given.

The CPR private governance system regulates the common pool problem before bankruptcy law applies. Moreover, unlike collateral, it is mainly enforced out of court and thus avoids enforceability problems. This also highlights one of its main benefits, namely its transnational character. Covenants and the CPR private governance system are not limited to national jurisdictions. Thus, their enforceability can be ensured without problems connected with state jurisdictions and court enforcement mechanisms. Questions about the applicable law and forum do not hamper the enforcement of covenants in the bilateral private governance system nor the CPR private governance system regulating the common pool problem. The transnational character of covenants and the CPR private governance system is further fostered by the standardisation process in the market due to the LMA and LSTA. This ensures that covenants and the event of default clause are internationally stipulated similarly. Moreover, the incentive structure surrounding covenants was found to be broadly alike in Germany and the US. Further qualitative research, however, should be conducted to support this theory. Generally, the transnational character allows for more certainty, even though the CPR private governance system functions in the shadow of the law.

The last Chap. 10 detailed the important implications of the interaction between the different spheres of regulation for the selected legal topics that have been exemplarily discussed, as well as the legal treatment of covenants and event of default clauses. Covenants cannot be seen as an alternative to institutional regulation on its own; instead the complete CPR private governance system and its interaction with institutional regulation must be taken into consideration. This change of perspective leads to the conclusion that covenants and the CPR private governance system are not a substitute for but rather a supplement to capital requirements. Only the initial minimum capital requirement seems to be dispensable. Moreover, covenant-secured creditors can also play an important role in corporate governance by mediating between short-term and long-term interests.

In addition, the legal treatment of covenants and event of default clauses in Germany must accept and respect the function of the CPR private governance system. They fill a gap in the tragedy of the commons regulation by bankruptcy law and collateral. Accordingly, covenants and event of default clauses must not be declared null under §138 BGB if in doubt. Rather, factual misbehaviour must be sanctioned under § 826 BGB to ensure that covenants can still fulfil their function. Also, more extensive mandatory duties can foster the CPR private governance system. Any covenant breach that is reasonably likely to cause an acceleration should lead to an ad-hoc duty for public companies to disclose substantial information about the covenant default under Art. 17 I of the Market Abuse Regulation. This could *de lege ferenda* include the date of the covenant default; a brief description of the loan agreement defaulted; a brief description of the covenant default; the amount involved and terms of acceleration; any other material obligations that might be affected by the covenant default; if waived, the time period waived for; and steps the company intends to take to cure or otherwise address the covenant default. More generally, a risk report and forecast according to § 289 HGB should similarly include substantial information about covenant defaults.

Chapter 12
Outlook

The findings of the work have also further implications for future research. Covenants and the CPR private governance system function in the shadow of the law. They were developed in a dynamic process and will continue to be shaped by national and international regulations. For example, when regulating banks, the national regulator affects the bank's conduct after a covenant default. Regulations may hinder the bank's discretion after a covenant default and impede necessary corrective actions. This will in turn, adversely impact the CPR private governance system. On the other hand, the trend "covenant-lite 2.0" should also be considered when regulating banks and other investors. Covenants and the CPR private governance system have a particular market function: They regulate the common pool problem in areas where property law and bankruptcy law are insufficient. If the trend continues, the CPR private governance structure looses its "teeth". This will lead to a lower level of protection for all creditors as well as to a shift of control in corporate governance towards short-term stakeholders. Thus, future research in the area of bank regulation must consider its interrelationship with covenants and the CPR private governance system. Also, the effect that the selling of loans on the secondary market has on the CPR private governance system must be further researched to better understand the limits of the CPR private governance system found. If the credit risk is transferred, the economic risk is decoupled from the control rights. Thus, after a loan is sold on the secondary market, there is no longer an incentive for the bank to monitor.

Moreover, research on covenant-secured creditors other than banks should be conducted. This may allow concretising, broadening or limiting the theory developed. In the same way, the perception of debtor companies and third-party creditors should be researched in detail. Particularly, future research should focus on the interrelationship of the CPR private governance structure and bankruptcy law; e.g. by interviewing bankruptcy administrator.

As mentioned earlier, the question should not be whether covenants and the CPR private governance system can substitute bankruptcy law, but how an efficient interaction between them can be ensured. This may also have consequences for

D. Matri, *Covenants and Third-Party Creditors*, DOI 10.1007/978-3-319-62036-7_12

the legal treatment of covenants—particularly for the debate about subordinating sophisticated creditors.[1] In light of the so-called "*atypisches Pfandgläubiger-Urteil*"[2] (atypical lienor judgment) a discussion about the subordination of covenant-secured loans in case of legal or *de facto* power to control the debtor company arose.[3] This discussion was resparked by the introduction of the MoMiG[4] because the new § 39 InsO called the criteria for subordination into question.

The prevailing view still requires that the creditor's position is comparable to that of a shareholder.[5] First, the covenant-secured creditor must partake of the debtor company's profit in an equity-like way. This can be assumed in the case of an equity kicker or mezzanine capital.[6] However, the nominal value of the profit participation should be higher than ten percent of the share capital.[7] Second, the covenant-secured creditor's ability to control the debtor company's management is required.[8] The threshold of control or influence needed for an equity-like position that justifies a subordination is, however, unclear. Principally, the concrete danger of equity-like influence should be sufficient.[9] However, the mere stipulation of financial covenants should not lead to an equity-like position since the headroom leaves the management some discretion.[10] The same is true for information undertakings, even though they provide the creditor with an information advantage.[11] However, the granting of rights to actively control or influence the management of the debtor company is problematic.[12] Regularly, such rights will already be assumed when contractual remedies are provided in case of a covenant default (event of default clause). Thus, if equity-like profit participation is given and a

[1]Servatius (2008), p. 426 et seqq.; *Engert*, ZGR (2012), 835; Majic (2013), p. 45 et seqq.

[2]BGHZ 119, 191 regarding the old law.

[3]Also relevant (regarding the old law), BGHZ 83, 341; BGHZ 106, 7; BGH, WM 1983, 594, 594 et seq.; BGH, WM 1985, 284, 284 et seq.; regarding the new law, BGHZ 193, 378, 385.

[4]*Gesetz zur Modernisierung des GmbH-Rechts und zur Bekämpfung von Missbräuchen* (Law for the Modernisation of the German Limited Liability Company Law and the Prevention of Misuse).

[5]Similar BGHZ 196, 220, 226, 227; cf. also Servatius (2013), 19. Servatius himself, however, even goes one step further and gives the requirement of equity-like profit participation up because he argues for a different double function (Servatius (2013), 19 et seqq.).

[6]Cf. Berger (2008), 103 et seq.; Engert (2012), 861 et seq.; Renner and Hesselbarth (2014), 13 et seq.

[7]Following § 39 V InsO. Nuanced Engert (2012), 862 et seq., 869.

[8]Kampshoff (2010), 901; Breidenstein (2010), 276; Fleischer and Schmolke (2011), 1015; Kleindiek, in: Lutter, Hommelhoff (eds) (2012), para. 121; Hoffmann (2012), 11; disagreeing Huber, in: Hommelhoff et al. (eds) (2007), p. 279 et seq.; *Habersack* (2008), 2387 et seq.; Krolop (2009), 400.

[9]BGHZ 193, 378, 385; Fleischer, in: Henssler, Strohn (eds) (2014), para. 25.

[10]Kampshoff (2010), 901.

[11]Ulbrich (2011), p. 401 et seq.; Kampshoff (2010), 901 et seq.; concerning the old legal framework, Servatius (2008), p. 526; Fleischer (1998), 319.

[12]Ulbrich (2011), p. 402; Kampshoff (2010), 902; Servatius (2008), p. 527 et seqq.

negative pledge clause or covenants and an event of default clause are stipulated, the loan should—according to some scholars—be subordinated.

This disregards the general CPR private governance system, which ensures cooperative behaviour between creditors. The fact that the concrete danger of such influence is sufficient for § 39 I no. 5 InsO may do the CPR private governance system no justice. It assumes that there is no other incentive structure than that for self-interested and opportunistic behaviour and that the creditor will misuse its powers. However, the empirical study indicates that this is not true. Moreover, the risk of subordination may adversely interfere with the CPR private governance system, as covenant-secured creditors may abstain from producing the CPR to avoid any potential risks of subordination and instead demand additional collateral. A better approach could be to sanction actual misbehaviour of covenant-secured creditors via tort law (§ 826 BGB). Nevertheless, as aforementioned due to the limited scope of the empirical study conducted further research is required.

In any case, the transnational character is a key advantage of covenants and the CPR private governance system as a creditor protection device. It allows for more certainty in international transactions. Particularly, in times of changing legal and political environments—for example, if the UK leaves the EU—covenants and the CPR private governance system provide stability and transaction security.

References

Berger KP (2008) Fremdkapitalnahe Mezzanine-Finanzierungen. ZBB:92 106

Breidenstein M (2010) Covenantgestützte Bankdarlehen in der Insolvenz. ZinsO:273–283

Engert A (2012) Drohende Subordination als Schranke einer Unternehmenskontrolle durch Kreditgeber. ZGR 41(6):835–874

Fleischer H (1998) Covenants und Kapitalersatz. ZIP:313–321

Fleischer T (2014) § 39 InsO. In: Henssler M, Strohn L (eds) Gesellschaftsrecht. Beck, München

Fleischer H, Schmolke KU (2011) Faktische Geschäftsführung in der Sanierungssituation. WM:1009–1016

Habersack M (2008) Die Erstreckung des Rechts der Gesellschafterdarlehen auf Dritte. ZIP:2385–2395

Hoffmann G (2012) Grenzen der Einflussnahme auf Unternehmensleitungsentscheidungen durch Kreditgläubiger. WM:10–19

Huber U (2007) Fianzierungsfolgenverantwortung de lege lata und de lege ferenda. In: Hommelhoff P, Rawert P, Schmidt K (eds) Festschrift für Hans Joachim Priester zum 70. Geburtstag. Otto Schmidt Verlag, Köln, pp 259–283

Kampshoff M (2010) Behandlung von Bankdarlehen in der Krise der GmbH. GmbHR 101 (17):897–904

Kleindiek D (2012) Anh zu § 64. In: Lutter M, Hommelhoff P (eds) GmbH-Gesetz Kommentar. Otto Schmidt, Köln

Krolop K (2009) Zur Anwendungder MoMiG-Regelungen zu Gesellschafterdarlehen auf gesellschaftsfremde Dritte. GmbHR 100(8):397–405

Majic M (2013) Covenants und Insolvenz: Risiken covenant-gesicherter Kreditgeber im Falle der Insolvenz des Kreditnehmers. De Gruyter, Berlin

Renner M, Hesselbarth M (2014) Grundzüge der Unternehmensfinanzierung. JuS:11–15
Servatius W (2008) Gläubigereinfluss durch Covenants. Mohr Siebeck, Tübingen
Servatius W (2013) Covenants in der Restrukturierung. Corporate Finance Law:14–22
Ulbrich M (2011) Die Abschaffung des Eigenkapitalersatzrechts der GmbH, vol 117. Schriften des Instituts für Arbeits- und Wirtschaftsrecht der Universität zu Köln. Nomos, Köln

Appendices: Empirical Research

Appendix 1: Interview Guideline

The mandatory or main questions provide the broader framework and were covered in all interviews. The subsequent questions were only posed if they have not already been answered under the main question or the subsequent question. So not every question has been posed and they might have been asked in a different order to facilitate the interview flow.[1]

[1]This is the standard procedure cf. *Bogner, Littig and Menz*, Interviews mit Experten. Eine praxisorientierte Einführung, 2014, p. 27 et seqq.

D. Matri, *Covenants and Third-Party Creditors*, DOI 10.1007/978-3-319-62036-7

Table 1 Interview guideline

Mandatory question		Subquestion question		Subquestion question	
English	*German*	***English***	*German*	***English***	*German*
What are your experiences with covenants in your day-to-day working life?	Wie sehen Ihre Erfahrungen mit Covenants im Berufsalltag aus?				
What is your understanding of the function of covenants?	Wie ist Ihr Verständnis von der Funktion der Covenants?	**How do you regard the relationship between covenants and collateral?**	Wie würden Sie das Verhältnis von Covenants und dinglicher Kreditsicherung beschreiben?		
		Why do you apply or recommend covenants?	Warum wenden Sie Covenants an?		
How effective do you regard covenants?	Für wie effektiv erachten Sie Covenants?	**Do you know of any problems regarding the enforcement of covenants?**	Welche Probleme gibt es bei der Durchsetzung von Covenants bekannt?	**How effective do you regard statutory creditor protection in comparison to covenants?**	Welchen Effektivitätsgrad würden Sie dem gesetzlichen Gläubigerschutz im Vergleich zu Covenants zuordnen?
		How do you ensure enforcement of covenants against third parties?	Wie wird die Durchsetzung von Covenants gegenüber Dritten erreicht?		
In the literature covenants are often said to have a free-riding effect for third-party creditors? How do you	In der Literatur wird in Bezug auf Covenants häufig von einem "free-riding" Effekt für Drittgläubiger	**Which mechanism do you know of, which ensure that third parties can**	Welche Instrumente sind Ihnen bekannt, mit denen die Informationsweitergabe bezüglich		

reflect on this topic from your practical experience?	gesprochen. Wie bewerten Sie diese Annahme aufgrund Ihrer Erfahrungen?	**learn about stipulated covenants?**	Covenants an Dritte gesichert werden kann?		
		Would you consider covenants as beneficial for third party creditors?	Inwieweit wirken sich Covenants auch positiv oder negativ für Drittgläubiger aus?		
		How effective would you consider the cross-default clause?	Für wie effektiv halten Sie die Cross-default Klausel?	**How do you ensure that you know about a cross-default?**	Wie erfahren Sie von einem Cross-Default?
				Which version of cross-default clauses do you recommend and why?	Welche Variante der Cross-default Klausel würden Sie empfehlen?
		Do you cooperate with other creditors?	Kooperieren Sie mit anderen Gläubigern?	***If yes*, would you like to expand that?**	Wenn ja, würden Sie das gerne ausbauen?
				***If no*, why not and would you like to change that?**	Wenn nein, warum und würden Sie das gerne ändern?
In your opinion in what way is there a race to assets in the twilight zone?	Inwieweit würden Sie Ihrer Erfahrung nach in dieser Situation von einem Wettlauf um Vermögenswerte sprechen?				
How would you consider the role of law firms, advisors and rating agencies in this process?	Wie bewerten Sie die Rolle von Rechtskanzleien, Beratern und Ratingagenturen in diesem Prozess?				

(continued)

Table 1 (continued)

Mandatory question		Subquestion question		Subquestion question	
English	*German*	***English***	*German*	***English***	*German*
How would you evaluate more transparency with regard to covenants and defaults?	Wie würden Sie mehr Transparenz bezüglich Covenants und deren Nichteinhaltung bewerten?				
Would you refrain from using covenants if your claim was subordinated because of them?	Würden Sie auf Covenants verzichten wenn ihre Forderungen in der Insolvenz nachrangig behandelt würden?				
We have covered a lot of aspects. Is there anything you would like to add or can you think of anything that should change with regard to the legal treatment of covenants?	Wir haben viele Aspekte von Convents behandelt. Gibt es noch etwas was Sie gerne ergänzen würden oder fällt Ihnen etwas bezüglich der rechtlichen Behandlung von Covenants ein, das geändert werden sollte?				

Appendix 2: Results

The following tables show the results from the author's coding process of the collected data. The complete material is available upon request. The translations are not literal[2] and only aim at making the statements accessible to all English speaking readers.

1 Private Governance: Enforcement Out of Court

Table 2 Commonness of enforcing covenants out of court

Category	Int. no.	Line	Statement	Translation[a]
Enforcement of covenants out of court is common	3	24	Usually, these things do not get played out in a court other than a bankruptcy court anyway	
	9	16	Und da sehen wir uns natürlich auch in der Rolle dem Kunden hier mal einen Hinweis zu geben, gleichwohl wir rein rechtlich gesehen nicht die Hoheit haben, den Kreditvertrag zu interpretieren. Letztlich könnte das nur vor Gericht geklärt werden, aber das ist eine rein theoretische Maßnahme. In der Regel konsultiert man dann final seinen Anwalt. Der Agent konsultiert den Anwalt des Konsortiums und daraus wird dann letztlich eine Meinung geformt	And here we naturally see ourselves in a position to give advice to our customers—even though, from a purely legal perspective, we don't possess the power to interpret the loan agreement. Ultimately it would be only possible to solve this before the court, but this is a purely theoretical measure. Generally, you end up consulting your lawyer—the agent consults the lawyer of the consortium—and an opinion will end up being formed from this
	13	42	Also ich bin jetzt seit acht Jahren Anwalt und in diesen acht Jahren war ich kein einziges Mal vor Gericht	I have been a lawyer for 8 years now and during these 8 years I was not once in front of a court
	14	14	*Interviewer:* Wie häufig hatten Sie schon gerichtliche Auseinandersetzungen oder Auseinandersetzungen vor Schiedsgerichten? *Interviewter:* Null	*Interviewer:* How often did you have court disputes or alternative disputes? *Interviewee:* Zero

[a]It is only a rough translation. The same is true for all translations within the findings

[2]This is a common procedure for international empirical research see *Behling and Law*, Translating Questionaires and other Research Instruments, 2000, p. 54 f.

1.1 Reasons for Enforcement Out of Court

Table 3 Reasons for private enforcements

Category	Int. no.	Line	Statement	Translation
Better for both parties	3	21	There are two other reasons, one of which you mentioned is relationship. It is particularly true for an investment bank in a sponsor deal or for that matter large companies that tend to go through bankruptcy but never go away: You do not want to run to the courts to enforce things if you can amicably work things out. [. . .] to the extent that the company is cooperating and you are working things out amicably you have a better shot at preserving enterprise value	
	9	34	[. . .] wenn man auch von der Kundenseite eine vernünftige Kommunikation pflegt, Dinge vernünftig erklärt, ist das auch kein starres Korsett, was unauflöslich ist, sondern eines das dann auch lebt mit Veränderungen, die während der Geschäftsbeziehungen, während der Kreditlaufzeit einfach passieren können	[. . .]when customer communication is good and matters are explained properly, there is no rigid corset that must be followed, but rather one can adapt to new circumstances, which can occur during the life of a credit agreement
	13	42	Von den Verträgen, die ich beraten habe, ist bis jetzt nach meinem Kenntnisstand kein einziger jemals vor Gericht gelandet, weil es meistens das Interesse beider Parteien ist, eine Lösung zu finden mit der beide Seiten leben können. Während ein Gerichtsverfahren in aller Regel dazu führen würde, dass erstens auf Jahre lang Unsicherheit besteht bis das Gerichtsverfahren wirklich in der letzten Instanz durch ist. Da vergehen Jahre. In diesen Jahren ist man dann möglicherweise schon in einer Insolvenz. Das heißt, es geht dann eh zum	According to my knowledge, no contract, that I have been advising on has ever ended up before a court because it is commonly in the interest of both parties to find a solution with which both can live. In contrast, a court trial regularly results in years of uncertainty until the matter is decided in the last instance. This takes years to happen, in which time a party might already become bankrupt. As a consequence you end up with an bankruptcy administrator or you have to build up reserves. No party is interested in doing that.

(continued)

Table 3 (continued)

Category	Int. no.	Line	Statement	Translation
			Insolvenzverwalter oder es müssen Rückstellungen gebildet werden und da hat dann keine der Parteien ein Interesse dran. [. . .] am Ende hat keine der beiden Parteien ein Interesse daran, das jetzt vor Gericht krähen zu lassen, weil dann im Zweifel beide pleite sind am Ende, weil beidc müssen über die Jahre Rückstellungen bilden [. . .]	[. . .] in the end nobody is interested in bringing the case before a court because in doubt both parties will be insolvent in the end since both have to build up reserves over the years [. . .]
	14	19	Die Summen, die wir beraten, die so umfangreiche Verträge darstellen, da sind die Werte, die da auf dem Spiel stehen, einfach viel zu hoch, als dass es sich ökonomisch lohnen würde darüber zehn Jahre vor drei Instanzen zu streiten. Da ist man schon um zwei Finanzkrisen weiter. Vielleicht gibt es ja die ein oder andere Bank in der Zeit gar nicht mehr [. . .] Auf jeden Fall ist ein Vergleich für alle die ökonomisch beste Lösung und das auch außergerichtlich	With those complex contracts, there, the sum that is in question is just too high so that it is not economical to fight over it before three instances for 10 years. At that point two economic crises will have come. Maybe one or the other bank won't exist till then [. . .] in any case a settlement is more economical for all parties and that is also the case if it is madc out of court
Legal enforcement of covenants is possible, but. . .	1	44	If you enforce them the way they are meant to be enforced, if you declare default and then you follow through with whatever it is that you say that you are going to do, then unless there is something wrong with the way that they were structured or written, then yes they are absolutely enforceable and can be used to increase interest rate or freeze a line of credit. Again, if your payments are current it is harder to declare default and accelerate	
	1	54	It is because—for whatever reason—it is just sort of the mind-set that if you are getting paid unless you can	

(continued)

Table 3 (continued)

Category	Int. no.	Line	Statement	Translation
			convince the judge that you are invoking a default under the general insecurity clause it is really hard—probably almost impossible—to enforce a financial covenant	
	13	61	Also, was mir auffällt, ist dass die vorhin von Ihnen angesprochenen Thematiken, AGB-Recht, faktische Geschäftsführung, Nachrangigkeit, dass das auf Seiten der Banken nicht immer auf den Schirmen ist, dass die Banken nicht selten Klauseln in ihre Darlehensverträge reinverhandeln/aufnehmen, deren tatsächliche Durchsetzbarkeit vor Gericht zumindest fragwürdig ist	The topics you mentioned earlier standard terms, *de facto* directorship and subordination are often not thought of by bankers and frequently clauses are included with at least questionable enforceability before court
	14	25	[. . .] dass es zwar furchtbar toll ist zwar auf mehreren Seiten dann Kündigungsgründe und sehr ausgefeilte Verträge zu haben, aber am Ende des Tages traut sich keine Bank letzten Endes vor Zahlungsverzug zu kündigen	[. . .] it is great to have reasons for acceleration stipulated on multiple pages and to have very sophisticated contracts. However, at the end of the day no bank dares to accelerate before payment default
Barriers to legal enforcement	14	19	Also es fängt schon mit der Sprache an: Nämlich ein englischer Vertrag. Im Moment ist ja noch die Gerichtssprache Deutsch. Außer vielleicht in Köln muss ich eine Übersetzung machen. Wie soll ich bitte 4000 Seiten übersetzten, da streite ich mich mit der Gegenseite zwei Jahre um eine autorisierte Übersetzung [. . .] Es gibt viele Bereiche, die macht der Markt einfach so. Da hat der Markt für sich einen Standard gefunden, der funktioniert. Der ist so vom	It already starts with the language—namely an English contract. At the moment, the language of the court is German. Except for maybe Cologne, you have to provide a translation. But how does someone translate 4,000 pages? Because we will fight with the other party over the appropriate translation for 2 years. [. . .] There are several areas self-regulated by the market. The market found a standard for itself that works. This standard has not yet been dealt with by current legal

(continued)

Table 3 (continued)

Category	Int. no.	Line	Statement	Translation
			Recht, von der Kommentarliteratur und von den Universitäten—deswegen freu ich mich so, dass sie hier sind—gar nicht so richtig aufgearbeitet worden, als dass darüber jemand unbefangenes Drittes sich so einlesen könnte oder einfinden könnte, dass er versteht, was da funktioniert	literature and the universities—that is why I am really happy that you are here. So it is nearly impossible for a third party to access the topic and understand what happens
Saving the status quo	14	13	Bei vielen übrigens nicht ganz unbewusst. Viele Finanzrechtler—Kollegen mit denen man sich unterhält—wissen ganz genau, dass es da gewisse Themen gibt, darüber wollen wir einfach nichts schreiben, weil man Angst hat, dass das dann ins Gegenteil verkehrt wird. Wo man einfach sagt: Da ist es besser—auch wenn es jetzt ein Zustand ist, der unbefriedigend ist—dieses Problem nicht zu problematisieren und in die Hände von Richtern oder so anzuvertrauen oder irgendjemandem anders würde uns noch mehr Probleme bereiten, als es im Moment der Status Quo ist	Many do that not entirely unintentionally. Many finance lawyers—colleagues you are talking with—know very well that there are topics we do not want to write about because the fear is there that it will have an adverse effect. In this situation you simply say: 'It is better—even though the situation is unsatisfactory—not to thematise this problem. To put it in the hands of judges or someone else would cause more problems than the current status quo'

1.2 Through Self-Enforcing Agreements

Table 4 Reasons for self-enforcement of covenants

Category	Int. no.	Line	Statement	Translation
Leverage based enforcement	1	16	Well, a good one is when you are kind of creating pain for the customer. A good way to do that is to have a default interest rate—meaning that the customer can disregard the covenant and can not pay any attention to it, but if the bank increases the interest rate by four hundred bases points, it gets their attention	
	1	18	If we fully enforced our rights, we would cost you to file with SEC certain documents. On the other hand, maybe there is something else that we can get that would make this more comfortable, where they would not have to file. So, that is a big plus if they are a public company	
	4	14	The interests of the borrower and of whoever is at the top of the capital structure are kind of aligned here because the first lien lenders do not want it to be necessary for the consent of the second lien lenders or the consent of bondholders to be needed. But the borrower does not want this either	
	6	15	Hier die Finanzkennzahlen, da ist man noch weit von einer Insolvenz entfernt, aber die führen dazu, dass man ein Kündigungsrecht hat und man dieses Kündigungsrecht nutzt, sodass man sagt: "Gut, wir verhandeln jetzt nochmal und lassen uns neue Sicherheiten geben—lassen uns diese erhöhte Risikoposition durch neue Sicherheiten untermauern."	The financial covenants, there one is still far away from bankruptcy but they [their breach] provide a right to accelerate. And if one uses this right to accelerate in a way that you say: "Well, we renegotiate and we want to receive collateral—we want the increased risk premium be compensated for by the new collateral."
	9	18	Ich habe in meiner Laufbahn bisher noch keinen Konsortialkredit gesehen, der faktisch gekündigt wurde. Sondern es ist letztlich immer nur der Mechanismus, den man	In my professional career I have not yet seen a syndicated loan that was *de facto* accelerated. But it is a mechanism one has to create a momentum in a specific situation—to actually

(continued)

Table 4 (continued)

Category	Int. no.	Line	Statement	Translation
			hat, um ein Momentum in eine Situation reinzubekommen—sich gemeinsam mit dem Kunden auch tatsächlich zusammenzusetzen, um eine Lösung für ein offensichtliches Problem herbeizuführen	get together with the customer to find a solution for an obvious problem
	13	16	[. . .] die Waiver werden von der Bank normalerweise nur ungern erteilt, beziehungsweise nur erteilt gegen Zahlung eines Preises. Preis im Sinne von natürlich erstens einer Waiver Gebühr, aber vielmehr auch eines sonstigen Entgegenkommens auf Seiten des Darlehensnehmers	Waivers are not handed out readily by banks, or rather only in return for payment of a price. Price in the sense of naturally first a waiver fee but more importantly other accommodations on the side of the debtor
	13	42	Und dann wird halt verhandelt und dann wird hart verhandelt und intensiv verhandelt und am Ende hat keine der beiden Parteien ein Interessen daran, das jetzt vor Gericht krähen zu lassen, weil dann im Zweifel beide pleite sind am Ende, weil beide müssen über die Jahre Rückstellungen bilden—über Jahre Geld einfach einbetonieren—und das würde keiner von beiden wirtschaftlich überleben	And then there will be negotiations, they will be tough and intensive and in the end no party is interested in bringing the case before the courts because in case of doubt both parties will be insolvent at the end since both have to build up reserves—to simply concrete money over years—and that will none of them survive economically
	14	27	Ein interessantes anderes Druckmittel gibt es ja noch, wenn sie noch Linien haben, die nicht ausgenutzt sind, beziehungsweise der Kreditnehmer noch ziehen will. In dem Moment liegt sozusagen bei einem rein ökonomischen Kräftemessen das Leverage, also der Hebel, bei der Bank	An interesting leverage is given, when there are still undrawn credit lines or the debtor still wants to draw. In that situation in case of a purely economically trial of strength the leverage lies with the bank
Relationship based enforcement	1	14	So, covenants can be really effective if your customer is tuned into them and they consider them to be an important part of that relationship. If they do not, then you have got problems	
	5	47	Wir wollen ein Relationship-Geschäft, wo wirklich jede einzelne Beziehung auf dem	We want a relationship transaction, where really every single relationship is put to the

(continued)

Table 4 (continued)

Category	Int. no.	Line	Statement	Translation
			Prüfstand steht. Und wenn man so nah dran ist, dann kriegt man in der Regel schon mit, wenn da irgendwas passiert	test. And when one is so close, one will usually latch on if something is wrong
	8	89	Weil wenn man sich auf Financial Covenants einlässt, dann geht es nur auch über die Relationship-Schiene	Because if one uses financial covenants, then this is only possible with the relationship-track
	8	91	Also ich glaube, Financial Covenants ohne "Relation" macht gar keinen Sinn. Ein sehr gutes Relationship braucht aber keine Financial Covenants	Well, I think that financial covenants without relation do not make any sense. A really good relationship, however, does not depend on financial covenants
	9	18	Ich kenne es eigentlich fast ausschließlich nur so, dass man dann gemeinsam versucht—vielleicht manchmal auch nach zähem Ringen—dann Lösungen zu finden, in denen man den Vertrag und mit ihm die Verpflichtungen und die Covenants so anpasst, dass sie wieder zu der Situation passen, in dem das Unternehmen sich befindet [. . .]	I know it actually only in that way, that both parties try—maybe after hard bargaining—to find a solution together in which one adapts the contract and with it the covenants in a way that they fit to the situation in which the company is [. . .]
	13	28	[. . .] weil diese stabilen Beziehungen, die man aufgebaut hat, das Vertrauensverhältnis, was über Jahre aufgebaut wurde, auch dazu führen, dass man leichter in Krisensituationen mit der Bank reden kann und die Bank auch mehr bereit ist mitzugehen, als wenn man im Prinzip keine jahrelang aufgebaute Beziehung hat	[. . .]these stable relationships and trust one has built also lead to better communication with the bank in times of crisis, and the bank is also more willing to go along with you than they would be without those years spent building a relationship
	13	40	Sondern ich glaube ein langfristiges Vertrauensverhältnis, wo man auch mal bereit ist zu geben oder wo man bereit ist irgendwo eine Lösung zu finden mit der beide Seite gut leben können, ist häufig eher im langfristigen	I believe that a long-term relationship of trust where one is also willing to give sometimes or to find a solution that both parties can live with is in the long-term interest of the debtor. And that is my experience with my customers. Some

(continued)

Table 4 (continued)

Category	Int. no.	Line	Statement	Translation
			Interesse des Darlehensnehmers. Und das ist auch mit meinen Mandanten so meine Erfahrung, dass die zum Teil bereit waren auch auf Forderungen der Banken zu leisten, die sie gar nicht hätten leisten müssen. Und zwar nicht ohne erheblichen Umfang. [. . .] der Darlehensnehmer hat trotzdem gesagt: "Nc, wir haben seit Jahren ein Vertrauensverhältnis mit der Bank und wir wollen das jetzt nicht wegen € 500.000 platt machen und wir leisten jetzt auf diese Vorfälligkeitsentschädigung, obwohl wir wissen, dass wir, wenn es zum Gerichtsverfahren kommen würde, allerhöchstwahrscheinlich obsiegen würden."	of them have been willing to comply with the demands of the bank even though they did not need to. And those demands concerned high sums. [. . .] one debtor even said: "No, we have had a relationship of trust for years—we don't want to ruin that because of €500,000. So we are going to pay the prepayment penalty even though we know that we would most likely win before a court."

1.3 Limits of Private Governance via Covenants

Table 5 Limits of private governance via covenants

Category	Int. no.	Line	Statement	Translation
Lack of motivation to monitor	1	28	If somebody has a commercial real estate building and you only test a covenant on an annual basis, or they give you information on a quarterly basis or semi-annual, obviously if they do not sent that information to you, you are back to the question what can you really do with that default if they are making their payments. You have got tangible collateral—it is this building you can see it every day and unless there is something going on with the building, deteriorating or some sort of maintenance issues, you are going to be less concerned about that	
Liability	1	40	But usually where the courts would find that the bank has to take a subordinated position or maybe their claims are somehow impaired by the court is if you are doing something that is beyond your scope and you are causing harm or you set up a course of dealing where you were doing something over a period of time and then you suddenly changed tag. If you are doing something completely different that the customer did not have enough time or the ability to adapt to. Lender liability is a big issue. We frequently get coaching. Our legal department will have regular discussions with lenders and will say: **"Here are a set of common mistakes or things you want to refrain from doing." Because the court can essentially impair your ability to collect or even sometimes they can wipe out your claim**	

(continued)

Table 5 (continued)

Category	Int. no.	Line	Statement	Translation
			completely. And where you caused harm to somebody, not only do you not get repaid but you pay them for damages	
Limiting leverage	14	27	Gibt dann auch Kreditnehmer, die wenn ein Covenant-Verstoß absehbar ist, vorher vorsichtshalber alle Linien nochmal komplett ziehen und ausnutzen, dass das Geld bei denen liegt	There are debtors, who if a covenant breach is immanent will draw all loan lines completely and who will utilise the fact that all money is already with them

2 *Negative Effects on Third-Party Creditors*

2.1 Debtor Pays Bank First or Only It

2.1.1 Not Likely

Table 6 Not likely that debtor pays bank first or only it

Category	Int. no.	Line	Statement
Feeling responsible towards other third-party creditors	2	42	If it comes to paying back the loan, it is about whom the customer is feeling more obligated to
Better relationship with other third-party creditor	2	7	If I have got to rely on the covenants at giving me pay back, that is a problem. I have been here thirty 5 years and I had people where there is no way they should have been able to pay me and they did. And people who had the capacity to pay and did not. So, character is still a big part of who you are dealing with. Again, I think that is one of the advantages of old people like me of being around and knowing who you are lending to and having a relationship as opposed to we are going to fly in and doing that to you and then we are out of here
	2	49	So, whomever he has the closest relationship to, is probably the one who is getting paid. Even though his loan documents may say that the other creditor is paid first

2.1.2 Likely

Table 7 Likely that debtor pays bank first or only it

Category	Int. no.	Line	Statement
Payment options limited by covenants	2	49	It depends on the creditor. Covenants may keep them in line but it also keeps them beholding to that other individual. I guess, when it comes down to whether pay me or them, then they probably pay them
	3	19	One of the things that you should always find in a first lien document is a junior debt prepayment covenant. That is what junior creditors do not like because that in essence says that the senior lenders are going to treat payments on debt that is junior to their own debt almost like it is an equity payment. In other words, there are going to be restrictions on your ability to, for example, prepay. There may also be limitations under subordination provisions where if there is a default—payment or bankruptcy default—under senior debt, the subordination provision may even stop interest payments. The subordinated debt typically does not have principal payments until maturity. But it will have semi-annual interest payment, which can usually freely be made. But if there is a bankruptcy or payment default, they are blocked. And for a covenant default on a senior debt they could have to stand by for a hundred and eighty days, typically—or at least for one interest payment; usually not more than one
	4	10	If you imagine the same borrower with and without a maintenance covenant. In one scenario the credit is deteriorating and the maintenance covenant kicks in and either the company is putting into proceeding or has to renegotiate some date. In the other scenario there is no maintenance covenant and, as a result, maybe the company can continue using a bunch of cash and they can go on and find other places where they can get some cash or sell assets and they can make some additional number of interest payment on junior debt that they otherwise would not be able to make. In a situation like that, it is conceivable to me that there are junior creditors at some level of the capital structure that might end up recovering more money overall in the absence of a maintenance covenants than they would if the maintenance covenant were there. [...] A maintenance covenants like that at least avoids a situation where from a perspective of a first lien creditor a company can bleed off money servicing other debt that is more junior in the capital structure before there is anything you can do about it

2.2 Exploiting Third-Party Creditors

2.2.1 Not Likely

Table 8 Not likely that bank exploits third-party creditors

Category	Int. no.	Line	Statement	Translation
Cross default clause	11	34	Die Fälle des Dominoeffektes gibt es. Oder, wo zumindest damit gedroht wird, dass es passiert. Das reicht ja schon. So, da muss man sehen, wie kriegt man die Interessen unter einen Hut?	Cases where the domino effect occurred do exist—or at least it was used as a threat. That is already enough. So you have to find a way to reconcile all interests
	13	20	Also wenn wir den Bereich haben, dass der Darlehensnehmer in wirtschaftliche Schwierigkeiten kommt, dann muss man immer mit allen Gläubigern verhandeln, weil über die Cross Default Klausel oder Most Preferred Klausel oder wie auch immer man sie im Einzelnen ausgestaltet oder welche Regelungen da insbesondere in Betracht kommen, da immer letztlich irgendwo alle Gläubiger mit im Boot sitzen	If we are faced with the situation that the debtor is in financial distress, one has to negotiate with all creditors because—due to the cross-default clause or most preferred clause or however one drafts those clauses—all creditors are finally in the same boat
Liability	10	76	Das ist ja nur eine Frage der Geschwindigkeit und wie schnell die Sachen greifen, aber prinzipiell bin ich ja in der Geschäftsführerhaftung, wenn ich jetzt die einen Gläubiger bediene und die anderen nicht und dann melde ich Insolvenz an. Dann kann ich alles, das was ich den einem Gläubiger zugeschoben habe, persönlich nachschießen	It is only a question of speed and how fast measures take effect. But generally one is liable as director or manager: when I satisfy one creditor and not the others and then I file for bankruptcy, I am personally liable for everything I transferred to the one creditor
Junior debt is nothing worth anyway	4	12	Usually, everyone gets more value out of the company if you can find a way—even if that means writing debt off that is junior in the capital structure (but usually that is not worth anything anyway)	
Ability to protect oneself	1	30	And then you might have other creditors that might not have a formal loan agreement but they supply something that is critical to the operational flow of the company. They probably do not	

(continued)

Table 8 (continued)

Category	Int. no.	Line	Statement	Translation
			have covenants. But on the other hand, they are usually delivering something on a relatively frequent basis to the customer that the customer needs to keep its doors open. So by the time a borrower gets a troubled credit and is in the situation where it finds out that it is 90 days past making payments to this supplier, everything delivered has to be paid for in cash	
	1	30	So, eventually the creditor finds out that the borrower has problems and they are taking their own steps to sort of mitigate their loss or at least to try to minimise it	
	7	70	Alle anderen Gläubiger, ganz grob, sind entweder Lieferanten, die über ihre Eigentumsvorbehalte gesichert sind oder es sind die Kreditgläubiger, die entweder gar keine Sicherheiten oder Sicherheiten im Bereich nach den Eigentumsvorbehalten haben oder im Immobilienbereich	Roughly, all other creditors are either suppliers, who can secure themselves via retention of title, or they are creditors who have either no collateral or collateral ranking subordinated to retention of title or in immovable property
	7	104	Wenn wir uns im Krisenvorfeld bewegen, kostet das natürlich. Und da sind diejenigen, die im Endeffekt die Covenant-Strukturen vereinbart haben, sicher im Vorteil zu Drittgläubigern. die mit Sicherheit wesentlich mehr Schwierigkeiten haben ihre Preise entsprechend anzupassen. Sofern es sich um die laufenden Lieferanten oder so weiter handelt, geht das, aber wenn andere mit ihren eher mittelfristigen Themen mit drin sind, glaube ich das eher weniger	If a company is in financial distress, it is expensive. And in that case creditors, who have stipulated covenants, certainly have an advantage over third-party creditors, who will struggle more to adjust their prices. Insofar as regular suppliers or similar creditors are concerned, it will be alright, but if a creditor is lending for a medium duration, it will be difficult
	8	22	In dem Moment, in dem ich die Krisensituation habe, habe ich zwangsläufig das Problem, dass Kleingläubiger die bekannten	The moment I find myself in financial distress, I inevitably face the problem of small creditors trying to obtain the

(continued)

Table 8 (continued)

Category	Int. no.	Line	Statement	Translation
			Nörgelprämien und Nörgeleinflüsse versuchen durchzusetzen	known 'nagging' premiums or 'nagging' influences
	11	30	Also, die Drittgläubiger, die wir sehen oder sehen könnten, das sind in der Regel dann Factor- und Leasingunternehmen, die in der Regel erstklassig und erstrangig an den dinglichen Sicherheiten besichert sind, die einfach da sind	We often see factor- or leasing creditors as third-party creditors, who are generally covered by first-class or first-ranking collateral
	1	30	But typically if you are in a syndication all of those senior creditors are sort of in the same boat	
Syndicated loan	12	2	Wobei man aber auch sagen muss, dass die Tendenz zu Konsortialkreditverträgen schon zunimmt. [...] Für die Banken bietet das ja auch noch mehr Schutz, wenn alle Banken in einem Boot sitzen [...]	The tendency towards syndicated loans increases. [...] This provides protection to banks because all banks are in the same boat [...]
	13	20	Wenn man diese Auflagen nimmt [...] bezüglich Veräußerung oder Fusionierung oder wie auch immer, dann ist es häufig so, dass entweder ähnliche Verpflichtungen in den Darlehensverträgen mit den verschiedenen Gläubigern oder Gläubigergruppen (das sind ja häufig Konsortialdarlehen) bestehen	If you look at the restriction on sales or mergers or other matters, you will often find similar conditions in loan agreements with different creditors or creditor groups (these are often syndicated loans)

2.2.2 Likely

Table 9 Likely that bank exploits third-party creditors

Category	Int. no.	Line	Statement	Translation
Additional risk premium	3	24	And in the meantime the senior debt can issue a waiver or amendment in exchange for fees and/or other covenant protections designed to get around this problem or they can be refinanced, as well	
	7	10	Das führt im Endeffekt natürlich häufig auch zu verstärkten Risikoprämien	In the end this often leads to additional risk premiums
	8	6	Die andere Rechtsfolge, die sie daraus ableiten können ist zu sagen: "Ich will eine höhere Risikoprämie dafür haben."	The other legal consequence that can be deduced is to say: "I want a higher risk premium."
	9	20	Dafür werden in der Regel Waiver-Fees gezahlt, weil die Banken haben in dem Moment das Kreditrisiko, was deutlich schlechter ist—was sich in den internen Ratings auch nach unten entwickelt	For that debtor companies have to pay waiver fees because banks have to bear the credit risk, which is definitely worse and which also becomes evident in internal ratings
	10	54	[...] eine Waiver Fee ist eigentlich die häufigste Maßnahme	[...] a waiver fee is the most common reaction
	11	22	Und wenn das Risiko gestiegen ist, möchte ich eben auch partizipieren und möchte meine Risikokosten auch wieder verdienen	And when the risk increases, I want to participate and be reimbursed for my risk costs
	13	16	[...] es ein Waiver-Verfahren gibt und die Waiver von der Bank normalerweise nur ungern erteilt werden, beziehungsweise nur erteilt werden gegen Zahlung eines Preises. Preis im Sinne von natürlich erstens einer Waiver Gebühr, aber vielmehr auch eines sonstigen Entgegenkommens auf Seiten des Darlehensnehmers	[...] a waiver process is in place and banks usually do not like to give a waiver or they only give it in return for payment of a price. A price not merely in form of a waiver fee but rather in form of any other accommodation on the part of the debtor
	14	41	Margenerhöhung auch	Margin increase, as well
	14	51	Selbst wenn der Kredit unbesichert sein sollte, hat natürlich in der Insolvenz die Bank, der Finanzgläubiger—	Even if the loan is unsecured, the bank will have *de facto* the most power in bankruptcy proceedings—just because

(continued)

Table 9 (continued)

Category	Int. no.	Line	Statement	Translation
			einfach weil er der größte Gläubiger sein wird—de facto die größte Macht. Er hat auch die Macht über Verhandlungen, Sanierungsverhandlungen außerhalb der Insolvenz. Und das größte Wort oder kann den größten Einfluss nehmen, weil er meistens den Finger am Abzug hat	the bank will be the biggest creditor. The bank has the power with regard to negotiations, reorganisation negotiations outside bankruptcy. And the bank has the biggest say or biggest influence because it has its finger on the trigger
Monetary premium if fully secured credit	4	12	But if you believe you are fully secured and you do not believe that the value of your debt is declining day by day, there may not be a tone of urgency around that. And the alternative to accelerate the debt is saying "OK. There is a problem here. You need relieve under the covenants, we can loosen the covenants but you will pay us more". So, there is some incentive to go ahead and collect some more money for the perceived additional risk on the debt	
Additional securities	5	13	Also dann gibt es häufig Nachverhandlungen und dann wird der Covenant-Bruch auch benutzt als Argument, um dann vielleicht andere Dinge durchzusetzen wie zum Beispiel Kreditsicherheiten	Then usually there will be renegotiations and the covenant breach will also be used to enforce other things like collateral
	6	15	Gut, wenn man sagt hier die Finanzkennzahlen, da ist man noch weit von einer Insolvenz entfernt, aber wenn die dazu führen, dass man ein Kündigungsrecht hat und man diese Kündigungsrecht nutzt, dass man sagt: "Gut, wir verhandeln jetzt nochmal und lassen uns neue Sicherheiten geben; lassen uns diese Risikoposition, diese erhöhte Risikoposition durch neue Sicherheiten untermauern."	Well, when you look at the financial ratios and see that the company is far away from bankruptcy but if these ratios entitle you to accelerate you do so and say "Well, we will renegotiate and we want additional collateral. We want to be protected from our increased risk by additional collateral."
	7	10	Also es führt nicht jeder Covenant-Bruch zu einer	Not every covenant breach leads to a corresponding increase in collateral

(continued)

Table 9 (continued)

Category	Int. no.	Line	Statement	Translation
			entsprechend verstärkten Sicherheitenbestellung	
	10	56	Wenn noch was da ist und es gibt einen Covenant Breach, ist die Nachbesicherung nicht weit entfernt	If there is something left and there is a covenant breach, the security is never far away
	11	28	Und je nachdem wie da die Situation ist, wird man möglicherweise auch ein höheres Absicherungsbedürfnis haben. Und dann kommt das Thema Nachbesicherung auf den Tisch	And, depending on the situation, there may be an increased need for credit protection. And then, the topic of additional security is on the table
	13	16	es ein Waiver-Verfahren gibt und die Waiver von der Bank normalerweise nur ungern erteilt werden, beziehungsweise nur erteilt werden gegen Zahlung eines Preises. Preis im Sinne von natürlich erstens einer Waiver Gebühr, aber vielmehr auch eines sonstigen Entgegenkommens auf Seiten des Darlehensnehmers. Also in der Bestellung einer zusätzlichen Sicherheit, eines höheren Zinssatzes, einer längeren Festlaufzeit, die man vielleicht nicht haben will als Darlehensnehmer, oder ähnlichem	[...] a waiver process is in place and banks usually do not like to give a waiver or they only give it in return for payment of a price. A price not merely in form of a waiver fee but rather in form of any other accommodation on the part of the debtor
	14	51	Also, wenn ich mir alles das, was nicht niet- und nagelfest am Unternehmen ist, an Sicherheiten nehme, habe ich entweder ein Aussonderungs- oder ein Absonderungsrecht in der Insolvenz und der andere geht leer aus. In dem Moment sind Drittgläubiger gefährdet	So, if I take everything that is not nailed down to the debtor company as collateral, I posses a higher ranking (either a right to separation from the estate ("Aussonderungsrecht") or a right for separate satisfaction ("Absonderungsrecht")) in bankruptcy proceedings and the other creditor will get nothing. In that moment third-party creditors are exposed
	9	84	Ich habe wenige Kredite gesehen, die sich aus Sicherheiten getilgt haben	I have seen few credits that were paid solely by securities

(continued)

Table 9 (continued)

Category	Int. no.	Line	Statement	Translation
Bondholders are too diverse	3	29	That is the other reason, why quite honestly in bank debt deals they allow others to pursue first-lien debt command but it is not going to be in the form of another bank debt. It has to be in the form of bonds because they know the first-lien bonds, while they rank equal in the capital structure, they cannot get their act together	

2.3 Domino-Effect

2.3.1 Not likely

Table 10 Not likely that domino-effect occurs

Category	Int. no.	Line	Statement	Translation
Insolvent anyway (no need for domino effect)	12	31	[...] die Bank; also das ist die größte Position und wenn die gekündigt wird, ist es eigentlich egal, wie sich das auswirkt auf den Dritten, weil wenn die echt gekündigt würde, und zurückgefordert werden würde, dann wäre das Unternehmen insolvent	[...] the bank, that is the biggest position and if that is accelerated, the effect on third-party creditors is irrelevant because if that is really accelerated and recalled, then the debtor company is insolvent anyway
	13	36	[...] egal wie solvent der Darlehensnehmer ist, wenn die Banken ihm die Finanzierung kündigen und zur sofortigen Rückzahlung fertig stellen, ist jedes Unternehmen pleite	[...] regardless of how solvent a debtor is, if the bank accelerates and immediately recalls its loan, every company is bankrupt
No better position in bankruptcy proceedings	9	82	Solange wir keine Sicherheiten haben, sind wir Senior Gläubiger neben anderen auch und müssen in der Insolvenz einfach schauen, was noch übrig bleibt	As long as we have no collateral, we are senior creditors besides others and have to see in bankruptcy what is left over
Biggest commitment	9	22	Und der Schuldschein hat ja ein Einzelkündigungsrecht und dann tritt das Problem auf. Ja, dann kommt es zum Cross-Default und die Konsortialbanken befinden sich in der Regel in der etwas unschönen Situation—da sie meistens die größten Commitments haben—den Fresh-Money-Einschuss zu leisten, damit die ganze Sache noch am Leben bleibt	The bond has an individual right to accelerate and then there is a problem. Then, there is a cross-default and the consortium banks are in the unattractive situation of having to provide the fresh money injection—because they commonly hold the greatest commitments—to keep the whole thing alive
	9	84	Und ich glaube man muss es eigentlich eher andersrum sehen: Dass Banken ein massives Interesse daran haben durch die hohen Commitments, die in der Regel alles übersteigen was andere Stakeholder haben, dass das Unternehmen irgendwo wieder	And I believe, one must look at it the other way around: due to their big commitments that regularly exceed what other stakeholders hold, **banks have a massive interest in putting the debtor company back into a reasonable situation to**

(continued)

Table 10 (continued)

Category	Int. no.	Line	Statement	Translation
			in eine vernünftige Situation zurückkommt und Cash Flows generiert, aus denen ein Kredit bedient werden kann	**generate cash flows out of which the loan can be paid**
Interested in going concern surplus	3	21	There are two other reasons, one of which you mentioned is relationship. It is particularly true for an investment bank in a sponsor deal or for that matter large companies that tend to go through bankruptcy but never go away: You do not want to run to the courts to enforce things if you can amicably work things out	
	4	12	And in a situation where people may believe that the debt is undersecured (So, let's say it is bank loan but it is trading at 80 cents on the dollar) in most of these situations it is very rare for there not to be a perception that you will get more out of the company if you help it as a going concern than you will if you chop it off	
	13	38	[. . .] aber natürlich auch durchaus im eigenen Interesse damit handeln, weil die Wahrscheinlichkeit, dass sie ihr Geld zurückbekommen bei einem Unternehmen das fortgeführt wird und die Sanierung schafft—wenn vielleicht auch mit quietschenden Reifen in der Kurve—deutlich höher ist, als wenn das Unternehmen einfach platt gemacht wird	[. . .] but of course banks act in their own interest, because the chances that the bank gets their loan principal back are higher, if a company continues and is recapitalised—even if so with screeching tires—than if the company is pushed in bankruptcy
No acceleration	2	17	But have we ever called a loan simply because they did not meet covenants? I do not think so	
	3	24	But are the lenders willing to push the nuclear button? Particularly, if you got a company that has significant junior debt and public bonds, the junior	

(continued)

Table 10 (continued)

Category	Int. no.	Line	Statement	Translation
			layers in the capital structure will typically have no cross-default clause but they will have a cross-acceleration clause. **So once the lenders actually accelerate, the lenders are no longer the only ones with a seat at the table**	
	5	10	Ob man eine Kündigung gleich immer umsetzt?, würde ich sagen in den wenigsten Fällen. Sondern meistens wird der Covenant-Bruch "gewaived", also man akzeptiert es als Bank, aber man behält sich eben seine Rechte vor	An acceleration is seldom the first response In most cases a covenant violation is waived. So, the bank accepts the covenant default but reserves its rights
	5	17	Man kann ja kündigen, aber hat man davon irgendwas? Bekommt man dann sein Geld zurück? Das ist damit noch lange nicht gesagt	You can accelerate but what do you get from it? Do you get repaid? That is not necessarily the case
	8	6	Dann stellt sich natürlich automatisch die Frage, wenn jemand einen Covenant bricht und Sie haben ein außerordentliches Kündigungsrecht und sie kündigen den Kredit, ob sie möglicherweise das Kapital überhaupt noch wieder erhalten. Also von daher ist das sicherlich erstmal eine theoretische Möglichkeit. Ich habe es in meiner beruflichen Karriere eigentlich noch nie erlebt, dass aufgrund eines Financial Covenants—also aufgrund des Bruchs eines Covenants—ein Kreditvertrag tatsächlich gekündigt wurde	If one breaches a covenant and you have a right to extraordinary notice and then you accelerate, the question arises whether the loan principal will be repaid. From that perspective, acceleration is certainly foremost a theoretical option. In my professional career I have actually never seen, that a credit was accelerated due to a covenant default
	9	18	Ich habe in meiner Laufbahn bisher noch keinen Konsortialkredit gesehen, der faktisch gekündigt wurde	So far in my professional career I have never seen that a syndicated loan was *de facto* accelerated
	9	52	Es ist ja nicht so, dass bei einem Verstoß gegen einen Financial Covenant gleich die Panik bei den Banken	It is not that every violation of financial covenant leads to banks panicking. Normally, one knows the cause and it is

(continued)

Table 10 (continued)

Category	Int. no.	Line	Statement	Translation
			ausbricht. In der Regel kennt man was die Ursache ist; es bleibt noch in bestimmten Rahmenbedingen. Da wird das Ganze einfach freigeschaltet per Waiver	within the basic conditions. Then, the whole thing gets waived
	12	31	Die wenigsten Covenant-Brüche führen zu einer Kündigung. Also die ganz überwiegende Zahl führt zu einem Waiver oder da, wo man davon ausgehen muss, dass es ein dauerhafter Bruch ist, kommt es zu einer Refinanzierung und Restrukturierung des Kredites	Few covenant defaults will lead to an acceleration. The overwhelming number lead to a waiver or in cases where the default is permanent a refinancing and restructuring of the loan
	14	25	[. . .] dass es zwar furchtbar toll ist zwar auf mehreren Seiten dann Kündigungsgründe und sehr ausgefeilte Verträge zu haben, aber am Ende des Tages traut sich keine Bank letzten Endes vor Zahlungsverzug zu kündigen	[. . .] it is great to have reasons for acceleration stipulated on multiple pages and to have very sophisticated contracts. However, at the end of the day no bank dares to accelerate before payment default
Ability to avoid cross-default	3	24	And in the meantime the senior debt can issue a waiver or amendment in exchange for fees and/or other covenant protections designed to get around this problem or they can be refinanced, as well	
	4	10	If a borrower then wants relieve from the tighter set of restrictions it can go out and get them and does not need the consent of the junior creditor	
	10	42	Jetzt ist die Frage, wie oft es zu so einem Cross Default kommt. Also das habe ich bisher immer verhindern können	Regarding the question, how often a cross-default occurs: So far I have been able to prevent that
	12	27	Weil die können verändert werden durch Verhandlungen des Konsortiums ohne dass ein Cross Default eintritt oder durch eine andere Refinanzierung	[. . .] because they can be changed through renegotiations with the consortium banks without triggering a cross-default or via a different method of refinancing

2.3.2 Likely

Table 11 Likely that domino-effect occurs

Category	Int. no.	Line	Statement	Translation
Cross default clause	5	28	Da hat man eine relativ schlanke vertragliche Basis für so ein Schuldscheindarlehen. Man hat in der Regel sehr viele verschiedene Investoren. Jeder Einzelne hat im Grunde genommen das Kündigungsrecht, wenn ein Covenant gebrochen ist. Das führt bei einer falschen Gestaltung von Covenants dazu—muss noch nicht mal falsch sein, generell gilt das aber erst Recht bei der falschen Gestaltung von Covenants gilt das—, dass man eben in so ein Kündigungsszenario reinkommt, was ein Unternehmen sofort in Liquiditätsengpässe bringen kann	There is a relatively narrow contractual basis for a bonded loan. That's why there are normally many different investors. Basically, each one of them has a right to accelerate when a covenant is violated. This means that if covenants are drafted incorrectly—it does not even have to be incorrect, but generally it is particularly true if covenants are drafted incorrectly—you enter a scenario of accelerations that immediately causes a liquidity shortage for the debtor company
	6	19	Und diese Cross-Default-Klauseln, die können dann so einen Dominoeffekt anstoßen, der möglicherweise der wahren Situation—die das Ganze aus der Tatsachensituation auslöst—nicht gerecht wird	And those cross-default clauses can cause a domino effect that may not reflect the actual situation—it is triggered by the situation on paper
	9	22	[...] ein zu hohes Gewicht auf Finanzierungen mit Einzelkündigungsrecht ist sicherlich ein Problem im Krisenfall. Auf jeden Fall. Da haben wir das Cross-Default-Problem. [...] Und der Schuldschein hat ja ein Einzelkündigungsrecht und dann tritt das Problem auf. Ja, dann kommt es zum Cross-Default und die Konsortialbanken befinden sich in der Regel in der etwas unschönen Situation—da sie meistens die größten Commitments haben—den Fresh-Money-Einschuss zu leisten,	[...] a high concentration of credits with individual acceleration rights is certainly a problem in a crisis situation. Certainly, there we will have a cross-default problem. [...] The bond has an individual right to accelerate and then there is a problem. Then, there is a cross-default and the consortium banks are in the unattractive situation of having to provide the fresh money injection—because they commonly hold the greatest commitments—to keep the whole thing alive

(continued)

Table 11 (continued)

Category	Int. no.	Line	Statement	Translation
			damit die ganze Sache noch am Leben bleibt	
	11	14	Also, Cross-Default ist Standard, weil das eigentlich die einzige Möglichkeit ist sich zu schützen, wenn von dritter Seite irgendetwas passieren sollte	So, the cross-default clause is standard because that is the only means to protect oneself, when something happens from a third party
	12	8	Cross Default ist immer auch Standard. Also ich glaub das ist mittlerweile in jedem Kreditvertrag, nicht nur in Bankverträgen, sondern grundsätzlich Standard	A cross-default clause is standard. I believe that nowadays it is not only standard in bank loan agreements but in loan agreements in general
	14	27	[. . .] also der Sachverhalt, wo ich gestern verhandeln war—da haben wir 26 oder 27 Banken, die bislang nicht durch eine Konsortialregelung vereint sind—, wenn da einer aus der Reihe schert, vielleicht da noch irgendwie durch so eine "unguided missile" von Anwalt irgendwie beraten ist, und dann fällig stellt, dann kann das einen Dominoeffekt verursachen	[. . .] the facts of the case, I had to deal with yesterday—there 26 or 27 banks were involved who are not syndicated so far—if somebody steps out of line there, maybe due to the advice of an "unguided missile" as lawyer, and recalls its loan, that can cause a domino effect
	14	45	Es gibt Leute, die behaupten, dass der Cross Default die Ausnahme wäre, aber das kann ich so nicht bestätigen	Some people claim that a cross-default clause is the exception but I cannot confirm that
Only cross-acceleration clause	3	24	But are the lenders willing to push the nuclear button? Particularly, if you got a company that has significant junior debt and public bonds, the junior layers in the capital structure will typically have no cross-default clause but they will have a cross-acceleration clause. So once the lenders actually accelerate, the lenders are no longer the only ones with a seat at the table It also goes back to the free-riding point. That is, because it is only cross-acceleration as opposed to a full cross-default for senior debt, the ability of the junior debt to in essence free-	

(continued)

Table 11 (continued)

Category	Int. no.	Line	Statement	Translation
			ride is more practical than legal because again they do not have a cross-default. It is not until the first lien lender does actually accelerate or the more senior lenders accelerate that they then have the same default. And in the meantime the senior debt can issue a waiver or amendment in exchange for fees and/or other covenant protections designed to get around this problem or they can be refinanced, as well	
	3	26	That is why the second lien and the more junior debt only have a cross-acceleration. The more senior lenders want to be the first at the table and potentially the only ones that need to be made happy before everybody leaves the table	
	13	10	Je nachdem, wie gut man verhandelt, schafft man als Darlehensnehmerseite Cross-Acceleration Klauseln rein zu verhandeln	Depending on how good one negotiates as debtor only a cross-acceleration clause is stipulated
But not seen in reality	13	36	Wobei ich jetzt die Erfahrung, dass eine Bank wirklich das Darlehen formal gekündigt hat und dann die anderen Banken denen gefolgt sind, als solches nicht hatte	I have not yet experienced that a bank actually accelerated a loan formally and that then other banks followed
Exit strategy	5	17	Man kann so etwas schon als Ausstiegschance sehen, wenn man mit dem Kunden eh nicht mehr so richtig glücklich ist. Dann kann man sagen: "Gut, wir haben jetzt das Recht auszusteigen. Er hat ein Fehlverhalten gezeigt, indem er eine andere Bank bevorzugt behandelt und wir können jetzt hier eine Kündigung aussprechen."	One can consider it also as exit strategy if you are no longer happy with the customer. Then you can say: "We have the right to exit. He has shown a wrongdoing giving privileged treatment to another bank and we can give him notice."
	5	30	Also in den Ausläufern der Finanzmarktkrise als sich die Unternehmen dann schwächer	In the offset of the financial crisis, when the companies performed worse than expected

(continued)

Table 11 (continued)

Category	Int. no.	Line	Statement	Translation
			entwickelt haben und natürlich auch die Finanzinstitute betroffen waren und jeder die Gelegenheit gesucht hat irgendwie rauszukommen, hat das erstens für die Kunden natürlich schnell Probleme ausgelöst, aber auch für die anderen Banken, die dabei bleiben wollten. Sprich, wir haben eigentlich keine Sorge mit dem Kunden gehabt, auch wenn seine Entwicklung ein bisschen negativ war in der Phase—das war ja erklärbar—, aber andere Banken haben sozusagen die Notbremse gezogen und man hat dann kaum die Möglichkeit aus dieser Situation rauszukommen	and the banks were also affected and everyone was looking for a way out, customers encountered problems—but so did the banks who wanted to continue the relationship. That is, we were not concerned about the debtor, even though his development was a little negative in that particular phase—and understandably so. But other banks activated the emergency brakes, so to speak, leaving little room to resolve the situation
	10	34	[. . .] dass die Banken dann ihre Linien einfrieren und oftmals führt das zu einer Insolvenz	[. . .] that banks freeze the credit lines and this often leads to bankruptcy
	13	12	Ich denke, das ist insbesondere die Angst der Banken, dass den letzten die Hunde beißen und die wollen natürlich, sobald es wirtschaftliche Probleme gibt—und ein Default in einem anderen Vertrag ist ja ein wirtschaftliches Problem—auch die Möglichkeit haben ihrerseits die Reißleine zu ziehen und irgendwo das zu beenden und möglichst schnell rauszukommen	I believe that banks in particular fear that the devil will take the hindmost. They naturally want to be able to pull the plug and make a fast to exit in case of financial distress—and a default under a different contract also constitutes financial distress
	13	38	Es kann aber auch negativ sein, ganz klar, dass zum Beispiel die Banken die Möglichkeit haben die Reißleine einfach frühzeitig zu ziehen und dann eben das Unternehmen in die Insolvenz zu treiben	It can also be negative, for sure: For example a bank uses the option to pull the plug too early and the company is pushed into bankruptcy

3 *Positive Effects on Third-Party Creditors*

3.1 Similar Rights for Third-Party Creditors

3.1.1 Not Likely

Table 12 Not likely that third-party creditors have similar rights to those of the bank

Category	Int. no.	Line	Statement	Translation
Bondholders are too diverse	3	29	That is the other reason, why quite honestly in bank debt deals they allow others to pursue first lien debt command but it is not going to be in the form of another bank debt. It has to be in the form of bonds because they know the first-lien bonds, while they rank equal in the capital structure, they cannot get their act together	
Only cross-acceleration clause	3	24	But are the lenders willing to push the nuclear button? Particularly, if you got a company that has significant junior debt and public bonds, the junior layers in the capital structure will typically have no cross-default clause but they will have a cross-acceleration clause. So once the lenders actually accelerate, the lenders are no longer the only ones with a seat at the table. It also goes back to the free-riding point. That is, because it is only cross-acceleration as opposed to a full cross-default for senior debt, the ability of the junior debt to in essence free-ride is more practical than legal because again they do not have a cross-default. It is not until the first lien lender does actually accelerate or the more senior lenders accelerate that they then have the same default. And in the	

(continued)

Table 12 (continued)

Category	Int. no.	Line	Statement	Translation
			meantime the senior debt can issue a waiver or amendment in exchange for fees and/or other covenant protections designed to get around this problem or they can be refinanced, as well	
	3	26	That is why the second lien and the more junior debt only have a cross-acceleration. The more senior lenders want to be the first at the table and potentially the only ones that need to be made happy before everybody leaves the table	
	13	10	Je nachdem, wie gut man verhandelt, schafft man als Darlehensnehmerseite Cross-Acceleration Klauseln rein zu verhandeln	Depending on how good one negotiates as debtor only a cross-acceleration clause is stipulated
Can be changed without consent of third-party creditor	3	18	If a borrower then wants relieve from the tighter set of restrictions, it can go out and get them and does not need the consent of the junior creditors. Or it can potentially refinance the first lien debt, if the credit quality is good enough for refinancing and it can possibly get a new lender to give him the flexibility	
	3	24	And in the meantime the senior debt can issue a waiver or amendment in exchange for fees and/or other covenant protections designed to get around this problem or they can be refinanced, as well	
	4	10	If a borrower than wants relieve from the tighter set of restrictions it can go out and get them and does not need the consent of the junior creditor	
	9	34	[. . .] wenn man auch von der Kundenseite eine vernünftige Kommunikation pflegt, Dinge vernünftig erklärt, ist das auch	[. . .]when customer communication is good and matters are explained properly, there is no rigid corset that must be

(continued)

Table 12 (continued)

Category	Int. no.	Line	Statement	Translation
			kein starres Korsett, was unauflöslich ist, sondern eines das dann auch lebt mit Veränderungen, die während der Geschäftsbeziehungen, während der Kreditlaufzeit einfach passieren können	followed, but rather one can adapt to new circumstances, which can occur during the life of a credit agreement
	12	27	Weil die können verändert werden durch Verhandlungen des Konsortiums ohne dass ein Cross Default eintritt oder durch eine andere Refinanzierung	[...] because they can be changed through renegotiations with the consortium banks without triggering a cross-default or via a different method of refinancing
Not enforced in a way that helps third-party creditors	6	7	"Du darfst niemanden besichern und für den Fall, dass doch, dann musst du uns gleich behandeln." Wenn man dann mitbekommt, jemand hat Sicherheiten bekommen, dann kann man sagen: "Da will ich jetzt partizipieren oder zumindest gleichwertige Sicherheiten bekommen." Und dann gerät man in so eine Situation, dass man dann einen Sicherheitenpool macht	'You are prohibited from collateralising anyone, but if you do then you have to treat us equally.' If you find out that someone got collateral, then you have to say: "I want to participate, or at least I want an equivalent collateral." And then you get into a situation where you create a collateral pool
	9	52	In der Regel ist es ja so, dass aber dann keine anderen Finanzierungspartner mehr da sind, die das auch noch haben oder man nimmt die eben mit rein. Dann wird da halt eine Sicherheitentreuhandschaft gebildet und die werden auch beteiligt an den Sicherheiten, aber dann wird die Sache schnell sehr komplex	Generally it is true that there are no other financing partners with a negative pledge clause left or you have to take them on board. Then a security trust is created and the collateral is shared. But then things fast get really complicated

3.1.2 Likely

Table 13 Likely that third-party creditors have similar rights to those of the bank

Category	Int. no.	Line	Statement	Translation
Negative pledge clause/Pari passu clause	6	12	Und das Gleiche ist natürlich gegeben, wenn es da eine Klausel gibt, die ihm auferlegt, seine Sicherheiten unbelastet zu lassen. Das führt ja im Endeffekt auch dazu dass es im Insolvenzfall der gesamten Gläubigerschaft zugutekommt—also dass es in die Insolvenzmasse fällt und kein Absonderungsrecht daran geltend gemacht werden kann, das ansonsten letztendlich nur den absonderungsberechtigten Gläubiger privilegiert	The same situation is given, when there is a clause that prohibits collateralising. That ultimately benefits all creditors if the debtor becomes insolvent—that is it goes into the pool of assets and there is no superior right to an asset, which only benefits the party holding the right
	9	42	Die Gleichbehandlung ist ein ganz, ganz wichtiges Thema. Das man da eben nicht plötzlich andere Banken mit einer Besicherung versieht ist klar	Equal treatment is a really, really important topic. It should go without saying that you do not suddenly provide another bank with collateral
	12	10	Und das kann ich dann auch nochmal für die Banken sagen: Sie fordern es nicht nur, sondern sie lassen es auch gegen sich gelten. Also wenn Sie der erste sind, der jetzt, also in bilateralen Verträgen, der sagen würde: "Ich möchte jetzt eine Besicherung haben."—und das ist eine Besicherung, die Sie im Grunde nur über ein Pooling mit anderen teilen können—dann (so ist das in unserem Hause zumindest, dann) sagen wir: "Pass auf, wir brauchen hier jetzt Sicherheiten und das mag sein, dass das die Forderung Warenlager sind. Aber die anderen haben auch gleichgeartete Kredite, also müssen die auch für andere gelten."	And I can say that for the banks: They do not only demand it but are also bound by it. So if you are the first in case of a bilateral contract who says "Now, I want collateral"—and that collateral can basically only be shared with other creditors by way of pooling—then (at least that is the way we do it) we say: "Look, we need a security and it may be that the claims are warehouse. But the others have similar credits and thus, the same must be true for them."
Must confirm with the strictest covenant	3	24	The company always needs to adhere to its stricter covenants. [...] The more strengthened covenants and the more senior	

(continued)

Table 13 (continued)

Category	Int. no.	Line	Statement	Translation
			the debt, the more they serve some practical protection for the junior lenders	
	4	10	Oftentimes, an issuer has both bank loans and bonds in its capital structure. So, effectively, the tighter of the two sets of covenants are the ones that control. There might be transactions that a borrower might want to undertake that it could under one set of covenants but it could not under the other, and the undertaking could be risky. Obviously the creditors behind the looser document are benefitting from the tighter of the two, as a practical matter	
	6	12	Also, wenn sich der Kreditnehmer gegenüber jemandem verpflichtet gewisse Finanzkennzahlen einzuhalten und das zu einer Situation führt, dass die finanzielle Situation des Unternehmens einfach stabiler wird, dass dann alle Gläubiger davon profitieren, liegt ja irgendwie auf der Hand	So, if the debtor is obliged to comply with certain financial ratios and that leads to a situation, in which the company's financial situation is more stable, the fact that all creditors benefit from it is self-evident
To ensure uniformity of conditions	9	28	In der Regel hat der Kunde auch meistens ein Interesse die Covenant-Definitionen gleichzufahren. Also, dass er zumindest nicht x-verschiedene Kennzahlen im Blick haben muss. Und wir teilen solche Einschätzungen auch und versuchen das dann auch so anzugleichen, dass es kreditmateriell vernünftig ist. Aber eben auch so, dass er nicht x-verschiedene Kennzahlen hinterher abarbeiten muss, weil da verliert man ja schnell den Überblick und das ist sicherlich nicht sinnvoll	Generally, the customer has an interest in concurrent covenant definitions. This means that at least the customer must not keep an eye on various different financial covenants. And we share those assessments too and try to assimilate them in a way that is also reasonable with regard to the credit quality. However, this is done in a way that ensures that the debtor must not work through various different financial ratios because then it is easy to lose track and that is not sensible
	13	26	Deswegen ist es auch aus Darlehensnehmersicht häufig sinnvoller unter einzelnen	That is why it is often sensible from the debtor's perspective to accept maybe slightly

(continued)

Table 13 (continued)

Category	Int. no.	Line	Statement	Translation
			Finanzierungsverträgen vielleicht ein bisschen strengere, ein bisschen engere Covenants oder Auflagen und Bedingungen zu akzeptieren, die aber dafür unter sämtlichen Finanzierungsverträgen einheitlich sind, sodass man sich im Prinzip nur eine Checkliste erstellen muss und nur diese eine Checkliste abarbeiten und prüfen muss	stricter or tighter covenants—but that are still homogenous in all financing agreements—so that basically all you have to do is create one checklist and work through it
	14	49	Da hatte die X-Bank und die XX-Bank ein Unternehmen finanziert und die hatten erst unterschiedliche Verträge und dann gab es eine Refinanzierungsrunde 2012 und dann haben die statt aus einem Vertrag einen Konsortialkreditvertrag zu machen, zwei bilaterale Verträge, die mehr oder weniger inhaltlich identisch sind, gemacht	The bank X and the bank XX first financed a company with two different contracts and then in 2012 during refinancing they did not opt for a syndicated loan but for two bilateral loan contracts with roughly the same content
Cross-default clause	1	22	The cross-default clause is an important thing to have. Even though it might not help you necessarily, it brings everybody to the table so you are able to discuss what the issues are with the credit	
	9	48	[...] denn auch das betrifft ja sozusagen die Urangst der Banken, dass jemand anderes sein Geld nimmt, durch die Tür marschiert und man selbst sitzt noch da und merkt nicht, dass sich die Situation massiv verschlechtert. Deshalb gibt es den Cross-Default und den sehen wir auch als ganz wichtigen Aspekt	[...] because that speaks to the banks' primal fear that somebody else takes their money and walks out of the door and you still sit there and do not realise that the situation has substantially worsened. That is why there are cross-default clauses and we regard them as important aspects
	11	14	Also, Cross Default ist Standard, weil das eigentlich die einzige Möglichkeit ist sich zu schützen, wenn von dritter Seite irgendetwas passieren sollte	So, the cross-default clause is standard because that is the only means to protect oneself, when something happens on the part of a third party
	11	32	Das heißt, Sie haben, wenn der Cross Default zwischen	That is, when a cross-default between a syndicated loan and

(continued)

Table 13 (continued)

Category	Int. no.	Line	Statement	Translation
			Schuldschein und Konsortialkredit läuft, die Situation, dass Sie zwar mit einer Bankenmehrheit den Konsortialkredit beherrschen können und ihn steuern können, aber Sie haben das Problem, dass Sie den Schuldschein komplett einfangen müssen. Und je heterogener die Schuldscheingläubigerstruktur ist, desto problematischer kann die Situation werden	bond occurs, you face the situation that you can control and steer the syndicated loan with a majority of consortium banks, but you must get all bondholders on board. And the more heterogeneous the bondholder structure, the more difficult it becomes
	12	8	Cross Default ist immer auch Standard. Also ich glaub das ist mittlerweile in jedem Kreditvertrag, nicht nur in Bankverträgen, sondern grundsätzlich Standard	A cross-default clause is standard. I believe that nowadays it is not only standard in bank loan agreements but in loan agreements in general
	13	12	Ich denke, das ist insbesondere die Angst der Banken, dass den letzten die Hunde beißen und die wollen natürlich, sobald es wirtschaftliche Probleme gibt und ein Default in einem anderen Vertrag ist ja ein wirtschaftliches Problem auch die Möglichkeit haben ihrerseits die Reißleine zu ziehen und irgendwo das zu beenden und möglichst schnell rauszukommen	I believe that banks in particular fear that the devil will take the hindmost. They naturally want to be able to pull the plug and make a fast to exit in case of financial distress—and a default under a different contract also constitutes financial distress
	14	45	Es gibt Leute, die behaupten, dass der Cross Default die Ausnahme wäre, aber das kann ich so nicht bestätigen	Some people claim that a cross-default clause is the exception but I cannot confirm that

3.2 Ensuring a Larger Pool of Assets

3.2.1 Not Likely

Table 14 Not likely that a larger pool of assets is ensured

Category	Int. no.	Line	Statement	Translation
Additional securities	5	13	Also dann gibt es häufig Nachverhandlungen und dann wird der Covenant-Bruch auch benutzt als Argument, um dann vielleicht andere Dinge durchzusetzen wie zum Beispiel Kreditsicherheiten	Then usually there will be renegotiations and the covenant breach will also be used to enforce other things like collateral
	6	15	Gut, wenn man sagt hier die Finanzkennzahlen, da ist man noch weit von einer Insolvenz entfernt, aber wenn die dazu führen, dass man ein Kündigungsrecht hat und man diese Kündigungsrecht nutzt, dass man sagt: "Gut, wir verhandeln jetzt nochmal und lassen uns neue Sicherheiten geben; lassen uns diese Risikoposition, diese erhöhte Risikoposition durch neue Sicherheiten untermauern."	Well, when you look at the financial ratios and see that the company is far away from bankruptcy but if these ratios entitle you to accelerate you do so and say "Well, we will renegotiate and we want additional collateral. We want to be protected from our increased risk by additional collateral."
	7	10	Also es führt nicht jeder Covenant-Bruch zu einer entsprechend verstärkten Sicherheitenbestellung	Not every covenant breach leads to a respectively increased collateral
	9	52	In der Regel ist es ja so, dass aber dann keine anderen Finanzierungspartner mehr da sind, die das auch noch haben oder man nimmt die eben mit rein. Dann wird da halt eine Sicherheitentreuhandschaft gebildet und die werden auch beteiligt an den Sicherheiten, aber dann wird die Sache schnell sehr komplex	Generally it is true that there are no other financing partners with a negative pledge clause left or you have to take them on board. Then a security trust is created and the collateral is shared. But then things fast get really complicated
	10	56	Wenn noch was da ist und es gibt einen Covenant Breach, ist die Nachbesicherung nicht weit entfernt	If there is something left and there is a covenant breach, the request for additional security is never far away
	11	28	Und je nachdem wie da die Situation ist, wird man möglicherweise auch ein	And, depending on the situation, there may be an increased need for credit protection. And

(continued)

Table 14 (continued)

Category	Int. no.	Line	Statement	Translation
			höheres Absicherungsbedürfnis haben. Und dann kommt das Thema Nachbesicherung auf den Tisch	then, the topic of additional security is on the table
	14	51	Also, wenn ich mir alles das, was nicht niet- und nagelfest am Unternehmen an Sicherheiten nehme, habe ich entweder ein Aussonderungs- oder ein Absonderungsrecht in der Insolvenz und der andere geht leer aus. In dem Moment sind Drittgläubiger gefährdet	So, if I take everything that is not nailed down to the debtor company as collateral, I posses a higher ranking (either a right to separation from the estate ("Aussonderungsrecht") or a right for separate satisfaction ("Absonderungsrecht")) in bankruptcy proceedings and the other creditor will get nothing. In that moment third-party creditors are exposed
	5	13	Also dann gibt es häufig Nachverhandlungen und dann wird der Covenant-Bruch auch benutzt als Argument, um dann vielleicht andere Dinge durchzusetzen wie zum Beispiel Kreditsicherheiten	Then usually there will be renegotiations and the covenant breach will also be used to enforce other things like collateral

3.2.2 Likely

Table 15 Likely that a larger pool of assets is ensured

Category	Int. no.	Line	Statement	Translation
Pari passu/ Negative pledge clause	6	7	"Du darfst niemanden besichern und für den Fall, dass doch, dann musst du uns gleich behandeln." Wenn man dann mitbekommt, jemand hat Sicherheiten bekommen, dann kann man sagen: "Da will ich jetzt partizipieren oder zumindest gleichwertige Sicherheiten bekommen." Und dann gerät man in so eine Situation, dass man dann einen Sicherheitenpool macht	'You are prohibited from collateralising anyone, but if you do then you have to treat us equally.' If you find out that someone got collateral, then you have to say: "I want to participate, or at least I want an equivalent collateral." And then you get into a situation where you create a collateral pool
	6	12	Und das Gleiche ist natürlich gegeben, wenn es da eine Klausel gibt, die ihm auferlegt, seine Sicherheiten unbelastet zu lassen. Das führt ja im Endeffekt auch dahin, dass es im Insolvenzfall der gesamten Gläubigerschaft zugutekommt—also dass es in die Insolvenzmasse fällt und kein Absonderungsrecht daran geltend gemacht werden kann. Das ansonsten letztendlich nur den absonderungsberechtigten Gläubiger privilegiert	The same situation is given, when there is a clause that prohibits collateralising. That ultimately benefits all creditors if the debtor becomes insolvent—that is it goes into the pool of assets and there is no superior right to an asset, which only benefits the party holding the right
	9	42	Die Gleichbehandlung ist ein ganz, ganz wichtiges Thema. Das man da eben nicht plötzlich andere Banken mit einer Besicherung versieht ist klar	Equal treatment is a really, really important topic. It should go without saying that you do not suddenly provide another bank with collateral
	9	52	In der Regel ist es ja so, dass aber dann keine anderen Finanzierungspartner mehr da sind, die das auch noch haben oder man nimmt die eben mit rein. Dann wird da halt eine Sicherheitentreuhandschaft gebildet und die werden auch beteiligt an den Sicherheiten, aber dann wird die Sache schnell sehr komplex	Generally it is true that there are no other financing partners with a negative pledge clause left or you have to take them on board. Then a security trust is created and the collateral is shared. But then things fast get really complicated

3.3 Keeping the Debtor Solvent

3.3.1 Not Likely

Table 16 Not likely that the debtor is kept solvent

Category	Int. no.	Line	Statement	Translation
No possibility to support debtor due to overregulation	8	81	Ich würde sagen, die Rolle der Banken hat sich heute extrem gewandelt, weil sie in vielen Bereichen einfach überreguliert sind und eigentlich fast überhaupt gar keine Möglichkeiten mehr haben. In manchen Situation würde ich alternativlos auch Unternehmer nicht mehr stützen können, was in der Vergangenheit noch ging, aber was heute eben nicht mehr geht aus Portfoliogesichtspunkten	I would say that the role of banks has extremely changed nowadays because in many areas they are overregulated and have nearly no opportunity for actions. In some situations I would be absolutely unable to support a company, which would have been possible in the past but not nowadays due to portfolio reasons
Additional risk premium	3	21	And in the meantime the senior debt can issue a waiver or amendment in exchange for fees and/or other covenant protections designed to get around this problem or they can be refinanced, as well	
	7	10	Das führt im Endeffekt natürlich häufig auch zu verstärkten Risikoprämien	That often leads to increased risk premiums
	8	6	Die andere Rechtsfolge, die sie daraus ableiten können ist zu sagen: "Ich will eine höhere Risikoprämie dafür haben."	The other legal consequence that can be deduced is to say: "I want a higher risk premium."
	9	20	Dafür werden in der Regel Waiver-Fees gezahlt, weil die Banken haben in dem Moment das Kreditrisiko, was deutlich schlechter ist—was sich in den internen Ratings auch nach unten entwickelt	For that debtor companies have to pay waiver fees because banks have to bear the credit risk, which is definitely worse and which also becomes evident in internal ratings
	10	54	eine Waiver Fee ist eigentlich die häufigste Maßnahme	[. . .] a waiver fee is the most common reaction
	11	22	Und wenn das Risiko gestiegen ist, möchte ich eben auch partizipieren und möchte	And when the risk increases, I want to participate and be reimbursed for my risk costs

(continued)

Table 16 (continued)

Category	Int. no.	Line	Statement	Translation
			meine Risikokosten auch wieder verdienen	
	13	16	[. . .] es ein Waiver-Verfahren gibt und die Waiver von der Bank normalerweise nur ungern erteilt werden, beziehungsweise nur erteilt werden gegen Zahlung eines Preises. Preis im Sinne von natürlich erstens einer Waiver Gebühr, aber vielmehr auch eines sonstigen Entgegenkommens auf Seiten des Darlehensnehmers	[. . .] a waiver process is in place and banks usually do not like to give a waiver or they only give it in return for payment of a price. A price not merely in form of a waiver fee but rather in form of any other accommodation on the part of the debtor
	14	41	Margenerhöhung auch	Margin increase as well
	14	41	Wir verzichten auf Forderungen erst einmal oder auf Zinszahlungen. Wenn es dann irgendwann besser läuft, gibt es das Plus—irgendwie einen netten Aufschlag nochmal "on top."	We first waive our claims or interest payments. If the financial situation increases, there will be a plus—kind of a nice premium "on top."

3.3.2 Likely

Table 17 Likely that the debtor is kept solvent

Category	Int. no.	Line	Statement	Translation
Sense of responsibility	9	86	Jetzt kommt es drauf an, das was noch da ist, das was gesund ist, noch irgendwie überleben zu lassen und, dass den Verpflichtungen auch irgendwie nachgekommen werden kann und dann auch letztlich Arbeitsplätze miterhalten werden können, denn darum geht es ja dann auch, weil es gibt ja dann noch eine ganze Reihe von Aspekten, die da dranhängen	Now we must focus on what is still there and healthy and to save it and that their obligations are met and that ultimately jobs are preserved because that must be considered as well since a number of different topics are attached to it
	11	46	Das Unternehmen ist darauf angewiesen, diesen Vertrag unbedingt verlängert zu bekommen, das Unternehmen ist auf die Fortführung eines Kredites angewiesen und damit eben auch auf diese Bankbeziehung und, weil es eben in einer besonderen Situation ist, gibt es vielleicht keine dritte Bank, die man dort ansprechen könnte und ich kann deswegen aus diesem Kreditverhältnis nicht grundsätzlich aussteigen. Dann ist es schon eine ethische Verantwortung der Bank, diese Machtposition nicht auszuspielen. Aber das sie natürlich versuchen wird für sich in dieser Situation die bestmögliche Verhandlungsposition zu bekommen, finde ich erstmal nicht verwerflich, sondern völlig normal	A company depends on the continuation of the credit and, thereby, on the relationship it has with the bank. And because the company may be in a special situation, perhaps there is no other bank the company could approach and therefore I basically cannot exit this relationship. It is an ethical responsibility of the bank not to abuse this position of power. However, it is not condemnable *per se* but actually normal that the bank should try to occupy the best negotiation position
	13	38	Wobei meine Erfahrung ist, dass die Banken sehr zurückhaltend damit sind,	My experience is that banks are really reluctant to drive a company into bankruptcy

(continued)

Table 17 (continued)

Category	Int. no.	Line	Statement	Translation
			die Unternehmen wirklich in die Insolvenz zu treiben, weil den Banken natürlich auch bewusst ist, dass sie da eine gewisse Verantwortung haben—sowohl der Gesellschaft als auch den Arbeitnehmern der Gesellschaft gegenüber	because banks are aware of the fact that they have a certain responsibility both to society and the employees of the company
Biggest commitment	9	18	Aber jede Bank muss sich selbst überlegen, ob das eine zielführende Maßnahme ist in einer solchen Situation, wenn man auch ein großes Commitment draußen hat, das Geld zurückfordert, was faktisch in der Regel nicht zurückgezahlt werden kann	However, every bank has to consider whether it is rewarding to recall the loan principal in such a situation when you have the biggest commitment outstanding and it is usually not paid back
	9	84	Und ich glaube man muss es eigentlich eher andersumsehen: Dass Banken ein massives Interesse daran haben durch die hohen Commitments, die in der Regel alles übersteigen was andere Stakeholder haben, dass das Unternehmen irgendwo wieder in eine vernünftige Situation zurückkommt und Cash Flows generiert, aus denen ein Kredit bedient werden kann. Ich habe wenige Kredite gesehen, die sich aus Sicherheiten getilgt haben	And I believe, one must look at it the other way around: due to their big commitments that regularly exceed what other stakeholders hold, banks have a massive interest in putting the debtor company back into a reasonable situation to generate cash flows out of which the loan can be paid. I have seen few credits that were paid solely by securities
	11	36	Ich bin Teilnehmer an einem Konsortialkredit und wir müssen davon ausgehen, dass das Unternehmen insolvent geht, wenn dieser Schuldschein komplett zurückgezahlt werden soll. Dann ist die Frage: Ok, wie viel Geld habe ich im Konsortialkredit drin und was steht dagegen an	I am part of a syndicated loan and we have to assume that the company will become insolvent if a bond has to be repaid. Then you have to answer the question: Okay, how much money have I invested in the syndicated loan and what is there in terms of assets, collateral and similar topics?

(continued)

Table 17 (continued)

Category	Int. no.	Line	Statement	Translation
			Vermögen, an Sicherheiten, an ähnlichen Themen?	
Going concern of the company is higher than chopping off value	4	12	And in a situation where people may believe the debt is under-secured (So, let's say it is bank loan but it is trading at 80 cents on the dollar) in most of these situations it is very rare for there not to be a perception that you will get more out of the company if you help it as a going concern than you will if you chop it off [. . .] Usually, everyone gets more value out of the company if you can find a way—even if that means writing debt off that is junior in the capital structure (but usually that is not worth anything anyway)	
	13	38	[. . .] aber natürlich auch durchaus im eigenen Interesse damit handeln, weil die Wahrscheinlichkeit, dass sie ihr Geld zurückbekommen bei einem Unternehmen, das fortgeführt wird und die Sanierung schafft wenn vielleicht auch mit quietschenden Reifen in der Kurve—deutlich höher ist, als wenn das Unternehmen einfach platt gemacht wird	[. . .] but of course banks act in their own interest, because the chances that the bank gets their loan principal back are higher, if a company continues and is recapitalised—even if so with screeching tires—than if the company is pushed in bankruptcy
Relationship investment	2	44	I got confidence in you; I believe you; I trust you. Those are all the things that come along with a personal relationship. But that being said if I go ahead and trust you, you have to be willing to commit everything to me	
	9	26	Schuldscheine insbesondere zeigen sich da oft relativ hartleibig, denn die haben ein anderes Interesse. Die haben in den meisten Fällen	Bonds are often difficult because they have a different interest. In most cases, there is no relationship

(continued)

Table 17 (continued)

Category	Int. no.	Line	Statement	Translation
			kein Relationship-Interesse, sondern sind reine Investoren	interest but they are pure investors
	9	32	Wir wissen, dass das Leben nicht nur aus Sonnenschein besteht und sind auch bereit solche Wege mitzugehen. Man muss einfach nur vom Kunden auch mitgenommen werden auf die Reise und rechtzeitig erfahren, wenn etwas ist, weil man kann aus seinen eigenen Erfahrungen heraus dem Kunden ja auch Hinweise geben—wie man damit umgehen kann; was vielleicht auch andere in der Situation gemacht haben	We know that life is not all sunshine and roses and we are ready to face those situations with companies. However, the customer has to take you on the journey with him and inform you on time when there is an issue because you can provide advice from your own experience to the customer—how you can tackle the problem; maybe also what others have done in similar situations
	11	20	Relationship-Lending machen wir sowieso eigentlich nur	We actually only do relationship lending
	11	48	Und das Schlimmste ist, dass die Regionalbanken und die Ortsbanken, die eigentlich ein viel besseres Relationship haben müssten vor Ort, diese Position überhaupt nicht spielen, sondern dieses Margengeschäft einfach voll mitmachen. Vielleicht auch mitmachen müssen, aber offenbar das Gehör auch nicht finden oder es noch gar nicht suchen, zu sagen: "Junge, das was du hier machst, du kannst es natürlich nehmen. Du kannst den billigen Kredit nehmen, aber es ist auf Dauer trägt es nicht, weil die die das Geld jetzt heute hinterherschmeißen, das sind die ersten, die es auch wieder wegziehen."	The worst thing is that regional and local banks—which should have a better on-site relationship—don't adopt that position, choosing instead to participate fully in the margin business. It's also possible that they have to participate, but apparently they are not heard when they say—or maybe they don't even try to say—"So, you can obviously go with this cheap loan, but in the long run it is not worth it because those who give the money today so easily are the first who take it away."
	13	28	[. . .] das, was man früher so klassischerweise als Hausbank benannt hat, aufzubauen und nicht möglicherweise auf der Jagd	[. . .] to develop what you classically call "house bank" and not to chase after the last quarter percentage points, higher or lower

(continued)

Table 17 (continued)

Category	Int. no.	Line	Statement	Translation
			nach dem letzten Viertelprozentpunkt, mehr oder weniger Zinsen, einfach ein Windowshopping zu machen und von einer Bank zur nächsten zu rennen, weil diese stabilen Beziehungen, die man aufgebaut hat, das Vertrauensverhältnis, was über Jahre aufgebaut wurde, auch dazu führen, dass man leichter in Krisensituationen mit der Bank reden kann und die Bank auch mehr bereit ist mitzugehen, als wenn man im Prinzip keine jahrelang aufgebaute Beziehung hat	interest rates and basically do window shopping and to run from one bank to another, because these stable relationships and trust one has built also lead to better communication with the bank in times of crisis, and the bank is also more willing to go along with you than they would be without those years spent building a relationship
	13	40	Sondern ich glaube ein langfristiges Vertrauensverhältnis, wo man auch mal bereit ist zu geben oder wo man bereit ist irgendwo eine Lösung zu finden mit der beide Seite gut leben können, ist häufig eher im langfristigen Interesse des Darlehensnehmers	I believe that a long-term relationship of trust where one is also willing to give sometimes or to find a solution that both parties can live with is in the long-term interest of the debtor
	14	35	Bei einem Kaufvertrag, das ist so ein "spot contract". Also man tauscht was aus: Ware oder Unternehmen gegen Geld. Dann gibt es vielleicht hinterher noch Gewährleistungsthemen, aber im Kern kommt man zusammen, geht auseinander. Das ist bei einer Finanzierung anders. Man hat mehrere Jahre miteinander zu tun und das weiß glaube ich auch jeder. Und deswegen ist man dann im Kern glaube ich konsensualer orientiert und hat weniger Konfliktpotenzial oder man streitet sich so, dass der eine sagt, "Mit dem will ich jetzt nicht mehr reden."	A sale contract is a spot contract. Meaning, you exchange things: goods or business against money. Then later on there may be issues of warranties but at the bottom you come together and part. This is different in financing. You deal with each other over years and that I believe everyone knows. And that is the reason why one is more consensual as a basic principle and there is less conflict potential nor does one fights in a way that one party says "With him I do not want to talk."

(continued)

Table 17 (continued)

Category	Int. no.	Line	Statement	Translation
Relationship rent	3	21	There are two other reasons, one of which you mentioned is relationship. It is particularly true for an investment bank in a sponsor deal or for that matter large companies that tend to go through bankruptcy but never go away: You do not want to run to the courts to enforce things if you can amicably work things out. [. . .] A lot of the investment banks are relationship lenders. They do a lot of things with these sponsors, more than just this one loan deal—M&A advisory and other things. You want to maintain the relationship as much as possible	
	14	39	[. . .] aber ich glaube die Intention ist schon da bei einer Bank aus einem Vertrag oder aus einer Sache mehr zu machen und das passiert auch recht häufig. [. . .] Und so ähnlich ticken Banken auch, weil der Aufwand, etwas zu akquirieren und sowas zu bekommen, hoch ist—der Wettbewerb ist gerade auch bei den Banken extrem hoch	[. . .] but I believe a bank's intention is always to make more out of a contract or something and that happens quite often. [. . .] And that is how banks work because the effort to acquire something or to get something is high—competition especially between banks is extremely high
Reduction of shareholder/lender conflict	3	15	The sooner the lenders and investors can get in front of the company when it is not doing good, the better it is for the lenders to be able to have a say in preserving equity value	
	9	84	Natürlich sind auch persönlich Situationen davon betroffen: Management und Gesellschafter. Und daraus kommen vielleicht bestimmte	Needless to say personally situations are concerned: management and shareholders. And this may result in certain sensitivities but sometimes one has to think

(continued)

Table 17 (continued)

Category	Int. no.	Line	Statement	Translation
			Befindlichkeiten, aber man muss da manchmal vielleicht auch einfach weiterdenken. Heute unpopuläre Entscheidungen treffen, die vielleicht im Nachhinein für alle Stakeholder zielführend sein können	further: today one makes an unpopular decision that may be expedient for all stakeholders in hindsight
	10	48	Covenants sind durchaus positiv, weil natürlich die Gläubiger davon ja in der Regel profitieren, dass sich da jemand genau das Unternehmen anschaut und auch zu Gegenmaßnahmen greift, falls es in die falsche Richtung geht	Covenants are positive because creditors generally benefit from the fact that somebody monitors the company and also intervenes if something goes in the wrong direction
	12	35	Das ist ja auch oft, dass man sagt: "Wir haben nicht den Eindruck, dass das Management das im Griff hat dieses Thema. Und das ist ein nachhaltiges Thema. Wir würden es begrüßen, wenn eine Unternehmensberatung sich das nochmal von außen anguckt."	It is often that one says: "We do not have the impression that the management copes with this problem. And this is a long-lasting topic. We would appreciate if a consultancy could look at it from an outside perspective."
	13	38	Es kann einerseits eine gewisse disziplinierende Wirkung haben—also Financial Covenants—, dass das Unternehmen schaut, dass es die Finanzzahlen in Auflagen und Bedingungen einhält, dass es halt einfach im Prinzip, was Investitionen angeht, nicht zu optimistisch rangeht, sich nicht vergaloppiert	On the one hand it—that is, financial covenants—can have a disciplinary effect that the company is anxious to comply with the financial ratios and that it is not too optimistic regarding investments—that it does not go down on the wrong track

3.4 Information Sharing

3.4.1 Not Likely

Table 18 Not likely that information about the debtor is produced for third-party creditors

Category	Int. no.	Line	Statement	Translation
First discussion without third-party creditors	4	14	The first discussion has to be had between the borrower and the creditors under the tightest piece of debt before you bring other people into the conversation	
	13	57	Dann spricht man normalerweise mit der Bank unter dessen Vertrag oder in deren Vertrag das verboten war und nicht noch mit den anderen Banken. Sondern dann regelt man es dann jetzt zum Beispiel mit der X-Bank und die Y-Bank lässt man außen vor und erst, wenn die X-Bank nicht bereit ist einen Waiver zu erteilen, dann würde man vielleicht irgendwann mit der Y-Bank sprechen	Then, you normally speak with the bank under whose contractual terms the matter was prohibited and not with other banks. You settle the problem with, for example, bank X, and bank Y is left out. Only if bank X is not willing to waive the default would you maybe start talking to bank Y
Companies dislike disclosure	1	20	So, you will see companies go private if they are in a work-out situation or if there is some strategy that they are trying to implement that might be viewed unfavourably by the investment community. And so they have private investors, obviously, that they have to answer to but there is less pressure to perform immediately. So you have got more flexibility to take a longer view or a longer tag if you need to	
Limits	1	24	Part of that is that the customer has certain rights where they can say "No, I do not want this information disclosed to this other vendor" and they might have valid reasons to do that	
	5	49	Und wenn ein Kunde es darauf anlegt, kann er das eine Zeit	And if a customer wants to conceal something then he can

(continued)

Table 18 (continued)

Category	Int. no.	Line	Statement	Translation
			lang auch sicherlich unter den Teppich kehren	definitely do that for some time
	6	22	Es wird eigentlich immer erst verhandelt, wenn das Kind schon in den Brunnen gefallen ist	Generally, negotiations take place too late: They lock the stable door after the horse had bolted
	11	16	Und insofern können Sie fast nur darauf vertrauen, dass der Kunde für die außerbilanziellen Finanzierungsinstrumente, ob es Leasingverträge oder andere Themen sind, dass der Kunde Sie informiert. Oder Sie warten tatsächlich bis Sie irgendwann tatsächlich von dritter Seite ein Informationsschreiben haben, dass Pfändungs- oder Überweisungsverbote oder ähnliche Themen auftreten	And insofar you can only trust that the customer will inform you with regard to off-balance sheet financial instruments, such as leasing contracts. Otherwise you wait until you get informed from a third party with an information letter regarding prohibition to seize or transfer or similar topics
	12	43	[...] wenn wir über eine nachhaltige Verschlechterung sprechen. Ja, dann müssen alle an den Tisch. Das kann natürlich nur das Unternehmen immer im Grunde initiieren. Wir haben da Bankgeheimnisse. Das können sie nie als Gläubiger von sich aus initiieren, selbst wenn sie die anderen kennen über die Bilanzunterlagen	[...] if we talk about lasting deterioration, then everybody must be at the table. However, only the company can initiate that. We have the banking secrecy. You cannot initiate that as a creditor, even if you know about the other from the accounting records
	14	13	Bei vielen übrigens nicht ganz unbewusst. Viele Finanzrechtler—Kollegen mit denen man sich unterhält—wissen ganz genau, dass es da gewisse Themen gibt, darüber wollen wir einfach nichts schreiben, weil man Angst hat, dass das dann ins Gegenteil verkehrt wird	Many do that not entirely unintentionally. Many finance lawyers—colleagues you are talking with—know very well that there are topics we do not want to write about because the fear is there that it will have an adverse effect

3.4.2 Likely

Table 19 Likely that information about the debtor is produced for third-party creditors

Category	Int. no.	Line	Statement	Translation
Via debtor	1	22	That is for what the cross-default clause is. It brings the measure transparency when the customer has to reveal those issues to you that maybe you did not know about or were not aware of; especially, when those vendors or other creditors have something that is critical to the customer's operations	
	1	26	[...] if you have got a cross-default clause, you typically will find out what the issue is with the other party and that is probably disclosed through the customer	
	6	2	Wenn das im Rahmen eines Konsortialkreditvertrags ist und je nach Größe des Unternehmens, wenn die dann schon sehen, dass sie einen Covenant brechen, dann kommen die oft schon vor Kreditablauf auf jemanden zu und sagen: "Pass auf, wir werden ihn vermutlich brechen", und bitten dann das Konsortium um einen Waiver	When that issue occurs under a syndicated loan and depending on the size of the company, if they spot that they will violate a covenant, then they will approach the consortium in advance and say "Look, we probably are going to violate that" and they will ask for a waiver
	9	32	In der Regel muss man sagen, sind da aber doch die meisten Kunden auch so, dass sie, wenn was droht, direkt die Banken informieren	Generally, one must say that most customers inform banks directly if something is imminent
	10	66	Also, wenn das Unternehmen schlau ist, wird es auch entsprechend transparent mit den anderen Gläubigern umgehen. Die anderen Gläubiger erfahren es ja so oder so	So if the company is smart, it will deal with other creditors in an appropriately transparent way. The other creditors will hear about it anyway
	11	30	Was wir jetzt gesehen haben, beispielsweise in einer großen Konsortialfinanzierung, die gerade im Waiver Prozess ist: Da wird es so sein, dass die	What we have just seen, for example in a big syndicated loan that is in a waiver process: There the banks demand that existing third-party

(continued)

Table 19 (continued)

Category	Int. no.	Line	Statement	Translation
			Banken verlangen, dass diese Drittgläubiger oder dass diese Linien, die dort vorhanden sind, offengelegt werden. Die Banken haben sich praktisch eine Komplettaufstellung geben lassen, nicht nur einen Bankenspiegel, sondern eine komplette Verbindlichkeitenaufstellung und werden verlangen, dass das Unternehmen eine Bestätigung abgibt, dass diese Linien nicht gekündigt sind und offen gehalten werden	creditors or those credit lines must be made transparent. The banks have obtained a complete list of all obligations. And they are going to demand a confirmation that those credit lines are not accelerated and are kept open
	13	55	Was es aber natürlich standardmäßig gibt—was in dem X-Bank Darlehensvertrag steht—, dass der Darlehensnehmer über einen Kündigungsgrund informieren muss. Und ein Kündigungsgrund wäre natürlich auch ein Cross Default, sprich unter dem Vertrag der Y-Bank ein Default vorliegt	It is standard practice—and will be stipulated in the loan agreement of bank X—to include a clause requiring the debtor to inform about any reasons for acceleration. And a cross-default constitutes, of course, a reason for acceleration—namely that there is a default under the loan contract of bank Y
	13	57	[. . .] wenn es wirklich ernsthafte wirtschaftliche Probleme gibt wir reden hier nicht vom Geschäftsbericht, den du statt nach 180 nach 200 Tagen vorgelegt hast und deswegen formell ein Default vorliegt—, dann ist die Bereitschaft und das Bewusstsein der Verpflichtung auf Darlehensnehmerseite mit der Bank wirklich zu sprechen schon sehr groß	[. . .] When there are serious financial problems—we do not talk about the financial statement that is handed in on day 200 instead of day 180 and that causes formal default—then the debtor's willingness and awareness of the obligation to really talk with the bank is high
	14	29	Da ist dann entweder das Unternehmen gefragt, weil nur die kennen, letzten Endes, alle ihre Gläubiger oder eben halt ein guter Berater	Then either the company due to its knowledge of all its creditors or a good consultant must act
Informal information exchange	1	24	If you get into that situation where you might find yourself trying to exchange information	

(continued)

Table 19 (continued)

Category	Int. no.	Line	Statement	Translation
			in case of a troubled credit, there might be a meeting of creditors called—informally, outside of court—where you have an exchange of ideas and all lenders are there. You are certainly not handing everybody what your loan agreements are but you could certainly say "I have got a default and I am willing to do this or that if I get X". Then, it is kind of a multi-party negotiation with the original borrower and the other creditors	
	1	26	[...] if you have got a cross-default clause, you typically will find out what the issue is with the other party and that is probably disclosed through the customer. **It is not direct communication necessarily with that other creditor although it can be**	
	1	56	In bankruptcy court proceedings there is a lot of opportunity cost and reputation cost involved. You essentially set up a structure that mirrors what you get in bankruptcy court but without that additional time, expense and money. If everyone is in agreement with it, it works out great. But it only takes one rogue lender or one party that maybe has a material interest so that it does not want to agree to that for the whole thing to fall apart	
	5	49	Man muss da schon irgendwo am Markt sein, am Kunden sein, wissen wer noch am Kunden ist, vernetzt sein. Sonst funktioniert das nicht	One has to be in the market, close to the customer and to know who is also close to the customer. Basically one must be networked. Otherwise it won't work
	6	34	Da fällt ein Finanzierer weg, der einem da was weiß ich wie	If a financer drops out, who financed who knows how

(continued)

Table 19 (continued)

Category	Int. no.	Line	Statement	Translation
			viel Millionen liefert, der ist weg und dann wird das Unternehmen erstmal hektisch nach Ersatz suchen und das spricht sich dann schon rum. Und dann sind die Leute da auch gut im Markt vernetzt und das, denke ich, spricht sich dann schon rum	many millions, then the company starts to hectically search for a replacement, then that will get about. And people are networked and I believe that news will get around
	6	36	Und die Betreuer, die könnten natürlich dann auch wissen, welche anderen Banken den Kunden versorgen. Ich meine, die kennen sich ja in der Regel. Da wird ja auch manchmal gesprochen	And the person in charge could know which other banks are creditors of the debtor. I mean, they usually know each other and sometimes they talk
	7	35	Also bei allen Krisensituationen—ich würde sagen in 99,9% der Fälle, in denen eine Vereinbarung gefunden wurde—sitzen wir mit allen anderen Banken am Tisch, auch Versicherungen je nachdem, und gegebenenfalls auch irgendwelche Lieferanten, wenn die in dieser spezifischen Situation notwendig sind	In all crisis situations—I would say in 99.9% of all cases that came to an agreement—we sit together with all other banks, as well insurers if any and if necessary in the specific situation suppliers
	9	26	Wir kennen es jetzt so, dass wir in der Regel uns mit den Banken zusammensetzen und versuchen die, die jetzt zum Beispiel Schuldscheine haben, oder bilaterale Kreditgeber auch reinzubekommen	We usually sit together with all banks and try to involve those with bonds and other bilateral loan creditors
	11	40	Also die Lieferantenkredite, die kann ich nicht im Auge behalten. Aber zumindest wenn Darlehensgeber, Leasinggeber und Schuldscheingeber mit am Tisch sitzen, dann ist das schon auch ein wesentlicher Schutz der da entsteht, dass man überhaupt auch wieder in der Lage ist, zu reagieren und miteinander zu reden	Well, I cannot keep tabs on trade credits. However, at least when loan creditors, leasing creditors and bondholders are sitting at the table, a substantial safety is ensured that one is able to react and to communicate with each other
	12	6	Andererseits sind alle Banken in einem Boot. Also sie wissen ganz genau, wenn was passiert,	On the other hand, all banks are in the same boat. So, they know exactly, when

(continued)

Table 19 (continued)

Category	Int. no.	Line	Statement	Translation
			dann sitzen alle an einem Tisch und alle müssen sich mit dem Problem auseinandersetzen, ohne dass sich einer vorher rausstehlen kann, weil er drei Tage vorher gekündigt hat	something happens they all sit at the table and all must tackle the problem without anyone being able to escape just because he accelerated three days earlier
	13	36	Also nach meinen Erfahrungen zu diesen Sanierungsfällen war es so, dass wenn in der Tat erhebliche wirtschaftliche Probleme beim Darlehensnehmer vorlagen—das heißt, erheblich gegen die Financial Covenants verstoßen wurde—, dass dann üblicherweise ziemlich schnell sämtliche Darlehensgeber, sämtliche Gläubiger, die irgendwo mit im Boot saßen und mit denen gemeinsam mitverhandelt wurde	According to my experiences in those restructuring cases, all creditors, who were in any way in the same boat, negotiated jointly when there were *de facto* substantial financial problems—that is a material violation of financial covenants
	14	27	[. . .] also der Sachverhalt, wo ich gestern verhandeln war, da haben wir 26 oder 27 Banken, die bislang nicht durch eine Konsortialregelung vereint sind—, wenn da einer aus der Reihe schert, vielleicht da noch irgendwie durch so eine "unguided missile" von Anwalt irgendwie beraten ist, und dann fällig stellt, dann kann das einen Dominoeffekt verursachen	[. . .] the facts of the case, I had to deal with yesterday—there 26 or 27 banks were involved who are not syndicated so far—if somebody steps out of line there, maybe due to the advice of an "unguided missile" as lawyer, and recalls its loan, that can cause a domino effect
	14	29	Es hat sich in Deutschland inzwischen auch etabliert, solche Gläubigerausschüsse zu bilden. [. . .] Wir haben da jetzt die Begriffe bei diesen Transaktionen, nennt sich Lenkungsausschuss und dann heißt das, das sind fünf oder sechs Banken aus diesem großen Kreis und es gibt halt noch eine Bank, die die Führungsrolle sozusagen übernimmt. Aber die müssen	By now, in Germany, such a committee of creditors has been established. [. . .] Now we have terms in these transactions—like a steering committee—and then that means five or six banks out of the big circle with one leading bank. However, they must form themselves; there are no legal means to force a formation

(continued)

Table 19 (continued)

Category	Int. no.	Line	Statement	Translation
			sich konstituieren. Da gibt es keine gesetzlichen Möglichkeiten, die sozusagen zusammen zu ihrem Glück zu zwingen	
	14	45	Deswegen immer, wenn ich jetzt Schuldscheine höre: Es gibt eine Vielzahl, die muss man als erstes einfangen, dass die konzentriert agieren und, dass es da keinen gibt, der da irgendwie rumläuft und Dinge tut, die er besser nicht tun sollte	That is why, when I hear bonds, I think: There are a great number of them, which you have to reel in first so that they act pooled and that there is no one, who does things he or she should better not do
	14	47	Und dass man sagt: "Ok, ich weiß die ist da auch mit drin, diese Bank. Ich kenne auch den Kollegen, den ruf ich jetzt mal an und tausche mich mal mit dem aus" oder eben das Unternehmen stellt die Kommunikation da tatsächlich her [. . .] Also alle Leute, die da Sanierungen, Restrukturierungen, Insolvenz Work-out, Special Situations,—wer weiß, was es da noch so für Namen für gibt—betreiben, die kennen sich einfach untereinander. Das ist auch ein spezieller Schlag von Mensch. Das ist so eine eingeschworene Gemeinde. Die greifen auch glaube ich direkt zum Hörer und fragen bei ihren Kollegen nach	And then you say: "Okay, I know this bank is also involved. I know the colleague and I will call him now and we are going to exchange ideas and experiences." Or sometimes the company initiates the exchange [. . .] Well, all people who work in financial restructuring, bankruptcy work-out or special situations—or who knows how it is called—know each other. That is a special type of person. That is a small and pledged community. They will also simply pick up the phone and ask a colleague
Third party as communicator	3	31	But information can be powerful for lenders and investors and a company like ours which actually goes through not only bank credit agreements but also high yield and high grade bonds actually serves a function to the market because we are outlining what each deal	

(continued)

Table 19 (continued)

Category	Int. no.	Line	Statement	Translation
			has in a way of covenant protections: What are the exceptions to the covenant protection? How significant are they? And we are providing extra commentary on top of that to help guide, educate and reinforce things along the way	
	7	47	Aber umgekehrt bei den Rating Agenturen, auch wenn ich das nicht definitiv weiß, kann ich mir vorstellen, dass es einen Einfluss hat, ob Sie dort das Thema beispielsweise Negative Pledge entsprechend weit für alle Gläubiger vereinbart haben: ja oder nein. Wenn dort also eine deutliche Bevorzugung bestimmter Gläubigergruppen besteht, kann das schon einen Einfluss haben	However, by the same token rating agencies may consider topics like negative pledge clauses, which are broadly stipulated for all creditors—but I do not know it definitely. When there is a preference of a creditor, then that will have an influence
	8	53	Also überall da, wo sie Cash Flow orientierte Finanzierungen haben, da haben die Financial Covenants wahrscheinlich—ich kann es nicht zu hundert Prozent sagen—wahrscheinlich Auswirkungen auf das Rating	Well, everywhere where you have financial ratios based on cash flow, financial covenants probably influence the rating—but I cannot say that for one hundred percent
	9	74	Auf der anderen Seite ist ja auch klar, wenn der Abschlussprüfer einen Bericht testiert, muss er auch die Fortführung positiv sehen, sonst gibt es ein eingeschränktes Testat. [...] Also, ist auch klar: Wer gegen Financial Covenants verstoßen würde und dafür keinen Waiver zum Abschlusszeitpunkt da ist, würde das im Testat drin stehen	On the other hand, it is clear that when an auditor certifies a report, he must also certify a positive continuance prognosis; otherwise he has to give a qualified opinion. [...] Well, it is also clear: If you violate a financial covenant and it does not get waived at the time of auditing, then this would be stated in the audit opinion

(continued)

Table 19 (continued)

Category	Int. no.	Line	Statement	Translation
Before bankruptcy courts	1	26	There is something in the U.S. called an involuntary bankruptcy and in certain circumstances three creditors can force a customer into bankruptcy court without their permission or willingness going to court. In that case everybody is laying all of their cards out on the table and you can know what is going on	
	1	54	Banks typically do not like to get into bankruptcy court. But sometimes you do, due to the fact that you have this general information sharing, and then you have a structure around what is occurring	

4 Influence of Third-Party Creditor on the Bilateral Private Governance System

4.1 Not Likely

Table 20 Not likely that third-party creditors can influence the behaviour of banks

Category	Int. no.	Line	Statement	Translation
Only cross-acceleration clause	3	26	That is why the second lien and the more junior debt only has a cross-acceleration. The more senior lenders want to be the first at the table and potentially the only ones that need to be made happy before everybody leaves the table	
	3	24	That is, because it is only cross-acceleration as opposed to a full cross-default for senior debt, the ability of the junior debt to in essence free-ride is more practical than legal because again they do not have a cross-default	
	13	10	Je nachdem, wie gut man verhandelt, schafft man als Darlehensnehmerseite Cross-Acceleration Klauseln rein zu verhandeln	Depending on how good one negotiates as debtor only a cross-acceleration clause is stipulated
Lack of information	5	41	Und irgendwer fängt dann schon an diesen Stein ins Rollen zu bringen und dann kriegen es nachher auch die Kleinen mit, weil sie dann eben um Zustimmung gebeten werden. Das ist natürlich eine denkbar ungünstige Situation, weil man dann selber nichts mehr beeinflussen kann	And someone will set the ball rolling and then later the small creditors will know about it at some point, because they will be asked for their permission. That is obviously an unfavourable situation because then you cannot influence anything anymore
	11	16	Und insofern können Sie fast nur darauf vertrauen, dass der Kunde für die außerbilanziellen Finanzierungsinstrumente, ob es Leasingverträge oder andere Themen sind, dass der Kunde Sie informiert oder Sie warten tatsächlich bis Sie irgendwann tatsächlich von dritter Seite ein Informationsschreiben haben, dass Pfändungs- oder	And insofar you can only trust that the customer will inform you with regard to off-balance sheet financial instruments, such as leasing contracts. Otherwise you wait until you get informed from a third party with an information letter regarding prohibition to seize or transfer or similar topics

(continued)

Table 20 (continued)

Category	Int. no.	Line	Statement	Translation
			Überweisungsverbote oder ähnliche Themen auftreten	
	11	46	Aber wo im Leben sind Rechte gleich verteilt? Fast in jeder vertraglichen Beziehung sind doch Rechte nicht gleich verteilt, weil Informationen auch nicht gleich verteilt sind	But where are rights ever distributed evenly? In nearly all contractual relationships rights are not split evenly due to information asymmetry
Bondholders are too diverse	3	29	That is the other reason, why quite honestly in bank debt deals they allow others to pursue first lien debt command but it is not going to be in the form of another bank debt. It has to be in the form of bonds because they know the first-lien bonds, while they rank equal in the capital structure, they cannot get their act together	

4.2 Likely

Table 21 Likely that third-party creditors can influence the behaviour of banks

Category	Int. no.	Line	Statement	Translation
Small community	8	34	Letztlich ist das, also mir kommt es immer vor, wie eine große Pokerrunde. Jeder kennt die Dokumente sehr genau, hat sich natürlich im Vorfeld der jeweiligen Sitzung gut drauf vorbereitet und jeder kennt seine Rechte und selbst diejenigen, die alle Trümpfe in der Hand halten, selbst diejenigen machen Zugeständnisse, weil sie genau wissen, wenn ich hier auch nicht den anderen Häusern entgegenkomme—in welcher Form auch immer—dann wird es einen zweiten Fall geben bei einem völlig anderen Unternehmen, wo wir auch miteinander zusammenstecken und dann hauen die mir da eine rein	In the end—at least this is my impression—it is like a round of poker. Everyone knows the documents in detail, is prepared well in advance and everyone knows their rights. And even those who hold all the aces will make concessions, because they know that "if I do not come up to meet the other banks—in which way whatsoever—then there will be a second case with a different company where we are interlinked again and then they are going to punch me in the face"
	9	36	Man sieht sich ja als Banken immer wieder und der Bankenmarkt in Deutschland ist trotz aller "Overbankedheit" überschaubar [. . .] Man kennt immer wieder die Kollegen bei anderen Häusern. Man trifft sich wieder bei anderen Kunden. Man sieht immer wieder ähnliche Konstellationen von Teams, die darauf arbeiten und so kennt man eben auch die Befindlichkeiten und weiß, dass man auch ein bisschen behutsam miteinander umgehen muss und auch immer mal wieder Verständnis haben muss für unterschiedliche Sichtweisen, die eine Bank auf ein bestimmtes Risiko haben kann [. . .]	As banks you always meet again and the bank market in Germany is despite being overbanked manageable [. . .] You usually know the colleagues from other banks. You meet again at different customers. You often see similar constellation of teams who work on that and for that reason you know about sensitivities and that you have to treat each other carefully and that you need to be understanding for different perspectives of a particular risk [. . .] Yes, however, you see each other for sure again and because of that you try to find a solution that is acceptable for all

(continued)

Table 21 (continued)

Category	Int. no.	Line	Statement	Translation
			Ja, aber dadurch, dass man sich eben sicherlich häufiger sieht, bemüht man sich da eben auch Lösungen zu finden, die für alle tragbar sind	
	11	38	Und fast alle Banken haben Spezialteams, die sich mit der Akquisitionsfinanzierung beschäftigen. Da treffen sich die gleichen Leute immer wieder [. . .] Und da sage ich mal, dass jetzt die Osnabrücker einen Herrn Y haben. Wenn der eine harte Kante spielt, dann ist es ihm egal, ob in Hannover gerade der Kollege Z mit uns irgendwas anderes verhandelt. Also, von daher, es kommt immer drauf an	And nearly all banks have specialised teams for acquisition financing. The same people keep meeting each other [. . .] Let's say, for example, that there is a Mr. Y at the bank in Osnabrück. If he wants to play tough, he won't care if we are also holding negotiations with his colleague Z in Hannover. So it always depends on the situation
	14	19	Auf jeden Fall, solange sich die Leute da kennen, funktioniert das Ganze. So ähnlich, ein bisschen komplexer ist es auch auf dem Finanzierungsmarkt. Das sind ein paar mehr Leute, die da unterwegs sind, aber es wird natürlich auch mit Begrifflichkeiten um sich geschmissen, wo nur Leute was von verstehen, die das schon 20 Mal irgendwo in Verträgen gelesen haben und sich dann da dieser berühmte Marktstandard herausgebildet hat	In any case, as long as the people know each other, the whole thing works. Similar but a little more complicated is it on the finance market. There are a few more people around there but they also use terms which are only understood by people who have read it like 20 times before somewhere in contracts and then the famous market standard evolved out of it
	14	35	Hier habe ich immer das Gefühl, dass die Parteien doch alle, ich glaube die gleiche Sprache sprechen. Ich will jetzt in keinster Weise implizieren, man tut es, ist deswegen miteinander freundlich oder es geht nicht so hoch her, weil das alles Vetternwirtschaft ist oder so. Das glaube ich gerade nicht. Jeder vertritt da schon die Interessen seiner eigenen Bank, seines eigenen Mandanten oder sonstiger	Here I always have the feeling that the parties speak the same language. I do not want to imply that you actually do it and that for that reason we are friendly or that there are no heated debates because all that is nepotism or so. I definitely do not believe that. Everybody represents the interests of their bank, their clients or other interests groups. However, because you meet regularly at the

(continued)

Table 21 (continued)

Category	Int. no.	Line	Statement	Translation
			Interessensgruppen. Das schon. Nur, weil man sich doch recht häufig sowieso irgendwo an Verhandlungstischen wiedersieht, beziehungsweise weiß, was im Bereich des realistisch Machbaren liegt, braucht man sich da jetzt nicht so zu kloppen	negotiation table and you know what is realistic, you do not need to fight so hard
Essential for operational business	1	30	And then you might have other creditors that might not have a formal loan agreement but they supply something that is critical to the operational flow of the company. They probably do not have covenants. But on the other hand, they are usually delivering something on a relatively frequent basis to the customer that the customer needs to keep its doors open. So by the time a borrower gets a troubled credit and is in the situation where it finds out that it is 90 days past making payments to this supplier, everything delivered has to be paid for in cash	
	9	26	In der Regel hat man in solchen Situationen eben auch dann eher die Kreditversicherer noch mit an Bord, weil die sorgen dafür, dass das aktive Leben auf der Lieferantenseite erhalten bleibt. So gibt es dann eben Bemühungen Lösungen zu finden, die für alle beteiligten Parteien dann irgendwo akzeptabel sind. Da ist eben manchmal der Kleinste derjenige, der relativ starken Ausschlag geben kann, und die Banken im Konsortium sind ja für sich erstmal aneinander gebunden	Generally, you have the trade credit insurer on board because they ensure the active life on the supplier side. For that reason, efforts are made to find a solution that is acceptable to all involved parties. There, the smallest is sometimes the one who can make the difference and the banks in bank consortiums are first bound together
	11	30	Da wird es so sein, dass die Banken verlangen, dass diese Drittgläubiger oder dass diese	What we have just seen, for example in a big syndicated loan that is in a waiver

(continued)

Table 21 (continued)

Category	Int. no.	Line	Statement	Translation
			Linien, die dort vorhanden sind, offengelegt werden. Die Banken haben sich praktisch eine Komplettaufstellung geben lassen, nicht nur einen Bankenspiegel, sondern eine komplette Verbindlichkeitenaufstellung und werden verlangen, dass das Unternehmen eine Bestätigung abgibt, dass diese Linien nicht gekündigt sind und offen gehalten werden. **Denn auch da besteht das große Risiko; Leasing-Verwertung wäre ein Risiko im Sinne von: Ist das Unternehmen denn überhaupt noch in der Lage weiter zu produzieren oder zu handeln?**	process: There the banks demand that existing third-party creditors or those credit lines must be made transparent. The banks have obtained a complete list of all obligations. And they are going to demand a confirmation that those credit lines are not accelerated and are kept open. **As there is also a big risk; making use of leased items would be a risk in the sense of: Is the company still able to produce or trade?**
	11	40	Also die Lieferantenkredite, die kann ich nicht im Auge behalten. Aber zumindest wenn Darlehensgeber, Leasinggeber und Schuldscheingeber mit am Tisch sitzen, dann ist das schon auch ein wesentlicher Schutz der da entsteht, dass man überhaupt auch wieder in der Lage ist, zu reagieren und miteinander zu reden	Well, I cannot keep tabs on trade credits. However, at least when loan creditors, leasing creditors and bondholders are sitting at the table, a substantial safety is ensured that one is able to react and to communicate with each other
	12	43	Eine ganz, ganz wichtige Gruppe, die nicht direkt auf der Bilanz ist, sind zum Beispiel die Kreditversicherer. In dem Moment, wo ein Kreditversicherer sagt "Um Gottes Willen, ich will nicht mehr", kann es dazu führen, dass sie nicht mehr beliefert werden und das Unternehmen operativ gar nicht mehr arbeiten kann [...] da ist eine große Position Lieferanten, dann würde man sagen: "Dann lade ich Kreditversicherer dazu ein", weil die müssen auf jeden Fall mitwirken	A really important group, which is not directly on balance sheet, is, for example, trade credit insurers. In that moment in which a trade credit insurer says: "For heavens' sake, I'm out", it's possible that delivery will stop is and the company may not be able to operate anymore

(continued)

Table 21 (continued)

Category	Int. no.	Line	Statement	Translation
	14	51	Die größte Macht haben allerdings in der Krise die Warenkreditversicherer	The biggest power in times of crisis lies with the trade credit insurer
Ability to drive debtor company into bankruptcy	1	22	The cross-default clause is an important thing to have. Even though it might not help you necessarily, it brings everybody to the table so you are able to discuss what the issues are with the credit	
	6	22	Bei den Schuldscheindarlehen hat ja jeder einzelne Schuldscheingläubiger ein eigenes Kündigungsrecht und wenn es natürlich zu so einem Dominoeffekt führt, dass jetzt einer kündigt und die anderen sagen: "Wir aber jetzt auch" Dann führt es früher oder später dazu—eigentlich faktisch, so meine Erfahrung—, dass dann derjenige, der diesen Schuldschein aufgesetzt hat, dann auch in diese Rolle kommt und die Restrukturierung übernimmt und da quasi versucht die Banken, die Teile eines Schuldscheins übernommen haben, wieder an einen Tisch zu bringen, um zu gucken: Wie kommen wir jetzt hier aus der Nummer raus, wie geht man mit dieser Situation um?	In case of bonded loans every single bonded loan creditor has an individual right to accelerate and if that leads to some kind of domino effect, that one accelerates and then the others say: "Then we want to accelerate as well" then this will sooner or later—in my experience it will definitely do so—lead to the situation that the one who drew up the bonded loans will be in charge of the restructuring and then tries to bring the banks, who hold part of the bonded loans, together at the table to see: How are we going to solve the thing?
	7	33	Das liegt einfach daran, dass wir in der Krisensituation uns in der Regel in einer Gesamtsituation bewegen, wo alle Banken im Vorfeld sehr schnell an den Tisch kommen und sich überlegen werden, ob Sie formalrechtliche Kündigungsmöglichkeiten ziehen. Weil in dem Moment sind wir bereits in einem Fahrwasser, was wir nicht mehr hundertprozentig kontrollieren können	That is due to the fact that we are in times of crisis usually in the overall situation in which all banks are really fast at one table well in advance and then they consider whether to accelerate the loan. Because at that point we are already in a position which we cannot control to 100%

(continued)

Table 21 (continued)

Category	Int. no.	Line	Statement	Translation
	7	35	Also bei allen Krisensituationen—ich würde sagen in 99,9% der Fälle, in denen eine Vereinbarung gefunden wurde—sitzen wir mit allen anderen Banken am Tisch, auch Versicherungen, je nachdem, und gegebenenfalls auch irgendwelche Lieferanten, wenn die in dieser spezifischen Situation notwendig sind	In all crisis situations—I would say in 99.9% of all cases that came to an agreement—we sit together with all other banks, as well insurers if any and if necessary in the specific situation suppliers
	9	22	[. . .] ein zu hohes Gewicht auf Finanzierungen mit Einzelkündigungsrecht ist sicherlich ein Problem im Krisenfall. Auf jeden Fall. Da haben wir das Cross-Default-Problem. [. . .] Und der Schuldschein hat ja ein Einzelkündigungsrecht und dann tritt das Problem auf. Ja, dann kommt es zum Cross-Default und die Konsortialbanken befinden sich in der Regel in der etwas unschönen Situation—da sie meistens die größten Commitments haben—den Fresh-Money-Einschuss zu leisten, damit die ganze Sache noch am Leben bleibt	[. . .] a high concentration of credits with individual acceleration rights is certainly a problem in a crisis situation. Certainly, there we will have a cross-default problem. [. . .] The bond has an individual right to accelerate and then there is a problem. Then, there is a cross-default and the consortium banks are in the unattractive situation of having to provide the fresh money injection—because they commonly hold the greatest commitments—to keep the whole thing alive
	9	26	Schuldscheine insbesondere zeigen sich da oft relativ hartleibig, denn die haben ein anderes Interesse. Die haben in den meisten Fällen kein Relationship-Interesse, sondern sind reine Investoren	Bonds are often difficult because they have a different interest. In most cases, there is no relationship interest but they are pure investors
	11	32	Das heißt, Sie haben, wenn der Cross Default zwischen Schuldschein und Konsortialkredit läuft, die Situation, dass Sie zwar mit einer Bankenmehrheit den Konsortialkredit beherrschen können und ihn steuern können, aber Sie haben das	That is, when a cross-default between a syndicated loan and bond occurs, you face the situation that you can control and steer the syndicated loan with a majority of consortium banks, but you must get all bondholders on board. And the more heterogeneous the

(continued)

Table 21 (continued)

Category	Int. no.	Line	Statement	Translation
			Problem, dass Sie den Schuldschein komplett einfangen müssen. Und je heterogener die Schuldscheingläubigerstruktur ist, desto problematischer kann die Situation werden	bondholder structure, the more difficult it becomes
	11	34	Die Fälle des Dominoeffektes gibt es. Oder, wo zumindest damit gedroht wird, dass es passiert. Das reicht ja schon. So, da muss man sehen, wie kriegt man die Interessen unter einen Hut?	Cases where the domino effect occurred do exist—or at least it was used as a threat. That is already enough. So you have to find a way to reconcile all interests
	11	36	Ich bin Teilnehmer an einem Konsortialkredit und wir müssen davon ausgehen, dass das Unternehmen insolvent geht, wenn dieser Schuldschein komplett zurückgezahlt werden soll. Dann ist die Frage: Ok, wie viel Geld habe ich im Konsortialkredit drin und was steht dagegen an Vermögen, an Sicherheiten, an ähnlichen Themen?	I am part of a syndicated loan and we have to assume that the company will become insolvent if a bond has to be repaid. Then you have to answer the question: Okay, how much money have I invested in the syndicated loan and what is there in terms of assets, collateral and similar topics?
	12	6	Andererseits sind alle Banken in einem Boot. Also sie wissen ganz genau, wenn was passiert, dann sitzen alle an einem Tisch und alle müssen sich mit dem Problem auseinandersetzen, ohne dass sich einer vorher rausstehlen kann, weil er drei Tage vorher gekündigt hat	On the other hand, all banks are in the same boat. So, they know exactly, when something happens they all sit at the table and all must tackle the problem without anyone being able to escape just because he accelerated three days earlier
	12	10	Und das kann ich dann auch nochmal für die Banken sagen: Sie fordern es nicht nur, sondern sie lassen es auch gegen sich gelten. Also wenn Sie der erste sind, der jetzt, also in bilateralen Verträgen, der sagen würde: "Ich möchte jetzt eine Besicherung haben."—und das ist eine Besicherung, die Sie im Grunde nur über ein	And I can say that for the banks: They do not only demand it but are also bound by it. So if you are the first in case of a bilateral contract who says "Now, I want collateral"—and that collateral can basically only be shared with other creditors by way of pooling—then (at least that is the way we do it) we say:

(continued)

Table 21 (continued)

Category	Int. no.	Line	Statement	Translation
			Pooling mit anderen teilen können—dann (so ist das in unserem Hause zumindest, dann) sagen wir: "Pass auf, wir brauchen hier jetzt Sicherheiten und das mag sein, dass das die Forderung Warenlager sind. Aber die anderen haben auch gleichgeartete Kredite, also müssen die auch für andere gelten."	"Look, we need a security and it may be that the claims are warehouse. But the others have similar credits and thus, the same must be true for them."
	13	20	Also wenn wir den Bereich haben, dass der Darlehensnehmer in wirtschaftliche Schwierigkeiten kommt, dann muss man immer mit allen Gläubigern verhandeln, weil über die Cross Default Klausel oder Most Preferred Klausel oder wie auch immer man sie im Einzelnen ausgestaltet oder welche Regelungen da insbesondere in Betracht kommen, da immer letztlich irgendwo alle Gläubiger mit im Boot sitzen	If we are faced with the situation that the debtor is in financial distress, one has to negotiate with all creditors because—due to the cross-default clause or most preferred clause or however one drafts those clauses—all creditors are finally in the same boat
	14	27	also der Sachverhalt, wo ich gestern verhandeln war, da haben wir 26 oder 27 Banken, die bislang nicht durch eine Konsortialregelung vereint sind—, wenn da einer aus der Reihe schert, vielleicht da noch irgendwie durch so eine "unguided missile" von Anwalt irgendwie beraten ist, und dann fällig stellt, dann kann das einen Dominoeffekt verursachen	[...] the facts of the case, I had to deal with yesterday—there 26 or 27 banks were involved who are not syndicated so far—if somebody steps out of line there, maybe due to the advice of an "unguided missile" as lawyer, and recalls its loan, that can cause a domino effect
	14	45	Deswegen immer, wenn ich jetzt Schuldscheine höre: Es gibt eine Vielzahl, die muss man als erstes einfangen, dass die konzentriert agieren und, dass es da keinen gibt, der da irgendwie rumläuft und Dinge tut, die er besser nicht tun sollte	That is why, when I hear bonds, I think: There are a great number of them, which you have to reel in first so that they act pooled and that there is no one, who does things he or she should better not do

(continued)

Table 21 (continued)

Category	Int. no.	Line	Statement	Translation
Sense of responsibility	9	86	Und ich glaube die Banken sind auf der anderen Seite auch in den meisten Fällen sehr verantwortlich, verantwortungsbewusst, und versuchen auf diese Weise auch in schwierigen Situationen das Ganze so zu managen, dass man eben allen gerecht wird	And I believe that banks, on the other hand, are very responsible in most cases and try to manage the whole thing in a way that is fair for everyone—even in difficult times
	11	46	Das Unternehmen ist darauf angewiesen, diesen Vertrag unbedingt verlängert zu bekommen, das Unternehmen ist auf die Fortführung eines Kredites angewiesen und damit eben auch auf diese Bankbeziehung und, weil es eben in einer besonderen Situation ist, gibt es vielleicht keine dritte Bank, die man dort ansprechen könnte und ich kann deswegen aus diesem Kreditverhältnis nicht grundsätzlich aussteigen. Dann ist es schon eine ethische Verantwortung der Bank, diese Machtposition nicht auszuspielen. Aber dass sie natürlich versuchen wird für sich in dieser Situation die bestmögliche Verhandlungsposition zu bekommen, finde ich erstmal nicht verwerflich, sondern völlig normal	A company depends on the continuation of the credit and, thereby, on the relationship it has with the bank. And because the company may be in a special situation, perhaps there is no other bank the company could approach and therefore I basically cannot exit this relationship. It is an ethical responsibility of the bank not to abuse this position of power. However, it is not condemnable *per se* but actually normal that the bank should try to occupy the best negotiation position
	13	38	Wobei meine Erfahrung ist, dass die Banken sehr zurückhaltend damit sind, die Unternehmen wirklich in die Insolvenz zu treiben, weil den Banken natürlich auch bewusst ist, dass sie da eine gewisse Verantwortung haben—sowohl der Gesellschaft als auch den Arbeitnehmern der Gesellschaft gegenüber	My experience is that banks are really reluctant to drive a company into bankruptcy because banks are aware of the fact that they have a certain responsibility both to society and the employees of the company

Table of Cases

1 German Case Law

1.1 Supreme Court of the (German) Reich

RG, judgment of 23 July 1937, *VII 36/1937*, BankArchiv 1937/38, 311.
RG, judgment of 09 April 1932, *IX 74/31*, RGZ 136, 247.
RG, judgment of 15 March 1935, *II 283/34*, RGZ 147, 321.

1.2 German Federal Supreme Court

BGH, judgment of 11 May 1953, *IV ZR 170/52*, BGHZ 10, 14.
BGH, judgment of 09 July 1953, *IV ZR 242/52*, BGHZ 10, 228.
BGH, judgment of 09 November 1955, *IV ZR 196/54*, BGHZ 19, 12.
BGH, judgment of 08 February 1956, *IV ZR 287/55*, BGHZ 20, 43.
BGH, judgment of 02 February 1955, *IV ZR 252/54*, WM 1955, 402.
BGH, judgment of 20 December 1955, *I ZR 171/53*, WM 1956, 217.
BGH, judgment of 21 December 1955, *VI ZR 192/54*, WM 1956, 283.
BGH, judgment of 03 March 1956, *IV ZR 334/55*, WM 1956, 527.
BGH, judgment of 30 April 1959, *VII ZR 19/58*, WM 1959, 964.
BGH, judgment of 21 January 1960, *VII ZR 170/58*, WM 1960, 576.
BGH, judgment of 28 November 1960, *VIII ZR 211/59*, WM 1961, 243.
BGH, judgment of 25 April 1961, *VI ZR 96/60*, WM 1961, 776.
BGH, judgment of 04 July 1961, *VI ZR 84/60*, WM 1961, 1103.
BGH, judgment of 18 September 1963, *VIII ZR 46/62*, WM 1963, 1093.
BGH, judgment of 14 April 1964, *VI ZR 219/62*, WM 1964, 671.
BGH, judgment of 22 June 1966, *VIII ZR 141/64*, WM 1966, 792.
BGH, decision of 30 January 1967, *III ZR 248/64*, WM 1967, 397.

D. Matri, *Covenants and Third-Party Creditors*, DOI 10.1007/978-3-319-62036-7

BGH, judgment of 30 September 1968, *II ZR 224/66*, WM 1968, 1214.
BGH, judgment of 17 December 1969, *VIII ZR 35/68*, WM 1970, 120.
BGH, judgment of 09 December 1969, *VI ZR 50/68*, NJW 1970, 657.
BGH, judgment of 29 January 1970, *VII ZR 34/68*, BGHZ 53, 174.
BGH, judgment of 05 July 1971, *II ZR 176/68*, BGHZ 56, 339.
BGH, judgment of 20 January 1971, *VIII ZR 129/69*, WM 1971, 441.
BGH, judgment of 25 September 1972, *VIII ZR 216/71*, BGHZ 59, 230.
BGH, judgment of 30 October 1973, *VI ZR 27/71*, WM 1974, 99.
BGH, judgment of 15 December 1976, *IV ZR 197/75*, WM 1977, 287.
BGH, judgment of 10 November 1977, *III ZR 39/76*, WM 1978, 234.
BGH, judgment of 08 November 1978, *IV ZR 179/77*, WM 1978, 1384.
BGH, judgment of 19 September 1979, *III ZR 93/76*, WM 1979, 1176.
BGH, judgment of 01 March 1982, *II ZR 23/81*, BGHZ 83, 341.
BGH, judgment of 24 January 1983, *VIII ZR 353/81*, BGHZ 86, 300.
BGH, judgment of 21 March 1983, *II ZR 139/82*, WM 1983, 594.
BGH, judgment of 26 March 1984, *II ZR 171/83*, BGHZ 90, 381.
BGH, judgment of 18 April 1984, *VIII ZR 50/83*, WM 1984, 931.
BGH, judgment of 17 December 1984, *II ZR 36/84*, WM 1985, 284.
BGH, order of 26 September 1985, *III ZR 229/84*, WM 1985, 1437.
BGH, order of 26 September 1985, *III ZR 213/84*, WM 1985, 1493.
BGH, judgment of 21 March 1988, *II ZR 194/87*, BGHZ 104, 44.
BGH, judgment of 07 November 1988, *II ZR 46/88*, BGHZ 106, 7.
BGH, judgment of 09 July 1991, *XI ZR 72/90*, WM 1991, 1452.
BGH, judgment of 12 December 1991, *IX ZR 178/91*, BGHZ 116, 319.
BGH, judgment of 13 July 1992, *II ZR 251/91*, BGHZ 119, 191.
BGH, judgment of 06 June 1994, *II ZR 292/91*, NJW 1994, 2220.
BGH, judgment of 16 March 1995, *IX ZR 72/94*, WM 1995, 995.
BGH, judgment of 13 July 1995, *IX ZR 81/94*, BGHZ 130, 314.
BGH, judgment of 26 September 1996, *I ZR 265/95*, BGHZ 133, 316.
BGH, judgment of 30 January 1997, *IX ZR 89/96*, WM 1997, 545.
BGH, judgment of 03 April 1998, *V ZR 6/97*, WM 1998, 1289.
BGH, judgment of 19 March 1998, *IX ZR 22/97*, BGHZ 138, 291.
BGH, judgment of 03 November 1999, *VIII ZR 269/98*, BGHZ 143, 104.
BGH, judgment of 25 February 2002, *II ZR 196/00*, BGHZ 150, 61.
BGH, order of 12 December 2002, *IX ZB 426/02*, BGHZ 153, 205.
BGH, judgment of 11 March 2003, *XI ZR 403/01*, BGHZ 154, 146.
BGH, judgment of 20 May 2003, *XI ZR 50/02*, WM 2003, 1416.
BGH, judgment of 18 December 2003, *IX ZR 199/02*, BGHZ 157, 242.
BGH, judgment of 19 July 2004, *II ZR 218/03*, BGHZ 160, 134.
BGH, judgment of 22 July 2004, *IX ZR 183/03*, WM 2004, 1837.
BGH, judgment of 14 September 2004, *XI ZR 184/03*, WM 2004, 2200.
BGH, order of 16 December 2004, *IX ZB 72/03*, WM 2005, 472.
BGH, judgment of 29 November 2007, *IX ZR 30/07*, BGHZ 174, 297.
BGH, judgment of 29 November 2007, *IX ZR 121/06*, BGHZ 174, 314.
BGH, judgment of 20 December 2011, *VI ZR 309/10*, WM 2012, 260.

BGH, judgment of 28 June 2012, *IX ZR 191/11*, BGHZ 193, 378.
BGH, judgment of 21 February 2013, *IX ZR 32/12*, BGHZ 196, 220.
BGH, judgment of 18 July 2013, *IX ZR 198/10*, WM 2013, 1504.

1.3 Higher Regional Court

Oberlandesgericht des Landes Sachsen-Anhalt (OLG Naumburg), judgment of 15 February 2006, *5 U 158/05*, WM 2006, 1677.
Schleswig-Holsteinisches Oberlandesgericht (OLG Schleswig), judgment of 27 April 2006, *5 U 176/05*, WM 2006, 1338.

1.4 Regional Court

Landesgericht Hamburg (LG Hamburg), judgment of 23 October 1984, *4 O 113/84*, WM 1985, 163.

2 European Union Case Law

CJEU, *Jean-Bernard Lafonta v. Autorité des marchés financiers* (2015) C- 628/13 ECLI:EU:C:2015:162.
CJEU, *Markus Geltl v. Daimler AG* (2012) C -19/11, ECR [2012] I-397.
ECJ, *Centros Ltd v. Erhvervs- og Selskabsstyrelsen* (1999) C-212/97, ECR [1999] I-1459.
ECJ, *Kamer van Koophandel en Fabrieken voor Amsterdam v. Inspire Art Ltd* (2003) C-167/01 ECR [2003] I-10155.
ECJ, *Überseering BV v. Nordic Construction Company Baumanagement GmbH* [2002] C-208/00, ECR I-9919.

3 US Case Law

3.1 US Supreme Court

Begier v. Internal Revenue Service, 496 U.S. 53 (1990).
Curry v. McClanless, 59 S.Ct. 900, 904 (1939).
Taylor et al. v. Standard Gas & Electric Co. et al., 59 S. Ct. 543 (Sup.Ct. 1939).

3.2 State Supreme Courts

Farmers Cooperative Elevator, Inc. v. State Bank, 236 N.W.2d 674 (Iowa 1975).
Gay Jenson Farms Co. v. Cargill, Inc., 309 N.W.2d 285 (Minn. 1981).
Jean Clark v. Harvey Rowe, Junior, & another, 701 N.E.2d 624, 627 (Mass. 1998).
J.R. Hale Contracting Co Inc v. United N. M. Bank at Albuquerque, 799 P.2d 581 (N.M. 1990).
Leaf v. Reynolds, 203 P. 458, 460 (Ida. 1921).
Rubin v. Pioneer Federal Savings & Loan Assn, 214 Neb. 364 (Neb. 1983).
Warren Mitchell v. Ford Motor Credit Company, 688 P.2d 42 (Okl. 1984).

3.3 Courts of Appeal

Alan's of Atlanta. Inc v. Minolta Corp, 903 F.2d 1414 (11th Cir. 1990).
Bondi v. Citigroup, Inc, 32 A.3d 1158 (N.J.Super.A.D. 2011).
Brown v. Avemco Inv. Corp., 603 F.2d 1367, 1375 et seqq. (9th Cir. 1979).
Capital Bank v. MVB, Inc., 644 So.2d 515, 521 (Fla. Dist. Ct. App. 1994).
Cenco Incorporated v. Seidman & Seidman, 686 F.2d 449 (7th Cir. 1982).
Citibank, N.A. v. Data Lease Financial Corporation, 828 F.2d 686 (11th Cir. 1987), cert. denied, 484 U.S. 1062 (1988).
Commonwealth Nat'l Bank of Dallas v. United States, 665 F.2d 743 (5th Cir. 1982).
Concrete Pumping Services Inc. v. King Construction Co. Inc., 943 F.2d 627 (6th Cir. 1991).
Graf et al. v. Hope Bldg. Corporation, 171 N.E. 884 (N.Y.App. 1930).
Harris v. Kessler, 12 P.2d 467 (Cal.App. 1932).
Harry G. Hager v. Ruth A. Gibson, Trustee for Preference, Ltd., 108 F.3d 35 (4th Cir. 1997).
Hoffman v. Lincoln National Bank and Trust Company, 636 N.E.2d 185, 188 (Ind.App. 5 Dist. 1994).
Indu Craft, Inc. v. Bank of Baroda, 47 F.3d 490 (2nd Cir. 1995).
In re Falcon Products, Inc., et al. v. First Insurance Funding, 381 B.R. 543 (8th Cir.BAP 2008).
In re Powerine Oil Company v. Koch Oil Company, 59 F.3d 969 (9th Cir. 1995).
In re SGL Carbon Corporation, 200 F.3d 154 (3rd Cir. 1999).
In re Tenna Corporation v. United States, 801 F.2d 819 (6th Cir. 1986).
In re W.T. Grant Company v. Charles Rodman, 699 F.2d 599, 610 (2nd Cir. 1983) cert. denied, 464 U.S. 822 (1983).
Kirke La Shelle Co. v. Paul Armstrong Co. et al., 188 N.E. 163 (N.Y.App. 1933).
KMC v. Irving Trust Co, 757 F.2d 752 (6th Cir. 1985).
Laws v. United Missouri Bank of Kansas City, 98 F.3d 1047 (8th Cir. 1996).
Murray Drabkin v. A.I. Credit Corporation, 800 F.2d 1153 (D.C. Cir. 1986).

Official Committee of Unsecured Creditors v. R F Lafferty & Co, Inc., 267 F.3d 340 (3rd Cir. 2001).
Ora Lee Williams v. Walker-Thomas Furniture Company, 350 F.2d 445, 449 (D.C. Cir. 1965).
Richards Engineer, Inc. v. Charles Spanel 745 P2.d 1031, 1033 (Colo.App. 1987).
Robert Sullivan v. William Willock, 854 F.2d 196 (7th Cir. 1988).
Sahadi v. Continental Ill. Nat'l Bank & Trust Co. of Chicago, 706 F.2d 193 (7th Cir. 1983).
Spatuzzi v. Star Auto Truck Exchange, Inc., 119 N.J.L. 377 (Ct.Err.&App. 1938).
State National Bank of El Paso v. Farah Manufacturing Co., 678 S.W.2d 661 (Tex.Ct.App.1984).
United States v. John Grayson, 879 F.2d 620, 623 (9th Cir. 1989).

3.4 District Courts

Bergquist v. First National Bank of St. Paul, 5 Bankr. 470 (Bankr.D.Minn.1980).
Coleman Tidwell v. Glenda Galbreath, 207 B.R. 309 (Bkrtcy.M.D.Ga. 1997).
In re American Lumber Company v. First National Bank of St. Paul, 5 B.R. 470 (Bankr.Minn. 1980).
In re Crawford and Braunstein v. Crawford and Kamphaus, 454 B.R. 262 (Bkrtcy. D.Mass. 2011).
In re Dolton Lodge Trust No. 35188, 22 B.R. 918 (Bkrtcy.N.D.Ill.1982).
In re Fedders North America, Inc. v. Goldman Sachs Credit Partners L.P., 405 B.R. 527, 542 ct scqq. (Bkrtcy.D.Dcl. 2009).
In re Jan McLendon Moss, 249 B.R. 411 (Bankr.N.D.Tex. 2000).
In re Johns-Manville Corporation, et al., 36 B.R. 727 (Bkrtcy.S.D.N.Y.1984) appeal denied 39 B.R. 234, reargument denied 39 B.R. 998, mandamus denied 749 F.2d 3.
In re Lease-A-Fleet, Inc. v. Donald L. Wolk, Setven C. Wolk, Robins Le-Cocq Corp., 151 B.R. 341 (Bkrtcy.E.D. Pa. 1993).
In re Schwinn Bicycle Co. v. Transamerica Insurance Finance Corporation 200 B.R. 980 (Bkrtcy.N.D.Ill. 1996).
In re T. E. Mercer Trucking Company, 16 B.R. 176 (Bankr.N.D.Tex. 1981).
In re Yellowstone Mountain Club, LLC v. Brian Glasser, 2014 WL 1369363 (Dist. Ct.D.Mont. 2014) appeal filed.
In the Matter of 7H Land & Cattle Co., 6 B.R. 29 (Bankr.D.Nev. 1980).
Robinson v. McAllen State Bank, 48 Banking Rep (BNA) 1004 (Tex.Dist.Ct. 1987).

MIX
Papier aus verantwortungsvollen Quellen
Paper from responsible sources
FSC® C105338

If you have any concerns about our products,
you can contact us on
ProductSafety@springernature.com

In case Publisher is established outside the EU,
the EU authorized representative is:
Springer Nature Customer Service Center GmbH
Europaplatz 3, 69115 Heidelberg, Germany

Printed by Libri Plureos GmbH
in Hamburg, Germany